The Sociology of Chinese Capitalism in Southeast Asia

Yos Santasombat
Editor

The Sociology of Chinese Capitalism in Southeast Asia

Challenges and Prospects

palgrave
macmillan

Editor
Yos Santasombat
Chiang Mai University
Chiang Mai, Thailand

ISBN 978-981-13-0064-6 ISBN 978-981-13-0065-3 (eBook)
https://doi.org/10.1007/978-981-13-0065-3

Library of Congress Control Number: 2018939739

Cover credit: Kevin Phillips

Printed on acid-free paper

This Palgrave Macmillan imprint is published by the registered company Springer Nature Singapore Pte Ltd.
The registered company address is: 152 Beach Road, #21-01/04 Gateway East, Singapore 189721, Singapore

Preface

This book is a companion to our previous volume *Chinese Capitalism in Southeast Asia: Cultures and Practices.* While the first volume provided integrated perspectives on the situated and diverse cultures and practices of Chinese capitalism in Southeast Asia, this second volume focuses on the challenges and prospects of Chinese capitalism within the context of China's rise and economic regionalism.

How does Chinese capitalism from China impact the Association of Southeast Asian Nations (ASEAN) integration and its attempts at community building? In what ways does Chinese capitalism from China interact with the diverse forms of Chinese capitalism in Southeast Asia? The penetration of new Chinese economic statecraft and the accompanying transnational Chinese business corporations and entrepreneurs have posed serious challenges to both Southeast Asian governments and local Chinese communities. On one hand, China's rise and its growing economic engagement with ASEAN has presented new investment and business opportunities for local Chinese communities in Southeast Asia. On the other hand, China's rise has also stimulated anxieties, ambivalences, and new politico-economic realignments.

Those challenges have triggered multiple and transformative changes to the modes of economic organization in Southeast Asia, a region already influenced by regionalization and globalization, as well as the cultural foundations of the overseas Chinese. Creative strategies through desinicization, resinicization, and rebalancing of economic relationships have been used by local Chinese communities and ASEAN countries to cope with the challenges of Chinese capitalism.

This volume, like the previous one, is the fruit of collective efforts made by a team of dedicated researchers who have worked with, argued with, and assisted each other for many years. I am grateful to all the researchers and contributing authors for their untiring research efforts, endurance, and cooperation. The researchers, authors, and I, as editor, have benefited a great deal from challenging and perceptive commentaries from Chulacheeb Chinwanno, Celia Lee, Chen Chung-An, Guanie Lim, Hui Yew-Foong, Kei Koga, Koh Keng We, Kong Tuan Yuen, Michael Montesano, Siriporn Wajjwalku, Wang Tingyan, Yow Cheun Hoe, and Zhou Taomo. A short visiting fellowship at the Institute of Southeast Asian Studies (ISEAS)-Yusof Ishak Institute in Singapore provided a stimulating intellectual environment as well as facilities for further research, writing, and editing. I would like to thank Director Tan Chin Tiong, Terrence Chong, Michael Montesano, and Benjamin Loh for providing me with this opportunity.

Research and workshops were made possible by financial and organizational support from the Thailand Research Fund. Special thanks to Prof. Dr. Isra Sarntisart, Program Director of Division 1, Thailand Research Fund, for his continuous support of our research; and to Prof. Dr. Suthipun Jitpimolmard, the director of the Thailand Research Fund. Special thanks are due to the staffs of Thailand Research Fund, particularly Ms. Rungnapa Lakkanapornwisit for her continuous and kind assistances. Palaiwan Srisaringkarn deserves special recognition and gratitude for her untiring organizational assistance to our team. Finally, we would like to thank Ms. Lara Johnson and the editorial team at Palgrave Macmillan for their invaluable contributions in editing this volume.

Chiang Mai, Thailand
February 2018

Yos Santasombat

Contents

Notes on Contributors

Jean Chih-yin Cheng received her M.A. in anthropology from National Tsinghua University, Taiwan. Her research focuses on the theatrical characteristics of the national cultural policy of Singapore and local community building projects in Taiwan.

Bien Chiang received his Ph.D. in anthropology from the University of Pennsylvania (1993). He is currently an Associate Research Fellow with the Institute of Ethnology, Academia Sinica, and holds a joint appointment position of associate professor of the Graduate Institute of Anthropology, National Tsinghua University, Taiwan. He has done research and published papers on the topics of social hierarchy, house, exchange, and trade among the Austronesian-speaking communities in Taiwan and Sarawak.

Danny Wong Tze Ken is currently Director of the Global Planning and Strategy Centre, University of Malaya, and Professor of History at the Department of History, Faculty of Arts and Social Sciences, University of Malaya where he teaches history of Indochina and Southeast Asia. He is also Director of the Institute of China Studies at the University. His research interests include the Chinese in Malaysia, China's relations with Southeast Asia, and the history of Sabah. He was Visiting Scholar at the Research Center for Social Science and Humanities, National Tsinghua University; Visiting Professor at the Center for Integrated Area Studies, Kyoto University; Visiting Scholar at Magdalene College, Cambridge

University; Visiting Lecturer at Ecole des Hautes Etudes en Sciences Sociales, Paris; and Visiting Professor at the Asia-Europe Institute. Among his publications are: *The Diaries of G.C. Woolley, Vol. 1: 1901–1907* (2015) *& Vol. 2: 1907–1913* (2016); *Historical Sabah: The War* (2010); *The Spirit of Borneo* (2009); *The Nguyen and Champa During the 17th and 18th Century* (2007), *Historical Sabah: the Chinese* (2005); *Historical Sabah: Community and Society* (2004); *The Transformation of an Immigrant Society: a Study of the Chinese of Sabah* (1998); and *Vietnam-Malaysia Relations during the Cold War* (1995). Professor Wong is a Member of the Board of Governors, Chinese Heritage Centre, Singapore and Council Member of the Malaysian Branch of the Royal Asiatic Society Member of the Board of Trustees, Southeast Asian Studies Regional Exchange Program Foundation, and Chairman of the United Nations Educational, Scientific and Cultural Organisation Southeast Asian Shared-History Textbook Technical Committee.

Romyen Kosaikanont is a lecturer in Economics at the School of Management and Vice Rector, Mae Fah Luang University, Chiang Rai.

Kian Cheng Lee is a Singaporean serving as lecturer with the Faculty of Political Science and Public Administration, School of International Affairs, Chiang Mai University, Thailand. His academic qualifications include B.Sc. (Physics), M.A. (Biblical Studies), M.Div., MA (Southeast Asian Studies), Th.M. (Asian Christianity), and Ph.D. (Social Sciences). He teaches Southeast Asian Studies, East Asian Studies, Religions of Asia, International Relations, Political Economy of Asia Pacific, and Seminars on Chinese in Southeast Asia. He is currently doing research entrepreneurship, tourism, cultural diplomacy, One Belt One Road Initiative, and religious networks in the context of the People's Republic of China transnationalism. Dr. Lee has served as a military officer with the Singapore Armed Forces. He is also a board director of Asian Pastoral Institute Ltd. which is based in Singapore.

Wasana La-orngplew is a lecturer at the College of Interdisciplinary Studies, Thammasat University (Lampang Campus). Her areas of research are China's influence in Lao People's Democratic Republic (PDR), and agrarian transformation in Lao PDR and Thailand.

Hong Liu is a Tan Kah Kee Endowed Professor of Public Policy and Global Affairs and Chair of the School of Social Sciences at Nanyang Technological University in Singapore. He was awarded the Eminent

Yangtze Scholar Award in 2007 by the People's Republic of China Ministry of Education in conjunction with the Li Kashing Foundation in Hong Kong. Professor Liu's professional and public services include serving as the Academic Consulting Advisor for the China State Council Overseas Chinese Affairs Office, Vice President of the Asian Association of World Historians, Vice Chairman of the Universities' China Committee in London, Academic Advisor for the London School of Economics (China in Comparative Perspective Network), and Member of the China Studies Syllabus Development Committee (Singapore Ministry of Education). He is the current Editor of the *Journal of Chinese Overseas* (Boston and Leiden) and co-editor of the *International Journal of Diasporic Chinese Studies* (Singapore), and is on the editorial board of the *Journal of Contemporary China* (Routledge), *Journal of Technology Management in China* (Emerald, UK), Routledge Monograph Series *The Chinese World* (London and New York), and Brill Chinese Overseas Monograph Series (Boston and Leiden).

Chinh Van Nguyen is Associate Professor of Social Anthropology and Deputy Director of the Centre for Asian and Pacific Studies, Vietnam National University, Hanoi. He received his doctorate from the University of Amsterdam, the Netherlands, and his academic interests focus on the issues of labor, education, migration, and cross-border ethnic groups in the Mekong region.

Austin Ong is a lecturer at the International Studies Department at De La Salle University where he teaches courses on China Modern Economy and Globalisation. His research interests include Great Powers Relations, the Association of Southeast Asian Nations, and Philippines Foreign Policy. He is also the founding president of the Philippines China Friendship Club.

Ellen Palanca is a Professor at the Department of Economics and Chinese Studies Program of the Ateneo de Manila University. Her research focuses on China's trade with East Asia, ethnic Chinese in the Philippines, and general socio-economic issues. She is also the director of the Confucius Institute at the Ateneo de Manila University.

Yos Santasombat is Professor of Anthropology, Department of Sociology and Anthropology, Faculty of Social Sciences, Chiang Mai University, and Senior Research Scholar, Thailand Research Fund. He is the author of numerous books, including *Lak Chang: A Reconstruction of Tai Identity in Daikong* (Canberra: Pandanus Books, ANU, 2001); *Biodiversity, Local Knowledge and Sustainable Development* (Chiang Mai: RCSD, 2003, 2014); *Flexible Peasants: Reconceptualizing the Third World's Rural Types* (Chiang Mai: RCSD, 2008); *The River of Life: Changing Ecosystems of the Mekong Region* (Chiang Mai: Mekong Press, 2011); as well as the edited volumes *Impact of China's Rise in the Mekong Region* (Palgrave Macmillan 2015) and *Chinese Capitalism in Southeast Asia: Cultures and Practices* (Palgrave Macmillan 2017).

Aranya Siriphon is currently an Assistant Professor in the Department of Sociology and Anthropology, Faculty of Social Sciences, Chiang Mai University. Her current research is centered on Chinese influence in mainland Southeast Asia and border and transborder studies. Her recent research projects are Chinese capitalism, Association of Southeast Asian Nations Economic Community and Oversea Chinese in Southeast Asia (Co-researcher, 2015–2016); The Impacts of Contemporary Chinese Mobility into Mainland Southeast Asia: Views of Thai Border Communities in northern Thailand (2013–2015). Among her publications are: "Border Guanxi: *Xinyimin* and Transborder Trade in Northern Thailand" In *Chinese Encounters in Southeast Asia: How People, Money, and Ideas from China Are Changing a Region*, edited by Pal Nyiri and Danielle Tan, Settle: University of Washington Press, pp. 59–79; The Qiaoban, the PRC Influence and Nationalist Chinese in the Northern Thailand, *International Journal of Asian Studies* 13, 1 (January) pp. 1–17 (2016).

Hsing-Chou Sung is Professor and Chairman of the Department of Political Science, Tunghai University, Taiwan. He is also Director of the Urban and Regional Development Research Center, College of Social Science, Tunghai University. His research interests include political economy, international relations, research methods, East Asian regionalism, and cross-Strait relationships (China and Taiwan).

Touch Siphat holds a B.A. in Sociology from the Royal University of Phnom Penh, Cambodia, and an M.A. in Sustainable Development from Chiang Mai University, Thailand. He has been working in the area of rural development in Cambodia for more than ten years and is fully experienced in capacity building for rural development workers, working with rural community people, and in the arrangement of training courses and workshops at different levels of participation. He has also carried out research on land and livelihood issues in Cambodian rural communities and impacts of Chinese assistance in Cambodia for international workshops, conferences, and publications.

Khine Tun is Senior Research Fellow at the Asia Development Research Institute (ADRI) of Myanmar. He received his master's degree in Economics from Kyung Hee University of Republic of Korea. After his 12-year career in the government sector, he conducted research and consultancy work in such organizations as the United Nations Development Programme, the United Nations Environment Programme, the Food and Agriculture Organization, the Sasakawa Peace Foundation, and the Economic Research Institute for ASEAN and East Asia. His latest research paper is entitled "Policy Recommendations for the Future Economic Development of Myanmar" in the publication on Economic Development in Transition Period of Myanmar.

Wasana Wongsurawat is an Assistant Professor of Modern Chinese History at the Department of History, Faculty of Arts, Chulalongkorn University. Wasana's research interests include diaspora history, transnational history, history of the Chinese overseas, global history, history of the Cold War, the nation, and nationalism. Wasana obtained her doctoral degree in history from the Oriental Institute, Oxford, in 2007. In addition to teaching at Chulalongkorn University, Wasana has also completed postdoctoral research fellowships at the Asia Research Institute of the National University of Singapore in 2007–2008, and at the Faculty of Humanities, Hong Kong Polytechnic University in 2011–2012. She has edited and contributed to two edited volumes: *Dynamics of the Cold War in Asia: Ideology, Identity and Culture* (Palgrave, 2009); and *Sites of Modernity: Asian Cities in the Transitory Moments of Trade, Colonialism, and Nationalism* (Springer, 2017).

Miao Zhang is a Research Fellow at the Institute of China Studies, University of Malaya. She obtained her Ph.D. in Economics from the University of Malaya in 2004. She has been studying China-Malaysia trade and investment, urban studies, and institutional economics. Her research spectrum also extends to the fields of industrial policy and technology innovation. Her previous writings have appeared in international journals such as *Journal of Contemporary Asia*, *Habitat International*, *Cities*, *Journal of Asia Pacific Economy*, *International Journal of China*

Studies, Institutions and Economies, and *Asia Pacific Business Review*. She has undertaken several consultancies for international agencies, including the United Nations Development Programme, Japan-Association of Southeast Asian Nations (ASEAN) Center and Economic Research Institute for ASEAN and East Asia. Dr. Zhang has frequently contributed commentaries to the *Financial Times* (Chinese), *Sin Chew Daily*, and *Oriental Daily*.

Yishu Zhou is a Research Associate at the Lee Kuan Yew School of Public Policy, National University of Singapore.

List of Figures

List of Tables

CHAPTER 1

Introduction

Yos Santasombat

Chinese Capitalism and ASEAN Economic Community

The Association of Southeast Asian Nations (ASEAN) was founded in 1967 to coordinate security policy during the Cold War as part of the anticommunist containment strategy led by the USA and North Atlantic Treaty Organization (NATO). Historically and geo-politically, China has always viewed ASEAN as an integral part of its security environment.

Over the past two decades, a changing global context has given rise to remarkable opportunities to forge closer relations between the People's Republic of China (PRC) and ASEAN countries. The constructive role played by the government of the PRC in dealing with the Asian financial crisis coupled with the changing US priorities in Asia during the 1990s have led to a marked improvement in relations between ASEAN and the northern neighbor. The considerable distrust that once defined their relations during the Cold War has evolved into a more positive and intimate economic and political rapport.

However, China's territorial claims in the South China Sea reveal its increasing naval capabilities and willingness to deploy them for politico-economic interests. Hence the contemporary relationship between China and ASEAN is marked by a combination of cooperation and

Y. Santasombat (✉)
Chiang Mai University, Chiang Mai, Thailand

Y. Santasombat (ed.), *The Sociology of Chinese Capitalism in Southeast Asia*, https://doi.org/10.1007/978-981-13-0065-3_1

tension. China's rise exerts a powerful gravity on ASEAN economies and an impetus for a resinicization of the overseas Chinese economic elite and their descendants in Southeast Asia. China has the potential to strengthen the ASEAN economies but also to create structural and political imbalances in the region. Since full enactment of the ASEAN–China Free Trade Area (ACFTA) in 2010, ASEAN's trade with China has gone from a surplus to a deficit that reached US$45 billion in 2013. China has become relatively more important to ASEAN as a trading partner than ASEAN is to China. More importantly, poorer ASEAN members depend heavily on China, particularly as a source of imports. Vietnam's share of Chinese export and import flows with ASEAN has increased substantially although Singapore's share has dropped. ASEAN–China economic relations are strategically important for regional development and stability. The asymmetry of size and power, in conjunction with territorial disputes, however, can be sources of anxiety and mistrust which hamper political relations.

ASEAN Regional Integration and Chinese Capitalism

The establishment of the ASEAN Economic Community (AEC) can be seen as an attempt to strengthen regional organization and its bargaining power. It has four objectives, namely the transformation of ASEAN into a single market and production base, creating a highly competitive economic region of equitable economic development and a region that would be fully integrated into the global economy by the end of 2015. As of early 2018, many indicators show that economic integration cannot be accomplished soon. A single market and production base requires that all members have a common interest and a high degree of cooperation. However, the authority of domestic political economy reigns over regional integration and cooperation. The political elite of the ASEAN countries tend to facilitate the monopoly of important domestic sectors to the Chinese economic elite, and their mutual interests are so intertwined that competition from neighboring firms are seldom tolerated. China's rising influence in the region, or what Jones (2016: 24) calls the 'the sinification of the ASEAN way', has profoundly and negatively impacted the capacity of ASEAN to strengthen its integration. ASEAN's connectivity master plan, for example, will be funded indirectly or directly by China to the extent that those infrastructural development projects serve Chinese interests, which are not necessarily those of

ASEAN. China's continuing attempts to dominate the South China Sea raise more critical issues that hinder regional integration. A shift in US foreign policy under a new leader drives another nail into the ASEAN regional integration coffin.

On his first day in office President Trump signed an executive order formally withdrawing the USA from the Trans-Pacific Partnership (TPP) trade deal. The abandonment of TPP marks the end of the US pivot toward Asia. TPP would have checked Beijing's penetrating politico-economic influence in Asia and regained the USA as an important leverage. The decision to discard TPP shows that the American leader has little concern for the geopolitics that offer choices to ASEAN nations. Donald Trump's transactional view of the world leads him to prefer 'deals' over global leadership. In terms of security relations, Trump's questioning of the established security relationship with NATO, Japan, and Korea, and how its economic burdens are shared marks the beginning of a decline of security commitments between the USA and old alliances. If long-established security relationships are subject to the strict calculus of economic self-interest, ties between old alliances may be weakened. The geopolitical map might collapse into the economic one, and China could become an even stronger player on the global political stage.

As the USA moves toward isolationist leaning under the "America First" banner, ASEAN countries are witnessing another round of power shifts in the global geopolitical landscape which could potentially lead to heightened tension between the superpowers on various issues ranging from currency manipulation to unfair trade and protectionism, Taiwan, North Korea, as well as territorial boundary disputes in the South China Sea. With the end of US President Obama's rebalance policy and TPP Free Trade Area, ASEAN countries will pragmatically have little choice but to accommodate China's bilateral relations. Individually, each country will negotiate to achieve the best possible deal with China. Growing bilateralism between China and ASEAN countries implies fragmentation rather than integration of the AEC. In turn, a low level of regional integration implies that convergence between ASEAN countries is limited and difficult to achieve. Additionally, regional and within-country inequality is high and in many countries steadily growing.

Within the context of ASEAN economic integration, this text asks the following questions: how will Chinese capitalism from China interact with ASEAN integration and its attempts at community building, and how will Chinese capitalism from China interact with diverse forms of

Chinese capitalism in Southeast Asia? In other words, what are the challenges and prospects of Chinese capitalism in Southeast Asia?

On one hand, China's rise and its growing economic engagement with ASEAN has presented new investment and business opportunities for local Chinese communities in Southeast Asia. On the other hand, China's rise has also stimulated anxieties, ambivalences, and new politico-economic realignments. What are some of the creative strategies–desinicization, resinicization, rebalancing–utilized by local Chinese communities and ASEAN countries to cope with the challenges of Chinese capitalism?

This book begins with a discussion of the relations between Chinese capitalism and the AEC from a perspective of desecuritization. In Chapter 2, Hsing-Chou Sung focuses on the meaning of security issues in Southeast Asia and the political realist friend/foe dichotomy that securitization brings. The author applies the desecuritization concept to the relationship between China and ASEAN countries and demonstrates how security is constructed in economic terms. Desecuritization concepts problematize security as discursively established, dismissing the idea of objective threats. The chapter defines desecuritization as a critical strategy that tries to relocate the question of power and domination to a context of economic integration and development in which political relations are not perceived on the basis of existential insecurity. With that perspective in mind, Sung asks what types of strategies are used by Beijing to remove obstacles if a mutual trust relationship exists between China and ASEAN member countries. Although China remains a vital security concern for ASEAN, despite the issue of territorial disputes and naval bases in the South China Sea, China still actively participates in every movement of regional integration.

Sung shows that Beijing appears aware of the complex intertwining between political and economic situations and tries to reshape the structure of distrust in the ASEAN perception of China as a regional threat. The way to achieve its overall policy goal is desecuritization based on regionalism and soft power. Since the 1997 Asian financial crisis, China has been able to dismiss the anxiety of an objective threat by the premise of economic cooperation (trade, investment, foreign aid), regionalization and global connectivity (One Belt One Road [OBOR]). China has taken advantage of the new regionalism and has become a skilled practitioner of "commercial diplomacy" (Frost 2007: 95). If China continues to lead the way in regional integration (state-led), Chinese capitalism will integrate into AEC and become China's essential strategy of desecuritization.

There is no doubt that China is now a superpower in global affairs. But how effectively does China make use of its growing power (resources, including the military) and influence (exercise of power) to achieve desirable goals? Drezner (2009) cogently argues that China was unable to exert much meaningful leverage over US financial policy despite its position as the leading holder of US debt. Similarly, China was unable (or unwilling) to change North Korea's nuclear policies despite increasing economic dependency. Additionally, China was unable to persuade Vietnam to deflect the territorial claims in the South China Sea. Conversely, increasing dependency on China has turned the Myanmar's Tatmadaw into a more balanced and diversified strategic relations with Japan, the USA, and Europe.

In economic terms, however, China has used its central position in regional production network and its huge market potential to influence ASEAN countries' choices. Its ultimate goal, however, is to consolidate its position as the region's economic driver by initiating East Asian regionalism (Ravenhill 2006), AEC (Jetin and Mikic 2016), and OBOR global economic order linking Asia to the Middle East, Africa, and Europe. It is using its economic influence to induce, coerce, and force ASEAN countries into actual regional economic integration. China has proliferated its economic power and influence over the AEC (Goh 2014: 834) in two fundamental ways: (1) by stimulating economic growth in the least developed countries in the region (see Chapter 9), and (2) by multiplying the more developed parts toward a trading bloc.

Chapter 3 by Liu and Zhou examine the historical and politico-economic contexts of Chinese capitalism in Southeast Asia and its relations with the Chinese diaspora. The authors contend that China's rapid growth in terms of economy and outward foreign direct investment (OFDI) has lent itself to a new wave of Chinese capitalism that increasingly blurs the boundaries between state, private, and public interests. This new Chinese economic statescraft or the state's intention to provide impetus for Chinese entrepreneurs to generate business ventures that are conducive to the state's and public interests has been the essence of China's outgoing policy aimed at promoting outward investment and elevating China's status as a global superpower.

How has the Chinese economic statescraft (Norris 2016) interacted with the AEC? Using Indonesia, Malaysia and Singapore (the more developed parts of AEC) as case studies of both private and state-sanctioned Chinese investments, Liu and Zhou delineate the geographical and sectorial distributions of Chinese OFDI and discuss how those Chinese enterprises penetrate ASEAN countries and with whom they have collaborated in their business endeavors.

From those cases, the authors found that the new Chinese capitalism is transnational and foreign. Although the overseas Chinese entrepreneurs were migrants who had settled down and integrated into their new "homes" and identified themselves as Chinese-cum-Southeast Asian, the new Chinese diaspora are highly mobile but retain a strong identification with the homeland. The rise of China and its economic power in terms of trade and investments provides an impetus for a resinicization process of the Chinese communities and a reproduction of Chinese cultures and identities among the ethnic Chinese in ASEAN countries.

The Chinese economic statescraft and the transnational Chinese entrepreneurs have not disrupted the preexisting structure of Chinese enterprises, but have been able to establish networks of cooperation in terms of joint ventures for the benefit of both sides. In their examination of the business practices of the top echelons of Chinese businesses, Liu and Zhou are optimistic that the new Chinese capitalism is reflective of both a different consciousness among China's big businesses and the state in their mutual goal of enhancing China's international image as a peaceful and responsible world power.

Domestic Politics and Economic Regionalism

The roles of the military, bureaucracies, and political elite will be important in shaping the business practices and policies of developing countries toward the world economy. Contrary to Yeung's assertion that the future of Chinese capitalism in the era of globalization will no longer be "sustained by politico-economic alliances with powerful political elites" (Yeung 2004: 254), we believe that the preexisting alliances between ethnic Chinese capitalists and ruling power elite have not been disrupted by China's rise. Additionally, the alliances have also been extended to include closer ties between new Chinese entrepreneurs and the power elite, with the ethnic Chinese serving as bridges. However, the political elite in ASEAN may have a greater ability than previously acknowledged to shape policy directions toward trade and investment. The question is how China's rising influence over regional integration affects the transformation of the ASEAN political elite and domestic politics. Lessons learned from Thailand, the Philippines, and Cambodia provide a partial answer to that question.

The Chinese have been the prominent economic minority in Thailand for hundreds of years. Traditional Thai political elite ethnicize key economic roles to the Chinese entrepreneurs while simultaneously denying them access to political power. In this context, the Chinese economic elite become what Hamilton (1978) calls 'pariah capitalists'. Contrary to popular contention, the Chinese have not been fully assimilated (Skinner 1957, 1958) to their host country. The Chinese in Thailand and elsewhere in Southeast Asia have developed double 'social embeddedness' (Liu and Na 2017: 58–59) reaffirming their Chinese identity while at the same time maintaining their Thai identity.

Chapter 4 by Wasana Wongsurawat portrays the life of Banharn Silpa-acha, a successful businessman, a former Thai Prime Minister, and a prominent leader of Chinese descent in Thai history. Banharn's life as both an economic and political elite testifies well to the process of resinicization of Chinese identities and cultures in Thailand. Banharn was born in 1932, when the patrimonial system was successfully challenged. The role of Chinese entrepreneurs as dependent subjects and agencies of the royal household who managed the tributary trade and tax collection had come to an end. Banharn was born in a family of Chinese migrants who made a comfortable living in the fabric business in Suphanburi province, northwest of Bangkok. His parents sent him to Bangkok to further his education at the secondary level, but World War II disrupted his education and he started to work for his elder brother before trying his luck in various businesses of his own.

In the 1950s, the Chinese constituted about half of the total population of the greater Bangkok area. The Chinese community focused inward upon itself, being controlled through ethnic associations, secret societies, and the Chinese Chamber of Commerce (Skinner 1957: 203–207). The question of loyalty of the *huaqiao*[1] and the fear of Communist China resulted in strained relations between the Chinese and the Thai communities throughout the successive military regimes from the 1950s to the late 1970s. Those military governments were short of economic capital and turned toward the Chinese-Thai entrepreneurs who could provide it. Leading Chinese-Thai businessmen (i.e. Chin Sophonpanich) could mobilize resources within the Chinese community through their connections, and those economic elite began to develop a new set of alliances with the military and the revitalizing monarchy.

Banharn's rise in business was made through the accumulation of social capital or personal connections with high ranking members of the military governments. Banharn started a construction company in the 1950s and used his connections with the military to win a lucrative ten-year monopoly to install tap-water pipes throughout Thailand. In the 1960s, Banharn used his newfound wealth to initiate development works—hospitals, schools, temples restoration, and construction—in his hometown. The internationalization and industrialization processes in the 1960s restructured the Thai economy toward the emergence of export-oriented sectors. Chinese-Thai manufacturing companies grew from joint ventures with partners in Japan, Europe, and the USA. Banharn also began a joint venture with a Japanese company. In 1976, Banharn was a candidate in his first election as a member of the conservative Chat Thai Party led by retired military elite. He gradually rose to become secretary and leader of the party. He served as a cabinet member in many governments and in 1995 became the twenty-first century prime minister of Thailand (Nishizaki 2011). Over the many decades of his political career, Banharn attempted to expand his base of support in Suphanburi by securing unprecedented amounts of state funds to build various local infrastructures and spent a great deal of his personal wealth building an impressive array of monuments, including the 'Dragon Descendants Museum', as part of an attempt to reaffirm his ethnic Chinese identity.

The story of Banharn is not one of economic or political success of an assimilated second generation Chinese descendant, but rather it is a story of ethnic reconstructions and of a dual social embeddedness with both Thai and Chinese cultural traditions. His life attests to the extraordinary ability of the Chinese entrepreneurs to adapt to a new home and embed themselves in a set of political alliances and economic networks. On the one hand, Banharn's expression of total submission to the monarchy and the royal family made him a trusted ally of the military and bureaucratic elite who were also exploiting their loyalty to maintain status quo. All successful Chinese tycoons of his generation (i.e. Sophonpanich, Sahapathanapibul, Charoenphokphand, Sirivadhanabhakdi) who dominated all sectors of the Thai economy expressed their loyalty to the monarchy and maintained strong alliances and partnerships with the military and bureaucratic elite. On the other hand, the story of Banharn testifies to the changing image of Chinese-Thais as a once stigmatized minority group and the overt reaffirmation of their Chinese cultural roots. With the rise of China and the growing economic power of transnational Chinese entrepreneurs, younger generations of Chinese-Thai economic elite are reclaiming their ethnicity and reconstructing it to fit regional and global definitions.

In Chapter 5, Ellen Palanca and Austin Ong demonstrate how the political elite and domestic politics may have greater ability to profoundly shape policy directions toward bilateral relations than previously acknowledged in the Philippines. The chapter is an attempt to demystify the dynamics of China–Philippines bilateral relations by disentangling the domestic factors from the external ones and by illustrating how bilateral relations have been shaped, influenced, and managed by domestic politics but tempered by the external forces of a global market. By examining the different trajectories of China–Philippines relations under the administration of different governments since Cory Aquino, Ramos, Estrada, with special emphasis on Arroyo, Aquino III, and Duterte, there has clearly been a lack of a coherent China policy and volatility of the bilateral relations.

After the Asian financial crisis and the deepening of China's economic involvement in Southeast Asia, during Arroyo's administration (2001–2010), China's charm offensive resulted in an unprecedented level of Chinese investments, economic partnerships, and joint ventures that developed rapidly in the field of infrastructures, power, mining, and agriculture. The Philippines was among three Southeast Asian countries with large China aid and investment projects reaching US$5.4 billion between 2002 and 2007 (Vietnam, US$3.4 billion; Burma, US$3.1 billion). In 2004, China's official development assistance represented 60% of the Philippines' total ODA. Despite China's economic power and strategic diplomacy, however, it had not been successful in obtaining the cooperation of the Philippines because China underestimated the strength of domestic politics and the effect of China's strong stance on territorial issues, which the Philippine side perceives as the flexing of the emerging state's newfound power. On the other hand, the Philippines' domestic politics prevented the country from fully capitalizing on China's economic charm offensive. Ultimately, that led to a roller coaster ride in the Philippines–China relationship—the manifestation is seen in how relations went from "Golden Age of Partnership" (Arroyo, 2000–2010), to antagonistic relations (Aquino, 2010–2016), and to friendly relations (Duterte, 2016–2022).

The authors conclude that the domestic factors manifested in personality-based politics and rampant corruption coupled with the negative public perception of China have largely driven the roller-coaster China policy that changes cycles with every new president. Although the territorial disputes paralyzed the economic relations in terms of the flow of major Chinese investments, other aspects such as trade were driven by global trends and market forces. The bilateral trade data are indeed better explained by global economic phenomena such as the impact of the global supply network, the global financial crisis, and the rebalancing of China's economy.

While the Philippines–China relations have changed with every new president, Cambodia's longest reigning authoritarian ruler has consistently moved on a pro-China trajectory over the past two decades. Cambodia is now without a doubt one of China's closest allies in Southeast Asia. The reasons behind Cambodia's embrace of China are complex and interwoven with political, security, and economic factors. China's bilateral ties with Cambodia comprise political and military alliances, business collaboration, and generous financial aid. In political and security terms, Cambodia's inexorable anxiety that Vietnam and Thailand's growing economic superiority will threaten its sovereignty has been a key reason for its embrace of China (Chong 2017). In economic terms, China is the top investor and a major aid provider in Cambodia. Chinese investment in Cambodia, in turn, has received political protection and privilege from the ruling elite (Chheang 2017).

Chapter 6 by Siphat Touch examines the relations between Chinese investments and the rise of the Cambodian-Chinese who serve as links between Cambodia and China. The Cambodian elite see the formation of the AEC as an opportunity for rapid economic development through foreign direct investment (FDI). The Chinese-Cambodian community has been prominent in the business sector for generations and continues to play a key role in current economic development. The rise of Chinese-Cambodians is contributing factor to Cambodia's embrace of China and increasing Chinese influence in the country. As a global economic power, China has been positioning itself as Cambodia's most important economic partner while Cambodia's elite need China as the key supporter for both economic and political reasons.

Over the past decades, the resiliency of ethnic Chinese in various Cambodian political regimes has allowed them to dominate the national economy. The ethnic Chinese integrated themselves into Khmer cultures through intermarriage and, except for the Khmer Rouge period, have been fully accepted as an integral part of society. Increasing economic regionalism creates further opportunities for the rise of Chinese-Cambodian power in the national economy as they become key players for the regional investment competition. Chinese-Cambodian business tycoons have served as intermediaries between the Khmer elite and transnational Chinese investors. Through them, direct investment from China has steadily increased particularly in real estate, energy, agriculture, textile, mining, railways, and highway construction. Political trust and strategic and economic interests are the basis of China–Cambodia relations. China is perceived as the most important strategic and economic partner to Cambodia in providing performance legitimacy and countervailing force against immediate neighbors perceived as threats to Cambodian sovereignty.

State-Owned Enterprises and Large-Scale Chinese Entrepreneurs

ASEAN leaders have by no means shed their anxiety about China's rise and its implications for Southeast Asia. ASEAN governments believe that they are competing with China for investment and that China is winning. The drive to achieve a more integrated regional market is a practical effort to rise on China's economic wave instead of drowning. The political elite are convinced that they have no choice but to be a part of a more integrated market with China to expand their own exports and make their economies more attractive to foreign investors.

China has taken advantage of the new regionalism to enhance its position through skillful use of commercial diplomacy within the context of an integrated market. Networks of economic cooperation in terms of mega-projects, concessions, and joint ventures between China's state-owned enterprises (SOEs) and ASEAN economic elite are fostering continued economic growth to the benefit of China and the AEC's business tycoons and large-scale entrepreneurs.

As ASEAN and China become increasingly integrated through trading and investment links, what are the drivers of Chinese multinational corporations' (MNCs) internationalization and the interactions with host-governments, local ethnic Chinese partners, and suppliers? Chapter 7 in this volume attempts to shed light on those questions by studying China's Chery Automobile Co. in Malaysia. That research shows that the local ethnic Chinese community has benefited from business engagement by playing an intermediary role between MNCs and politically dominated government-linked companies (GLCs) in Southeast Asia. Nevertheless, local ethnic Chinese firms have not developed a strong production capability by extensively collaborating with China's manufacturers to forge a regional production network. Therefore, despite Chinese firms having increasingly invested in Southeast Asia, the domestic business environment facing the local ethnic Chinese business community has not fundamentally improved. On the contrary, Chery's experience in navigating a set of complex state-society relations in Malaysia leads to the conclusion that Chinese MNCs tend to be more attracted by hostile developing countries where productive alliances can be established in institutional settings that are not necessarily transparent and well governed.

Similarly, Chapter 8 by Romyen Kosaikanont shows that political connections are fundamentally important for joint ventures between Chinese SOEs and the economic elite of ASEAN. The chapter examines China's Going Out Policy in practice and how a joint venture between a Chinese SOE and a Thai large-scale business enterprise has developed by using the Thai-Chinese Rayong Industrial Zone. This site was chosen as a case study because it is one of the 56 Chinese government-supported cooperation zones situated worldwide while Zhongce Rubber (Thailand) Co., Ltd. was chosen because it is the largest SOE in the rubber sector outside of China.

Romyen uncovers that the Going Out Policy has in practice been a part of Beijing's grand strategies of OBOR or the Belt and Road Initiative (BRI) and has received various support from the government, namely (1) BRI and related policy implementation, (2) institutional infrastructural establishment and setting up the mechanism to facilitate the trajectory of going out, (3) the subsidies by state and local government, and (4) network of support from various ministries and departments. The motivation from the Thai side is to find ways and means of uplifting the economy from the middle-income trap through the implementation of the newly invented development model of Thailand 4.0, which can be interpreted as a welcoming message for the coming in of Chinese investments for the much-needed FDI. The political support of the Thai government and Thailand's Board of Investment can be a mechanism for the Chinese establishment of their business in Thailand.

Zhongce Rubber (Thailand) Co., Ltd. positively generated more than 2000 jobs for the Thai and Chinese. However, the working conditions and practices of running businesses are still unclear. Chinese management style clearly divides Thai and Chinese employees in space management and unequal treatment and creates friction and conflict rather than building people up under the BRI. The study also found that the joint venture received support from both the Thai and Chinese governments.

Thailand has received political support in participating in a government-initiated business matching and subsequent tax privileges provided by the Board of Investment. Regarding China, both national and local governments of Hangzhou provided subsidies as part of the Going Out Policy. Chinese investors have strategically used political and business connections with the Rayong Chamber of Commerce, the Chinese Embassy, Thai politicians, as well as a cluster of Chinese suppliers to minimize business investment risks. Additionally, Chinese investors are directly linked and benefit from the grand strategy of the Chinese government going global and the BRI. Romyen shows that the joint venture is highly profitable to investors on both sides but that the local community has gained limited benefits from this industrial zone.

Large-scale investment from China remains in close contact with and to a large degree is directed by the state. Interacting in the foreign market opens up space for Chinese investors to be more innovative in creating business opportunities by establishing new connections among Chinese diaspora abroad, linking with the crony capitalists and political elite in the host country, maximizing the privileges provided by the host country. State-led Chinese capitalism perceives the entire world as its playing field. The support of going global along with the BRI strategy through the establishment of Industrial Zones in Southeast Asia and other regions is an indicator that China is strategically moving closer to becoming a world economic superpower.

As seen in the chapters on Singapore, Malaysia, and Thailand, ethnic Chinese MNCs have captured the opportunity to serve as "connectors and bridges" between the host countries and China (Suryadinata 2006: 4) and have benefited from the joint ventures and business investments. The impact of new Chinese capitalism on the small and medium enterprises (SMEs) in the AEC member countries, however, has not been equally positive.

SME Transnational Chinese in Southeast Asia

Trade, investment, and foreign aid between China and ASEAN countries, particularly the least developed countries, have been expanding rapidly since the turn of the millennium. Megaprojects resulting from economic cooperation have stimulated increasing numbers of 'overland' Chinese migrants[2] (Siriphon 2015) flowing into the region, particularly to Cambodia, Laos, Myanmar, and Vietnam (CLMV) countries.

The flow of those new Chinese migrants are closely related to the Going Out Policy and the many ways the Beijing and provincial governments have subsidized and supported the movement of the new transnational Chinese diaspora (Santasombat 2015: 2–3; Liu 2016: 313). Chapter 9 by Nguyen Van Chinh explores the complexity of the new Chinese diaspora to CLMV countries within the context of China's rising political and economic power in the region. In line with Sung's desecuritization concept, Nguyen contends that China has forged closer ties to her former Southern 'adversaries' through increasing economic cooperation. From the late 1990s to 2010, China's bilateral trade and investment in the CLMV countries have increased dramatically. China has gradually become the largest economic partner in terms of trade, investment, and foreign aid, and with those economic transitions, Southeast Asia has also witnessed increasing numbers of Chinese diaspora in the region. Supported and encouraged by the central and provincial governments, those new transnational Chinese (mostly SMEs) are becoming one of the most economically powerful groups in the region. Through the powerful Chinese diaspora and their networks with overseas Chinese, China is actively participating in every movement of regional integration. Chinese diaspora plays an increasingly pivotal role in the future of the AEC.

How has China's increasing penetration into the region affected the local Chinese communities and their economic activities? Chapter 10 by Khine Tun discusses the impact of economic regionalism on the Myanmar-Chinese SME businesses and their adaptive strategies. Over the past decades, China has been the largest trading partner for Myanmar and the increase of bilateral trade contributed to the SMEs in both positive and negative ways. Those SMEs whose businesses are involved in border trade have benefited from expanding volumes of trade while those in production of related products to the imports of Chinese entrepreneurs have lost their share of the business. From cases studies of local Chinese entrepreneurs, the author finds that many Myanmar-Chinese SMEs feel they are at risk in open competition with the incoming transnational Chinese entrepreneurs because of limited access to capital investment and technology. Local SMEs contend that they must be more flexible and adaptive to cope with increasing competition with the transnational Chinese. One local entrepreneur told Khine Tun that the inflow of Chinese sweaters into the local market has a great impact on his business. Chinese sweaters are cheaper, more modern, and desirable. The market for local production has reduced 70% over the past few years and within a few more years, locally produced sweaters will be losing the entire market. That entrepreneur is shifting to the tourism business to capitalize on the increasing number of Chinese tourists coming into Myanmar.

Chapter 11 by Wasana La-orngplew about Lao PDR also reflects the concerns of the local Chinese entrepreneurs over the future of their businesses following the arrival of new Chinese migrant traders. The author begins by painting a picture of business trajectories of new Chinese migrants in Pakse, Champasak Province in Southern Laos. The first trajectory is the establishment of business through interpersonal connections with pioneers. The second involves new migrants who are employed as wage laborers in Chinese shops to accumulate capital for future business investments. The third path, which is the least common, is that of the migrants who travel to and explore the potential for business investment in Laos.

From interviews and data collection from small-scale traders at Daoheuang market in Pakse, the author reconfirms the observation previously made by Chiang and Cheng (2015) and Siriphon (2015) that the biggest group of overland Chinese migrant traders in Laos came from Hunan Province. The presence of Hunan migrant traders is related to the success of the pioneer migrants from the same area and their extended business networks that attract other Chinese migrants to find business opportunities in Laos where there is a perception of less pressure and competition. The increasing numbers of Chinese diaspora, however, has led some local merchants to be worried about the future of local business. Some local Chinese traders are concerned that their businesses could soon be replaced by new migrant businesses. New Chinese diaspora are also facing business difficulties or suffering losses due to increasing competitive business environment.

The voices of small-scale Chinese migrant traders in Myanmar and Laos do not speak uniformly but make conflicting and overlapping claims from many perspectives arising from their differing positions in the structures of inequality in class, gender, and age found in China and Southeast Asia. For example, a few small businesses complain that China's policy and development projects seem to provide benefits for large-scale business enterprises rather than their small business. Those small entrepreneurs feel left out and must depend on their family networks to survive in the business world. In Laos, Chinese migrant families are normally composed of husband, wife, and young children. Women do the work, from taking care of the shop, selling merchandise, cooking, cleaning, and tending to the children while their husbands play the strategic role of establishing business *guanxi* networks. Women often say that their lives are not better than in China and complain that in the new setting they lack the support of their families and friends.

Small-scale businesses are indeed centered on family and family networks. Family (plus relatives and friends) is the basis of capital accumulation not only in terms of money but also for social (networks) and cultural (knowledge and skills) capital. Many Chinese families who intended to do business in Southeast Asia send their children to schools and universities abroad to accumulate cultural capital (degree/language skills) and social capital (networking with local friends). If conditions there are more advantageous, then there is a good chance the family will relocate to start a business. That strategy of 'flexible capitalism' (Nonini 2003: 83) thus characterizes the transnational practices of new migrant businesses in the setup of independent small-scale trade enterprises managed by family members with the father or the oldest son in charge. The size and scale of those enterprises usually remain at the lower end due to a scarcity of money to invest. If the family enterprises do well, the size and scale of trade will expand, if not, the family moves their business to a new location across regions or even national borders.

In contrast to Myanmar and Laos, most new SMEs Chinese migrant entrepreneurs in Thailand are from middle-class backgrounds. They are better educated, well-informed, technology-oriented, more individualistic, and highly mobile. Chapter 12 by Aranya Siriphon examines the increasingly important impact of Chinese migrant entrepreneurs in tourism-related businesses in Chiang Mai, Thailand, their business strategies, and the role of Chinese and Thai state policies on tourism. Siriphon contends that those group of migrants are a part of an emerging transnational entrepreneurial class of Chinese capitalism. As middle-class migrants, they share common entrepreneurship strategies in applying professional and western-style modern managerial practices, organizational structures, and adopting technology advancement.

Those Chinese entrepreneurs usually travel back and forth between China and Thailand. They employ Thai and Western employees and professionals to assist them in both routine jobs and specific tasks of sales, marketing, and management. They apply high-tech equipment such as online closed-circuit television surveillance systems at their offices, restaurants, and hotels to monitor their staff from afar. They use online booking systems for guesthouses and hotels and allow customers to use electronic bill payment systems and money transfer of credit cards, or online payment platforms like *wechat* pay, *alipay* service to support the convenience of customers' new lifestyles and at the same time facilitate managers and owners in dealing with accounting and electronic bill paying systems as well as data record gathering on daily accounting audits. Technological equipment and advancement not only allow the Chinese migrant entrepreneurs to take care of their businesses from afar, they also reduce the risk of encountering cash flow issues because they can audit their daily income through online linking. Some Chinese entrepreneurs are exploring a new electronic commerce market for buying and selling merchandise from Thailand to China. The author also found that the new transnational Chinese entrepreneurs in Thailand tend to diversify their business and investment, develop multiple social embeddedness, and redefine *guanxi* relations to support their positive business images.

Another important finding in the chapter is that the roles of the Chinese and Thai states and their policies are different. While the Chinese state has the proactive role in advancing policies and strategies to encourage recent Chinese emigrants to pursue their businesses, the role of the Thai state, in contrast, is slow to respond to the increasing flow of transnational Chinese entrepreneurs in Thailand. The ineffectiveness of the Thai state leads to increasing concern for the Thai entrepreneurs in tourism-related businesses who are confronted with increasing competition with transnational Chinese entrepreneurs and their business ventures in Thailand.

How do the local Chinese-Thai entrepreneurs cope with the influx of new transnational Chinese entrepreneurs? Chapter 13 by Lee Kian Cheng focuses on the Thai-Yunnanese SMEs and their multiple strategies to mitigate the challenges and maximize opportunities posed by the deepening penetration of new Chinese diaspora in Northern Thailand. His data are based on in-depth case studies of four medium-scale Yunnanese entrepreneurs who have various types of business enterprises and perform different adaptive strategies.

Like the small-scale entrepreneurs in Laos and Myanmar, Yunnanese medium-scale entrepreneurs in Chiang Mai are concerned with increasing competition from new PRC entrepreneurs with greater financial resources. However, the Thai Yunnanese entrepreneurs demonstrate great versatility in their adaptive strategies against the challenges posed by Chinese entrepreneurs. For instance, one Yunnanese entrepreneur employs the institutional and interpersonal networking tactics and greater local knowledge to mitigate the effect of predatory business tactics of transnational Chinese entrepreneurs, while another utilizes the Thai legal framework to gain the upper hand in collaborations with Chinese investors. In other words, the Yunnanese entrepreneurs are not passive receptors of PRC encroachment and economic regionalism but apply a multiplicity of negotiation strategies to cope with the increasing challenges, and in the process, have benefited from competition and cooperation with the new Chinese diaspora.

One of the issues regarding Chinese capitalism revolves around the competing assumptions that ethnic Chinese business success in Southeast Asia relies *either* on ethnic affiliation and shared cultural values, or on strategic deployment of resources, power relations, and cooperation. Chapter 14 by Bien Chiang and Jean Chih-yin Cheng sheds light on how "Chineseness" works to contribute to the economic and business strength in Singkawang, an Indonesian city in the Province of West Kalimantan. With ethnographic examples from the Sino-Indonesian business community of Singkawang, the authors illustrate how "Chineseness" works as both a liability and an asset to their business operations. They argue that "Chineseness" retained by the Sino-Indonesian entrepreneurs allows them to convert the accumulated fiscal capital into cultural capital, which is then commodified to generate further business revenue. The Sino-Indonesian community of Singkawang arrives at their current economic and political statuses by surviving decades of government persecution, social expulsion, and secondary diaspora. The "Chineseness" they manage to retain, though in a sense closely embedded in their cultural identity, is at the same time a capital-cum-commodity that has significant value in the neoliberal market of the earlier twenty-first century.

Dynamism of Chinese Capitalism

Our research on Chinese capitalism in Southeast Asia has served as a type of canvas upon which various ideas, concepts, and experiences from different AEC member countries have been painted. Dynamism of Chinese capitalism in Southeast Asia is predicated upon four interrelated factors: Chinese economic statecraft, transnational Chinese entrepreneurs, the ethnic Chinese, and AEC regionalism.

In many Southeast Asian economies, where Chinese capitalism has been a dominant institutional form of economic organization, the penetration of new Chinese economic skill and the accompanying transnational Chinese business corporations and entrepreneurs have posed serious challenges to the ethnic Chinese and have triggered multiple and transformative changes to the organization and dynamics of Chinese capitalism in the context of increasing regionalization and globalization (Fig. 1.1).

The Going Out Policy initiated in 1999 by the PRC to promote investments abroad has introduced much support to assist domestic companies in developing a global strategy to exploit and utilize opportunities in the expanding local and international markets. Since the launching of the Going Out Policy, interest in overseas investment by SOEs and private companies has increased exponentially. Some of the most prominent Chinese business and professional institutions are expanding their investments in the international markets and, along with this expansion, the world has encountered a massive movement of PRC Chinese from their homeland. Far from a tightly structured political organization which controls every fabric of social life of its citizens, the new Chinese economic state and its Going Out Policy have been a proactive, coordinated machine with all its agents acting in unison to facilitate transnational flow of the Chinese to go global. Since 2001, the economic policy of the PRC has pushed its SOEs and national champions to go global to develop Chinese brands that can conquer the world market (Callahan 2011).

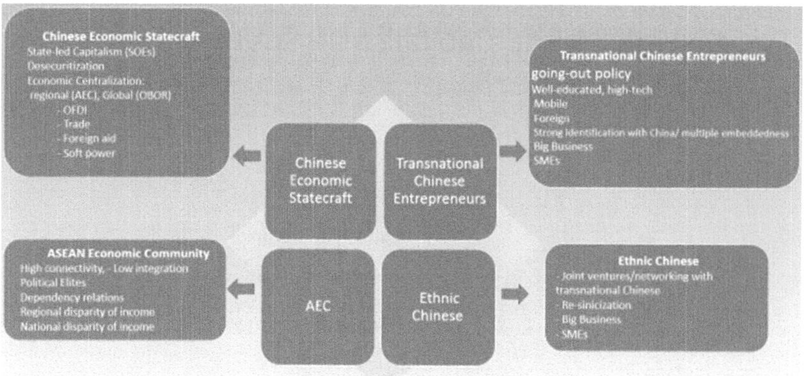

Fig. 1.1 Dynamism of Chinese capitalism in Southeast Asia

The rise of China as an economic power coupled with increasing regionalization and globalization has presented opportunities for changes and dynamism of Chinese capitalism over the past two decades. In response to China's rise, Southeast Asia has witnessed increasing complexity and variations of 'hybrid capitalism' (Yeung 2004), including the alliances between state-led capitalism, transnational entrepreneurships emanating from China's Going Out Policy and the ethnic Chinese (Fig. 1.2).

In between complex variations of global/transnational and local forms we can highlight three forms of Chinese capitalism in Southeast Asia: neoliberal capitalism, flexible capitalism, and Confucian capitalism. These forms are by no means mutually exclusive but have intermingled to produce variations of hybridized local forms under different socio-economic conditions.

Neoliberal capitalism is broadly generalizable to how large-scale Chinese businesses operate in all the AEC member countries. This form of capitalism integrates the financial resources of the state-led enterprises and market-oriented upper-class CEOs investing heavily in infrastructure mega-projects and export-oriented industrial development projects promoted by state investment policies and often operated by SOEs-private sector joint ventures. Chinese neoliberal capitalism is redistributive in a sense that it strategically exploits political connections and joint investment with the host country's GLCs or ethnic Chinese MNCs to obtain a contract, concession, AC, or project with highly favorable business

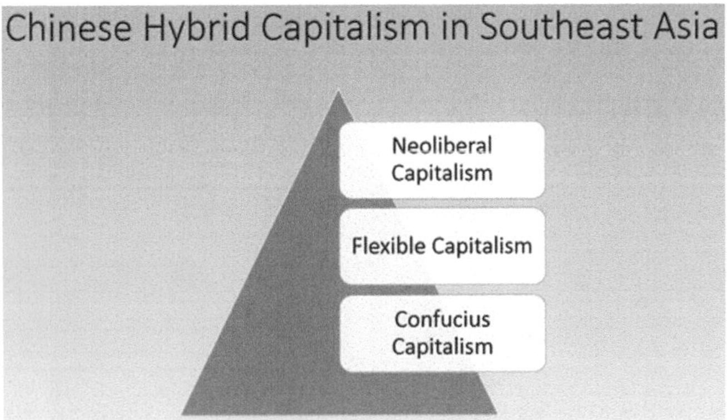

Fig. 1.2 Chinese hybrid capitalism in Southeast Asia

conditions. Chinese SOEs and MNCs are motivated by the Going Out Policy and the preferential trading arrangements such as ACFTA and economic regionalism to relocate operations in Southeast Asia. Local ethnic Chinese big businesses serve as links between China and host countries. Neoliberal SOEs and MNCs tend to be more attracted by authoritarian countries where productive alliances can be fostered in an institutional setting that favors connections and patronages to minimize investment risks.

Large-scale business investment from China remains in close contact with, and to a large degree is directed by, the state. Interacting in the foreign market opens up business opportunities by establishing new connections among the ethnic Chinese economic elite whom, in turn, link the transnational large-scale investors with the crony capitalists and political elite, thereby maximizing the privileges provided by the host countries. The Golden Triangle Special Economic Zone (SEZ) on the northern Laos border run by Chinese tycoon Zhao Wei (Laungaramsri 2015), Union Development's Seven Dragon SOE in Koh Kong, Cambodia (Siphat 2015), and the high-speed railways in Laos and Thailand (Zhenhua and Haynes 2015) are just a few examples of large-scale neoliberal capitalist investments which can be seen all over Southeast Asia.

Flexible capitalism is broadly generalizable to small- and medium-scale operations by transnational Chinese entrepreneurs in all AEC member countries. The term 'flexible capitalism' is used interchangeably with synonyms such as adaptability and versatility. The middle-class Chinese transnational entrepreneurs in Southeast Asia are well-educated, well-traveled, highly individualistic, high-tech oriented, highly mobile and risk-taking investors. They are highly flexible in terms of diversifying their businesses. They can constitute new labor forces and readily set diverse business processes in motion in response to market demand, yet quickly move their capital to new lines of business or trade when the market changes. A greater dispersal of investment, production, and recruitment of labor allows for greater flexibility in terms of capital accumulation, the production process, and the organization of labor.

In recent years, those transnational entrepreneurs have turned their increasing attention to the 'creative economy' and 'innovative industries' that are the crossroads of art, culture, business, and technology. The creative economy can be highly transformative in terms of expanding jobs, building exports, and generating income. Postmodern product design and production process come to entail higher measures of specialization such as 'tailor-made', 'chic', boutique, 'nuvo', 'fusion', 'niche market', and online trading, that require a high level of skills. Flexible capitalism undermines work as a source of identity, thereby traditional social relationships, groupings, and identities erode (Kjaerulff 2015). New transnational entrepreneurs no longer ascribe to the kind of economy that can provide a measure of stability but embrace a process of individualization and fragmentation which spans the workplace and the global space in which individuals live. Electronic payment systems, credit cards, or online payment platforms facilitate the transnational entrepreneurs in dealing with accounting and electronic bill paying systems as well as data record gathering on daily accounting audits and allow those Chinese flexible entrepreneurs greater mobility to take care of their multiple business settings from afar.

Confucian capitalism is broadly generalizable to small-scale overland Chinese businesses constructed around family connections in Laos, Myanmar, and Vietnam. Those small-scale Chinese migrant entrepreneurs are arguably the epitome of Confucian capitalism (Yao 2002). They use *guanxi* relations and connections to develop trust and mutual assistance between themselves and others in business arrangements. Those small-scale entrepreneurs rely equally on family and ethnic affiliation and shared cultural values as well as strategic deployment of resources, power relations, and cooperation. What is witnessed in those small-scale entrepreneurs is a mixture of pragmatism and strategic use of Chinese cultural values in establishing and maintaining their businesses.

Those new migrant small-scale entrepreneurs originally came as contracted workers and technicians working on road construction, rubber plantations, and industrial development projects. Many stayed and set up small businesses from personal and family savings. Some small-scale entrepreneurs worked as shop assistants while others stayed after visiting friends and relatives already settled in the host countries. Some are petty traders who load commodities in trucks and sell them in rural villages and local market fairs. It is common that while Chinese entrepreneurs may settle down in a city, they all have relatives, friends, or family members running a similar business in another place. The main commodities sold in Chinese shops are mostly inexpensive, low-quality products including clothes, home appliances, mobile phones, cosmetics, automobile and motorbike parts and accessories, sports equipment, agricultural tools, and machineries. The increasing numbers of small-scale migrant entrepreneurs in many urban centers have led to intensifying business competition. A result of vulnerabilities to increasing competition and related insecurity of trade is an inexorable tendency toward mobility and increasing exploitation of family members and hired laborers (Yao 2003; Nonini 2003).

In many parts of the Mekong Region, the small-scale Confucian capitalism is rapidly shifting. The future is an open-ended question. In fact, all forms of economic arrangements and organizations under the label of Chinese capitalism are drifting and strategically adapting to the ever-changing socio-political and economic situation. The trajectories of Chinese capitalism transformation in the AEC member countries are deeply linked to the regional integration of those economies with the growing economy of China through trade and investment flows. It remains to be seen whether those forms of Chinese hybrid capitalism are stable and enduring in the context of accelerated regionalization.

There is a growing concern within the context of economic regionalism whether ASEAN economies will be increasingly centralized and absorbed into the state-led economic organization of China. There is also a great deal of anxiety over the ASEAN resilience in the face of a rapidly shifting balance of power in the Asia-Pacific. In the years to come, the AEC will have to face new tests of how to avoid falling into the peril of the Thucydides trap.

Thucydides Trap

Thucydides, an Athenian historian, once lamented on the Greek war that it was the rise of Athens and the fear that it inspired in Sparta that made war inevitable (Hanson 2005). The phrase 'Thucydides trap' therefore refers to the tensions between an established hegemon and the rising challenger. Over the past decades, ASEAN countries have witnessed increasing tensions in US–China relations on a wide range of issues and areas. The defining question of global and regional order in the years ahead will be whether the USA and China can escape the Thucydides trap to strike a balance between competition and cooperation, and work together to rectify and improve the global economic, political, and security challenges.

China's rise and expanding political and economic interests have resulted in a drastic change in the regional order. China has adopted a more assertive approach toward multilateral organizations which it sees as controlled by Western powers, and toward ASEAN, its southern neighbors. Are we witnessing the formation of a regional economy which is specifically Chinese and dominated by the PRC? The extension of Greater China Economic Zones which originally comprised China, Taiwan, Hong Kong, and Singapore to cover other Southeast Asian countries?

The China's Dream project–OBOR–can be seen as the extension and "institutionalization" of Chinese capitalism which will naturally lead to the speculation that an extremely powerful and extensive Chinese trade network is likely to develop across Asia, the Middle East, Africa, and Europe. That economic centralization is also a project of transnational governance, a Chinese version of the world economic order, and a resinicization of regional and global economies. The OBOR represents both a symbolic and a direct challenge to the world economic order established and sustained by the USA and is a potential reason for increasing competition.

Increasing competition between the USA and China is of grave concern for AEC member countries. Changing US priorities in Asia over the past decades coupled with China's increasing efforts to deepen its relations with ASEAN are factors mitigating US influence in the region. Increasing ties between new Chinese diaspora/investors and old regional Chinese economic elite are leading ASEAN Chinese communities toward a resinicization process and an increasingly positive value of China as an economic partner. China's desecuritization and economic centralization strategies are designed to reassure AEC member countries that China continues to value close relationships with its southern neighbors despite uncertain and changing global politics and US-China continuing competition.

Notes

1. In Thailand, the term *huaqiao* refers to overseas Chinese and their descendants who have the legal right to reside in their host country but retain their loyalty and passion for the homeland. During the Japanese invasion, many Chinese families sent their children to fight for or provide financial support to China. Ties between the *huaqiao* and China were disrupted during Mao's era of communist ideology.
2. This book uses the term 'Chinese migrant', 'PRC Chinese', 'transnational Chinese' and 'Chinese diaspora' interchangeably to refer to the new waves of Chinese entrepreneurs and investors who migrated from mainland China to start the diverse forms of businesses and investments in Southeast Asia after 1978.

Bibliography

Callahan, William. 2011. "Introduction." In *China Orders the World: Normative Soft Power and Foreign Policy*, edited by William Callahan and Elena Barabantseva. Washington, DC: Woodrow Wilson Center Press.

Chheang, Vannarith. 2017. "The Political Economy of Chinese Investment in Cambodia." *Trends in Southeast Asia*, no. 16.

Chiang, Bien, and Jean Chih-yin Cheng. 2015. "Changing Landscape and Changing Ethnoscape in Lao PDR: On PRC's Participation in The Greater Mekong Subregion Development Project." In *Impact of China's Rise on the Mekong Region*, edited by Yos Santasombat, 85–117. New York: Palgrave Macmillan.

Chong, Terence. 2017. "The Politics Behind Cambodia's Embrace of China." *ISEAS Perspective*, no. 59.

Drezner, Daniel W. 2009. "Bad Debts: Assessing China's Financial Influence in Great Power Relations." *International Security* 34, no. 2: 7–45.

Frost, Ellen L. 2007. "China's Commercial Diplomacy in Asia: Promise or Threat." In *China's Rise and the Balance of Influence in Asia*, edited by William W. Keller and Thomas G. Rawski, 95–120. Pittsburgh: University of Pittsburgh Press.

Goh, Evelyn. 2014. "The Modes of China's Influence: Cases from Southeast Asia." *Asian Survey* 54, no. 5: 825–848.

Hamilton, Gary G. 1978. "Pariah Capitalism: A Paradox of Power and Dependence." *Ethnic Groups: An International Periodical of Ethnic Studies* 2: 1–15.

Hamilton, Gary G. 2006. *Commerce and Capitalism in Chinese Societies*. London and New York: Routledge.

Hanson, Victor D. 2005. *A War Like No Other: How the Athenians and Spartans Fought the Peloponnesian War*. New York: Random House.

Liu, Hong, and Ren Na. 2017. "Transnational Social Underpinning of New Chinese Capitalism: Immigrant Entrepreneurship in Singapore." In *Chinese Capitalism in Southeast Asia: Cultures and Practices*, edited by Yos Santasombat, 57–84. New York: Palgrave Macmillan.

Jetin, Bruno, and Mia Mikic, eds. 2016. *ASEAN Economic Community: A Model for Asia-Wide Regional Integration?* New York: Palgrave Macmillan.

Jones, David M. 2016. "ASEAN's Imitation Economic Community: The Primacy of Domestic Political Economy." In *ASEAN Economic Community: A Model for Asia-Wide Regional Integration?* edited by Bruno Jetin and Mia Mikic, 11–33. New York: Palgrave Macmillan.

Kjaerulff, Jen. 2015. "Introduction." In *Flexible Capitalism: Exchange and Ambiguity at Work*, edited by Jens Kjaerulff, 1–42. New York and Oxford: Berghahn Books.

Laungaramsri, Pinkaew. 2015. "Commodifying Sovereignty: Special Economic Zones and the Neoliberalization of the Lao Frontier." In *Impact of China's*

Rise on the Mekong Region, edited by Yos Santasombat, 117–146. New York: Palgrave Macmillan.

Liu, Hong. 2016. "Opportunities and Anxieties for the Chinese Diaspora in Southeast Asia." *Current History* 11, no. 784, November: 312–318.

Nishizaki, Yoshinori. 2011. *Political Authority and Provincial Identity in Thailand: The Making of Banharn-Buri*. Ithaca, NY: Cornell Southeast Asia Program.

Nonini, Donald M. 2003. "All Are Flexible, but Some Are More Flexible Than Others: Small Scale Chinese Business in Malaysia." In *Ethnic Business: Chinese Capitalism in Southeast Asia*, edited by Brian Fok and Jomo K.S., 73–92. London and New York: Routledge.

Norris, William J. 2016. *Chinese Economic Statecraft: Commercial Actors, Grand Strategy and State Control*. Ithaca, NY: Cornell University Press.

Ravenhill, John. 2006. "Is China an Economic Threat to Southeast Asia?" *Asian Survey* 46, no. 5: 653–674.

Santasombat, Yos. 2015. "Introduction." In *Impact of China's Rise on the Mekong Region*, edited by Yos Santasombat, 1–21. New York: Palgrave Macmillan.

Siphat, Touch. 2015. "Patterns and Impacts of Chinese Assistance in Cambodia." In *Impact of China's Rise on the Mekong Region*, edited by Yos Santasombat, 195–225. New York: Palgrave Macmillan.

Siriphon, Aranya. 2015. "*Xinyimin*, New Chinese Migrants, and the Influence of the PRC and Taiwan on the Northern Thai Border." In *Impact of China's Rise on the Mekong Region*, edited by Yos Santasombat, 147–166. New York: Palgrave Macmillan.

Skinner, William. 1957. *Chinese Society in Thailand*. Ithaca, NY: Cornell University Press.

Skinner, William. 1958. *Leadership and Community in the Chinese Community of Thailand*. New York: Cornell University Press.

Suryadinata, Leo. 2006. "Introduction." In *Southeast Asia's Chinese Businesses in an Era of Globalization: Coping With the Rise of China*, edited by Leo Suryadinata, 1–12. Singapore: ISEAS.

Yao, Souchou. 2002. *Confucian Capitalism: Discourse, Practice and the Myth of Chinese Enterprise*. New York: Routledge Curzon.

Yao, Souchou. 2003. "The Cultural Limits of 'Confucian Capitalism': Power and the Invention of the Family among Chinese Traders in Sarawak." In *Ethnic Business: Chinese Capitalism in Southeast Asia*, edited by Brian Fok and Jomo K.S. London and New York: Routledge.

Yeung, Henry. 2004. *Chinese Capitalism in a Global Era: Towards Hybrid Capitalism*. London and New York: Routledge.

Zhenhua, Chen, and Kingsley E. Haynes, ed. 2015. *Chinese Railways in the Era of Highspeed*. Bingley: Emerald Group.

CHAPTER 2

Chinese Capitalism and the Development of the ASEAN Economic Community: A Perspective of Desecuritization

Hsing-Chou Sung

Introduction

The establishment of the Association of Southeast Asian Nations (ASEAN) Economic Community (AEC) is an important milestone in regional economic integration. It is envisioned to be a single market and production base for the free flow of goods, services, investment, capital, and skilled labor within the ASEAN (ASEAN Secretariat 2008). ASEAN already accounts for more than 5% of the world's gross domestic product (GDP) and the International Monetary Fund predicts GDP growth will remain above 5% during 2015–2020 (ASEAN Secretariat 2015). Following the recent boom in efficiency-driven markets, particularly Brazil, Russia, India, China, and South Africa, attention is now shifting to the Southeast Asian region.

After adopting the *ASEAN Vision 2020*, ASEAN members tried to create a stable, prosperous, and highly competitive region with equitable economic development, reducing poverty and socio-economic disparities

H.-C. Sung (✉)
Department of Political Science, Tunghai University, Taichung, Taiwan

Y. Santasombat (ed.), *The Sociology of Chinese Capitalism in Southeast Asia*, https://doi.org/10.1007/978-981-13-0065-3_2

(ASEAN 1997). At the Bali Summit in October 2003, ASEAN leaders declared that the AEC shall be the goal of regional economic integration (*Bali Concord II*) by 2020. Leaders signed a *Declaration on the AEC Blueprint* at the 13th ASEAN Summit in Singapore. According to the declaration, leaders determined to achieve higher levels of economic dynamism, sustained prosperity, inclusive growth, and integrated development of ASEAN, while simultaneously promising their collective commitment to accelerate the establishment of the ASEAN community, including its AEC pillar, to 2015. In that regard, trade liberalization will serve as a key factor in improving working conditions directly through the rise of common standards among competing countries, and indirectly through rising productivity, job creation, and technological change.[1]

It is widely recognized that the economy will be the dynamic force that causes interdependence between ASEAN and China (ASEAN Secretariat 2016). China can provide a mega domestic market and direct foreign investment for ASEAN. Likewise, China's domestic "growing pains" of rising labor costs, land costs, and slowing economic growth has seen it turn to ASEAN as its new production and market base overseas. In other words, reaching out to ASEAN and other regional countries is not a want, but a need. As China tries to deal with its limited economic growth, ASEAN is a natural partner given their geographic and historic ties (Cheng 2013).

ASEAN regional integration continues to be influenced by China's perceived threat and security concerns, including the territorial disputes in the South China Sea (Cheng-Chwee 2005), which results in questioning how China can manage a crisis in trust. Strategies used by Beijing are a form of a "desecuritization" strategy to persuade ASEAN countries to change their perception of China as a threat.

The Copenhagen School (CS) argues that security is established through discourse or, more specifically, through a speech act by a securitizing actor. It is the act of *naming* an existential threat that legitimizes the players to take extraordinary measures, and to break the rules that normally bind them (Buzan et al. 1998).

This chapter has three sections. The first section has an overview of the studies of desecuritization and Chinese capitalism including important critiques that challenge assumptions, methods, and assertions. In the second section the development of AEC and the desecuritizing strategies used by Beijing in each phase of development are discussed and examines the theoretical and practical possibilities for desecuritization. The third section is an analysis of how China's economic participants have desecuritized the threat atmosphere in Southeast Asia since the 1990s, particularly with regard to the AEC and Chinese capitalism.

Desecuritization and Its Strategic Implication

In the decades following the end of the Cold War, dominant paradigms of security studies have been challenged by academics unsatisfied with existing concepts looking to explain security in a transformed world. Primarily, they sought to move security studies beyond theories that recognized only military threats as challenges to national security. One leading approach to reconceptualize security is the CS and their theory of securitization. That approach to world politics is to understand how international issues become securitized, or taken out of the sphere of normal, deliberative politics, into the realm of emergency politics and extraordinary measures (Buzan et al. 1998). That view of securitization is generally a negative one, as it allows the players to justify all sorts of policies to deal with a discursively constructed threat. Seeing security as doing more harm than good, desecuritization aims to diminish languages of emergency measures or existential threats (Hansen 2012).

Buzan et al. (1998) present the theory to understand how issues become securitized, focusing on the role of speech in the framing of threats. The securitization theory looks at how security dynamics are discursively established rather than looking at the objective reality of threats perceived out there (Floyd 2007). To understand threats as subjectively constructed, the theory disavows security analysts' ability to show what is and what is not a threat. However, that does not mean they see all securitizations as equally illegitimate. Instead, they maintain that by seeing all threats as subjective, they restrict players' ability to legitimize harmful policies based on the threatening nature of an issue (Balzacq 2005).

In this context, securitization means turning a specific issue from the realm of normal politics to conceptualizing threats as existentially threatening. Furthermore, securitizing allows the players to rise above the norms that would normally bind them to eliminate a perceived existential threat. This view of securitization is that securitization allows the players to justify all sorts of policies to deal with a discursively constructed threat. In the same vein, they argue that the aim of desecuritization should be for moving issues out of emergency mode and into the normal bargaining process of the political sphere (Buzan et al. 1998).

Security, Securitization, and Desecuritization

Although the securitization theory is a social constructivist understanding of threats, the methodology is fairly objectivist, choosing methodological collectivism over analysis at the individual level. Additionally, unlike some other nontraditional schools of security studies, they refrain from establishing an emancipatory ideal (McSweeney 1996). In other words, the theory does not define what security *is*, rather chooses to focus on understanding how security is constructed and what security does (Mackenzie 2009).

Theoretically, any player can speak on behalf of a referent in a securitizing move. Practically, however, securitizations are always carried out by the traditional elite (Buzan et al. 2009). Furthermore, securitizations may fail if, for example, the securitizing agent fails to convince the relevant audience that an issue is existentially threatening, or if the referent is deemed not worthy of being saved (Buzan et al. 1998).

The concept of securitization entails the construction of threats following a "grammar of security" (in Buzan's terms). Consequently, no issue is a threat per se, but anything could be constructed as one by utilizing discourse constructions. Buzan et al. (1998) identified three factors that influence the likelihood that the audience will accept the securitizing claim:

1. The demand internal to the speech act of following the grammar of security and constructing a plot with existential threat, point of no return, and a possible way out;
2. The social conditions regarding the position of authority for the securitizing player–that is, the relationship between speaker and audience and thereby the likelihood of the audience accepting the claims made in a securitizing attempt; and
3. Features of the alleged threats that either facilitate or impede securitization.

The emphasis on authority is significant in that securitization can only be carried out by coercive and persuasive power, institutional or other. There is admission that power relations between subjects inevitably play a role in a securitizing move, they claim that such power is never absolute, and no one is theoretically excluded from challenging a securitization. Furthermore, they argue that a securitization reveals itself once a relevant audience has accepted that an issue must be dealt with outside of the rules that would otherwise have to be obeyed.

Securitization establishes a logic by which authorized players can escape the normal realm of deliberative politics, embracing a state of exceptionalism of expedient decision-making to deal with a perceived existential threat. In that regard, security is a realm outside of politics and the usual laws and norms that bind players' decisions. By contrast, desecuritization is the optimal long-range option because it means not having issues phrased as threats against which have had countermeasures saved (Buzan et al. 1998).

Ole Wæver (2000) theorizes three strategies of desecuritization as follows:

1. Not speaking about an issue as a threat at all.
2. Managing a securitization so that it does not spiral.
3. Moving the securitized issue back into normal politics.

However, there is no general strategy for desecuritization, and some strategies will undoubtedly work better than others because desecuritization strategies aimed at the restoration of normal politics do not seem to share the same idea about what constitutes normal politics. Consequently, they do not follow the CS theory in viewing normal politics as subjective, but rather posit normative ideas on what those politics should be.

This theoretical framework of securitization and desecuritization will be used in the following sections to investigate China's desecuritization strategies for reshaping its external environment of development and integrating itself into the regional economy.

Regionalism

China is a constructive participant in Asian regionalism with its own characteristics. Since President Xi Jinping came to office at the end of 2012, China has been pushing through a new type of regionalism.

China's regionalism in Asia started in the 1990s and went through three major evolutions (Xiaotong and Xiaoyue 2014).

1. Preliminary stage: from hostile to active: China was hostile to Asian regionalism represented by ASEAN, claiming that ASEAN was an anti-communist tool used by imperialists. Since the late

1970s, and particularly after the end of the Cold War, China has gradually changed its negative attitude toward ASEAN. Since the mid-1990s, China has started to actively participate in Asian regionalism.

2. Mature stage: enlarging its geographic area: previously, China's regionalism was confined to East Asia, but now has expanded to all areas in Asia, including Central and South Asia. More specifically, China is now advancing its regionalism on two fronts: westward across the Eurasian continent and southward toward the Indian Ocean (Wanandi 2004).
3. Transformation stage: actively participating in and contributing to regional affairs. When the People's Republic of China (PRC) was founded in 1949, China was playing the role of a revolutionary state, which refused to accept the regional arrangement dominated by the USA and its anti-communist allies. From the mid-1990s, China started to become an active participant and contributor to the existing regional mechanisms, and now China is transforming itself into a great power in Asia's regionalism.

China started to seek a community-building type of regional cooperation since 2012. It is characterized by efforts at deeper regional integration through calls for historical and cultural empathy among Asian neighbors. It is the very first time that China has systematically sought to integrate itself into the whole region through historical and cultural links, rather than just through economic links. On October 25, 2013, Xi Jinping delivered an important speech at a symposium on diplomatic work in China's neighborhood (including Central Asian countries and Southeast Asian countries) and stressed, "strive for a good surrounding environment for our country's development, push forward the development of our country that benefits neighboring countries more" (Wanandi 2004).

Subsequently, China is calling for the building of the Silk Road Economic Belt as well as advancing the Maritime Silk Road. In 2013 China commemorated the 10th anniversary of the establishment of a strategic partnership between China and ASEAN. When Premier Li Keqiang visited the China–ASEAN Expo on September 4, 2013, he proposed establishing the Maritime Silk Road (*Xinhuanet* October 11, 2013). When Xi Jinping gave a speech on April 1, 2014 during a visit to Europe, he mentioned building a silk road linking the two ends of the Eurasian continent. Using the ancient Chinese concepts of a land-based silk road and a maritime silk road, China has proposed a new model for its regional cooperation.[2]

Regionalism for Desecuritization and Confidence Building

China is seeking an innovative way for regional cooperation, mainly in the form of community building. It is emphasizing cultural and historical exchanges as much as transport links. China believes that this type of regional cooperation would be softer, deeper, and easier for its neighbors to accept and reflects a new approach with Chinese characteristics in economic regionalism, but it is too early to tell whether China's new economic regionalism works (Cheng-Chwee 2005).

China's involvement with ASEAN is an extension of its "Good Neighbor" policy. However, with its increased economic power and persistent maritime claims, China's relations with Asian countries are not so straight forward as rhetoric would suggest. Rather, relations have become a complicated web of rituals, risks, and rivalries in which China interacts on multiple levels to influence respective member states without being overpowered by ASEAN (Papatheologou et al. 2014).

Far from being overpowered, some see China as riding the tide of an ASEAN wave that is viewed as "the center of gravity for maintaining a stable economic and geopolitical order in the region" (Yamei 2016). By utilizing more intensive economic engagement, China can lead that regional order. Southeast Asian states engage with China to earn economic incentives and their hope is that American security commitments with member states will balance the influence of China (Shamsul and Lei 2013). In other words, regionalism can help speed up the process of desecuritization and guarantee mutual confidence.

Soft Power

China's growing use of soft power in Southeast Asia, that is, non-military inducements including culture, diplomacy, foreign aid, trade, and investment has been the ongoing trend shaping relations between China and ASEAN countries.

China's Soft Power Strategy in Southeast Asia

Throughout history, Southeast Asia has been a natural target for China to extend its sphere of influence. China has been trying to counter the image of a "China threat" in Southeast Asia by reshaping preferences in the region using soft power diplomacy. Since the 1997 Asian economic crisis, China's policy in Southeast Asia can be described as soft power diplomacy. The PRC is using the soft power, wielded power through diplomacy and admiration of China as a model for development and ancient culture, to build its image in Southeast Asia as a responsible regional power (Lum et al. 2008).

Beijing's soft power policy in the region is based on economic engagement, diplomatic tactics, trade and investment, and cultural and educational exchange. Instead of resorting to military action, China began to use a less confrontational approach to resolve its issues with ASEAN states. Furthermore, China is one of the major trading partners of ASEAN states and provides economic aid and technological assistance to countries like Cambodia, Myanmar, Indonesia, the Philippines, and Laos (Hwang 2008).

The normalization of relations created a platform for a new era of regional cooperation which resulted in the signing of the China–ASEAN Free Trade Area (CAFTA) agreement in 2002 and the ASEAN Treaty of Amity and Cooperation in 2003.

Soft Power as the Core of Desecuritization

Womack's (2004) article explains that China is successfully using its soft power policy to extend its influence in the Southeast Asian states. China's billion-dollar investment in soft power has become successful in rebuilding its image and strengthening its influence in the region. Beijing's growing influence in Southeast Asia is being perceived as a natural progression and beneficial for the peaceful development in the region (Womack 2004). When the USA loses its influence in the region because of its unpopular unilateral foreign policy, China is gaining from the US decline. In fact, Beijing's charm offensive is the result of Chinese soft power. "China Studies" has become the new fad and shows no sign of dissipating. Confucius Institutes and Chinese culture schools are being established throughout the region (Hwang 2008).

Undoubtedly, China's growing economy permits Beijing to play a key role in the region. China has already made a significant impact on the regional politics in Southeast Asia by implementing its soft power, such as the "Good Neighbor" policy, trade, investment, development aid, cultural interaction, and educational exchanges. Beijing's rhetoric of a win-win foreign policy, along with the strong political economic and cultural initiatives, has amplified the effectiveness of its soft power and enhanced China's ability to extend its influence in the Southeast Asia region (Schmidt 2008).

Chinese Capitalism and Regional Economic Integration

Chinese state capitalism has proved its effectiveness and continued to be attractive following economic depressions such as the Asian financial crisis. Recently, theoretical and empirical literature is exploring the concept of Chinese state capitalism. Some important characteristics are summarized below.

ORIGIN OF CHINESE CAPITALISM

The concept of state capitalism is demonstrated in *The State and Revolution* written by Vladimir I. Lenin (1976). In the spring of 1918, during a brief period of economic liberalism prior to the introduction of war-based communism, and again during the New Economic Policy of 1921, Lenin justified the introduction of state capitalism controlled politically by the dictatorship to further centralize control and develop productive forces. To Lenin, that form of capitalism did not mean that the state would run the economic affairs; rather it was intended as a temporary economic system for transforming to a communist society operated by the workers (Gabriel et al. 2008).

From 1956 to the late 1970s, Mao's Communist Party of China (CPC) often described the Soviet Union as state-capitalist, essentially using the accepted Marxist definition, albeit on a different basis and in reference to a different span of time from either the Trotskyists or the left-communists. During his summer financial workshop in 1953, Mao wrote a note on an official document which defined state capitalism as a specific economic system. In Mao's opinion, state capitalism did not provide service for capitalists' interest, but for the people and state under the governing of a people's government. The Maoists and their descendants used the term and emphasized its socialist essence (Mao 1977).

After Mao's death, state capitalist formulation translated little to a different meaning. To save both socialism and the PRC regime, China embedded market mechanisms into the socialist economy for enhancing the efficiency of national economic activities in the late 1970s (Coase and Want 2013). In 1978, that innovative approach to economic reform was termed "socialism with Chinese characteristics", advocated by Deng Xiaoping. Eventually, that hybrid form of capitalism not only revitalized China's economy, but also reshaped the CPC political economic system without eliminating the one-party dictatorship.

In response to China's surging economy during the era of the global financial crisis, there are some contemporary analysts who assert that China is exemplary of state capitalism in the twenty-first century. Being a pioneer researcher of China state capitalism, Ian Bremmer (2008) describes China as the primary driver for the rise of state capitalism and a challenge to the free market economies of the developed world. In his definition, governments which adopt state capitalism use state-owned enterprises (SOEs) to manage the exploitation of resources as the state's crown jewels to create and maintain employment. Bremmer argued that China's ultimate motive is not wholly economic, but also political and interested in maximizing state power and leadership survival (Bremmer 2009).

Paul D. Aligica and Vlad Tarko (2015) made a similar argument. They argue that state capitalism, in countries like modern-day China and Russia, is an example of a rent-seeking society. Following the realization that the centrally planned socialist systems could not effectively compete with capitalist economies, the former CPC political elite are trying to engineer a limited form of economic liberalization that increases efficiency, while still allowing them to maintain political control and power.

Du Julan and Chenggang Xu (2009) argued that the contemporary economic system of the PRC represents a state capitalist system as opposed to a market socialist system. Their reason for the categorization is the existence of financial markets in the Chinese economic system, which are absent in the market socialist literature and in the classic models of market socialism. Furthermore, the "Chinese model" doesn't take welfare into consideration because state profits are retained by enterprises rather than being equitably distributed among the population.

In summary, research indicates the trend of moving away from market socialism. Christopher A. McNally (2012) replaces state capitalism with sino-capitalism which is based on a combination of top-down state coordination, bottom-up entrepreneurial networks, and focused global integration. He argues that China is getting used to managing production under the rule of market-liberal form with norms according to the World Trade Organization (WTO). Yasheng Huang (2008) provided a similar analysis that described China as a system of 'commanding-heights capitalism' and claimed that it has been transformed into a fully functioning market economy.

State Owned Enterprises

SOEs have become the focus of recent research on China's state capitalism as a key element of China's recent economic growth. Following the Chinese state capitalism arrangement, the market-oriented reforms led to a rapid expansion of the private sector, however, SOEs remained a large part of the economy (Pearson 2015). From 2001 to 2011, China's total GDP rose from the sixth to the second in the world, with an annual average growth rate of approximately 10%. Most strikingly, on average, China's SOEs seemed to outperform non-SOEs after around 2001 (Li et al. 2015).

China's SOEs have been the core of economic reform since 1978. China's central government made the historical decision for reform and adopted a gradual, experimental, and pragmatic approach to improve performance of SOEs without changing state ownership and control (Naughton 2007). During the 1980s, the first SOE reforms of increasing enterprise autonomy where started. Those reforms required managers to meet performance targets in return for retained profit and the system initially improved the performance of SOEs (Wei 1997). However, it quickly ran into trouble because of loose regulations imposed on the SOE managers and the increasing competition from non-SOEs, such as foreign-investment enterprises as well as township and village enterprises (Naughton 2007).

Deng Xiaoping's 1992 southern tour marked the next set of economic reforms. During the Third Plenum of 14th Chinese Communist Party Congress in 1993, the central government endorsed creation of a socialist market economy based on public ownership. In 1995, the scale of privatization of SOEs and resultant layoffs of workers rose when the central government formally pushed the policy of nurturing the large and letting the small go (*zhuada fangxiao*). The central government explicitly pursued the strategy of retaining state control of 500–1000 large SOEs in strategic sectors, where competition was severely restricted through administrative regulation, meanwhile closing or privatizing small- and medium-sized SOEs. Those smaller SOEs were typically in downstream industries such as footwear and apparel (Green and Liu 2005).

Throughout those reforms, SOEs had successfully consolidated their monopoly positions and reinforced their industrial advantages even further. Because the upstream industries are generally in non-tradable or regulated sectors, SOEs can always be shielded from competition after entering the WTO. By contrast, non-SOEs face fierce competition in the largely liberalized downstream industries which are typically tradeable and open to foreign direct investment (FDI). According to the Financial Supervision and Evaluation Office of PRC (2015), central enterprises realized total revenue of 25.1 trillion yuan, an increase of 3.8% in 2014; the cumulative total amount of taxes turned over 2.1 trillion yuan, an increase of 4.4%; total profit of 1.4 trillion yuan, an increase of 4.2%; attributable to owners of the parent net profit of 626.92 billion yuan, an increase of 6.9%.

Regional integration and infrastructure contracts provide SOEs fertile ground for growth. China then participated in the Regional Comprehensive Economic Partnership (RCEP), and initiated the Asian Infrastructure Investment Bank (AIIB) which started operation after the agreement entered into force on December 25, 2015. According to the agreement, AIIB is an international financial institution that aims to support the building of infrastructure in the Asia-Pacific region. As the regional integration and infrastructure contraction, SOEs will become the vehicle to extend China's economic power and state capitalism (Szamosszegi and Kyle 2011).

Ethnic Chinese Business Networks

Overseas Chinese business continues to grow, taking advantage of China's reform and economic development. For centuries, overseas Chinese networks have gradually integrated into local society. The transformation of the overseas Chinese economy has been successful in contributing to economic development of the Southeast Asian countries (Li 2000). Overseas Chinese in ASEAN countries, most notably Singapore, have formed a noticeable political, economic, and cultural influence. Most overseas Chinese continue to keep or retain a basic traditional Chinese culture and identity, whereas subsequent generations integrate as they become more familiar with the local economic, political, and investment environment. China aims to bolster foreign investment by gaining the support of overseas Chinese business networks. Through the reform in policies toward overseas Chinese, the Chinese government can increase SOE mergers and acquisitions overseas, as well as improve investment and operations to reduce risk. Southeast Asian Chinese have experience in overseas investment coupled with open trade networks to exchange information between enterprises. The networks provide a broad platform to achieve the optimal allocation of global resources. The above factors are useful resources for Chinese enterprises to implement the Chinese government's "going out" (*zou chuqu*) strategy (Sundaram 2003).

The establishment of CAFTA has significantly augmented economic ties. Southeast Asian Chinese who take part in transnational investment activities provide experience and investment for China's SOEs. The earlier establishment of overseas Chinese enterprises in Southeast Asia has been exploited by large Southeast Asian Chinese enterprises. The Southeast Asian Chinese enterprises are like China's enterprises following similar development processes and modes of operation which has enabled China's enterprises in Southeast Asia to expand overseas business. China's domestic enterprises can align with overseas Chinese enterprises or to establish outsourcing to expand business (Bun 2000).

To better respond to the investment of trade protectionism and trade negotiations, the Chinese government strengthens cooperation with overseas Chinese enterprises in Southeast Asia which further enables China's SOEs and private companies to overcome the barriers to entry, reduce cross-border transaction costs, and consolidate foreign markets (Gomez and Hsiao 2001).

The widely distributed overseas Chinese businesses are globally the key to expansion of domestic interests. In recent years, more and more China domestic enterprises obtain information and mechanisms of foreign investment. At the same time, the Chinese government promotes the exchange of overseas Chinese and domestic entrepreneurs (Hong 1998).

The overseas Chinese businesses are one of the largest and most enduring diasporas in the world today and are expected to shape the political and economic landscape of the twenty-first century. That transnational Chinese community may prove to be one of the main determinants in securing Xi' Jinping's China Dream in Southeast Asia. The Confucian-rooted concept of "*guanxi*" has facilitated Chinese business groups in setting up transnational, regionally focused operations based on the relationships with other Chinese player. With the blueprints of Beijing's geo-economic strategy, the worldwide network of businesses is likely to continue to play a rejuvenated role that bolsters the One Belt One Road (OBOR) initiative (Wijaya 2016).

AEC and China's Proactive Participation of Desecuritization

Until the mid-1990s, China was not very active in regional cooperation. It was reluctant to join any regional organization because it was not sure what the effects would be. That changed during the 1997–1998 financial crisis because China became active in regional economic integration.

China's Changing Attitude Toward Regional Economic Integration

In 2010, China surpassed Japan as the world's second-largest economy which led to closer ties with the countries in East Asia bolstered by free trade agreements (FTAs). Based on successful economic reform, China has been less afraid of fully opening its market to the outside world because it has gained from the initial policy of opening and will gain even more from accession to the WTO and the negotiation of regional FTAs. The Asian financial crisis and the European experience have shown the importance of regional cooperation in preventing and relieving financial turmoil. At the 1999 ASEAN + 3 summit, China endorsed full regional economic cooperation, including financial and monetary cooperation; it also sponsored the Chiang Mai Initiative and actively participated in the swap agreements (Minqi 2003).

China's economic growth inevitably causes concern to neighboring countries because of its huge population and vast territory. Nevertheless, its sustainable growth needs regional peace and security. China tries to persuade neighboring countries that it is a responsible and positive force in the region and is their friend. Typical examples of that attitude are the maintenance of a stable exchange rate during the 1997–1998 East Asian financial crisis, and the willingness to make concessions in settling border disputes with neighbors. Moreover, China supports the enhancement of political and security cooperation in the ASEAN + 3 framework and, since the late 1990s, has been active in promoting regional FTAs. In free trade negotiations with ASEAN, China took the initiative despite incurring some immediate costs.

Such examples illustrate China's strategy for peaceful development within the region and for a role as an active and positive player in region affairs. The Chinese government now supports the idea of a pan East Asia FTA and a mechanism to stabilize currency exchange rates among East Asian economies. China is interested in regional investment cooperation to promote capital flow and is considering joint mechanisms for the surveillance of financial markets and the establishment of an early crisis signaling system.

Economic Participation as an Effective Strategy for Desecuritization

The 1997–1998 Asian financial crisis made China cognizant of the necessity of a peaceful and dynamic international environment for the sustainability of its economic development. Consideration over its long-term economic objective, which was formulated in the Ninth Five-Year Plan, aimed to quadruple the per capita gross national product (GNP) of 1980 by the year 2000 and double the GNP of 2000 in 2010. That encouraged China to reformulate its regional foreign policy and develop friendly relations with other East Asian economies. Only by having security, with a stable political and economic environment, can China concentrate on its economic, socio-cultural, and political development.

The Asian financial crisis also provided an opportunity for China to actualize its "Good Neighbor" policy. China participated in a US$16 billion international package to bail out the Thai financial system by pledging to lend Thailand US$1 billion in 1997. Its decision to not devalue the *renminbi* (RMB), which experienced a drastic sincere appreciation against East Asian currencies, prevented the Asian crisis from becoming more severe and safeguarded the crisis-hit countries from deeper competitive devaluation. That decision relieved the fears of both the USA and European Union (EU) that a depreciation of the RMB would make Asian export became cheaper and lead to huge job losses in the USA and the EU. More than just becoming a good partner, China demonstrated its potential good will as a responsible regional leader (Tan and Zhang 2005).

More significantly, in 1996 China leveled up its status from a consultative dialogue partner to a full dialogue partner of ASEAN. The First Meeting of the ASEAN–China Joint Cooperation Committee was held in Beijing on February 26–28, 1997, and agreed to promote deeper cooperation. In December 1997, China's President Jiang Zemin and ASEAN leaders agreed to establish a twenty-first century oriented partnership of good neighborliness and mutual trust between China and ASEAN. In the Ninth Five-Year Plan formulated in 1996, China was willing to be "a friendly elephant" and considered "neighbors as partners and with cordiality" (Cheow 2005).

During that time, China had a changing attitude toward security policy. At the Fourth ASEAN Regional Forum (ARF) in July 1997, Chinese Foreign Minister Qian Qichen spoke about China's new security concept. The concept was subsequently explicated in the 1998 China's National Defense white paper and discussed frequently in various forums (Thayer 2003). That marked a post-1997 China declaring its preference for the promotion of mutual respect for sovereignty and peaceful coexistence leading to the strengthening of economic cooperation and encouraging mutual understanding. Additionally, China could create opportunities to secure resources from its neighboring countries and convert the China threat perception into a benign one (Cheow 2005).

Since the beginning of the millennium, China's central government has encouraged domestic companies to think globally and invest overseas. In 2001, Vice Premier Wu Bangguo encouraged competitive enterprises to invest abroad and "go global".[3] As outlined by former President Jiang Zemin at the 16th National Party Congress, the government hoped the "Going Out" strategy would "bring about a number of strong multinational enterprises and brand names".[4] Furthermore, economic incentives had also led the government toward the "Going Out" investment strategy in recent years. Increasing overseas direct investment (ODI) could help cool China's investment-driven economy and diminish excess liquidity (Freeman Briefing 2008).

The rising power improved China's bargaining position enabling greater influence on international institutions. In the case of ARF, China influenced members to respect the One-China Policy in relation to the Taiwan issue thereby reducing international support to Taiwan's independence (Leifer 2001). It also used leader meetings during the Asia-Pacific Economic Cooperation (APEC) Summit to gain support from other members for China's WTO accession. Until the late 1990s, China had participated in several regional institutions including the ARF, APEC, APT (ASEAN Plus Three, including China, Japan and South Korea), Asian Cooperation Dialogue, Asia–Europe Meeting, and Council for Security Cooperation in the Asia-Pacific. China also hosted several summits, such as the APEC Summit in 2001, Asian Cooperation Dialogue, and Boao Forum for Asia in 2002 (Samson 2012).

Charming Power to Eliminate the Perception of a China Threat

The ASEAN–China Free Trade Area (ACFTA) represents ASEAN's ambition to push toward signing preferential trade agreements outside the multilateral framework of the WTO (Kawai and Wignaraja 2013).

ASEAN members have since signed dozens of individual FTAs within and beyond the Asia region, including with major economies in Europe and North America. ASEAN has led an initiative to combine individual FTAs (with Australia and New Zealand, China, India, Japan, and Korea, respectively) into the RCEP, launched in November 2012 and slated for completion by year-end 2015 (Yoshimatsu 2012)–subsequently delayed to 2016 or 2017.

There is divided opinion of the RCEP. Proponents of RCEP argue that it could deepen economic integration in the region and detractors counter that RCEP is just like ACFTA, likely to be a shallow agreement amenable to the heterogeneous ASEAN member states and as such will not make a major impact on regional economic ties. RCEP excludes many of the advanced trade provisions promoted by the USA, such as those governing regulatory convergence, digital goods and services, and intellectual property. Furthermore, despite China's official policy to defer to ASEAN as the leader in regional integration, China may come to dominate the development of RCEP (Fukunaga and Isono 2013).

Significantly, four ASEAN countries, namely Brunei, Malaysia, Singapore, and Vietnam, are parties to the Trans-Pacific Partnership (TPP) led by the USA (USTR 2015). TPP sets itself apart from RCEP in terms of the scope and depth of its provisions and does not include China. Furthermore, the TPP could have an indirect bearing on the balance of power in the Asia region in terms of solidifying US partnerships in the face of China's growing influence as part of the US rebalance strategy of Pivot to Asia (Guoqiang and Zhenyu 2014). However, although 12 Pacific Rim countries signed the TPP in February 2016, US President Donald Trump began carrying out his campaign pledges in January 2017 to withdraw from the TPP.[5] That withdrawal helped the RCEP initiate and boost China to fill the political economy vacuum.

Most (75.8%) of ASEAN's trade in 2013 was with countries outside the bloc, a testament to the region's trade openness (Salidjanova and Koch-Weser 2015). China shared 14% of ASEAN trade and was the largest individual trading partner, while the USA was fourth (8.2%). Although ACFTA suggests mutually beneficial economic relations, the reality is that since full enactment of the agreement in 2010, ASEAN's goods trade with China has gone from a surplus to a US$44.731 billion deficit by 2013. Meanwhile, several ASEAN members have established integrated supply chains with both China and Northeast Asia, largely as a function of China's emergence as the world's manufacturing and assembly hub.

Several new initiatives such as the upgrading of the ASEAN–China FTA, the setting up of AIIB, and the OBOR strategy will further promote cooperation between both regions. The total trade between China and ASEAN had risen tenfold from US$41 billion in 2000 to an estimated US$492 billion in 2015. As a share of ASEAN's total global trade, China accounted for 5.1% in 2000 which had more than tripled to 17.2% in 2015. Based on research prediction, China's share of ASEAN's total trade could reach 25%, or US$1.85 trillion, by 2030.

Beyond the Milestone: Chinese Capitalism as a Dynamic of AEC?

AEC and the New Economic Order

China has been playing an active role in building trade and investment relations with ASEAN over the past decade. In 2013, China's President Xi Jinping mooted the idea of the New Silk Road, or the Maritime Silk Road that starts from Fujian province and links all the littoral countries of the region. From the perspective of trade and investment, the Maritime Silk Road concept will further deepen China's connection with ASEAN, with AEC serving as a main catalyst afterward because when China faces its domestic "growing pains" of rising labor costs, land costs, and appreciating currency, ASEAN will be the natural destination given the geographic and historic ties.

To date, China has been playing a rising role in ASEAN. China's share in ASEAN's total trade has more than doubled from 5% in 2000 to 14% in 2010, and to 16% in 2013. Similarly, China's push in recent years to invest overseas (to balance out investment inflows and partly to reduce appreciation pressure on the RMB) has seen ASEAN as a main beneficiary of the FDI which has resulted in both inflows and outflows of China's direct investment closing the gap on what was the case ten years previously. Furthermore, China's ODI has accelerated since 2007 (see Fig. 2.1). Of note is that Asia represents the bulk of China's annual ODI flow to the world, accounting for 73% in 2012.

China's share could rise to 14% by 2030, with a flow of US$185 billion, or six times greater compared with that in 2013 (UOB 2014). The rise of China, coupled with the establishment of the AEC in 2015, is expected to provide new catalysts for growth in ASEAN. At the same time, domestic factors such as population growth and the rise in the

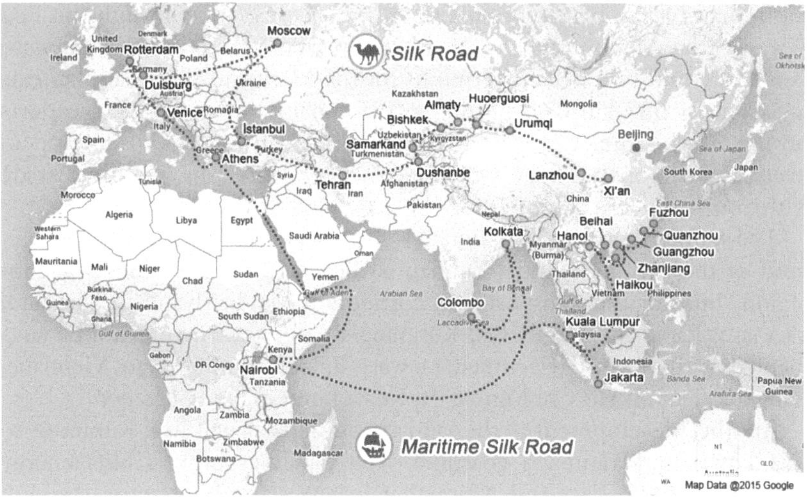

Fig. 2.1 One belt one road official map (*Source* "The Belt and Road: the Silk road Economic Belt and the 21st Century Maritime Silk Road," Xinhua Finance Agency, August 20, 2016, http://en.xinfinance.com/html/BR/)

middle-income class in ASEAN will pave the way for AEC's promise of an integrated production platform and market.

It is predicted that ASEAN's share of global total trade will rise from 6.7% in 2013 to nearly 8% by 2030, which is no small feat given that other larger trading groups such as EU will be seeing a dwindling share of global trade. At the same time, the shift in domestic conditions in China is propelling further outward orientation, which will result in closer integration and relations with ASEAN through trade and investment. Those two channels could see ASEAN's total trade with China rising to US$1.5 trillion and investment inflows from China rising to US$185 billion, from US$405 billion and US$31 billion, respectively.

New Opportunity: OBOR Synergize with AEC Blueprint 2025

In late 2013, during his trip to Malaysia and Indonesia, Xi announced the new agenda of the twenty-first century Maritime Silk Road initiative, thereby expanding port access to support maritime trade across the Indian Ocean to the Persian Gulf, East Africa, and through the Red Sea into the Mediterranean (Arase 2015). From a geo-economic view, Guangxi could be a perfect terminus for the Maritime Silk Road, benefiting from its 637-km land border with Vietnam and three deep seaports on the South China Sea. The Maritime Silk Road focus is to develop an overseas port operated by Chinese firms for managing maritime trade with Southeast Asia (Hong 2016).

The southern province of Yunnan is slated to be China's strategic bridgehead of the OBOR agenda. Yunnan is the GMS (Greater Mekong Subregion) hub for the transportation corridors through Myanmar, Thailand, Vietnam, Laos, and Cambodia. Kunming Road infrastructure will be augmented with planned electrified railways linking Kunming to Vientiane, Bangkok, Hanoi, Ho Chi Minh City, Kuala Lumpur, and Singapore.

Another development is the land corridors that will link Kunming to Kyaukpyu on Myanmar's coastline. The pipelines bring China energy from the Middle East and Africa that bypasses the long route through the Malacca Strait and South China Sea. Additionally, an 868-km railway is to be built between Kunming and Kyaukpyu, as well as a highway. Plans to implement the Bangladesh–China–India–Myanmar Economic Corridor began in December 2013. The 2800-km highway will link Kunming to Kolkata in India. Special customs, trade, and industrial zones along the route are intended to develop industry and build supply chains across China, Myanmar, Bangladesh, and India (Wang 2015).

President Xi Jinping and Premier Li Keqiang recently revamped the OBOR strategy, shifting from an outward market and investment expansion toward a more controlled approach around exporting Chinese equipment and high-value goods and services. Industrial upgrade has been one of the Xi Jinping administration's top priorities, and the new China 'Going Out' policy plays a key role in the transition toward higher value manufacturing and technology. Exporting high value-added products like high-speed railways promotes China's image abroad and showcases its newfound competitiveness. OBOR is the capstone of Xi Jinping and Li Keqiang's new 'Going Out' policy that will create stronger and more competitive Chinese SOEs, expanding into sectors traditionally dominated by Western firms, and exerting influence in many regions.

Zimmerman argued that the OBOR geo-economic scheme would spontaneously integrate China's neighbors more closely with the Chinese economy, enmeshing them in a network of trade ties, transportation links, and multilateral regional institutions, enhancing Beijing's influence over the weaker, poorer nations that surround it. The AIIB is one such mechanism and will assist in funding some of the projects that will be a part of the new Silk Roads (Zimmerman 2015), and can be interpreted as a desecuritization platform influencing ASEAN members to adjust their policies to reflect those potential interests in a realistic manner, although many believe that ASEAN members cannot be too dependent on China (Phoak 2015).

Potential Challenge: Territorial Disputes in South China Sea

China has expedited its building of islands and facilities in the South China Sea. In 1947, the nationalist Chinese government put forward claim to the South China Sea on a map containing 11 dotted lines. The map was adopted by the CPC when they took power and later Premier Chou Enlai deleted two lines in the Gulf of Tonkin to make the 11 dots into nine (Brown 2009). Because most of the territory that is controlled in the South China Sea was once limited to sandbars or chunks of reef that barely qualified as islands, China has been rapidly piling sand onto reefs in the South China Sea, creating seven new islets in the region (Watking 2015). The US Department of Defense's annual report to Congress in 2016 on China's military estimated that the Chinese have fashioned at least 3200 acres of new land in the Spratly Islands over the past several years. Adm. Harry Harris Jr., head of the US Pacific Command, has dubbed the Chinese building spree a "Great Wall of Sand" (Beech 2016).

For the sake of regional peace and security, the USA, India, and Japan kicked off the annual joint Exercise Malabar in June 2016, which was perceived as a maritime containment toward China (Kubo 2016). The Philippines formally initiated arbitration proceedings against China's territorial claim on the "nine-dash line" in January 2013, and the five arbitrators of the tribunal agreed unanimously with the Philippines in July 2016. They argued that there was no evidence that China had historically exercised exclusive control over the waters or resources; hence there was no legal basis for China to claim historic rights over the nine-dash line. China, however, refused to participate in the arbitration (Lockett 2016). Obviously, disputes regarding the South China Sea have been potential challenges to China–ASEAN relations.

Conclusion

Beijing appears well aware of the complex political economy of the situation in the ASEAN region and tries to reshape it. The way to achieve its overall foreign policy goals is through desecuritization based on regionalism and soft power. Desecuritization can correct shortcomings because it starts from an implicit premise of cooperation (both genuine and instrumental), integrates contextual factors beyond pure capabilities, and is process oriented. Although China often runs into difficulties with ASEAN countries in territorial disputes, Beijing is familiar with using diplomatic rhetoric of desecuritization to correct bilateral relations. For instance, China and ASEAN members agreed on a South China Sea code of conduct in May 2017, which was still a draft, but gave no details of its contents.[6] In summary, China's desecuritization combines regionalism and soft power and is certainly the key to fix chasms among regional countries. As China continues to participate in regional economic integration (i.e. RCEP and OBOR), Chinese capitalism will further merge into AEC and become China's most important desecuritizing strategy.

Notes

1. The characteristics and elements of AEC include: (1) single market and production base; (2) competitive economic region; (3) equitable economic development; and (4) integration into the global economy. See: 13th ASEAN Summit Press Statement: Blueprint for the ASEAN Economic Community (AEC), January 2008. http://asean.org/wp-content/uploads/archive/5187-10.pdf.
2. "President Xi's speech at the College of Europe," Bruges, April 1, 2014. http://www.china.org.cn/world/2014-04/04/content_32004856.htm.
3. "Go Global Investment Strategy Needed for Chinese Enterprises," *CHINA.ORG.CN*, September 12, 2001. http://www.china.org.cn/english/GS-e/19033.htm.
4. "Full Text of Jiang Zemin's Report at 16th Party Congress," *CHINA.ORG.CN*, November 17, 2002. http://www.china.org.cn/english/features/49007.htm.
5. "Trump Signs Order Withdrawing U.S. from Trans-Pacific Trade Deal," *Reuters*, January 23, 2017. http://www.reuters.com/article/us-usa-trump-executiveorders-idUSKBN1572.
6. Reuters. "China, ASEAN agree on framework for South China Sea code of conduct," *Reuters*, May 18, 2017. http://www.reuters.com/article/us-southchinasea-china-philippines-idUSKCN18E1FS.

Bibliography

Aligica, Paul D., and Vlad Tarko. 2015. *Capitalist Alternatives: Models, Taxonomies, Scenarios*. London: Routledge.

Arase, David. 2015. "China's OBOR: Implications for Southeast Asia." *LSEAS Perspective*, no. 2.

ASEAN Secretariat. 1997. "ASEAN Vision 2020." ASEAN. http://asean.org/?static_post=asean-vision-2020.

ASEAN Secretariat. 2005. *ASEAN Economic Community Blueprint*. Jakarta: ASEAN Secretariat, 2008.

ASEAN Secretariat. 2008, January. "13th ASEAN Summit Press Statement: Blueprint for the ASEAN Economic Community (AEC)." http://asean.org/wp-content/uploads/archive/5187-10.pdf.

ASEAN Secretariat. 2015. "The ASEAN Economic Community: Can the Reality Match the Vision?" EY. http://www.jakarta.diplo.de/contentblob/4589178/Daten/5756752/downloadaecstudie.pdf.

ASEAN Secretariat. 2016. "AEC: The China-ASEAN Connection." UOB Global Economics & Markets Research. http://www.uobgroup.com/assets/pdfs/research/ASEAN-Focus_2q16.pdf.

Balzacq, Thierry. 2005. "The Three Faces of Securitization: Political Agency, Audience and Context." *European Journal of International Relations* 11, no. 2: 171–201.

Beech, Hannah. 2016. "What's New on China's Artificial Islands in the South China Sea? Basketball Courts." *Time*, May 22. http://time.com/4341510/south-china-sea-artificial-islands/.

Bremmer, Ian. 2008. "The Return of State Capitalism." *Survival: Global Politics and Strategy* 50, no. 3: 55–64.

Bremmer, Ian. 2009. "State Capitalism Comes of Age: The End of the Free Market?" *Foreign Affairs* 88, no. 3: 40–55.

Brown, Peter J. 2009. "Calculated Ambiguity in the South China Sea." *Asia Times*, December 8. http://www.atimes.com/atimes/Southeast_Asia/KL08Ae01.html.

Bun, Chan Kwok, ed. 2000. *Chinese Business Networks: State, Economy and Culture*. Singapore: Prentice Hall.

Buzan, Barry, and Lene Hansen. 2009. *The Evolution of International Security Studies*. Cambridge: Cambridge University Press.

Buzan, Barry, Ole Wæver, and Jaap De Wilde. 1998. *Security: A New Framework for Analysis*. London: Lynne Rienner.

Cheng, Joseph. 2013. "China's Regional Strategy and Challenges in East Asia." *China Perspectives*, no. 2: 53–65.

Cheng-Chwee, Kuik. 2005. "Multilateralism in China's ASEAN Policy: Its Evolution, Characteristics, and Aspiration." *Contemporary Southeast Asia* 27, no. 1: 102–122.

Cheow, Eric T.C. 2005. "ASEAN+3: The Roles of ASEAN." In *ASEAN-China Relations: Realities and Prospects*, edited by Saw Swee-Hock, Sheng Lijun, and Chin Kin Wah, 49–67. Singapore: ISEAS.

CHINADAILY. 2013. "Xi Jinping: China to Further Friendly Relations with Neighboring Countries." *CHINADAILY*, October 26. http://usa.chinadaily.com.cn/china/2013-10/26/content_17060905.htm.

Coase, Ronald, and Ning Wang. 2013. *How China Became Capitalist*. London, UK: Palgrave Macmillan.

Corry, Olaf. 2012."Securitisation and 'Riskification': Second-Order Security and the Politics of Climate Change." *Millennium: Journal of International Studies* 40, no. 2: 235–258.

CSIS. 2008. "China's 'Going Out' Investment Policy." *Freeman Briefing*, May 27. https://csis-prod.s3.amazonaws.com/s3fs-public/legacy_files/files/publication/080527_freeman_briefing.pdf.

Du, Julan, and Chenggang Xu. 2009. "Which Firms Went Public in China? A Study of Financial Market Regulation." *World Development* 37, no. 4: 812–824.

Financial Supervision and Evaluation Office of PRC. 2015. "Central Enterprises 2014 Annual Operation." January 23. http://www.sasac.gov.cn/n86302/n326735/n326745/c1587997/content.html.

Floyd, Rita. 2007. "Towards a Consequentialist Evaluation of Security: Bringing Together the Copenhagen and the Welsh Schools of Security Studies." *Review of International Studies* 33, no. 2: 327–350.

Fukunaga, Yoshifumi, and Ikumo Isono. 2013. "Taking ASEAN+1 FTAs towards the REEP: A Mapping Study." *ERIA Discussion Paper Series*, ERIA-DP-2013–02. http://www.eria.org/ERIA-DP-2013-02.pdf.

Gabriel, Satya, Stephen A. Resnick, and Richard D. Wolff. 2008. "State Capitalism versus Communism: What Happened in the USSR and the PRC?" *Critical Sociology* 34, no. 4: 539–556.

Gomez, Terence E., and Hsin-Huang Michael Hsiao, eds. 2001. *Chinese Business in Southeast Asia: Contesting Culture Explanations, Researching Entrepreneurship*. Surry: Curzon.

Green, Stephen, and Guy S. Liu, eds. 2005. *Exit the Dragon? Privatization and State Control in China*. Oxford: Blackwell.

Guoqiang, Tang, and Wang Zhenyu. 2014. "Prospects for Asia Pacific Economic Integration." *China International Studies*, January/February, no. 1: 63–87.

Hansen, Lene. 2012. "Reconstructing Desecuritisation: The Normative-Political in the Copenhagen School and Directions for How to Apply it." *Review of International Studies* 38, no. 3: 525–546.

Hong, Liu. 1998. "Old Linkages, New Networks: The Globalization of Overseas Chinese Voluntary Associations and Its Implications." *The China Quarterly* 155: 582–609.

Hong, Zhao. 2016. "China's One Belt One Road: An Overview of the Debate." *Trends in Southeast Asia*, no. 6. Singapore: ISEAS Publishing. Accessed June 25, 2016. http://cic.nyu.edu/sites/default/files/zimmerman_new_silk_road_final_2.pdf.

Huang, Yasheng. 2008. *Capitalism with Chinese Characteristics: Entrepreneurship and the State*. New York: Cambridge University Press.

Hwang, Edward F. 2008. "China's Soft Power and Growing Influence in Southeast Asia." MA thesis. Monterey, CA: Naval Postgraduate School.

Kawai, Masahiro, and Ganeshan Wignaraja. 2013. "Political-Economy Considerations of Asian Free Trade Agreement." *Policy Studies*, no. 65: 42–54.

Kubo, Nobuhiro. 2016. "China Spy Ship Shadows U.S., Japanese, Indian Naval Drill in Western Pacific." *Reuters*, June 15. http://www.reuters.com/article/us-usa-pacific-exercises-idUSKCN0Z10B8.

Leifer, Michael. 2001. "Taiwan and South-East Asia: The Limits to Pragmatic Diplomacy." *The China Quarterly* 165 March: 173–185.

Lenin, V.I. 1976. *The State and Revolution: The Marxist Teaching on the State and the Tasks of the Proletariat in the Revolution*. Peking, PRC: Foreign Languages Press. http://www.marx.be/sites/default/files/documents/EN/texts/sr_and_sq.PDF.

Li, Peter S. 2000. "Overseas Chinese Networks: A Re-assessment." In *Ethnic Chinese: Their Economy, Politics and Culture*, edited by Yu Chunghsun. Tokyo: The Japan Times.

Li, Xi, Xuewen Liu, and Yong Wang. 2015. "A Model of China's State Capitalism." HKUST IEMS Working Paper, 2015–2012.

Lockett, Hudson. 2016. "Timeline: South China Sea Dispute." *Financial Times*, July 12. http://www.ft.com/cms/s/0/aa32a224-480e-11e6-8d68-72e9211e86ab.html#axzz4IM052V2b.

Lum, Thomas, Wayne M. Morrison, and Bruce Vaughn. 2008. "China's Soft Power in Southeast Asia." *CRS Report for Congress*, RL 34310, January 4.

Mackenzie, Megan. 2009. "Securitization and Desecuritization: Female Soldiers and the Reconstruction of Women in Post-conflict Sierra Leone." *Security Studies* 18, no. 2: 241–261.

Mao, Tse-tung. 1977. *Selected Works of Mao Tse-tung*. Beijing: People's Publishing House.

McNally, Christopher A. 2012. "Sino-Capitalism: China's Reemergence and the International Political Economy." *World Politics* 64, no. 4: 741–776.

McSweeney, Bill. 1996. "Identity and Security: Buzan and the Copenhagen School." *Review of International Studies* 22, no. 1: 81–93.

Minqi, Xu. 2003. "East Asian Economic Integration: China's Perspective and Policy." *Pacific Economic Papers* 341: 9–11.

Naughton, Barry. 2007. *The Chinese Economy: Transitions and Growth*. Cambridge: The MIT Press.

Papatheologou, Vasiliki, Rizwan Naseer, and Musarat Amin. 2014. "China's Engagement with Regionalization in South and Southeast Asia: A Comparative Perspective." *South Asian Studies* 29, no. 1: 281–290.

Pearson, Margaret M. 2015. "State-Owned Business and Party-State Regulation in China's Modern Political Economy." In *State Capitalism, Institutional Adaptation, and the Chinese Miracle*, edited by Barry Naughton and Kellee Tsai, 27–45. The Cambridge University Press.

Phoak, Kung. 2015. "Why ASEAN Should Embrace Chinese Initiatives." *East Asia Forum*, October 2.

Reuters. 2017. "China, ASEAN Agree on Framework for South China Sea Code of Conduct," *Reuters*, May 18. http://www.reuters.com/article/us-southchinasea-china-philippines-idUSKCN18E1FS.

Reuters. 2017. "Trump Signs Order Withdrawing U.S. from Trans-Pacific Trade Deal." *Reuters*, January 23. http://www.reuters.com/article/us-usa-trump-executiveorders-idUSKBN1572.

Salidjanova, Nargiza, and Iacob Koch-Weser. 2015. *China Economic Ties with ASEAN: A Country-by-Country Analysis.* U.S.-China Economic and Security Review Commission Staff Research Report. https://www.uscc.gov/sites/default/files/Research/China%27s%20Economic%20Ties%20with%20ASEAN.pdf.

Samson, Anna. 2012. "A Friendly Elephant in the Room? The Strategic Foundations of China's Multilateral Engagement in Asia." *Security Challenges* 8, no. 3 (Spring): 57–82.

Schmidt, Johannes D. 2008. "China's Soft Power Diplomacy in Southeast Asia." *Copenhagen Journal of Asian Studies* 26, no. 1: 22–49.

Shamsul, Khan, and Yu Lei. 2013. "Evolving China–ASEAN Relations and CAFTA: Chinese Perspectives on China's Initiatives in Relation to ASEAN Plus I." *European Journal of East Asian Studies* 12, no. 1: 81–107.

Sundaram, Jomo Kwame. 2003. "Chinese Capitalism in Southeast Asia." In *Ethnic Business: Chinese Capitalism in Southeast Asia*, edited by Jomo Kwame Sundaram and Brian C. Folk. New York: Routledge.

Szamosszegi, Andrew, and Cole Kyle. 2011. *An Analysis of State-Owned Enterprises and State Capitalism in China.* Washington, DC: U.S.-China Economic and Security Review Commission. http://www.uscc.gov/sites/default/files/Research/10_26_11_CapitalTradeSOEStudy.pdf.

Tan, S., and Y. Zhang. 2005. "China's Regional Strategy." In *Power Shift: China and Asia's New Dynamics*, edited by D. Shambaugh, 48–70. Berkeley: University of California Press.

Thayer, Carlyle A. 2003. "China's New Security Concept and Southeast Asia." In *Asia-Pacific Security: Policy Challenges*, edited by David W. Lovell. Singapore: Institute of Southeast Asian Studies.

UOB Group. 2014. *AEC and China: The Key Drivers in Trade and Investment into the Next Decades.* UOB Global Economics & Markets Research.

USTR. 2015. "Summary of the Trans-Pacific Partnership Agreement." 4 October 2015. https://ustr.gov/about-us/policy-offices/press-office/press-releases/2015/october/summary-trans-pacific-partnership.

Waever, Ole. 2000. "The EU as a Security Actor: Reflections from a Pessimistic Constructivist on Post-Sovereign Security Orders." In *International Relations Theory and the Politics of European Integration: Power, Security, and Community*, edited by Morten Kelstrup and Michael C. Williams. London: Routledge.

Wanandi, Jusuf. 2004. "China and Asia Pacific Regionalism." In *The Rise of China and a Changing East Asian Order*, edited by Kokubun Ryosei and Wang Jisi. Tokyo: Japan Center for International Exchange.

Wang, Ben Yunmo. 2015. "China 'Going Out' 2.0: Dawn of a New Era for Chinese Investment Abroad." *The Huffington Post*, June 11. http://www.huffingtonpost.com/china-hands/china-going-out-20-dawn-o_b_7046790.html.

Watking, Derek. 2015. "What China Has Been Building in the South China Sea." *The New York Times*, October 27. http://www.nytimes.com/interactive/2015/07/30/world/asia/what-china-has-been-building-in-the-south-china-sea.html?_r=0.

Wei, Li. 1997. "The Impact of Economic Reform on the Performance of Chinese State Enterprises, 1980–1989." *Journal of Political Economy* 105, no. 5: 1080–1106.

Wijaya, Trissia. 2016. "Can Overseas Chinese Build China's One Belt, One Road?" *East Asia Forum*, June 2. http://www.eastasiaforum.org/2016/06/02/can-overseas-chinese-build-chinas-one-belt-one-road/.

Womack, Brantly. 2003–2004. "China and Southeast Asia: Asymmetry, Leadership and Normalcy." *Pacific Affairs* 76, no. 3: 529–548.

Xiaotong, Zhang, and Li Xiaoyue. 2014. "China's Regionalism in Asia." *The Asan Forum*. http://www.theasanforum.org/chinas-regionalism-in-asia/.

Xinhuanet. 2013. "China to Pave Way for Maritime Silk Road," *Xinhuanet*, October 11. http://news.xinhuanet.com/english/china/2013-10/11/c_132790018.htm.

Yamei, Shen. 2016. "Strengthening Regional Order in the Asia-Pacific: An Analysis of China–Japan–US Perspectives." *China International Studies* 3 (May/June): 87.

Yoshimatsu, Hidetaka. 2012. "ASEAN and Evolving Power Relations in East Asia: Strategies and Constraints." *Contemporary Politics* 18, no. 4: 410–411.

Yuan, Wen Jin. 2012. "The Trans-Pacific Partnership and China's Corresponding Strategies." CSIS: A Freeman Briefing Report, June, 4–6. http://csis.org/files/publication/120620_Freeman_Brief.pdf.

Yunling, Zhang, and Tang Shiping. 2005. "China's Regional Strategy." In *Power Shift: China and Asia's New Dynamics*, edited by David Shambaugh, 48–70. Berkeley: University of California Press.

Zhang, Yunling. 2010. "East Asian Cooperation: Path & Approach." In *China and Asian Regionalism*, edited by Yunling Zhang. Singapore: World Scientific.

Zhu, X. 2012. "Understanding China's Growth: Past, Present and Future." *Journal of Economic Perspective* 26, no. 4: 103–124.

Zimmerman, Tomas. 2015, October. *The New Silk Roads: China, the U.S., and the Future of Central Asia*. New York: Center on International Cooperation.

CHAPTER 3

New Chinese Capitalism and the ASEAN Economic Community

Hong Liu and Yishu Zhou

Introduction

Since the formation of the Association of Southeast Asian Nations (ASEAN) in 1967, ASEAN leaders have tried various means to establish regional cooperation among their members. That has included the establishment of the Preferential Trading Agreement in 1977, ASEAN Free Trade Area in 1993, and the ASEAN Trade in Goods Agreement in 2010. The most ambitious attempt at economic integration has been the establishment of the ASEAN Economic Community (AEC) in December 2015. With the newest agreement, the ASEAN leaders aimed to achieve unprecedented levels of trade liberalization and market integration, with the goal to set up a single-market production base with a free flow of goods, services, investment, skilled labor, and freer movement of capital (ASEAN 2008).

H. Liu (✉)
Public Policy and Global Affairs and Chair of the School of Social Sciences, Nanyang Technological University, Singapore, Singapore

Y. Zhou
Lee Kuan Yew School of Public Policy, National University of Singapore, Singapore, Singapore

Y. Santasombat (ed.), *The Sociology of Chinese Capitalism in Southeast Asia*, https://doi.org/10.1007/978-981-13-0065-3_3

The process of greater regional integration has developed alongside the economic rise of China that began following its 'Reform and Opening' policies in 1978, and its membership in the World Trade Organization (WTO) in 2001. While the nature of the emergent and fast-growing Chinese economy has made it a popular destination for foreign direct investment (FDI), China has also been making rapid strides in overseas FDI (OFDI). The country's OFDI has grown from US$7 billion in 2001 to US$101 billion in 2013 and US$116 billion in 2014 (Sauvant and Nolan 2015). According to figures released in September 2016 by the Chinese Ministry of Commerce, China's outward FDI flows in 2015 reached US$145.7 billion (up 18.3% year over year), making it the world's second-largest source of FDI second only to the USA (US$300 billion) but higher than third-placed Japan (US$128.7 billion).

China has also taken a pointed interest in the development of ASEAN and has been ASEAN's largest trading partner since 2011. That has been largely facilitated by the signing of the ASEAN–China Free Trade Area (ACFTA) in 2002, which was subsequently upgraded to the ASEAN–China trade pact in 2015 to further ease cooperation and enhance transparency in trade transactions (ASEAN 2015). Mainland Chinese companies have become a particularly prominent presence in ASEAN's infrastructure development landscape, and more than US$50 billion in infrastructure projects with an expected completion date between 2013 and 2017 are associated with Chinese enterprises. Although most of those companies are state-owned enterprises, private companies such as Huawei also participate. China–ASEAN relations reached a new apex with the announcement of the One Belt One Road (OBOR) initiative in 2013, which is envisioned to galvanize economic development and connect China to regions spanning Southeast Asia, Central Asia, Europe, and Africa. In Southeast Asia, the OBOR initiative can be linked to China's 'three-pronged strategy on regional connectivity' that has been interpreted as a counterbalance to the USA's 'Pivot to Asia', as well as to leverage upon its extensive diasporic network.

While the presence of Chinese capitalism and Chinese entrepreneurs in the Southeast Asian political economy has been a prominent and historically meaningful one, stretching as far back as the 1920s, the economic rise of China and the growing clout of its OFDI has lent itself to a new phenomenon of what can be considered a wave of 'new Chinese capitalism' that increasingly blurs the boundaries between private economic interest and the public nationalistic interests of Chinese state-building. The new Chinese companies that venture into Southeast Asia are representative not only of China's economic strategies, but its foreign policy as well as its soft power. That is referred to by Norris as 'economic statecraft', or the intentional attempt of the state to incentivize commercial players to act in a manner that generates externalities that are conducive to the state's interests; it can be best understood as Chinese President Xi Jinping's reworking of China's Going Out Policy to a more focused and streamlined agenda, one that would promote outward investment and establish China's status as a key global power. At a broader level, the development of new Chinese capitalism is in tandem with the emergence of state capitalism that has shaped the political economy of East Asia (Kurlantzick 2016; Norris 2016).

New Chinese capitalism thus presents itself both as a huge opportunity and potential hindrance to economic community building of ASEAN. While the call for greater regional integration in ASEAN was largely perceived as a buffer to China's growing attractiveness as an FDI recipient, the rise of China has also provided ASEAN with greater sources of investment and opportunities for business expansion. It is therefore worthwhile to consider how new Chinese capitalism will interact with the increasing regionalism of ASEAN and its attempts at community building, the particularities of its political economy, and its relationship with preexisting forms of ethnic capitalism. In doing so, this chapter will also contribute to the emerging field of 'Capitalism Studies', which trades the concept of 'history from below' in studying the power relations that exist among the bosses, entrepreneurs, and businessmen that run the economy.

This chapter will first contextualize the phenomenon of new Chinese capitalism against an understanding of the political economy of Southeast Asia, and the role of Chinese capitalism and the diaspora Chinese. It will then discuss the regional architecture of the AEC and its implications for the preexisting and deeply ingrained politico-economic relations prevalent in Southeast Asia. Using cases of both private and state-sanctioned Chinese investments in Malaysia, Indonesia, and Singapore, this chapter will delineate the geographical and sectoral distributions of Mainland Chinese OFDI, as well as explain how those Chinese enterprises make an inroad into ASEAN and with whom they have collaborated in such endeavors. In doing so, this chapter will draw some conclusions on the characteristics of new Chinese capitalism in the context of an emerging AEC.

New Chinese Capitalism in Southeast Asia

Nesadurai (2012) argued that economic development in Southeast Asia is largely shaped by two features: the significant role played by the economy in politics, and the close government-business relations embedded within patronage networks that shape many economic policy choices. MacIntyre (2010) also stressed that the interdependent relationship between government, business, and economic development is a particularly pronounced one. Such interdependencies are deeply ingrained into the countries' political-economic landscape, and are supported by and work in the favor of select groups of the social and political elite. Thus, the progression of economic development in much of Southeast Asia is shaped as much by formal, institutional frameworks, as they are by informal, flexible arrangements and exchanges. That creates an inevitable tension between the institutional and regulatory nature of regionalism and the malleable and localized nature of power that governs domestic socio-political relations.

The prominence of alternative forms of power relations in Southeast Asia, which pervades all economic and political dealings, must necessarily consider the role of ethnic capitalism, primarily Chinese capitalism. A recurrent feature in the political economy of Southeast Asian countries, despite their heterogeneity, is the significance of Chinese capitalism and Chinese businesses. Originally modeled after Weber's concept of the Protestant Ethic, Chinese capitalism was envisioned as an 'economic culture' and the 'dominant mode of economic organization in Southeast Asia today' (Redding 1990). It is embedded in a peculiar form of political economy in which the ethnic Chinese rule the host economy and leave the political sphere to the reign of indigenous ethnic groups. The sheer diversity of economic activities and the prowess with which they are controlled and coordinated by ethnic Chinese has enabled them to become the very foundation of the Asian economies in which they are contained.

Liu (2012) argued that the external conditions in which Chinese capitalism emerged in Southeast Asia necessitated that Chinese entrepreneurs resort to various forms of formal and informal networks to survive in an indigenous-dominated (save for Singapore), and frequently hostile, environment. In Southeast Asia, particularly in countries such as Malaysia and Indonesia, entrepreneurial minorities were crucial to the growth of the commercial economy on the one hand, and the absolutist state on the other hand. The Chinese as a minority remained distinct from the majority populations in culture, religion, residence, and law, partly by choice and partly through the policies of government that found the distinctiveness useful. That formed the basis of laws such as the ***bumiputera*** affirmative action policies in Malaysia, and the proliferation of anti-Chinese legislation during Indonesia's Suharto era from 1966 to 1998. Because of such hostile political environments, the diasporic Chinese in Southeast Asia have had to enter into various types of formal and informal alliances to overcome numerous institutional and political barriers, thus translating into a distinctive type of flexibility and networking that has come to characterize Chinese capitalism.

Increasingly, diaspora Chinese capitalism also takes its cue from China's growing role in the globalization phenomenon, thus allowing it to leverage upon transnational networks and a growing repository of diasporic communities. Economically, China has become reliant on international trade and FDI, institutionalized through membership of both the International Monetary Fund and the World Bank. Politically, China has cooperated more closely with the international community, especially since its WTO membership in 2001 and partnership with the Group of 8. Liu and van Dongen (2016) thus call for a view of Chinese capitalism from the perspective of transnational governance, referring to one which incorporates the perspectives and mechanisms of various players, and which understands the Chinese state as one that is simultaneously global while strengthening its domestic foothold, thus reconciling the relationship between domestic Chinese politics and diaspora relations. That is conceptualized by Gamlen (2006) as a reinscribing of the nation as a transnational social field, and is exemplified by the Xi Jinping administration's 'firm but flexible' international strategy, which is aimed at enforcing China's domains of 'hard power' in the areas of the economy and the military, while incorporating greater considerations of 'soft power' befitting of a country generally considered to be a new 'world power'.

Three Case Studies

At the 9th ASEAN Summit held in Bali in 2003, ASEAN leaders agreed to establish an AEC by 2020. In many ways, it was perceived as the deepening and extension of the regional economic integration project that ASEAN had embarked on since the establishment of the ASEAN Free Trade Area in 1992 and formally came into existence December 31, 2015.

It was envisaged that the Asian Economic Community would help to bring about a stable, prosperous, and highly competitive ASEAN economic region in which there is a free flow of goods, services, investment, and a freer flow of capital, equitable economic development, and reduced poverty and socioeconomic disparities (Hew 2005).

Conscious of common criticisms of ASEAN's perfunctory form of 'shallow integration' that has allowed political objectives to take precedence over economic integration and trade policy, the AEC aimed at being the most stringent and objective of regional agreements. That was exemplified in the 2007 AEC Blueprint. It sets forth the long-term and short-term goals of the AEC process, along with specific actions indicated on a timeline. Its four main characteristics are as follows:

- A single market and production base
- A competitive economic region
- Equitable economic development
- Integration into global economy

While the AEC Blueprint laid out a detailed and ambitious set of goals and was endorsed by the ASEAN leaders, it remained a political document, not a legally binding one. Compliance has always been the biggest obstacle for ASEAN's institutional architecture, and ASEAN member states are well known for resisting any form of centralized authority to manage or complete the integration process. Even with the establishing of the AEC Scorecard mechanism in 2008, which aimed to monitor the achievement of milestones indicated in the AEC Blueprint's Strategic Schedule, it remained a self-assessment tool that would be hard pressed to provide any objective and balanced insight. Thus, the 'strategic schedule' remains saddled with loopholes and 'flexibility' hedges, which fails to set strict standards and objectives for member states. Most significantly, there is no mechanism for exerting peer pressure or enforcing sanctions when the AEC targets are missed. The country-based scorecards are kept confidential, which effectively rules out peer pressure and makes it difficult for working committees or expert meetings to assess and address implementation bottlenecks (Menon and Melendez 2017). Indeed, it has been observed that despite the growing economic ties between China and Southeast Asia over the past decade, "the choices made by individual ASEAN countries will be influenced by political and strategic factors as much as economic ones" (Booth 2016).

Hawes and Liu argued that the political economy of Southeast Asia must incorporate a view of the power balance between three different, yet closely connected, variables—the state, the domestic capitalist class, and the international economy (Hawes and Liu 1993). To that end, the new regionalism of the AEC must work in conjunction with-sometimes interacting with, sometimes circumventing-the delicate balance of power relations that underscore socio-political relations in Southeast Asia. That would involve an understanding of the contestations and negotiations between the formal, institutional apparatus of the AEC that is representative of the pressures of globalization and neoliberalization; and the informal, unstructured ways in which much of Southeast Asian development has progressed thus far, that is representative of the importance of structural and historical factors in understanding the local political economy.

Malaysia: Strong Links with the State

The history of Chinese entrepreneurs in Malaysia has been largely defined by the fraught racial politics in Malaysia, particularly the social rift between the *Bumiputera* Malays and ethnic Chinese. The New Economic Policy (NEP), introduced in 1970 by ruling party United Malays National Organization, was ostensibly a 20-year plan to achieve greater national unity by way of greater state intervention in the economy. That was aimed at offsetting the inequitable distribution of wealth among the Malays and Chinese, with the minority Chinese community owning a disproportionate amount of wealth. The government thus enlisted many government-linked companies (GLCs) to venture into major sectors of the economy on behalf of the ethnic Malays (Gomez 2013). That led to the decision in the 1980s to implement state-led ISI (Import Substitution Industralization) in heavy industries such as automobiles, steel products, and cement. During the 1997 Asian financial crisis, the government renationalized key projects, and GLCs remain highly overrepresented in the construction sector until today (Lim 2015).

The NEP also engendered the widespread practice of intra-ethnic networking, which was perceived by Chinese businessmen as the most viable option to ensure the well-being of their businesses. Chinese entrepreneurs thus decided that to develop their enterprise, it was important also to establish interethnic business ties, preferably with well-connected *Bumiputera* businessmen. Those enterprises operated predominantly in primary commodity production or resource-based industries that relied heavily on local sourcing and local support. They thus congregated most in the banking, manufacturing, and property and real estate sectors. Khoo argued that the leading Malaysian-Chinese business groups appear to have chosen a two-prong strategy in developing their enterprise: working closely with *Bumiputera* political patrons to achieve business success within Malaysia, while at the same time building relations with non-Malaysian capital, preferably other so-called 'overseas Chinese' capital, that can serve as a potential source of wealth (Khoo 2006).

The tendency of Chinese firms to select coalition partners that would best benefit their businesses, with a firm understanding of the relationship between politics and business, is also reflected in the behavior of new Chinese multinational corporations (MNCs) investing in Malaysia. Large mainland Chinese MNCs have been gaining steady momentum in terms of their contributions toward FDI in Malaysia. The property development sector in Malaysia has attracted growing interest from Chinese developers, with three major Chinese companies developing properties in Iskandar, a Special Economic Zone that borders Johor and Singapore. China's Guangzhou R&F Properties is investing RM$4.5 billion to build condominiums in Iskandar, while Country Garden Holdings is investing RM$900 million in 45 condominium towers, offering a total of 9500 units. Greenland Holdings is also investing RM$2.4 billion in its Iskandar property development (Chew 2016). One of the most prominent development projects in Iskandar is Country Garden's Forest City, a man-made island that will include apartments, schools, hospitals, and a special financial administrative region. Country Garden has pledged to invest a total of 250 billion yuan over 20 years on the project. The Country Garden Pacific View project is being developed in partnership with Esplanade Danga 88, of which the largest shareholder is Johor's Sultan Ibrahim Ismail—thus making Forest City a joint venture between the Guangzhou-based Country Garden and the Johor Monarch (Zhen 2017). That is a significant development in that it represents both a continuity of the past practice of ethnic Chinese capitalists collaborating with the local elite and power holders, and a change in that the Chinese are 'foreigners' in the true sense of nationality and country of origin.

Guanie Lim's study on mainland Chinese firms in Malaysia demonstrates that a sizeable portion of the mainland Chinese firms have cooperated with GLCs (50% of all firms) in their cross-border investments, while a smaller percentage have cooperated with ethnic Chinese firms (28% of all firms), and other entities, for example neither the GLCs nor the ethnic Chinese firms (33% of the firms). The mainland Chinese firms' preference for coalition partners also differs across different economic sectors. While the preference for the GLCs is most palpable in the construction sector (76%), the preference for ethnic Chinese companies is most perceptible in the manufacturing, finance, and information and communications sectors (33–43%). That reinforces the view that Chinese firms are adept at selecting coalition partners that best benefit them—the GLCs occupy a monopolistic position in the construction sector, while the majority of Chinese-owned small- and medium-sized enterprises (SMEs) are in the manufacturing and finance industries. Jakobsen refers to this as 'shallow' business networks—shallow in terms of time-depth and not necessarily confined to intraethnic relations. While ethnic differentiation and discrimination formed the historical context in which Chinese capitalism emerged, its hybridized nature also implies that the reference points of its extensive informal network sought to continually update and manifest itself to assimilate not only with the local economy, but the international political economy at large (Jakobsen 2015).

An even more striking, and in equal measure polarizing, example of Chinese economic statesmanship has been the state-owned China General Nuclear Power Corp's purchase of all the energy assets of 1Malaysia Development Bhd. (1MDB), amounting to US$2.3 billion. Those assets, known as Edra, consist of 13 power plants across five countries from Malaysia to Egypt and Bangladesh (Venkat 2015). The deal would not only afford China greater influence in Malaysia, but is in line with China's OBOR initiative, by providing access to other emerging economies in North Africa and South Asia. Despite the controversy surrounding 1MDB and its founder, Prime Minister Najib Razak, the Chinese company's willingness to buy the assets signals certain apathy to politics, while at the same time its decisions are intensely political. More significantly, mainland Chinese companies are uniquely attuned to the conditions of doing business in emerging economies and less developed countries, where corporate governance standards are comparatively weak, in ways that North American or European companies may not be. Lim argued that as those Chinese firms first had to cut their teeth in the cutthroat business environment of the mainland, that 'baptism of fire' has allowed them to familiarize themselves with more challenging business environments, and in negotiating complex state-society relations and patron-client networks. That in turn allows them a unique advantage when doing business in developing countries.

Indonesia: Interplay Between Politics and Ethnicity

The so-called 'Chinese Question' in Indonesia dates to the colonial period under Dutch rule, and has undergone several iterations. The ethnic Chinese issue became a major obstacle affecting diplomatic relations between China and Indonesia, with formal diplomatic ties being frozen during the New Order era under Suharto. Chua asserts that during the New Order government of President Suharto, Chinese capitalism flourished through extensive patronage links (Chua 2008). However, in the post-Suharto era of *Reformasi*, the former politico-bureaucrats that wielded power over the Chinese capitalists became much less necessary. Conversely, politicians became increasingly dependent on businessmen and entrepreneurs, such that corporate moguls could beget political power through the bureaucrats, inside the institutions, thus effectively exercising control over the state. The social demarginalization of ethnic Chinese gave capital the opportunity to present itself inside the reformed political system. Ethnic Chinese and other businessmen were no longer rarities in the political landscape of post-Suharto Indonesia, from local institutions to the national government (Hoon 2006).

Chinese-Indonesian businessmen also became much more open about identifying as ethnically Chinese, making use of their diasporic relations to China when the situation benefited them. Interviews with several ethnically Chinese business moguls in Indonesia detail their conviction that the Chinese will dominate the economy in the future, participation in the Chinese Indonesian Association INTI, and printing bilingual business cards (Chua 2008). Currently, the top listed Indonesian conglomerates with the highest market capitalization have all been founded by ethnic Chinese businessmen. The four groups consisting of the Astra Group, the Salim Group, the Lippo Group, and the Sinar Mas Group, have expanded from small trading businesses into mega-conglomerates that have business lines in finance, property development, manufacturing, and even media and information and communications. Combined, all listed companies controlled by those four groups account for 17.5% of total market capitalization in Indonesia.

The past decade has witnessed rapid growth of Chinese FDI in Indonesia. The majority of Chinese OFDI comes from state-owned enterprises, with the remaining from regional governments and private firms. In the case of joint ventures, their local partners are mostly local Chinese, except in the infrastructure, mining and energy sector where their local partners are Indonesian state-owned enterprises. The manufacturing sector remains the most important sector in China's FDI in the country, reflecting the important drivers of Chinese OFDI: "gaining access to and building markets, securing natural resources, acquiring strategic assets, burgeoning foreign exchange reserves, proactive government policies, international competitive dynamics, and extra-productive motives" (Gammeltoft and Tarmidi 2011). China was ranked as the tenth source country of FDI in Indonesia in 2015. It quickly jumped to second (overtaking Japan and behind Singapore) in 2016—with US$1.075 billion realized investments from China in the final quarter of the year, nearly five times what it was a year earlier (Suzuki and Maulia 2017).

The financial sector has become increasingly visible and prominent in China's overall FDI composition. Apart from the Bank of China which had branches in Indonesia from as early as the 1930s, the Industrial and Commercial Bank of China (Indonesia) Co., Ltd. (ICBC) was established in 2007 as a foreign exchange licensed commercial bank, with more than a dozen branches located in three big cities (Jakarta, Bandung, and Surabaya). The ICBC took over 90% of the shares of an Indonesian private commercial bank, the Bank Halim, owned by an Indonesian-Chinese individual. China Minsheng Investment Corp (CMI), a private equity firm, announced in 2015 that it would guide dozens of leading private enterprises in China's advantageous industries to invest US$5 billion in Indonesia to construct CMI Indonesia's industrial parks, and the investment scale is expected to surpass US$10 billion in the short term. Citing Indonesia's strategic location as a maritime power, population size, and sound China–Indonesia relations, CMI CEO Li Huaizhen said that the 'going global' of scores of domestic private companies from China would bring multiple beneficial programs to Indonesia to help support it in its middle to late period of industrialization (Lin 2015). CMI Chairman Dong Wenbiao had also stated that by building a platform to facilitate Chinese companies to 'go global' en masse, they will be able to cut costs and risks and create greater efficiency, returns, and competitiveness. Developing overseas in groups would also allow companies to blend into the local economy and society in a brief period of time (Jakarta Post 2015).

The apparent ease with which Chinese investors such as CMI are making gains in Indonesia is reflective of the indispensability of Chinese capital to Indonesian politics. The increasing economic importance of China will help to bolster the status of Chinese businessmen in

Indonesia, while also foregrounding the instrumentalist view of ethnicity that is prevalent in Indonesia. While during the Suharto-era Chinese businessmen were regarded as pariahs that engaged in patronage relations as part of social and political protection and were rarely vocal about their Chinese heritage, they are now using it to establish partnerships with mainland Chinese firms. As such, CMI's key partner in Indonesia is the Indonesia China Business Council, which actively helps to facilitate and encourage business development between Indonesia and China. Liu and van Dongen argue that diasporic Chinese organizations such as the Indonesia China Business Council help contribute to transnational governance that has resulted in China's 'augmented institutionalization'. Those organizations help create interactive platforms where state, society, and capital interact, and ensures that the Chinese state maintains a certain level of influence among businesses of China origin in Indonesia.

Suryadinata notes that the president of the Indonesia China Business Council, Alim Markus, is a second-generation Indonesian-Chinese who was elected based on his strong business connections with China (Suryadinata 2012). He is active in many local Chinese organizations and has served as the general chairman of the Indonesian Fuqing Organization, general chairman of the Indonesian Lim Surname Association, and permanent honorary chairman of the Indonesia Hakka Association. As the head of MNC Maspion, he has also played a part in local politics, acting as consultant to President Abudurrahman Wahid and to Speaker of the House Agung Laksono. The ability to occupy a role both in the Chinese business sphere and the Indonesian national political sphere is reflective of what Ren and Liu refer to as a 'dual embeddedness' (Ren and Liu 2015), typically exemplified as immigrants or members of a diaspora, in their ability to be involved in both their origin and settlement societies. Thus, Chinese diasporic entrepreneurs frequently utilize both transnationalism and integration as business strategies. Local economic or social resources in the host society can be converted into transnational economic or social resources in the home society, and vice versa.

Indonesia also plays a pivotal role in China's OBOR initiative. Many mainland Chinese companies are involved in the construction of power plants, ports, and road and rail infrastructure through various projects that began in 2013. Chinese investors are developing a China–Indonesia Industrial Investment and Cooperation Zone and other railway projects in the country. Sinopec is building an oil storage terminal in the Batam

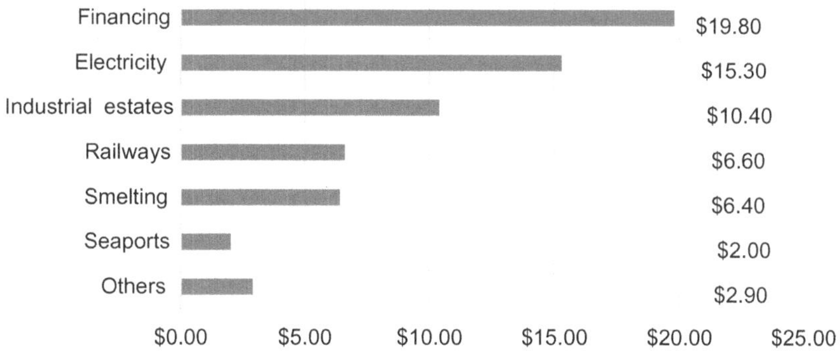

Fig. 3.1 Potential Chinese investment and financing in Indonesia (In billions of dollars)

Free Trade Zone that is estimated to cost approximately US$850 million. China Power Investment and Anhui Conch Cement are involved with a US$17 billion hydropower project in North Kalimantan. Other Chinese companies such as the China Railway Group, the China Honggiao Group, and the China Communications Construction Group are involved with transport, power, and communication projects in Indonesia. A consortium of Indonesian companies, in conjunction with the China Road and Bridge Corporation and China Harbor Engineering, constructed the 5.4-km, $445 million Suramadu Bridge connecting Surabaya with Madura (ASEAN 2015). There have also been talks of an impending US$63 billion investment deal with China, which would not only bolster President Joko Widodo's goal of building infrastructure, but also China's 'three-pronged strategy on regional connectivity', as part of the greater OBOR initiative. The $63 billion will likely be funneled into financing, electricity, and industrial estates projects (Otto 2015) (Fig. 3.1).

Singapore: Financial Hub and Interdependency

Singapore differs significantly from the previous cases of Malaysia and Indonesia as the ethnic Chinese occupy a significantly more favorable standing in the country's political and economic landscape and are also the racial majority (75% of the total population). The investment relationship between Singapore and China is an interdependent and long-standing one. By November 2013, 140 Chinese companies were listed on the Singapore stock exchange (SGX), with a market capitalization of approximately SGD$32 billion, although there are many mainland firms delisting from the SGX due to low interest and value added to their portfolios. In 2013, China became Singapore's number one trading partner with bilateral trade worth SGD$115.2 billion. The bilateral trade between China and Singapore accounts for 11.8% of Singapore's total trade (Ren and Liu), and Singapore has been China's largest foreign investor country since 2013, when its investments in China hit US$7.23 billion. As a result, there have been extensive interactions between the Chinese communities in Singapore (both old and new) and China in the transnational social, economic, and cultural arenas.

A study conducted by Chan and Ng (2004) identified three main categories in which ethnic Chinese business in Singapore may be categorized. The first is SMEs, which are mostly labor-intensive in their operations and oriented primarily toward the small domestic market. By 2006, SMEs comprised more than 90% of total establishments, employ 51% of the workforce and generate 34% of total output (Ng 2006). The second group is large business conglomerates that are involved in a host of industries ranging from light manufacturing, real estate and property, to hotels and banking. The third group of ethnic Chinese businesses in Singapore, in contrast to the previous two groups, is less culturally oriented, and mostly do not depend on traditional family lineage. Many may have worked previously with MNCs or GLCs, and have ventured out in industries such as computer technology, e-commerce, and knowledge-based operations. However, this third category remains a comparatively small percentage of the total businesses in Singapore. Yet, the developing of companies in the high technology and computer industry is becoming increasingly important for the continued growth of mature economies such as Singapore, in comparison with the emerging economies of Malaysia and Indonesia (Aggarwal 1985).

It is therefore no coincidence that some of the most prominent and popular MNCs of Chinese origin in Singapore belong to the internet and technology sector. The technology sector in China is growing at a remarkable pace, with companies such as Alibaba, Tencent, and Xiaomi carving out increasingly broad brand recognition and legitimacy not only domestically, but internationally, putting them on par with some of the most popular Western technology companies. In their efforts toward expansion, Chinese technology companies are drawing closer to

Southeast Asia. Eddie Wu, senior vice president of the Alibaba Group, claims that 'in five to ten years, the relationship between Chinese internet companies with Southeast Asian internet companies will be more important than Southeast Asian internet companies with European and American companies' (Lee 2016).

Within Southeast Asia, Singapore is well positioned to be the first choice for Chinese investment. Its strategic location makes it an essential connecting hub in Southeast Asia, a 'regional headquarters' for engaging with China, and a hub for gathering talent. Singapore also boasts a stringent and transparent regulatory framework and a friendly business environment, making it easier to wade through red tape for possible investments, setting up offices, and making hires. In terms of internet access, Singapore is a highly wired nation with a mobile penetration rate of 147% as of October 2017 (IMDA 2018). Importantly, the Singaporean government is eager to establish close ties with China, recognizing it as a site of great opportunities. Launched in 2007 and founded by late Prime Minister Lee Kuan Yew, Business China is a Singaporean organization that aims to nurture an inclusive and bicultural group of Singaporeans through extensive use of the Chinese language to develop a cultural and economic bridge linking the world and China. It has spurred the development of programs such as FutureChina, Apex, and Go East, all of which seek to deepen China–Singapore ties and allow Chinese enterprises in Singapore to exploit their dual identity as ethnic Chinese and Singaporean. On the one hand, they can play out their Chinese identity to enhance *guanxi* with Chinese government officials and mainland Chinese businesses. On the other hand, they, as Singaporeans, can take advantage of the fact that they are different from mainland Chinese, and pose themselves as attractive business partners and associates. On top of that, Singapore ethnic Chinese business can even use the 'brand state' of modern Singaporean developmentalism and incorruptibility to enhance their business reputation (Ng 2006).

In 2014, Hugo Barra, Vice President for Xiaomi Global, announced that the company would be expanding into Singapore—its first country in Southeast Asia and third country after launching in Hong Kong and Taiwan. In the same year, Chinese e-commerce giant Alibaba launched its Taobao marketplace in Singapore, similarly after having made progress in Hong Kong and Taiwan. In April 2016, Alibaba acquired a controlling stake in Singapore-based online retailer Lazada for about US$1 billion, its largest overseas investment to date. Lazada operates sites in six

Southeast Asian markets, including Indonesia and Malaysia, and the deal brings Alibaba closer to the goal of getting at least half the company's revenue from overseas.

The nature and characteristics of those fast-rising Chinese internet companies in Singapore is indicative of another type of Chinese MNC that differs significantly from notions of the Chinese-owned company as a traditional, hierarchical, family-owned type of operation. A report conducted by the World Economic Forum uncovered that leading Chinese companies are making innovation a strategic priority in their business models to stay competitive in global markets (World Economic Forum 2015). In analyzing how innovation contributes to those companies' globalization efforts, the report unraveled a dual-path framework. In the first path, companies become successful innovators in the domestic market at first and then leverage their advantage in innovation on the global market. In the second path, companies successfully expand within the global market first and then leverage its resources to enable innovation for long-term development. The first path is the one most commonly adopted by technology and internet companies, while large state-owned or formerly state-owned companies adopt the latter.

Conclusion

Looking at the cases of Indonesia, Malaysia, and Singapore, it is apparent that the new wave of Chinese capitalism should be differentiated from the previous manifestations of ethnic Chinese capitalism in Southeast Asia. First, new Chinese capitalism is 'foreign' both in the sense of nationality and country of origin, whereas the previous wave of Chinese capitalists were immigrants who had established roots and families in their host countries and identified foremost as Southeast Asians (Liu 2016).

Second, new Chinese capitalism must be considered along with the global presence of China as a new super power, which has not only made ASEAN countries much more welcoming of Chinese investment, but has also allowed the ethnic Chinese residing in those countries to reconsider their hyphenated identities.

Third, new Chinese capitalism does not posit to disrupt or dislodge the preexisting order of Chinese enterprise in their host countries, but instead are able to establish links and networks to make use of the resources best available to them. Reflecting the business knowledge obtained through years of operating in China's unique political economic environment, many of the Chinese firms exhibited high operational flexibility and adaptability to the host country's business conditions, and made sure that their business objectives were beneficial to the country's overall growth and economy.

Finally, new Chinese capitalism is reflective not only of a new growing consciousness among China's businesses, but also as part of the state's ambitions of 'going global' and strengthening China's international image. As such, the new brand of Chinese capitalists are not only businessmen and investors helping to fortify the country's economy by venturing into untapped markets, but are also 'diplomatic ambassadors' who would help to brand China as a peaceful and responsible great power, and an impending world power.

Bibliography

Aggarwal, Raj. 1985. "Emerging Third World Multinationals: A Case Study of the Foreign Operations of Singapore Firms." *Contemporary Southeast Asia* 7, no. 3: 193–208.

ASEAN. 2008. *ASEAN Economic Community Blueprint*. Jakarta: ASEAN Secretariat.

ASEAN. 2015. *A Blueprint for Growth ASEAN Economic Community 2015: Progress and Key Achievements*. Jakarta: ASEAN Secretariat.

Chan, Kwok Bun, and Beoy Kui Ng. 2004. "Singapore." In *Chinese Business in Southeast Asia: Contesting Cultural Explanations, Researching Entrepreneurship*, edited by Terence Gomez and Michael Hsiao, 38–61. London: Routledge.

Booth, Ann. 2016. "The Changing Pattern of China's Economic Relations with Southeast Asia." SOAS Department of Economics Working Paper Series No. 200.

Business China. "About Us." https://www.businesschina.org.sg/en.php/about.

Chew, Amy. 2016. "China Becomes Malaysia's Biggest Foreign Investor, Thanks to 1MDB Purchases." *South China Morning Post*, January 12.

Chua, Christian. 2008. *Chinese Big Business in Indonesia: The State of Capital*. London: Routledge.

Das, Sanchita Basu. 2015. *The ASEAN Economic Community and Beyond: Myths and Realities*. Singapore: ISEAS-Yusof Ishak Institute.

Ding, Sheng. 2008. "To Build a "Harmonious World": China's Soft Power Wielding in the Global South." *Journal of Chinese Political Science* 13, no. 2: 193–213.

Gamlen, Alan. 2006. "Diaspora Engagement Policies: What are They and What Kinds of States Use Them?" Working Paper 32, Centre on Migration, Policy, and Society, University of Oxford.

Gammeltoft, Peter, and L. Tarmidi. 2011. "Chinese Foreign Direct Investment in Indonesia." CIBEM Working Paper Series.

Gomez, Edmund Terence. 2013. "Nurturing Bumiputera Capital: SMEs, Entrepreneurship and the New Economic Policy." In *The New Economic Policy in Malaysia: Affirmative Action, Ethnic Inequalities and Social Justice*, edited by Edmund Terence Gomez and Johan Saravanamuttu, 87–115. Singapore: NUS Press, ISEAS Publishing.

Hawes, Gary, and Hong Liu. 1993. "Explaining the Dynamics of the Southeast Asian Political Economy: State, Society, and the Search for Economic Growth." *World Politics* 45, no. 4: 629–660.

Hew, Denis. 2005. "Introduction: Roadmap to an ASEAN Economic Community." In *Roadmap to an ASEAN Economic Community*, edited by Denis Wee, 1–12. Singapore: Institute of Southeast Asian Studies.

Hoon, Chang-Yau. 2006. "Assimilation, Multiculturalism, Hybridity: The Dilemmas of the Ethnic Chinese in Post-Suharto Indonesia." *Asian Ethnicity* 7, no. 2: 149–166.

IMDA. 2018. Infocomm Media Development Authority. *Mobile Penetration Rate.*

Jakobsen, Michael. 2015. *Ethnic Chinese Entrepreneurship in Malaysia: On Contextualisation in International Business Studies.* London: Routledge.

Khoo, Boo Teik. 2006. "Malaysia: Balancing Development and Dower." In *The Political Economy of South-East Asia: Markets, Power and Contestation*, edited by G. Rodan, K. Hewison, and R. Robison, 170–96. Oxford: Oxford University Press.

Kurlantzick, Joshua. 2016. *State Capitalism: How the Return of Statism is Transforming the World.* Oxford: Oxford University Press.

Lee, Xin En. 2016. "Chinese and Regional Tech Firms Drawing Closer." *Straits Times*, July 21.

Lim, Guanie. 2015. "China's Investments in Malaysia: Choosing the 'Right' Partners." *International Journal of China Studies* 6, no. 1: 1–30.

Lin, Zhou. 2015. "China Minsheng Investment: Build an Industrial Park in Indonesia." *China Today*, August 25.

Liu, Hong. 2012. "Transnational Chinese Sphere in Singapore: Dynamics, Transformations and Characteristics." *Journal of Current Chinese Affairs* 41, no. 2: 37–60.

Liu, Hong. 2016. "Opportunities and Anxieties for the Chinese Diaspora in Southeast Asia." *Current History* 115, no. 784: 312–317.

Liu, Hong, and Els Van Dongen. 2016. "China's Diaspora Policies as a New Mode of Transnational Governance." *Journal of Contemporary China* 25, no. 102: 805–821.

MacIntyre, Andrew. 2010. *Business, Government and Development: Northeast and Southeast Asian Comparisons*. London: Routledge.

Menon, Jayant, and Anna Cassandra Melendez. 2017. "Realizing an Asean Economic Community: Progress and Remaining Challenge." *The Singapore Economic Review* 62, no. 3: 681–702.

Nesadurai, Helen E.S. 2012. "Trade Policy in Southeast Asia: Politics, Domestic Interests and the Forging of New Accommodations in the Regional and Global Economy." In *Routledge Handbook of Southeast Asian Politics*, edited by Richard Robison, 315–29. Oxon and New York: Routledge.

Ng, Beoy Kui. 2006. "Ethnic Chinese Business in an Era of Globalization: The Singapore Case." In *Southeast Asia's Chinese Businesses in an Era of Globalization: Coping with the Rise of China*, edited by Leo Suryadinata, 289–320. Singapore: ISEAS.

Norris, William J. 2016. *Chinese Economic Statecraft: Commercial Actors, Grand Strategy, and State Control*. Ithaca: Cornell University Press.

Otto, Ben, and I. Made Sentana. 2015. "Indonesia Banks on $63 Billion from China." *Wall Street Journal*, April 1.

Redding, S.G. 1990. *The Spirit of Chinese Capitalism*. Berlin: Walter de Gruyter & Co.

Ren, Na, and Hong Liu. 2015. "Traversing Between Transnationalism and Integration: Dual Embeddedness of New Chinese Immigrant Entrepreneurs in Singapore." *Asian and Pacific Migration Journal* 24, no. 3: 298–326.

Sauvant, Karl P., and Michael D. Nolan. 2015. "China's Outward Foreign Direct Investment and International Investment Law." *Journal of International Economic Law* 18, no. 4: 893–934.

Sulisto, Suryo Bambang. 2015. "China to Build $5 Billion Industrial Park in West Java." *Jakarta Post*, October 29.

Suryadinata, Leo, ed. 2012. *Southeast Asian Personalities of Chinese Descent: A Biographical Dictionary*. Singapore: Institute of Southeast Asian Studies.

Suzuki, Wataru, and Erwida Maulia. 2017. "China Overtakes Japan in Indonesia Direct Investment." *Nikkei Asian Review*, January 25.

Venkat, P.R., and Rick Carew. 2015. "Malaysia's 1MDB to Sell Energy Assets to China Nuclear Firm." *Wall Street Journal*, November 23.

World Economic Forum. 2015. *Emerging Best Practices of Chinese Globalizers: Develop the Innovation Models*. Geneva: World Economic Forum.

Yeung, Henry Wai-chung. 2004. *Chinese Capitalism in a Global Era: Towards a Hybrid Capitalism*. London: Routledge.

Zhen, Summer. 2017. "Country Garden's Ambition in Malaysia Backed by Johor's Royal Family." *South China Morning Post*, July 7.

CHAPTER 4

The Social Capital of Being Chinese in Thai Politics

Wasana Wongsurawat

Introduction

Banharn Silpa-acha is probably the most well-known political leader of Chinese descent in modern Thai history, second only to King Taksin (1767–1782). Banharn was born in 1932 as Bei Teksiang (马德祥) to Chinese parents in the province of Suphanburi. Elected as a member of Parliament in 1976,[1] he became Thailand's 21st Prime Minister in 1995 (1995–1996). Banharn was intimately connected with the ethnic Chinese community as he rose through the intricate mechanisms of the Thai political scene (Manthira 1995). His tenure as the nation's premier witnessed contradictory events related to his Chinese roots. For example, the official inauguration of the 'Dragon Descendants Museum' in his home province of Suphanburi represented respect paying homage to the Prime Minister's ethnic and cultural heritage. On the other hand, he faced a vehement series of attacks and accusations from the opposition party (the Democrat Party) questioning the authenticity of his Thai citizenship and, consequently, his qualification to hold office as the country's Prime Minister. Those allegations played a key role in the Democrat

W. Wongsurawat (✉)
Chulalongkorn University, Bangkok, Thailand

Y. Santasombat (ed.), *The Sociology of Chinese Capitalism in Southeast Asia*, https://doi.org/10.1007/978-981-13-0065-3_4

Party's no-confidence debate in September 1996. Ultimately, although it did not result in an explicit no-confidence vote, Banharn's regime succumbed to pressure and dissolved the parliament within a week after the debate (Sathaporn 2012). That led to the November 17, 1996 general election which saw the rise of northeastern-dominant political parties: the New Aspiration Party, under the leadership of General Chavalit Yongchaiyudh. Banharn would continue be elected as a member of parliament through the party list system up to the very last election of his life in February 2014, two years before his death in 2016.

When Banharn passed away on April 23, 2016, the political mood toward his ethnic Chinese origins appeared to be very different from what it was when he was forced out of office in 1996. Heartfelt obituaries and glorifying eulogies were published in every major Thai newspaper and distributed online. He was hailed as the most distinguished son of Suphanburi and the pride of the nation's Chinese community. The Dragon Descendants Museum has become a major site of pilgrimage for visitors from China. Banharn's Chinese background is recognized because China has increasing influence in the country and those eulogies had rare mention of the previous controversy around his Thai citizenship as Prime Minister. Public opinion instead expressed sympathy toward Banharn, with criticism targeting Democrat Party leaders, including former Prime Minister Abhisit Vejjajiva, for unscrupulously fabricating hateful evidence during his premiership. The past decade has been turbulent in Thailand with military coups in 2006 to oust Prime Minister Thaksin Shinawatra and again in 2014 to oust his sister, Prime Minister Yingluck Shinawatra.

This chapter examines the influence of Chinese ethnicity in the context of Thai politics. Banharn's life appears to represent the social implications of being Chinese in Thai politics, albeit with different consequence because of changing perceptions and political players. Born the same year as the Siamese Revolution (1932) and the formation of a constitutional monarchy, his life followed Thailand's contemporary political development. During some periods, it was beneficial to be part or completely Chinese, while during other times being Chinese proved to be detrimental. The socio-economic and political context of Thailand, both domestic and international, had influence on the social capital of being ethnic Chinese in Thai politics. Understanding those facts makes it possible to understand and prepare for major changes that have already begun with the rise of People's Republic of China (PRC) influence in Thailand.

Citizenship and Different Ideals of the Nation-State

The matter of citizenship only became a factor in Thai politics when nationalism became a matter of the people rather than the ruling elite following the Siamese Revolution and coup d'etat of 1932. That argument is built on the crucial transformation of the concept of national territory and nationalism changing from the rule of a royalist absolutist regime to a revolutionary constitutionalist regime of the People's Party (*Khana Ratsadon*). That transformation was profoundly influenced by the final abolition of extra-territoriality by the People's Party government in 1938 (Mektrairat 1997).

Since the ratification of the Bowring Treaty in 1855, the existence of extra-territorial rights for colonial subjects in Siam categorically denied the kingdom from the possibility of transforming into a modern nation-state. Regardless of how the national borders might have been geographically determined, there would remain a sizable population within those boundaries that were beyond the control of the Siamese judicial system. In other words, the borders might have been marked, but if the government did not enjoy absolute sovereignty within those borders, the borders that were established in late nineteenth-century Siam were not recognized. A sizable population of colonial subjects were economically influential and of Chinese origins (Wongsurawat 2016).

King Vajiravudh Rama VI propagated his own brand of royalist nationalism as the fundamental policy of his reign. Contrary to the popular interpretation of Vajiravudh's nationalism, I believe that Rama VI's royalist nationalism was designed to include, not exclude, the economically influential Chinese colonial subjects to the monarch's nation-building. Vajiravudh's nation was identified by the subjects in the monarchy instead of geographic territories or birth right. To allow rich Chinese, whose extensive business interests were transnational in the colonial territories,[2] to contribute to the nascent Siamese nationalism, they had to be defined by devotion to the monarch and not solely about actual geographical residency or ethnic/cultural origin (Matichon 2015).

Vajiravudh's version of nationalism was elitist and less democratic compared with the new territorial version of the People's Party regime of the 1930s. The complete abolition of extra-territoriality was among the top priorities of the revolutionary government. That was to enable their vision of a more egalitarian nation that was defined by its people and territorial boundaries rather than by the highly elitist measure of a person's connection to the monarch. That also meant that the formerly highly transnational Chinese colonial subjects were forced to identify their political allegiance in a far more substantial manner than was required of them in the previous régime. No doubt, that was a more democratic definition of the nation, yet it was also more unavoidably racist. When local elections eventually followed in 1933, voting rights were determined largely by residency and citizenship. Rights to run for and hold political positions were similarly defined. That was decidedly the point in time when being Chinese started to hold some negative implications in Thai politics (Sattayanurak 2002).

The egalitarian and idealistic People's Party's version of the territorial nation was short-lived. Dreams of a people's nation came crashing down just as quickly as the territories in French Indochina were forcibly returned to France in 1941. The royalist conservative leader of the pro-Allied Free Thai Movement, M.R. Seni Pramoj, and wartime Thai minister to Washington, DC returned to be the first postwar Prime Minister of Thailand from 1945 to 1946, and again in 1975 and 1976. The kingdom quickly descended into military dictatorship and became a dedicated supporter of the USA during the Cold War. At that time, a quarter of a century since Vajiravudh's passing, his ideological design of 'nation, religion, monarch' became a powerful ideology behind the conservative autocracy in Thailand through much of the Cold War period.

The royalist concept of the nation-state and nationalism returned during the Cold War era as a crucial aspect of the military regime's anti-Communist policies. It is important to note that the Thai nation, and the socio-political context of the world that surrounded it, had been transformed through the course of the two world wars and the highly disruptive collective process of decolonization. Save for a few anachronistic anomalies—namely, Hong Kong and Macau—the latter half of the twentieth century had little tolerance for the colonial world order. The Cold War was truly an era of building of the nation-state. Extraterritoriality had been abolished in most parts of the region and the nation-states were geographically defined by internationally recognized national borders (Wongsurawat 2016). At that time, citizenship became more important in defining the rights and identities of people residing in territorial borders of each nation and Thailand was hardly an exception. Although the political influence of the monarchy was systematically increased through much of the postwar period, Thailand continued to be a territorial nation. Citizenship continued to be an important condition for receiving various forms of state support, protection, and recognition, and it became a fundamental part of political life. For the (not entirely democratic) elections that occurred through the Cold War years, citizenship was required both for voting and running for office. Citizenship was required for joining the armed forces, which, for many, was a quicker and more secure way to access political power (Kasetsiri 2016).

It is important to note that during that time, ethnic Chinese entrepreneurs gained much of their privileged position vis-à-vis the working-class masses. In addition to regaining dominance with the return to political power of conservative elite allies, leading ethnic Chinese entrepreneurs managed to secure their business advantages by cultivating connections with the ruling military government. In similar fashion to how the Chinese served as the Crown's business agents during the colonial period, the Chinese-Thai of the Cold War era were the business agents for military regimes. As corporations began to have influence, they were protected from harassment and secured a stable and continuous flow of government contracts by keeping powerful generals on their payroll as honorary board members. Small- and medium-sized enterprises in the provinces acted like local gentry, making profit through implementing state policy while engaging in philanthropy and public service to maintain an amiable relationship with the masses whom they were exploiting (Wongsurawat 2009). Not surprisingly, many ethnic Chinese tycoons assumed the leading positions in their local communities and easily dominated provincial elections. It was within that transformed territorial nationalist context that Banharn Silpa-acha entered national politics for the first time.

Banharn Silpa-acha: A Provincial Narrative that Overpowered the National Scene

Banharn Silpa-acha's colorful life story and impressive political achievements are an example of the channels of negotiation and compromise that enabled ethnic Chinese entrepreneurs to forge necessary alliances with the military and the conservative elite to ascend to the top echelons of Thai politics.

Banharn's story began in the very typical manner of most regional second-generation Chinese business families. Born only months after the Siamese Revolution, he was the fourth of six children (third of four sons) in a family of Chinese migrants who made a comfortable living in the fabric business in the city of Suphanburi. Like most sons of any respectable Chinese family of the provinces, after completing his primary education in his home province, Banharn traveled to Bangkok to further his education at the secondary level. Unfortunately, the Great East Asia War broke out and interrupted young Banharn's education. He had to leave school and entered the job market, first as an assistant in his older brother's company and later trying his hand in various businesses of his own. His first major break in the capital's business scene came in the early 1970s when his company, Sahasrichai Chemical Co. Ltd., won contracts to sell chlorine to the Thai Bureau of Public Works and the Metropolitan and Regional Waterworks Authorities (Silpa-acha 2016).

State-awarded business contracts were garnered through personal connections with high ranking members of the military government who oversaw the Bureau of Public Works as well as high-ranking civil servants among the conservative elite who dominated the waterworks authorities. That was a classic way of businesses from the ethnic Chinese community to gain a competitive edge in major businesses. Banharn was outstanding in that he managed to build on that initial success in business to quickly orchestrate a political breakthrough for himself. In 1974, in the capacity of a successful business personality with good connections in military political circles, he was appointed as one of the government-selected Senators to draft a new constitution following the upheavals of the October 1973 student movement. By 1976, Banharn Silpa-acha had managed to get himself elected as parliamentary representative of his hometown in Suphaburi (Choetcharatfa 1995).

Banharn capitalized on his Chineseness and Chinese connections to enhance his political position throughout his political career. He was Chinese before the rise of China and he continued to profess his Chineseness even at times when he was being attacked vehemently for his family roots. Banharn started his political career very much in the manner of a respectable member of the local gentry. That is, he positioned himself as the intermediary agent between the political elite in Bangkok and the masses of his hometown in Suphanburi. He made his fortune through business ventures supported by his colleagues and connections in military government and then spread his wealth via numerous philanthropic projects throughout his home province. When he came to lead the team of Suphanburi Parliamentarians, Banharn was famous for channeling public funding to his province and making Suphanburi the province with the best infrastructure in the country throughout the 1980s and 1990s. From highways to schools to public parks, nearly every significant institution in the province bore the name of Banharn and his wife Chaemsai, so much so that many mockingly call the province 'Banharn-buri' (Silpa-acha 2016).

Among the most popular analogies in the numerous existing narratives of Banharn's formidable ties with his hometown is the story of his vow to the City Pillar Shrine. He first made his declaration as he was leaving Suphanburi for Bangkok for the first time in 1949. The story that is told is that young Banharn, at the age of 17, was heading off to seek his fortune in the capital and stopped to pay respect to the City Pillar Shrine of Suphanburi where he vowed to return to restore the shrine to greater glory once he had succeeded in his business in Bangkok. Banharn returned to be the lead sponsor in the enlargement of the City Pillar Shrine in 1964. When he rose to the height of his political career as Prime Minister in 1995, Banharn went even further to make good on his vow to the City Pillar Shrine. He announced, as one of his foundational policies in foreign affairs and globalization, the plan for the nation's largest Chinese diaspora museum: Museum of the Descendants of the Dragon. That museum is built on the grounds of the Suphanburi City Pillar Shrine to commemorate the 20th anniversary of Thailand's formal diplomatic relations with the PRC. Despite his short-lived premiership, much of the museum project was realized only after Banharn left office in 1996. Most of the funding came from him personally and the Silpa-acha Family Foundation. The Museum of the Descendants of the Dragon, along with the surrounding Gardens of the Heavenly Dragon, was completed with a grand opening ceremony on Christmas eve of 2008 (Loetrattanawisut 2009).

The grand opening of the Museum of the Descendants of the Dragon and the Gardens of the Heavenly Dragon was arguably the point in which the localized Chinese identity of Suphanburi province officially overshadowed the national narrative of Suphanburi as the heart of the Thai nationalist narrative. The completion of the Museum of the Descendants of the Dragon in 2008 marked the transformation of Suphanburi from the hometown of nationalist legends[3] to become the nation's foremost center of the Chinese diaspora and leading site of pilgrimage for mainland Chinese tourists to Thailand. To understand the logic and significance of that transformation, it is important to investigate the brief history of the restoration of the Suphanburi City Pillar Shrine and the development of Suphanburi within the context of the Thai nationalist narrative from the late nineteenth century through much of the twentieth century.

Suphanburi City Pillar Shrine: From Legend of National Unity to Site of Diasporic Domination

Recognition and restoration of the Suphanburi City Pillar Shrine provides many intriguing clues regarding the Thai nation-building. What is known as the city pillar itself is a pair of stone figures of the Hindu God Vishnu of the Dvaravati Period (sixth to thirteenth centuries). It is unclear when the figures came to be venerated as the city pillar, but by the time Prince Damrong first visited Suphanburi in 1892, it was already recognized within the province of Suphanburi as the city pillar. The story of Prince Damrong's visit to Suphanburi is quite telling of the city's significance in the Thai nationalist narrative. There is a legend that has been circulating at least since the establishment of Bangkok as the capital city in 1782 under the rule of the Chakri Dynasty. The legend purported that should any member of the royal family visit or travel through Suphanburi, he or she would die. So deeply ingrained was this superstitious belief that, up to the Fifth Reign of the Chakri Dynasty, there was no official trip of any members of the Chakri royal household to Suphanburi. Hence, when Prince Damrong, who was a son of King Mongkut Rama IV and half-brother of King Chulalongkorn Rama V, decided to visit Suphanburi in 1892, it was considered a heroic act for the Chakri royal household (Damrong 2006).

It is no coincidence that Prince Damrong's first visit to Suphanburi in 1892 took place only a few years before the first stage of centralization was achieved through the *Monthonthesaphiban* (a hierarchical governing system composed of provinces, cities, districts, and *tambon* and *muban* villages) promulgated in 1897. The historical arrival of Prince Damrong in Suphanburi was key to Rama V's centralizing reforms. Prince Damrong had the grand project of producing the first national history of the Kingdom of Siam represented as a modern nation-state. Damrong's first official visit to Suphanburi proved the myth false of the city being forbidden to the royal family. Moreover, upon his return to Bangkok, he proposed to the monarch to symbolically and officially demonstrate his sovereign power over Suphanburi by extending royal patronage to the gods of the city pillar. King Chulalongkorn eventually followed Prince Damrong's lead and visited Suphanburi in person. He sponsored the first restoration of the city pillar shrine of Suphanburi in 1904. The City Pillar Shrine of Suphanburi came under the patronage of the royal government in Bangkok. Even after the Siamese Revolution, the shrine was among the first to be registered as a national heritage and put under the care of the Fine Arts Department in 1935.[4]

From the perspective of the mainstream nationalist historical narrative of Thailand, Suphanburi has figured prominently in the royalist-nationalist narrative of Prince Damrong from the late nineteenth century up to the Siamese Revolution in 1932. Luang Wichitwathakan's fascist-popularist narrative of the Wartime Phibunsongkhram Regime reinforced that narrative until the return of the royalist narrative of the Cold War and post-Cold War eras of Thai history. According to Prince Damrong's narrative, the greatest of all Ayutthayan battles is of King Naresuan's elephant-back duel with the Burmese Prince in 1593 that occurred in Suphanburi. The most well-known and well-loved Thai folktale from the Ayutthayan through early Rattanakosin period (the tale of *Khun Chang Khun Phaen*) was based on the lives of leading characters who were from Suphanburi (Baker and Phongpaichit 2012).

In both the royalist and territorialist narratives of Thai nationalism, Suphanburi is presented as the heartland of the Thai nation, a place that was Thai even before there was the idea of the nation-state. The royalist-nationalist narrative of Prince Damrong would describe Suphanburi as a loyal supporter of Ayutthaya, the capital of the Kingdom of Siam (1351–1767) and the anachronistic imagination of what Bangkok and the Chakri Dynasty would have been at the time of the greatest hero of the Siamese people, King Naresuan. The tale of *Khun Chang and Khun Phaen*, despite all the romantic and bloody intrigue, has been presented as, first and foremost, a story of the common people of Suphanburi and their loyalty toward the Ayutthayan Crown. The post 1932 constitutional regime managed to use Suphanburi in their unroyalist nationalist propaganda. The most distinct example would be *Luead Suphan* [lit. Suphan Blood], a historical play by Luang Wichitwathakan that was first staged in 1936. The play recounted the bravery of the men and women of Suphanburi who sacrificed their lives to protect the kingdom from invading Burmese troops. The narrative of *Luead Suphan* highlighted the heroism of the common people and their patriotic devotion to the nation as opposed to the royalist-nationalist narrative of the earlier era that celebrated the monarch as the representation of the nation and equated loyalty to the crown as one and the same as devotion toward the nation. Even after the fall of the People's Party's constitutional regime with the defeat of Japan at the end of World War II, *Luead Suphan* still managed to make a comeback in 1951 in the form of a highly acclaimed motion picture designed to boost patriotic sentiments at the height of the politically motivate 'Red Scare' in the early Cold War years (Sattayanurak 2002).

While the province of Suphanburi remained prominent in the Thai nationalist narrative through much of the Cold War years, it was not until 1964 that the local community had the opportunity and sufficient funds to mobilize their first restoration project of the City Pillar Shrine. The restoration of 1964 was carried out mainly by the Foundation of the City Pillar Shrine along with the personal funds of Banharn Silpa-acha and his family. The first local-funded restoration project kept the traditional Thai architectural structure of the pavilion that housed the city pillar figures designed during the earlier restoration by Prince Narit in 1937. However, it added traditional Chinese architectural dressings to archway entrances and the walls surrounding the square-shaped property of the shrine. That local-led restoration is indicative that the richest and most influential group in the province were the ethnic Chinese community.

It was not until 1987, after more than a decade of success in national politics, that Banharn Silpa-acha managed to mobilize another restoration project for the City Pillar Shrine of Suphanburi. The 1987 restoration would see the City Pillar Shrine of Suphanburi transform completely into a Chinese shrine in both architectural style and ritualistic function. Banharn ordered the construction of a traditional Chinese shrine building to encompass the smaller old traditional Thai architectural structure designed by Prince Narit. Banharn also bought a sizable piece of land (approximately 7 rai or 2.7 acres) adjacent to the property of the City Pillar Shrine to support traditional Chinese shrine activities such as traditional dances and alms giving, and a smaller shrine for the Chinese locality god or '*Puntaogong*' was established. The 1987 restoration represents a major turning point in the identity of the City Pillar Shrine of Suphanburi from a site of royal Siamese patronage to that of influential ethnic Chinese families (Sapphaitun 2000).

Suphanburi's position as the historical center of the rise to dominance of the ethnic Chinese community in Thailand coincided with Banharn's rise in political prominence. Among his earliest policies, the idea to build the Museum of the Descendants of the Dragon was enabled by the visit of Prime Minister Kukrit Pramoj to Beijing in 1975 and his historic meeting with the elderly and ailing Chairman Mao Zedong of the Chinese Communist Party. For several reasons, that should be considered a most crucial turning point in both the history of Suphanburi province, the Thai nation, and the history of Sino-Thai relations. First, it represents a national undertaking at the provincial level, outside of Bangkok, to commemorate a relationship with a rising superpower, China. That was a crucial decision that would result in the province rising to challenge Bangkok as the most important center of Chinese tourism and the Chinese diasporic history in Thailand (Silpa-acha 2016).

The fact that the decision was included as part of the national government's policy in 1995 was largely a result of the influence of the Chinese diaspora on Banharn's political identity and success in national politics. It was also a time when the Chinese economic influence was expanding rapidly, but before the PRC became a dominant global economic superpower. Banharn's bold yet highly visionary decision to invest in the propagation of his own and Suphanburi's socio-cultural and economic ties with the PRC at that initial period put the province ahead of the game in comparison with other major centers of the Chinese diaspora throughout Thailand. Despite ultimately being inaugurated around the same time as the Yaowarat Chinatown Heritage Center in Bangkok, Banharn's Dragon Museum was in the planning stages nearly a decade earlier.

Those two museums represent a divergence in political identity and alliance of the Bangkok-based Chinatown business community and that of Banharn's supporters in the Chinese diaspora. The Bangkok-based Yaowarat Chinatown Heritage Center was dedicated as part of the celebration of the late King Bhumibol Rama IX's 80th birthday in 2007. The narrative of the Bangkok Chinatown museum was largely related to the community's longstanding intimate relationship with the monarch and the royal family, which positioned the museum as representing an ethnic neighborhood in Bangkok. The Yaowarat museum laid claim of being the center of the Chinese diaspora largely through its connection to the Chakry dynasty and, indirectly, through connections to members of the royal family which also represent connection to the PRC government. The Museum of the Descendants of the Dragon, on the other hand, was planned from its very inception to be the site of commemoration of the 20th anniversary of the formal diplomatic relations between Thailand and China. The exhibitions narrate the stories, not so much of the history of the Chinese diaspora in Thailand, but of the shared historical and cultural foundations between the Chinese communities in Thailand and those in other Chinese communities around the world.

That dedication and narration, therefore, positions Banharn's Dragon Museum, not simply as a provincial ethnic museum, but as the national center of the ethnic Chinese community vis-à-vis the global network of Chinese diaspora.

At its grand opening in 2008, the Museum of the Descendants of the Dragon was inaugurated along with the opening of the Gardens of the Heavenly Dragon and a Chinese market community near the Suphanburi City Pillar Shrine (OPS Ministry of Tourism and Sports). Barely months after the conclusion of the Beijing Olympics, the newly inaugurated compound of the City Pillar Shrine and Dragon Museum became popular to Chinese tourists. It was the perfect combination for attracting twenty-first century Chinese tourists: superstitious folklore; religious practice in the City Pillar Shrine; magical, legendary, soft history presented with audio/visual effects; and shopping and enjoyment of local delicacies in the Chinese market town next door. With the continuous political turmoil in Thailand following the coup in 2006 and the chronic economic stagnation that has come to define the twenty-first century, Chinese tourists provide an important contribution to the economy.

Conclusion

The role of Chinese identity in provincial and national Thai politics is demonstrated in the life of Banharn Silpa-acha. The Thai political context is ever-changing with coups and military regimes disrupting democratic elections that would allow for Chinese premiers such as Banharn. The transformation of public opinion toward the Chineseness of Banharn Silpa-acha between the years he was politically active, his short-lived premiership, and the outpouring of condolences and nostalgic admiration surrounding his death is a telling social transformation which represents the rise of influence that PRC China has in Thailand. His life and related monuments can provide insight into what it will mean to be Chinese in Thailand during the politically volatile early twenty-first century.

In conclusion, there are three major transformations relating to the social capital of being Chinese in Thai politics that can be surmised from the case study of Banharn Silpa-acha's business life and political career. The first, and perhaps at the most personal level, is that the possession of Thai citizenship or lack thereof has gone from being most fundamental to an individual's political rights and potential in the early twentieth century. In the current post-Democratic era in Thailand, individual political rights have little meaning. The reason for that is the lack of fundamental democratic rights that could be expressed through the process of political elections, under a military regime. One of the most fundamental issues regarding the legitimacy of Banharn's premiership was his citizenship, affecting his right to run for office, which would in turn affect the possibility of his election as Prime Minister of Thailand. The extended implications of those suspicions regarding Banharn and his father's citizenship is that if the ethnic Chinese could easily obtain Thai citizenship, they could contribute to the outcome of the elections favorable for ethnic Chinese candidates. Banharn Silpa-acha openly and consistently capitalized upon his Chinese connections in his political campaigns. Under military rule, that would amount to a moot point because the efficacy of social capital within a political system that does not depend on a majority vote, or even public opinion of the masses, need not worry about which group has voting rights or the right to run for elections.

Another important factor observed through Banharn's life and political career is that the very strong socio-economic and legal pressure for the ethnic Chinese to acquire Thai citizenship to be able to reside and make a livelihood in Thailand through much of the World War and Cold War periods. In the current era, under the Prayuth Chan-Ocha government, China has increasing influence investing in PRC-nominee companies with labor, expertise, management, and materials imported from China. With the rise in political and economic influence of the PRC in mainland Southeast Asia, the possession of Chinese citizenship might be more beneficial in transnational and transregional business activities. That phenomenon is observed from the rise of the so-called 'New Chinatown' of *Huay Khwang* district in Bangkok where large numbers of Chinese nationals congregate in the neighborhood of the Chinese Embassy and reside and engage in various business activities with no intention of assimilating or acquiring Thai citizenship at any time in the foreseeable future.

The second major transformation is related to the decreasing/disappearing incentives to assimilate among Chinese nationals residing and doing business in Thailand. In the same way that western European, American, and Japanese migrants have been residing and making a living in Thailand throughout the Cold War period, Chinese nationals in the post-Cold War era are no longer perceived to pose a serious threat to national security. Instead of being constantly under suspicion of possibly being malicious agents of the Chinese Communist Party looking to overthrow 'nation, religion, and king' in Thailand, Chinese nationals currently represent purchasing power of a neighboring economic superpower. Consequently, an individual's socio-economic and cultural connection with Chinese communities within Thailand—both ethnic Chinese communities of people with Thai citizenship and communities of transnational migrant workers and entrepreneurs with Chinese citizenship—is no longer perceived with suspicion or a probable cause for political legitimacy, but instead as an invaluable asset that could encourage foreign investments as well as boost the local economy through growth in the tourism and hospitality industries.

Finally, as national identity becomes more of an asset for economic growth in the globalized world of the twenty-first century, Banharn Silpa-acha was indeed thinking ahead of his time in promoting his ethnic Chinese identity with the ethnic Chinese community and the rising economic influence of the PRC. The Museum of the Descendants of the Dragon in commemoration of the 20th anniversary of the establishment of formal diplomatic relations between Thailand and the PRC in 1995 represents that foresight. The royalist and anti-Communist nationalist identity of Suphanburi in the Cold War is no longer potent enough to allow Suphanburi to stand out as a special and crucial part of the national narrative of Thailand and Thai identity. The Suphanburi that the central power in Bangkok would desire to adopt as part of its grand narrative in the twenty-first century is not the province that claimed to be the center of the ancient Dvaravati civilization or the origin of the Ayutthayan Suphanaphum Dynasty, instead it is the Suphanburi province that could claim to be the heartland of the Chinese diaspora in Southeast Asia. Although there are no general elections for Banharn's descendants to run or his loyal constituency of Suphanburit to vote for, the central governing power in Bangkok, in the form of the military government, would appear to be following Banharn's lead in encouraging socio-economic and cultural connections between Thailand and the PRC. In an era when Chinese tourists are among the most powerful forces driving the Thai economy, even the unelected military government needs to capitalize on whatever Chinese connections they could claim to have.

Postscript: The Funeral Memorial Volume

When Banharn's memorial volume was finally published after the extended mourning and funerary rites had been completed in November 2016, it came in the form of two hefty hardcover books neatly arranged in a precisely fitting silver-colored cardboard box. The first book was an autobiography of Banharn, taken from his last long interview with the editors of the volume, which was originally planned to be featured in the former premier's 84th birthday volume had he not passed away only days following the interview in April 2016. A photograph of a smiling Banharn during the peak of his political career adorned the cover of the first book and provided a complete and personal narrative of Banharn's life from his family background, the moment he was born, his courtship and marriage with childhood friend Khunying Chaemsai, his business career, his entry into politics, his short reign of power as Prime Minister, the plan and construction of the Dragon Museum, political turmoil of the post-Thaksin Shinawatra period, all the way up to early April 2016 when he announced that he would once again lead his party in the next election—whenever that should happen. The second book in the silver memorial box is a picture book. Its off-white cover is adorned with a golden sketch of the same giant dragon that has been constructed as the façade of Suphanburi's famed Museum of the Descendants of the Dragon, which Banharn considered to be one of his life's greatest achievements. The picture book tells a similar story to the autobiography, but with pictures instead of printed words (Silpa-acha 2016).

The pictures in Banharn's memorial volume read like a photo essay of the transformation of political power from the most personal level of his own family and the provincial community of Suphanburi, to national electoral politics, the regional arena of Southeast Asia, the PRC looming at the transregional level, all the way up to the global politics of world leaders visiting Thailand under Banharn's premiership. It is not only a memorial volume for a former Prime Minister's funeral, but also one of a bygone era. The picture book memorializes a time when politicians still walked the streets and held rallies in the local temple, the long-gone era when politicians, no matter how corrupted, were still being elected into office. The volume prominently featured His Majesty the late King Bhumibol Rama IX in his regal capacity of providing advice and approval to the civilian government. It was a time when the Association of Southeast Asian Nations (ASEAN) still mattered and the province of Chiang Mai hosted the Southeast Asia Games. Pictures from Prime Minister Banharn's various state visits to neighboring Southeast Asian countries and of ASEAN heads of states visiting Thailand were presented as important moments in the history of that Prime Minister. However, toward the very end, we see a hint of what will become of paramount importance in the future. The memorial volume that was published in November 2016 ended in a detailed narrative of the sinification with restoration of the City Pillar Shrine of Suphanburi and the construction of the Museum of the Descendants of the Dragon and the Heavenly Dragon Village. Warawuth Silpa-acha, his youngest and only son, claimed in the obituary he wrote for his father that "Banharn is the spirit of Suphanburi",[5] and Suphanburi represents the past, present, and future of the Thai nation, and all of that, including the memory of Banharn himself, is culturally, economically, and politically Chinese.

If the social capital of being Chinese in Thai politics in the case of Banharn Silpa-acha can provide any indication to regional and transregional politics in that part of the world, it should be the obvious tendency toward a continuous rising role and influence of the PRC and the waning of relevance of ASEAN in Thai politics. Sino-Thai relations is on a steady path toward outweighing every other relationship and ASEAN will only matter for Thailand (and perhaps most of its other member states) in as much as it enhances Thailand's position vis-à-vis the PRC. It is yet unclear if and when Thailand would ever have an elected Prime Minister again, but it is almost certain that whoever should rise to become the country's political leader within the foreseeable future would require an intimate and amiable relationship with China.

Notes

1. Barnharn Silpa-acha was elected a member of parliament of Suphanburi a combined total of eight times (in 1976, 1983, 1986, 1988, 1992/1, 1992/2 [before and after the 'Black May Incident' of 1992], 1995, and 1996). After the 1996 election, Banharn continued to be elected as a member of parliament through the party list system.
2. Siam was not officially colonized, but there were a sizeable number of ethnic Chinese capitalists who were operating in Siam during that period who were colonial subjects (either born or resided in other European colonies in Asia prior to moving to Siam) and enjoyed extraterritorial rights. It was the Siamese court's intentions to attract those Chinese colonial subjects to invest and do business in Siam to contribute to the Siamese economy and enhance Siam's ability to compete with other economies (all of which were parts of major European empires) in the region.
3. Suphanburi legends include King Naresuan's elephant-back duel with the Burmese Prince, the most well-known and well-loved lore of *Khun Chang–Khun Phaen*, and the origins of one of the most important Ayudhayan dynasties (1370–1388), and the Suphannaphum Dynasty (1409–1569).

4. Later in 1937, the royal artist Prince Narit led the project to expand the City Pillar Shrine of Suphanburi to include an entrance archway, a pavilion for worshipers, and built a wall around the square-shaped property.
5. "When I miss my father, I only need to drive to Suphanburi province and I would feel like I am with him. Today I feel that father never left us. He only changed his vehicle from the body that had served him faithfully for the past 83 years to a new state that is free from all bondages. He continues to take care of his beloved Suphanburi. It is such a coincident that this thought is one and the same as the slogan of Suphanburi Football Club that father had revived years ago and is flourishing to this day. I think this is the best slogan for my father, who had devoted his life, his body, and heart to Suphanburi province. Today, Banharn Silpa-acha, my beloved father, is the spirit of Suphanburi." (Memorial Volume for Banharn Silpa-acha's Funeral. *Suphanburi Dragon Returns to Heaven* [Mangkon Suphan Khuen Fa]. Nonthaburi: Matichon Press, 2016, p. 84).

Bibliography

Baker, Chris, and Pasuk Phongpaichit. 2012. *The Tale of Khun Chang Khun Phaen*. Seattle: University of Washington Press.

Choetcharatfa, Khomdeaun. 1995. *Chiwaprawat lae thatsana Banharn Silpa-acha* [Biography and Perspectives of Banharn Silpa-acha]. Bangkok: Soithong.

Damrong, Prince. 2006. *Nithanboranakhadi* [Archeological Stories]. Bangkok: Thai Quality Books.

Kasetsiri, Chanvit. 2016. *A Political History of Siam, 1932–1957*. Bangkok: The Foundation for the Promotion of Social Science and Humanities Textbook Project.

Loetrattanawisut, Prasong, ed. 2009. *Mangkon Deng kamsuan padsipet pi maime wan tai* [Passions of the Dragon, the 81-Year-Old Immortal]. Bangkok: Matichon.

Manthira, Ruj, ed. 1995. *Senthang Su Nayok khong Deng Siao Han* [The Path to Premiership of Banharn Silpa-acha]. Bangkok: Namfon Press.

Matichon, Thep Boontanond. 2015. *Kanmuang nai kanthahan samai rachakanthibok* [Politics in the Military During the Sixth Reign]. Bangkok: Matichon.

Mektrairat, Nakarin. 1997. *Siamese Revolution 1932*. Bangkok: Amarin Wichakan.

Office of the Permanent Secretary, Ministry of Tourism and Sports. *Grand Opening of the Gardens of the Heavenly Dragon and the Museum of the Descendants of the Dragon*. http://secretary.mots.go.th/.

Post Today. 2016. อาลัย "บรรหาร ศิลปอาชา" *83* ปี มังกรการเมือง .... อ่านต่อได้ที่. August 14. http://www.posttoday.com/analysis/report/448546.

Sapphaitun, Athiwat, ed. 2000. *Senthang chewit Banharn Silpa-acha* [The Life Path of Banharn Silpa-acha]. Bangkok: Pathomakan Press.

Sathaporn, Santisuk. 2012. *Banharn Silpa-acha: Yodlaikhram Mangkonsuphan* [Banharn Silpa-acha: the Greatest of Suphan Dragons]. Bangkok: Bangkok Books.

Sattayanurak, Saichon. 2002. *Chatthai lae khwampenthai doi Luangwichitwathakan* [The Thai Nation and Thai-ness by Luang Wichit Wathakan]. Bangkok: Matichon.

Silpa-acha, Banharn. 2016, November. Phatara Khamphitak and Intharachai Phanichakul, eds. *Banharn Silpa-acha lao rueang khrang sutthai* [Banharn Silpa-acha Tells His Story One Last Time], memorial volume.

Wongsurawat, Wasana. 2009. "From Yaowaraj to Phlabphlachai: The Thai State and Ethnic Chinese in Thailand During the Cold War." In *Dynamics of the Cold War in Asia: Ideology, Identity and Culture*, edited by Vu Tuong and Wasana Wongsurawat, 165–186. New York: Palgrave Macmillan.

Wongsurawat, Wasana. 2016. "Beyond Jews of the Orient: A New Interpretation of the Problematic Relationship Between the Thai State and Its Ethnic Chinese Community." *Positions: Asia Critique* 24, no. 2, May: 555–582.

Wongsurawat, Wasana, ed. 2016. *Sites of Modernity: Asian Cities in the Transitory Moments of Trade, Colonialism and Nationalism*. Hong Kong: Springer.

CHAPTER 5

Philippines–China Relations: Interplay Between Domestic Politics and Globalization

Ellen Palanca and Austin Ong

Introduction

In 2016, the Philippine government headed by Rodrigo Duterte ushered in a new chapter in the Philippines–China bilateral relations. Duerte's first major state visit within months of assuming office was to China. The state visit generated US$24 billion worth of economic pledges in the form of increased investments, trade, tourism, and financial cooperation (Romero 2016). That development in bilateral relations was a dramatic shift from relations just months prior when Philippines–China relations deteriorated to their "lowest-point" when, in 2013, the Philippines sued China in the Permanent Court of Arbitration under the preceding administration of Benigno S. Aquino III (2010–2016). Consequently, there were no Chinese investments in the Philippines during that time. The tumultuous cycle of the Philippines–China relations is further

E. Palanca (✉)
Ateneo de Manila University, Quezon City, Philippines

A. Ong
De La Salle University, Manila, Philippines

Y. Santasombat (ed.), *The Sociology of Chinese Capitalism in Southeast Asia*, https://doi.org/10.1007/978-981-13-0065-3_5

demonstrated by the fact that the bilateral relations had been described as the "Golden Age of Partnership" under Aquino's immediate predecessor, Gloria Macapagal Arroyo (2001–2010). During that time, the Philippines was China's largest recipient of investment in the region. Those sixteen years demonstrate the Philippines' relations with China as a swing from the "Golden Age of Partnership" to no investment to the current state of friendly relations.

Relations between the Philippines and China are very much influenced by two main factors: (1) the strong alliance with the USA, and (2) the Philippines' domestic politics characterized by personalized politics, patronage bureaucracy, and weak institutions. The Philippines' alliance with the USA spans a period of approximately 120 years. Although political independence was granted in 1946, the Philippines continues to have strong ties with the USA through the Mutual Defense Treaty established in 1951. Economic ties, as well as social and cultural affinities, have continued to grow with migration. The Philippines' politics and foreign policy echo the US ideology of democracy.

The politics and patronage bureaucracy with weak institutions contribute to the lack of formal and strategic foreign policy. As a result, the president has control over relations with China (and other foreign interests) which has resulted in a more volatile relationship, as seen over the past 15 years, when compared with the USA.

Entangled in relations between China and the Philippines is the sensitive issue of the South China Sea (SCS). For decades, territorial disputes strained relations, particularly during Benigno Aquino III's term. The role of the private sector and global interests have played a moderating effect on bilateral relations by separating economic from political relations. For example, the Philippines signed on as a founding member of the China-led Asian Infrastructure Investment Bank (AIIB) despite the country's troubled relationship with China over the disputed SCS Islands and demonstrates the profit-driven interests surpassing politically driven ambitions.

Regional and global trade developments are taking precedence over bilateral relations. For example, the Philippines have signed on to participate in China's One Belt One Road (OBOR), the AIIB, and the Regional Comprehensive Economic Program (RCEP). In this chapter, we illustrate how Philippines–China relations have been shaped by the Philippines' domestic politics but tempered by external market forces and globalization.

Formal diplomatic ties between the Philippines and China were first established in June 1975 during the martial law era of Ferdinand Marcos which took place shortly after the US reestablishment of diplomatic relations with China in 1972. The diplomatic change was relatively swift and immediate under the Marcos dictatorship.

The Philippines has been a staunch ally of the USA since World War II. Relations with the USA, as colonizer for almost 50 years (1898–1946) "rests on a wide and substantive social basis with solid political, economic, military, and social bonds" (Rueda 2012). Filipinos are the second largest ethnic minority group in the USA, after the Hispanics. Active American influence in the 1950s and 1960s in the fields of education, institutional and organizational building promoting anti-communist policies, and activities led to a pervasive distrust of the then communist China.

Under the Mutual Defense Agreement of 1951, the USA has provided a de facto security umbrella for the Philippines that continues until today. As the USA established diplomatic relations in 1972, the main resistance to build closer relations with China came from Taiwan. When the Communist Party took over China in 1949, the Philippines maintained diplomatic ties with the exiled government in Taiwan as the legitimate representative of China. During the Cold War period, the Kuomintang (KMT) of Taiwan had substantial influence in the Philippines, particularly among the ethnic Chinese, due in part to the presence of a US military alliance with an anti-communist drive. Under the Treaty of Amity signed in 1947, Taiwan was able to supervise and control all Chinese schools in the Philippines.[1] Taiwan focused on anti-communism in those schools. Taiwan also had strong influence on the Federation of Filipino Chinese Chambers of Commerce, Inc., established in 1954, as the primary business organization of the Filipino Chinese. The KMT maintained influence over the Federation through the 1990s.

Because of those factors, and despite the Philippines being one of the early countries to establish formal diplomatic relations with China, which resulted in some friendly engagements and trade exchanges in favor of the Philippines,[2] China posed a lingering threat as a communist and an underdeveloped country. During Corazon Aquino's term (1986–1992) the Philippines wavered on the One China Policy because of the economic benefits that Taiwan offered.[3]

The Philippines missed the opportunities presented by China's rapid economic growth during the six-year period of Corazon Aquino's term. Lim (1999) explained that "the Aquino government was so single-minded in seeking Taiwan economic support that it overlooked the phenomenal rise of China's economy and therefore failed to utilize it as benevolent stimulus to the Philippines's economic growth." However, by the early 1990s, amid the flurry of regional economic development, China's economic growth could not be ignored. The Philippine government, under Fidel Ramos who succeeded Corazon Aquino, focused on economic "developmental diplomacy" aligned to a more practical approach toward China (Pattugalan 1999). The Balance of Trade Policy was terminated, which led to an increase of trade with China with an almost ten-fold increase from 1992 to 1998.[4] Trade and investments increased significantly during that period, largely driven by the force of globalization. The Philippines became a member of the World Trade Organization (WTO) in 1996 and China joined in 2001.

Relations with China were relatively calm during the early 2000s as President Joseph Estrada, who succeeded Fidel Ramos, had a short-lived presidency. China's ascent in the global stage unavoidably convinced the leaders of the Philippines, for the most part, to see the importance of maintaining the balance of power in the region and to seek to engage China and at the same time maintain the traditional alliance with the USA. Furthermore, The China–Association of Southeast Asian Nations (ASEAN) Free Trade Agreement inaugurated regional aspirations.

During the 2000s, the Philippines became a major source of China's new found economic dynamism. During the Arroyo administration (2001–2010), unprecedented levels of Chinese investments and official development assistance (ODA) entered the Philippines. Beginning in 2002, economic partnerships and joint ventures developed rapidly in diverse fields including energy, infrastructure, mining, and agriculture. The Philippines was among three largest recipients of China aid among Southeast Asian countries, reaching US$5.4 billion between 2002 and 2007 (Vietnam was $3.4 billion and Burma $3.1 billion) (Landingin 2010). In 2004, China represented 60% of the Philippines' total ODA.[5] Two of the largest projects, the Northrail Project and the National Broadband Network (NBN)—Zhong Xing Telecommunications Equipment (ZTE) Project, are highlighted below to illustrate China's early charm initiatives in the Philippines.

Northrail Project

Reported to be China's single largest aid project in Southeast Asia at that time, the North Luzon Railway Project ("Northrail") signed in 2004, was a major infrastructure project that was to build a commuter train service that could ferry 150,000 passengers per day between the capital and surrounding provinces. It was awarded to China National Machinery and Industry Corp. (later renamed to Sinomach) in 2003 for an initial US$431 million, which was to be funded by China's Export-Import Bank. It was reported to be the first 20-year concessionary loan ever extended by China to any government at 3% interest including a 5-year grace period. It was followed by a second loan of US$500 million, which was signed but never used (Landingin 2010). After six years, not a single kilometer of rail was built. The succeeding government halted and eventually cancelled the project and China then demanded the repayment of the loan.

NBN-ZTE

Another major project to be financed by China was the NBN project with Chinese state firm ZTE Corporation. It was a US$330 million contract to be funded by the Export–Import Bank of China to build a NBN linking the national offices and barangay (village) municipal offices. The contract was signed in April 2007, suspended by September 2007, and canceled by October 2007.

Under Arroyo's term, the Philippines was poised to be an early beneficiary of China's charm offensive with the entry of a deluge of mega-projects to be funded by China. The funding of those projects included foreign direct investments and ODA. Regardless of the classification, those major state-to-state projects were packaged in such concessional rates that according to a Philippine economic officer, the rates China extended were rates the Philippine government had to negotiate from other funding countries, which added to its attractiveness.[6]

Despite China's economic power and strategic diplomacy, it had not been successful in getting the cooperation of the Philippines and in fact got into more trouble with all its efforts, partly because China underestimated the strength of domestic politics and the effect of China's strong stance on territorial issue, which the Philippines perceived as the flexing of the emerging state's newfound power. The Philippines' domestic politics prevented the country from fully capitalizing on China's altruism and economic charm offensive.

Domestic Politics and the Philippines–China Relations

The domestic political landscape of the Philippines has been described as personality-based which leads to policy changes whenever a new president is elected—the Philippine president has a six-year term limit in office. Change may also occur within an administration due to internal politics as in the case of relations with China during the Arroyo and Aquino terms. Additionally, the Philippines lacks a long-term national development policy that can transcend presidential administrations. The personality-based politics and weak institutions concentrate the decision and management of foreign policy to the President, who is considered the chief architect of foreign policy. Consequently, bilateral agreements initiated by the president when relations are good may altogether be derailed or canceled by the next president when relations turn sour, and vice versa. Ultimately, that was demonstrated in the Philippines–China relationship change from a "Golden Age of Partnership" under Arroyo (2000–2010) to a cessation under Aquino (2010–2016), and finally friendly relations under Duterte (2016–2022).

China Policy Formulation

The Philippines has traditionally been dependent on the West for much of what it needed in political, economic, and security terms. For example, the USA has provided de facto external security needs for the country under the 1951 Mutual Defense Treaty. Economically, the USA and Japan have been the top trading partners of the Philippines. China was traditionally not a major trade partner but that changed, and in 2017 became the top trading partner. American brands and media influence are ubiquitous in the Philippine market and demonstrate the extensive reach of America's soft power. For the most part, the Philippines' foreign policy remains tightly linked with the USA. Wurfel (1990) believed that the Philippines has not had full foreign policy restructuring because of the US cultural and strategic colonial vestiges. Resulting from those factors, the Philippines has traditionally not had the sense of urgency to craft a strategic or a coherent China policy.

In extension, the Philippines, for the most part—unlike other countries that have established long-standing, even government-funded, research institutes or think tanks with whom the government can regularly consult—has not seen the importance of establishing institutions that research or study China extensively. Because of that, policymakers or architects of foreign policy lack the pool of resources provided by institutional memory or sinologists that understand China and all her complexities. Therefore, the absence of a long-term China policy has been responsible for the Philippines' "missing the boat" or fully capitalizing on China's economic growth since the 1990s. For example, the Philippines focused on its relationship with Taiwan in the early 1990s just when China's economy took off. It initially did not sign on to the "Early Harvest Program" of the China–ASEAN Free Trade Area in 2003 although the nine other ASEAN members already had (China Embassy 2004). Among the major ASEAN countries, the Philippines is one of the lowest in trade, tourism, and student exchanges with China. It also almost missed being part of the AIIB and OBOR when the Philippine government expressed concerns that China might use participation to those programs as leverage on the territorial dispute—the threat perception was only reinforced when Chinese maps presenting the planned routes did not include the Philippines. More importantly, whenever bumps or challenges in the bilateral relationship develop, management of the relations easily go askew—or worse, cascade into a crisis.

That is what transpired in the 1995 Mischief Reef dispute. The Philippines was caught off guard when China suddenly occupied the area. In the 2012 Scarborough Shoal Incident, the Philippines lost effective control of the area to China after the US-brokered negotiations did not materialize (Greiten 2016). Moreover, Manila could not prevent the political impasse from spilling over and adversely affecting the health of the economic relations between the two countries.[7]

In the absence of a firm strategic foreign policy, the foreign relations of a country can easily be dictated or altered with the change of leadership. Personality-based politics in the shaping of foreign policy is mainly concerned with the divergent interests of leaders who shape or make policies—in the case of the Philippines, the president is the chief originator. According to Mesquita, "the choice of foreign policy interactions is generally constrained to be incentive-compatible with the motivations of national leaders to maintain their hold on political power" (Beuno de Mesquita 2017). In the case of the Philippines, the absence of a firm

China policy has seen the incumbent president adopt the "China-card" based on his or her personal need or political expediency. That can best be demonstrated by how each president can single-handedly alter the Philippines' SCS position, as the examples below illustrate.

Macapagal-Arroyo served nine years as president from 2001 to 2010. Her administration began to warm up to China when relations with the USA cooled after she pulled the Philippines out from then US President Bush's "coalition of the willing" for the war in Iraq to save the life of an overseas Filipino hostage. The succeeding years would see Arroyo travel to China an unprecedented 11 times and on the 30th anniversary of bilateral relations in 2005, both sides toasted to the "Golden Age of Partnership".[8] At that time, China became a major part of the Philippines' foreign relations. However, domestic challenges to Arroyo's legitimacy from local stakeholders would continually overshadow her foreign policy. From the start, her taking over the presidency from Estrada was viewed as an underhanded power grab. The maneuver also pitted her, who represented the society's elite, against the poor masses (Estrada was a "president of the poor" and experienced a similar "coup" as Thailand's Thaksin Shinawatra). Upon winning the election in 2004, she was overshadowed with accusations of election fraud which would hound her for the rest of her administration.

South China Sea Disputes

The perennial SCS issue was addressed during Arroyo's term with the establishment of the Joint Maritime Seismic Understanding (JMSU)-a tripartite agreement including the Philippines, China, and Vietnam signed by Arroyo in Manila in March 2005. The proponents contended that the agreement was scientific in nature with the aim of gathering pre-exploratory seismic data on possible oil reserves. The agreement was initially hailed as a breakthrough in dispute resolution. However, it would soon be dragged into the political quagmire that hounded Arroyo's term. Opponents criticized the nontransparent action taken with the negotiations and questioned the reasoning behind the trilateral approach when the SCS dispute involved more claimants. Additionally, critics questioned whether political concessions made under JMSU were a quid pro quo for China's generous economic packages that were coming into the country and were said to fund Arroyo's development projects. Political opponents further accused her of bartering away Philippine national security interests, and the clamor eventually led to a full-blown Senate inquiry. The deal was made to lapse on July 1, 2008 foregoing the option to extend the agreement to its second phase.

Benigno Aquino III (son of Corazon Aquino) took over the presidency in 2010–2016. Branding his government as the antithesis of his predecessor—he had campaigned on an anticorruption campaign and went on a crusade to implicate Arroyo—his administration halted or canceled most of the infrastructure projects signed by the previous administration. He would later be criticized for arbitrarily canceling projects that would have contributed to the developmental needs of the Philippines (Tiglao 2012). Despite that, Aquino's initial overtures to China appeared to start off relations on a fresh start. His first state visit was to China where the two leaders agreed to strengthen economic and trade cooperation while minimizing the impact of disputes in the SCS.[9] Aquino also sent his close friend and Interior Secretary to negotiate the repayment of the loans for the canceled Northrail Projects and even placed his international reputation at risk when he decided not to attend the 2010 Nobel Peace Prize ceremony in support of the Chinese government that was boycotting the event. Fourteen Taiwanese online fraudsters were deported from Manila to Beijing amidst the protest of Taipei. From the Philippine perspective, those efforts demonstrated Aquino's early friendly overtures toward China.

Philippines–China relations quickly went from bad to worse. At around the same time, Aquino faced early challenges in his presidency that were coincidentally directly or indirectly linked to the Philippines–China relations. Several examples include the botched rescue operation to save a bus filled with Hong Kong tourists in Manila in 2010, the shooting of the Taiwanese fishermen by the Philippine Coast Guard in mid 2013, and the execution of Filipino drug mules by the Chinese despite appeals for clemency by the Philippine President.[10] The SCS issue then erupted which inevitably cascaded into a crisis in relations when the highest level of communication was halted. The SCS disputes were at the center of relations. He criticized Arroyo's JMSU and said it "shouldn't have happened as it encroached into the country's territorial waters" (*ABS-CBN News* 2011).

The government of President Aquino decided to adopt a unidimensional approach to manage relations. The turning point was the April 2012 Scarborough Shoal Incident that ended with China gaining effective control of the disputed area that caused a loss of confidence on both sides. Consequently, Philippine–China relations inevitably became less cordial, even hostile. The following year in 2013, the Aquino administration decided to file the historic arbitration case against China in the United Nations Permanent Court of Arbitration. The last two years of Aquino's presidency, bilateral relations went into a stand-still and were described to have reached the "lowest point" (Baviera 2012).

The unanimous decision that voted in favor of the Philippines in the arbitration case was made a few months after President Duterte assumed office in replacement of Aquino in mid-2016. Duterte decided to be friendlier with China by not forcing China to deal with the legal aspect of the SCS issue and instead to adopt a multidimensional approach in the relations—demonstrating the contrasting approaches of the two presidents, but more importantly how the personal decisions of a leader can single-handedly alter the country's China foreign policy.[11]

One of Duterte's domestic governance platforms was anchored on his "war on drugs". The US government under the Obama Administration criticized Duterte for his human rights violations which led Duterte to question the long-standing alliance between the Philippines and the USA and announced his intention to craft an independent foreign policy which included a pivot to China.[12] Within a few months he sent an informal but high-level delegation to Hong Kong, led by former president Ramos. That historical meeting was a significant inroad because it was the first high-level meeting between the two countries since high-level talks were called off under Aquino. That was followed by Duterte's first state visit to Beijing and he would visit China twice within the first year of his administration. That state visit highlighted the renewed focus on the economic relations and pledges made that totaled US$24 billion.[13] Within a few months, the Joint Commission on Economic and Trade Cooperation, which was discontinued under Aquino, was reconvened to fast track the implementation process.

Some of the immediate developments brought about by the friendlier relationship initiated by Duterte included the Chinese government lifting of the ban on the imports of Philippine tropical fruits such as bananas and pineapples followed by the purchase of US$1.5 billion worth of Philippine goods destined for China's markets—the largest such deal China has made for an Asian country. The travel warning for the Philippines issued in 2014 by the Chinese was also lifted leading to an increase in arrivals from about 490,000 in 2015 to 670,000 in 2016, and aimed for 1 million in 2017 (Xinua 2017).

Filipino fishermen could return to their fishing activities in Scarborough Shoal only a few weeks after Duterte's state visit, which China had made off limits in the aftermath of the 2012 Scarborough Shoal Incident (Hunt 2016).

Public Perception of China

There is a widely shared public distrust of China among the Philippine populace which also pervades among the government leaders and bureaucrats. On one hand, the pervasive public perception that Chinese-funded projects are of low quality and prone to corruption and, on the other hand, the ongoing territorial dispute inevitably tied any economic engagements as somehow politically motivated. Since scientific opinion polling began in the Philippines, the net-trust rating of China by Filipinos has been perennially the lowest among the traditional foreign partners of the Philippines—the USA is the most trusted followed by Japan (Mangahas 2016). In fact, despite the increasing pledges China has made to invest in the Philippines and the Philippines' more amicable relations with China under President Duterte, survey results continue to show negative public perception of China, only better than North Korea (Mangahas 2017). That is not surprising because as seen before, the US–Taiwan influence on the Philippines has resulted in a zero-sum mentality approach toward China. Further contributing to the negative public perception is the SCS territorial dispute and corruption issues that hound Chinese-funded projects that vested interest groups and political opposition also use to attack the seated president.

That negative perception may partly explain why even when political relations were good under Arroyo or Duterte, closer economic engagements were still slow in fruition or can be derailed entirely. The domestic aversion to China-funded projects is evident when compared with other sources of foreign funding (i.e. from the USA, Japan, or South Korea). Closer economic relations with China are often portrayed as posing a political or security risk, especially vis-à-vis the issues connected to the SCS dispute. In fact, the friendlier positions of Presidents Arroyo and Duterte toward China were even claimed to be too easy on, or even selling out to, China.

The situation is exacerbated when political relations deteriorate which can be seen under President Aquino when applications of Chinese investments, both public and private, were not being processed.[14]

Institutions and Bureaucracy

As in most countries, the Philippine President is considered the chief originator of foreign policy. However, unlike other countries with strong institutions that can provide some objectivity or continuity that transcends the limits of a presidential term, the Philippine bureaucracy is characterized by patronage politics, weak institutions, and rampant corruption which have had a cumulative effect on Philippines–China relations as well. For instance, given the traditionally US ideology-based foreign policy framework and the lack of resources for policy formulation coupled with the President's "power of the purse", in general the oversight powers of the legislative and judicial branches of government on the President's foreign policy are weak or simply defer to the presidential prerogative (Tuazon 2014). Moreover, the lack of political will and manpower allocations prevent the Department of Foreign Affairs and Foreign Trade attachés to develop specializations to better manage informal power structures as well as vested interest of pressure groups to wield a stronger influence on foreign relations.

One manifestation of weak institutions is the rampant corruption in the bureaucracy. That has a debilitating effect on the country from fully capitalizing on its foreign relations in general, and with China in particular. Amid allegations and controversies of corruption, even escalating to the highest officials in government, major projects meant to have been funded by China have been ultimately halted or canceled. (It must be noted that other projects from other foreign partners that were mired in corruption were also halted or canceled.)

The initial excitement surrounding the Northrail Project deteriorated when reports surfaced that massive corruption permeated throughout the negotiations. Layers of contractors and subcontractors were used to create a labyrinth of signatories that doomed the project from the start.[15] Moreover, President Macapagal-Arroyo's weakened hold on power meant she was unable to defend the ongoing Northrail Project which was subsequently passed on to the next administration. Subsequently, upon taking office the Aquino's government froze the project in mid 2010 and eventually canceled it saying it is "an expensive project that became even more expensive after renegotiation…with fewer public benefits".[16] China then asked for the repayment of the loan that had already been released to the Philippines (Burgonio 2012). Because that developed during the deterioration of political relations because of the SCS issue, China's demand for repayment was perceived as politically motivated.

The NBN-ZTE deal was another major casualty. The contract was signed, suspended, and canceled within six months by Arroyo because of allegations that key people in her administration, including her husband and elections chief, received kickbacks of as much as 200 million pesos to guarantee the deal. Her political survival was put in jeopardy when she was attacked by her predecessors, cabinet members, civil society, and even the military and resulted in a government directive in 2008 that halted ODA and loans for 11 major projects with a total worth of US$2.6 billion, half of which were meant to be funded by China.

Amid the public clamor and growing opposition for a series of China-funded projects, Ms. Arroyo would eventually form a panel called the China Projects Oversight Panel to review all Chinese government-funded projects in the country and placed a moratorium on additional loan transfers and eventually suspended other projects in the pipeline to stave off the domestic pressure being mounted on her. Her fate was sealed in the court of public opinion when the media reported about a photo of president Arroyo playing golf in Shenzhen with the Chinese businessmen connected to the NBN-ZTE deal. In October 2007, she met with Chinese President Hu Jintao in Shanghai to explain her "difficult decision" to cancel the controversial ZTE deal and suspend other projects to be funded by China.[17]

Although the weaknesses of Philippine domestic politics have prevented the country from fully benefiting from China's economic overtures, there have been successful China-funded development projects. One common pattern among those projects is that they worked with established institutions and linked on the developmental objectives of cooperation and delinked from politics. Some projects were even begun under one president and completed under the successor, including the Agno River Integrated Irrigation Project, the Angat Water Utilization and Aqueduct Improvement Project, and the Philippine-Sino Center for Agricultural Technology—projects that also finished several months ahead of schedule. Most of those projects were passed through the ministerial or organizational level on a somewhat smaller scale (a few million dollars compared with hundreds of millions of dollars).[18]

The largest Chinese investment in the Philippines, the National Grid Corporation of the Philippines (NGCP), is another well-illustrated case. Although there were many aspects to the initial success, one factor stands out: it anchored on established institutions.

China State Grid

In 2007, State Grid of Corporation of China (also called China State Grid), a Chinese state-owned enterprise and the world's biggest power company, won the 25-year contract (extendable to 50 years) to manage and operate the Philippines' entire electricity grid in what was then the first overseas investment for the company.[19]

The deal was made with two local partners—Monte Oro Grid Resources Corporation led by port tycoon Enrique Razon, Jr., who would later enter the gaming industry and build the Philippines' largest casino resort venture, and Calaca High Power Corporation led by businessman Robert Coyuito, another tycoon. The domestic players each own 30% while China's State Grid owns the remaining 40%.[20] The consortium was established as the NGCP. In 2010, Henry Sy Jr. of the SM Group and the Philippines' richest family bought out the 30% stake of Monte Oro Grid Resources. The typical business model entails the international partner to provide financial and technical assistance to the local partner.

The choice of institutional Filipino names by the Chinese investors suggests that was part of the strategy to partner with established players. It was initially dubbed as the country's biggest government auction conducted in efforts to reform the local power sector, nonetheless, it is not without its critics. The deal was criticized for the supposed nontransparent and biased conduct that surrounded the bidding. Despite the local opposition, even by some Philippine officials, a law was passed in 2008 that legalized the role of NGCP in the "franchise to operate, manage, and expand the electric transmission business of the country",[21] which further institutionalized the presence of the China State Grid.

It must be noted that the successful auction came after four failed attempts since 2001 and was part of the Philippine government's program to revive a troubled initiative to sell power-generating and grid assets to settle over $7 billion in debt at the Philippines' insolvent state power company (Landingin and McGregor 2007). Additionally, the privatization was a product of the Philippine domestic law known as the Electric Power Industry Reform Act of 2001. Finally, the company contends that it won the contract through public competitive bidding, in which other major local and foreign players had equally participated in.

Privatizing the state-owned utility was subsequently criticized as posing a grave national security threat under the administration of Aquino and took place amid the deteriorating political relationship of the two countries resulting from the SCS conflict post 2012. In 2015, the Philippine government refused to grant a work visa extension to 18 Chinese technical experts. The head of the Department of Energy acknowledged that the decision not to extend the working visas stemmed from the uncertainty surrounding a territorial dispute between the two countries. However, he also acknowledged that the government's concern might be unfounded as other countries where China State Grid had invested such as Europe, Australia, and Brazil had not posed such concerns (Tabeta 2017).

Philippine legislators continue to voice their concerns regarding the participation of a Chinese state-owned enterprise in the Philippines' national grid even under the Duterte administration, who has since established good relations with China. Amid reported profits, lawmakers have recently questioned the role of China State Grid and have proposed legislations to amend or rescind Chinese ownership (Palaña 2017). The plight of the NGCP is an unfolding story. However, the initial achievements of the joint venture testify to the successful partnerships that may be had when the parties involved operate professionally and with established institutions of the host country.

Global Trends and Market Forces

The Philippines–China economic relations are unavoidably linked to global market forces. Despite unstable bilateral political relations, global economic developments provide a cushioning effect on the evolution of Philippine–China bilateral relations.

With the help of globalization, China has become completely integrated with the global economy and engages with practically all the countries in the world. In just a matter of decades following its Open-Door Policy, China emerged from being a secluded, isolated, and self-reliant economy to one of the most globalized economies in the world. In less than a generation, it has propelled itself to becoming the second largest economy and is forecasted to overtake the USA by 2020. During the Asian financial crisis in the late 1990s, it demonstrated its economic resilience and capability as well as its willingness to assist countries affected by the crisis. While also affected by the global financial crisis, China prevented the crisis from deepening into a global recession. For instance, in the Philippines, the decrease in exports to western markets was compensated by an increase in exports to China during the period from 2007 to 2009 (Palanca 2016). Conversely, China's economic slowdown since early 2010 has caused a significant impact on the global economy. For example, in the aftermath of the global financial crisis, the weakening demand for raw commodity and fuel from China resulted in the global slump in prices for those items.

Traditionally, it was assumed that good political relations translated to good economic relations and bad political relations to bad economic relations. However, the forces of globalization and regionalization are changing the rules of the game. For instance, Philippine–China trade has continually been growing despite the health of their bilateral relations, only slowing or decreasing because of the effects of the global supply network, global financial crisis, and "China's new normal" (Palanca 2016).

Beyond State-State Investments

For the most part, data show that when political diplomatic relations go awry, it is from the non-state-to-state engagements where investments continue.[22] That is because non-state players are more concerned about their economic and social welfare than with political disagreements or the territorial dispute (Ang See 2016). Non-state-to-state commercial players that are considered here include Chinese transnational corporations, private Chinese and Philippine corporations, and entrepreneurs.

Playing a vital catalyst in trade and investments are the new migrants of overseas Chinese. Their growing presence is clearly felt in the retail business but has also been seen in real estate, mining, and infrastructure. The role of the new migrants in the economic relations represents one of the significant, yet unrecognized, factors in globalization. In fact, as testament to their growing influence in the Philippine economy, during Ms. Arroyo's time, the new migrants established their own business associations: Migrant Chamber of Commerce and Industry by the retailers in 2007 and the Philippine Chinese Chamber of Commerce and Industry by the larger enterprises in the same year. At that time, the government as well as the biggest and most active chamber of commerce, the Federation of Filipino Chinese Chambers of Commerce and Industry established by the old migrants in 1954, encouraged the new migrants to form their own organization.

The new migrants' main purpose was to find opportunities and make money. Many of them initially establish themselves in the most low-profile manner in small-scale positions such as traders, retail merchants, and small-scale miners. Those entrepreneurs ventured into far-flung provinces that traditional Filipino businessmen had shied away from thus providing them with less competition compared with the metropolis. Due to their aggressiveness, entrepreneurship, and connections to suppliers in China, they have been able to disrupt the traditional business models and have experienced unprecedented growth in their investments.[23] That has been a big boost for the Filipino retailers and consumers in the provinces because they no longer need to travel to Manila for goods. Some of those provincial new migrants have since thrived and diversified their businesses from retail and wholesale to property development and mall operation. Furthermore, global opportunities abound as business can be done with China as their source and market.

As bigger Chinese businesses, with greater resources or access to capital, look outside of China for opportunities, coupled with China's Go-Global program announced in the mid 2000s, the global presence of Chinese enterprises will continue. Chinese-owned telecommunications companies Huawei and Fiberhome, for example, have established business operations in the Philippines as part of their global expansion even when political bilateral relations began to deteriorate, albeit in a more low-key manner. The Bank of China in the Philippines has since expanded operations to better service the needs of the growing network of business of both Chinese and Filipinos.[24]

In a 2014 Investment Forum in Beijing coorganized by the Philippine embassy with the China Overseas Federation, it was noted that many Chinese enterprises had decided to locate their operations in the Philippines as they went global to be "closer to the market either to mitigate foreign trade friction, and/or to curb potential trade protectionism" (Philippine Embassy News 2014). It is evident that when political bilateral relations are bad, the private sector picks up the slack as the states lessen their economic cooperation. Moreover, in the countries where Chinese businesses venture, Chinese entrepreneurs follow to facilitate business transactions and often take up residency in the host countries where they end up purchasing a condominium residence, renting an office, hiring local personnel, and eventually immigrating—ultimately creating more dynamism in the host's domestic economy. That may partly explain why the real estate prices in Southeast Asia particularly, have continued to show strong growth (JLL 2013).

China and ASEAN Markets

Other groups representing the private sector are the Filipino (ethnic and Chinese Filipinos) private companies and entrepreneurs who do cross-border business. Unlike in China where the biggest industry players are usually state-owned enterprises, the Philippines is largely dominated, if not monopolized, by private businesses. The latter group, especially those who linked with China's burgeoning economy during the early years, has benefited substantially from China. The Filipino conglomerates have also benefitted through the availability of cheaper manufactured and industrial goods as those have contributed to the lower cost of doing business in the home market. For instance, players in real estate, construction, and infrastructure development have exploited the record-low prices of steel, cement, aluminum, flat glass, and shipbuilding supplied by China's excess production as they have since been able to successfully bid for government projects being able to significantly lower their costs or establish joint ventures with technical Chinese partners.[25] For the more aggressive Filipino companies, the business opportunities have also expanded not only in the Philippines but across ASEAN, particularly with the entry of the ASEAN Economic Community in 2015.

Foreign diversification of Philippine firms is largely privately led and has mostly taken place after 2010 (Rodriguez and Sandoval 2016). Filipino conglomerates decide to do business in China or the ASEAN, based on the opportunities to profit from a market or as part of its regional strategy. For example, one of the Philippines' largest conglomerates, Ayala Group of Companies, invested in electronics manufacturing and the real estate business in China. The conglomerate's latter business took advantage of the booming housing market in China's second tier cities but then divested its stake when the housing market matured and transferred its investment to ASEAN. The former business continues to manage the manufacturing sites and sales offices on the mainland to support its global supply chain. One of the most well-known snack food manufacturers in China is the Filipino-owned Oishi brand of the Liwayway Group of Companies. It has factories all over China that import managers and machineries from the Philippines. Oishi was one of the first Filipino companies to venture into China in the early 1990s when land and labor were very cheap. It went on to replicate the same model in Southeast Asian countries. Another example is the International Container Terminal Service, Inc. (ICTSI), the country's biggest container port operator controls a port in Shandong, China as part of its global network. The company then diversified into the hotel and gaming industry, opening a casino complex in the Philippines to cater to the Chinese high rollers. Those are just some examples of Filipino players finding their niche in that regional marketplace.

Only a handful of companies had invested early in China as part of their corporate strategy. Noteworthy examples include the San Miguel Corporation in beer (Guangzhou 1990), ETON in real estate properties (1993), Unilab in pharmaceuticals (Shanghai 1995), the SM Group in malls (Xiamen 2001), the Ayala Group of Companies in real estate (as mentioned above) (Tianjin 2010), and Metrobank in banking (Shanghai 2010), which are some of the oldest, largest, and most diversified Philippine conglomerates—and finally, the privately-held Liwayway Corporation, also mentioned above (Shanghai 1993).

More recently, Filipino companies have skipped China altogether and focused on the ASEAN market instead. The early ASEAN diversifiers include Universal Robina Corporation and Zesto Corporation in snack food and beverage manufacturing; Jollibee in the fast food chains; Unilab in pharmaceuticals; Petron in oil refining; Philweb in online gambling; Metro Pacific Manila Toll Roads in road construction, and Manila Water and Manila Electric Company in utilities. Some of the late entrants such as Zesto had initially attempted to penetrate the China market but withdrew when they found the barriers to entry insurmountable.[26] The general perception was that the China market was too competitive and cutthroat, the government regulations were too difficult to manage, and growth prospects were slowing due to a maturing market. In contrast, the ASEAN market provides a large market, geographic proximity, cultural similarities, and more favorable regulatory treatment as members of the bloc, and the favorable growth prospects of the region. Although the developments are still preliminary, the momentum of the ASEAN Economic Community only provides additional impetus for additional players to invest in ASEAN. Interestingly, most publicly listed companies with new plans to diversify abroad have explicitly acknowledged the desire to establish a foothold in the emerging ASEAN market (Rodriguez and Sandoval 2016). With a population of 100 million, the Philippines has a young and educated workforce and second largest population in ASEAN, after Indonesia. The Philippines is viewed as being strategically situated to benefit from the regional integration. Based on those examples, it is evident that the movement of Philippine investors from China to ASEAN is motivated more by economic market diversification than bilateral political considerations.

China's Global and Regional Charm Offensive

Contemporary developments signal China's desire to take a more pronounced role in global and regional affairs, demonstrated by OBOR and AIIB to contribute to global infrastructure investments. It has also taken the driver's seat in the RCEP, first proposed in the 2012 ASEAN Summit in Cambodia and initially considered as the region's response to the US-led Trans-Pacific Partnership (TPP), it has since been infused with renewed dynamism ever since the TPP lost steam when President Trump withdrew the USA from the partnership.

The OBOR is China's formal declaration of its intent to take on a more active global role. On the one hand, the critics warn that the OBOR carries geopolitical and security designs by China, on the other hand the program includes packages that align with the economic needs of the regional members, such as Asia's need to fill its infrastructure development gap of an estimated US$26 trillion until 2030 (Endo 2017). However, from China's perspective the OBOR is expected to develop China's less developed provinces, find markets for excess capacity such as steel, cement, aluminum, and capital surplus as well as technical capabilities. It also hopes to develop its industries by establishing standards in infrastructure and trade developments (Cai 2017). A more prosperous region and the establishment of industry standards will contribute to the development and stability of China's domestic economy.

During the height of the territorial dispute which coincided with Xi Jinping's first announcement of the OBOR in 2013, China seemed to have sidelined the Philippines with observers pointing out that the early maps of the OBOR route issued by China bypassed the Philippines.

Under President Aquino, the Philippines was the last-minute founding member of the AIIB. That took place after debates within the Aquino government regarding whether it was prudent to join the AIIB amid the political impasse of the SCS dispute and concerns regarding China's geo-political ambitions. The decision to join suggests that although the Philippines was involved in territorial disputes with China in the SCS, and even though the USA and Japan opted out, the Philippines had also recognized China's influence in the global economy.

A converging development was seen when under Duterte, the Philippines had recalibrated its foreign policy toward closer economic relations with China. One example of the renewed dynamism in the relationship was demonstrated when his Secretary of Finance strongly backed the Philippines' membership in the AIIB, which, he said, would provide the government "another source of long-term funding at very reasonable interest rates" (DOF 2016). In 2016, the AIIB agreed to co-finance two projects in transportation and flood-control projects in the metropolis with the Asian Development Bank and World Bank, respectively—perhaps signaling the changing norms in global developmental financing.

Conclusion

Because of colonial vestiges and dependency on the USA, early anti-communist sentiments, strong lobbying of Taiwan, and weak institutions, the Philippines was not able to prepare itself for the rise of China. The lack of institutions that study China have prevented the Philippines from crafting a coherent China Policy. Therefore, the domestic factors manifested in personality-based politics and rampant corruption, coupled with the negative public perception of China, have largely driven the roller coaster China Policy that cycles with every new president. One of the consequences is that the Philippines has not been able to fully capitalize on China's economic ascent, particularly vis-à-vis its ASEAN neighbors.

China's early charm offensive in the Philippines had several milestones including the latter being the recipient of the largest ODA in Southeast Asia during 2002–2007 and the first foreign destination of the China Grid Corporation's major outward investment. The story of the investment of the China Grid Corporation in the Philippines represents a successful case of Chinese investments and established Filipino institutions working together.

Although the territorial spat that culminated in the Philippines filing the arbitration case against China paralyzed the economic relations in terms of the flow of major Chinese investments, other aspects such as trade were tempered, if not driven, by global trends and market forces. Indeed, the bilateral trade data are better explained by global economic phenomena such as the impact of the global supply network, global financial crisis, and the rebalancing of China's economy. Additionally, investments continue within the private sector—supporting the truism that business is profit driven. Furthermore, the increasing shift of investments by Filipino businessmen to ASEAN from China, is due more to the growing attractive economic opportunities the regional market presents rather than political considerations. The role of the new migrants has also contributed to continuous trade and renewed economic activities in local industries such as retail. The health of bilateral political relations has a bigger impact on other forms of economic relations such as state loans and overseas development assistance.

The OBOR and the AIIB underlies China's newfound strategic initiatives to take on a larger role in global affairs. For the ASEAN region, its efforts to further integrate their market with the ASEAN Economic Community, and to a larger extent, with the Regional Economic Comprehensive Program, signal the growing dynamism taking place in the region. That is also affirmed by President Trump's "America First" Policy that seems to signal a retreat in US global leadership. The vacuum created by the junking of the TPP provides an opening for China to take the driver's seat as manifested in its renewed initiatives in the RCEP. As shown in the aforementioned cases, the biggest challenge for the Philippines is largely dependent on the weaknesses on the domestic front: to get its own house in order. For China to be more successful in its determination to cement its influence in the world, a more nuanced management of bilateral relations, beginning with understanding the domestic politics of the partner country, becomes more vital.

For the Philippines, its role in regional and bilateral development will depend on how institutions are strengthened and transcend the endemic problems of personality-based foreign policy, patronage politics, and rampant corruption. Deep-seated perceptions will not disappear easily. Given the friendlier relations under Duterte, the question moving forward is whether that amiable relationship can be sustained or institutionalized beyond the personal leadership of the sitting president. Given that domestic factors drive bilateral relations, the questions that need to be answered to address the people's concerns about sovereignty and security issues will depend on what happens to the friendly relations when Duterte's term ends in 2022, and how Duterte handles the SCS dispute. The next president may decide to bring the SCS issue and the international arbitration decision to the center of discussions. It is not inconceivable to consider that because of the continuation of personalistic politics and weak institutions, the roller coaster ride may continue.

Notes

1. Up until 1975, the Chinese schools followed a bi-curricula system: the English curriculum of the Philippine education system, and the Chinese curriculum similar to those used in Taiwan.
2. Upon the normalization of diplomatic relations with China in 1975, then First Lady Imelda Marcos secured concessional prices from China on much-needed oil exports to the Philippines. The oil crisis and the end of the trade agreement with the USA at that time prompted Marcos to explore markets in the socialist countries. In exchange, the Philippines exported coconut oil, lumber, sugar, copper ore, and other metals to China.
3. When Marcos was replaced by Cory Aquino, Taiwan offered many benefits to the new government. In addition to economic exchanges, which were allowed under the memorandum with Taiwan for economic and cultural exchanges, the Taiwanese government also invited top government officials to visit Taiwan in an official capacity and publicized the visits which violated the One-China Policy. Diplomatic protests from Beijing prompted the Philippine Congress to raise the issue and to reinterpret the One-China Policy to allow more engagement with Taiwan.
4. Trade between the two countries was traditionally restricted by the "Balance of Trade" Policy adopted by the Philippines to prevent a high deficit in its trade with China.
5. Chinese loans and ODA to the Philippines are considered together because Chinese loans to the Philippines thus far have been concessional in nature. Concessional funding from China, often financed through the Export and Import Bank of China, include RMB Yuan and US Dollar denominations at a 2–3% annual interest rate with 20-year maturity and inclusive of a 5-year grace period.
6. Interview with National Economic Development Authority Officer, 2016. That is supported in studies such as John Cooper's "China's Foreign Aid and Investment Diplomacy" (p. 30) and by Benito Lim, professor of Chinese Studies at the Ateneo de Manila University, when he said: "China lends money without imposing condition on opening markets or trade liberalization, which makes it an attractive alternative to loans from the WB, ADB and most Western lenders".
7. It was unable to address Beijing's travel advisory of Chinese tourists to the Philippines issued on two occasions and an importation ban placed on Philippine bananas. In response, the Philippine immigration made it difficult or refused to renew the working visas of volunteer Mandarin teachers and Chinese technical experts who were assisting Filipino organizations. Investments and tourism numbers fluctuated due to the deterioration of good will and confidence on both sides. In comparison, Japan and Taiwan

continue to receive several millions of Chinese investments and tourists annually, and vice versa, despite their ongoing political challenges with China.

8. In 2005, in celebration of the 35th anniversary of the establishment of bilateral relations, the presidents of the Philippines and China toasted to the "Golden Year of Partnership" to usher in the friendly relationship that was unfolding.
9. The two sides had pledged to double trade volumes to US$60 billion in five years, a sixfold rise from 2010. Additionally, Aquino returned triumphantly announcing nearly $13 billion worth of actual and planned Chinese investments in the Philippines.
10. The unfortunate incidents were wholly unrelated to the SCS dispute, but more domestic security lapses that unfortunately involved the lives of people, in this case of Chinese citizens.
11. As of this writing, the Duterte government is still in its early years, therefore, it is difficult to make any conclusive analysis. However, the study includes Duterte because it provides examples on how the Philippine President can single-handedly alter the Philippines' China Policy.
12. One of China's early overtures to the new administration was the donation of funds for the construction of rehabilitation centers to address the growing number of drug users arrested. Additionally, China also signified its intention to contribute to the new government's goal of fast-tracking infrastructure investments in the whole country. Duterte's China pivot is part of a broader shift as he has also reached out to Japan, ASEAN, and Russia to help the Philippines diversify its foreign partners. Because the Philippine economy is dependent on dollar earnings from the overseas Filipino workers in the USA and the outsourcing operations of American companies, the victory of Donald Trump, forecasted to lead to more US protectionist policies, and how it will affect the Philippine economy became a concern.
13. US$15 billion worth of investment included railways, ports, infrastructure, flood control, transportation, mining energy, telecommunications, real estate and agricultural projects; and US$9 billion in the form of soft loans including a $3 billion credit line with the Bank of China.
14. Interview. Knowledgeable sources who requested to remain anonymous.
15. Interview with Mr. Franics Chua, Honorary Chairman of the Philippines Chamber of Commerce and Industry, 2015.
16. President Aquino's Third State of the Nation Address. July 23, 2012.
17. *GMA News*, October 2, 2007. http://www.gmanetwork.com/news/news/nation/62860/arroyo-stops-deal-with-zte-china-prexy-accepts-decision/stor.
18. Interview. Knowledgeable source who requested to remain anonymous.
19. The company is reported to control 80% of the China's power transmission assets. It generates more revenue than Apple Inc. and Boeing Co.

combined (James Paton, "China Builds an Empire of Electricity with Australia as Target," *Bloomberg* [2016]. http://www.bloomberg.com/news/articles/2016-03-31/chinese-power-behemoth-with-global-ambitions-targets-australia).
20. The 40-60 rule is a provision in the Philippine Constitution for foreign ownership of selected industries, including the power industry.
21. Republic Act No. 9511 states "An Act Granting the National Grid Corporation of the Philippines a Franchise to Engage in the Business of Conveying or Transmitting Electricity through High Voltage Backbone System of Interconnected Transmission Lines, Substations and Related Facilities, and for Other Purposes."
22. Data show the number of Chinese locators in the Philippines' special economic zones increased, even during the political tensions under the term of President Aquino (2010–2016). (Ellen Palanca, "PH-CH Economic Relations," Presentation in the APPFI Forum held at the University of the Philippines, 2016).
23. Interviews, small- and medium-sized entrepreneurs, several dates from 2014 to 2016.
24. Interview with Mr. Deng Jun, Country Manager of Bank of China-Manila, 2016.
25. Interview with Mr. Deng Jun, Country Manager of Bank of China-Manila, 2016.
26. Interview with Mr. Alfredo Yao, President of Zest-O Corporation, 2015.

Bibliography

ABS-CBN News. "PNoy: JMSU with China, Vietnam 'Shouldn't Have Happened'." 2011. *Abs-Cbn News*. Accessed June 30, 2017. http://news.abs-cbn.com/nation/01/04/11/pnoy-jmsu-china-vietnam-shouldnt-have-happened.

Ang See, Teresita. 2016. "Migration Trends and Their Socio-Economic Implications: The Ethnic Chinese Community." Presentation in the Asia Pacific Pathways for Progress Foundation Forum Titled "In Search of a China Strategy: Unpacking the Bilateral and Regional Dynamics of Philippine-China Relations." August 15, 2016.

Asia Sentinel. 2012. "The China-Philippine Banana War." *Asia Sentinel*, June 06, 2012. http://www.asiasentinel.com/society/the-china-philippine-banana-war/.

Associated Press. 2015. "Metro Manila Traffic Costing PH P3 Billion a Day." *Philstar*, September 16, 2015. Accessed on August 10, 2016. http://www.philstar.com/headlines/2015/09/16/1500512/metro-manila-traffic-costing-philippines-p3-billion-day.

Baviera, Aileen. 2012. "The Influence of Domestic Politics on Philippine Foreign Policy: The Case of Philippines-China Relations since 2004." RSIS Working Paper No. 241.

Bueno de Mesquita, Bruce. 2017. "Foreign Policy Analysis and Rational Choice Models." Accessed July 30, 2017. https://pdfs.semanticscholar.org/54af/a0ca13faca35a5623288deb3f94f08d3a2e8.pdf.

Bueno de Mesquita, Bruce, and Alastair Smith. 2012. "Domestic Explanations of International Relations." *Annual Review of Political Science* 15: 161–181.

Burgonio, T.J. 2012. "China Duns PH for $500 M for NorthRail Loan." *Inquirer*, September 26, 2012. http://globalnation.inquirer.net/51282/china-duns-ph-for-500-m-for-northrail-loan.

Business World. "China Port Operations Consolidated." *Business World*, May 21, 2014. www.bworldonline.com/content.php?section=Corporate&title=china-port-operations-consolidated&id=87725.

Cai, Peter. 2017. *Understanding China's Belt and Road Initiative*. Lowy Institute For International Policy 2017. https://www.lowyinstitute.org/sites/default/files/documents/Understanding%20China%E2%80%99s%20Belt%20and%20Road%20Initiative_WEB_1.pdf.

Chen, Jie. 2002. *Foreign Policy of the New Taiwan: Pragmatic Diplomacy in Southeast Asia*. Cheltnham: Edward Elgar Publishing Limited.

China Business Philippines. "Chinese Investments in the Philippines." *China Business Philippines*. Accessed January 10, 2016. http://www.china-businessphilippines.com/index.php?option=com_content&view=article&id=111:chinese-investments-in-the-philippines-&catid=39:investment-update&Itemid=63.

China Embassy. 2004. "Is the Early Harvest Good for RP?" Accessed July 5, 2017. http://ph.china-embassy.org/eng/sgdt/t171568.htm.

Cooper, John. 2016. *China's Foreign Aid and Investment Diplomacy*. New York: Palgrave Macmillan.

Davis, Alex. 2015. "Biggest Nickel Producer Can't Mine Enough to Satisfy China." *Bloomberg*, April 30, 2015. http://www.bloomberg.com/news/articles/2015-04-30/world-s-top-nickel-producer-can-t-mine-enough-to-satisfy-china.

DOF. 2016. "AIIB Eager to Finalize PHL Projects for Bank Financing." December 19, 2016. Accessed February 2017. http://www.dof.gov.ph/index.php/aiib-eager-to-finalize-phl-projects-for-bank-financing/.

Dumlao-Abadilla, Doris. 2015. "Top Filipino Firms Build ASEAN Empires." *Philippine Inquirer*, December 23, 2015. http://business.inquirer.net/204522/top-filipino-firms-building-asean-empires.

Endo, Jun. 2017. "Asia Needs $26tn for Infrastructure Through 2030: ADB Report." *Nikkei Asian Review*, February 28, 2017. https://asia.nikkei.com/Politics-Economy/Economy/Asia-needs-26tn-for-infrastructure-through-2030-ADB-report.

Greiten, Sheena Chestnut. 2016. "The US-Philippine Alliance in Year of Transition: Challenges & Opportunities." Brookings Working Paper.

Gungwu, Wang. 2005. "China and Southeast Asia: Changes in Strategic Perceptions." In *China and Southeast Asia: Global Changes and Regional Challenges*, edited by Ho Khai Leong Ku and Samuel C.Y. Ku. Singapore: Institute of Southeast Asian Studies.

Guthrie, Doug. 2006. *China and Globalization: The Social, Economic and Political Transformation of Chinese Society*. New York: Routledge.

Haacke, Jürgen. 2005. "The Significance of Beijings Bilateral Relations: Looking Below the Regional Level in China-ASEAN Ties." In *China and Southeast Asia: Global Changes and Regional Challenges*, edited by Ho Khai Leong Ku and Samuel C.Y. Ku. Singapore: Institute of Southeast Asian Studies.

Holstag, Jonathan. 2015. *China's Coming War with Asia*. Cambridge: Polity Press.

Hunt, Katie. 2016. "China Allows Philippines Fishermen Access to Disputed Shoal in South China Sea." *CNN*, October 31, 2016. Accessed October 30, 2017. http://edition.cnn.com/2016/10/31/asia/philippines-china-scarborough-shoal-fishermen/index.html.

Inquirer. "Exploring the Middle Kingdom." 2016. *Inquirer*, October 16, 2016. http://business.inquirer.net/216779/exploring-the-middle-kingdom.

JLL. 2013. "Strong Growth in SEA Real Estate Markets to Support ASEAN Economic Integration by 2015." *JLL*, June 4, 2013. http://www.jll.com/news/154/strong-growth-in-southeast-asian-real-estate-markets-to-support-asean-economic-integration-by-2015.

Kurlantzick, Joshua. 2007. *Charm Offensive: How China's Soft Power is Transforming the World*. New York: Yale University Press.

Landingin, Roel. 2008. "Manila Halts Fresh ODA Loans from China." *Ft.com*, February 19, 2008. http://www.ft.com/cms/s/0/1d1aa3ea--defa--11dc--91d4--0000779fd2ac.html.

Landingin, Roel. 2009. "Secrecy, Rush Mark Tender of Biggest MWSS Dam Project." Philippine Center for Investigative Journalism. Accessed September 1, 2016. http://pcij.org/stories/secrecy-rush-mark-tender-of-biggest-mwss-dam-project/.

Landingin, R. 2010. "Chinese Foreign Aid goes Off-track in the Philippines." *South-South Development Cooperation: A Challenge to the Aid System*, edited by The Reality of Aid Management Committee, 87–94. Quezon City: Ibon Books.

Landingin, Roel. 2012. "Angat Aqueduct: Rare Success in China-Funded Infra Projects in PH." *Rappler*, July 16, 2012. http://www.rappler.com/business/8639-angat-aqueduct-rare-success-in-china-funded-infra-projects-in-ph.

Landingin, Roel. 2016. "Chinese Foreign Aid Goes Off-track in the Philippines." Philippine Center for Investigative Journalism, 2010: 87–91. Accessed September 1, 2016. http://www.realityofaid.org/wp-content/uploads/2013/02/ROA-SSDC-Special-Report8.pdf.

Landingin, Roel, and Richard McGregor. 2007. "China State Grid Group Wins Philippine Auction." *Ft.com*, December 12, 2007. https://www.ft.com/content/f385a5d6-a88d-11dc-ad9e-0000779fd2ac.

Lim, Benito. 1999. "The Political Economy of the Philippines-China Relations." Philippine APEC Study Center Network. Discussion Paper No. 99-16, page 291.

Lim, Joseph. 2016. *Impact of China's New Normal on the Philippines*. Unpublished.

Lim, Narzalina. 2016. "Tourism Prospects & Challenges." Presentation in the Asia Pacific Pathways for Progress Foundation Forum titled "In Search of a China Strategy: Unpacking the Bilateral and Regional Dynamics of Philippine-China Relations." August 15, 2016.

Malig, Jojo. 2011. "Arroyo Corruption Scandal Weakened China Influence—WikiLeaks Cables." *ABS-CBN News*, August 29, 2011. http://news.abs-cbn.com/-depth/08/29/11/arroyo-corruption-scandal-weakened-china-influence-leaked-us-cables-say.

Mangahas, Mahar. 2016. "Trust in the US versus China." *Philippine Inquirer*, October 22, 2016. http://opinion.inquirer.net/98411/trust-in-the-us-versus-china.

Mangahas, Mahar. 2017. "Filipinos Don't Pivot." *Philippine Inquirer*, May 27, 2017. http://opinion.inquirer.net/104326/filipinos-dont-pivot.

Palaña, Aberon. 2017. "Lawmakers Wants NGCP Back in Filipino Hands." *Manila Times*, March 8, 2017. http://www.manilatimes.net/lawmaker-wants-ngcp-back-filipino-hands/316081/.

Palanca, Ellen. 1999. "China's Changing Trade Patterns: Implications for ASEAN-China Trade." In *China's Economic Growth and the ASEAN*, edited by Ellen H. Palanca. Philippine APEC Study Center Network and Philippine Institute for Development Studies (15): 1–51. https://pascn.pids.gov.ph/files/Discussions%20Papers/1999/pascndp9920.pdf.

Palanca, Ellen. 2015. "China's Trade with East Asia." In *The Rise of China: Three Essays on China's Economy and "Soft" Power*, edited by Joseph Y. Lim. Philippines: Philippine Association for Chinese Studies.

Palanca, Ellen. 2016. "Ph-Ch Economic Relations." Presentation in the APPFI Forum Held at the University of the Philippines, August 15, 2016.

Pattugalan, Gina Rivas. 1999. "A Review of Philippine Foreign Policy Under the Ramos Administration." *Kasarinlan: Philippine Journal of Third World Studies* 14, no. 3: 108–134.

PBGEA. 2015. "Banana Trade with China". APPFI Roundtable Discussion on PH-CH Trade and Investment Relations, June 11, 2015.

Philippine Embassy. 2014. "Ph Investment Forum Co-organised with China Overseas Investment Federation." *Philippine Embassy News*. Accessed March 5, 2016. http://investphilippines.gov.ph/philippine-investment-forum-co-organised-with-china-overseas-investment-federation/.

President Aquino's Third State of the Nation Address. 2012. Accessed July 25, 2016. http://www.gov.ph/2012/07/23/benigno-s-aquino-iii-third-state-of-the-nation-address-july-23-2012[21]/.

Rodriguez, Rafael, and Sandoval, Benjamin. 2016. "Foreign Diversification of Philippine Firms." *Philippine Management Review 2016*, 23: 17–26.

Romero, Alexis. 2016. "Philippines, China Sign $24-B Deals." *Philstar*, October 22, 2016. http://www.philstar.com/headlines/2016/10/22/1636102/philippines-china-sign-24-b-deals.

Rueda, Nimfa. 2012. "Filipinos 2nd Largest Asian Group in US, Census Shows." *Inquirer*, 2012. http://globalnation.inquirer.net/30477/filipinos-2nd-largest-asian-group-in-us-census-shows.

Satake, Minoru. 2015. "Philippine Conglomerate Ready to Take ASEAN." *Nikkei Asian Review*, June 1, 2015. http://asia.nikkei.com/Business/AC/Philippine-conglomerate-ready-to-take-on-ASEAN.

Saw, See. 2007. "Asean-China Economic Relations: A Review." In *ASEAN-China Economic Relations*, edited by Saw Swee-Hock, 1–12. Singapore: Institute of Southeast Asian Studies.

Sayson, Ian. 2014. "Nickel Shortage Propels Philippines Mining Boom: Southeast Asia." *Bloomberg*, December 22, 2014. http://www.bloomberg.com/news/articles/2014-12-21/nickel-shortage-propels-philippines-mining-boom-southeast-asia.

Sheng, Lijun. 2007. "China's Economic Relations with ASEAN: Developments and Strategic Implications." In *ASEAN-China Economic Relations*, edited by Saw Swee-Hock, 295–317. Singapore: Institute of Southeast Asian Studies.

Simeon, Louise Maureen. 2016. "Global Ferronickel Targets More Exports to China." March 29, 2016. *Philippine Star*, March 29, 2016. http://www.philstar.com/business/2016/03/29/1566995/global-ferronickel-targets-more-exports-china.

Suryadinata, Leo. 2005. *China and the ASEAN States: The Ethnic Chinese Dimension*. Singapore: Marshall Cavendish Academic.

Tabeta, Shunsuke. 2017. "China Power Giant Gobbling up Foreign Players." *Nikkei Asian Review*, January 25, 2017. http://asia.nikkei.com/Business/Companies/China-power-giant-gobbling-up-foreign-players.

Tiglao, Rigoberto. 2012. "Aquino Axed Key Flood-Control Project in 2010." *Philippine Daily Inquirer*, August 15, 2012. http://opinion.inquirer.net/34831/aquino-axed-key-flood-control-project-in-2010.

Trinidad, Dennis. 2016. "Institutional Mismatch and Chinese Aid in the Philippines: Challenges and Implications." *Asian Perspective* 40, no. 2, April–June: 299–328.

Tuazon, Bobby. 2014. "The Highs and Lows of PH-CH Relations: Current Situation and Prospects." Lecture Paper for GASS/ISEAS. Accessed July 30, 2017. http://www.cenpeg.org/pol-study/int/PAPER%20FOR%20GASS%20ISEAS%20lecture%20of%20April%2018%202014.pdf.

Tubeza, Philip. 2011. "Aquino Back Home with $13-B Deals." *Inquirer*, September 03, 2011. Accessed July 3, 2016. http://globalnation.inquirer.net/11553/aquino-back-home-with-13-b-deals.

Wang, Vincent Wei-cheng. 2005. "The Logic of China-ASEAN FTA: Economic Statecraft of Peaceful Ascendancy." In *China and Southeast Asia: Global Changes and Regional Challenges*, edited by Ho Khai Leong Ku and Samuel C.Y. Ku. Singapore: Institute of Southeast Asian Studies.

Wurfel, D. 1990. "Philippine Foreign Policy." In *The Political Economy of Foreign Policy in Southeast Asia*, edited by David Wurfel and Bruce Burton. London: Palgrave MacMillan.

Xinhua. 2017. "Gov't Figure Shows More Ch Tourists Visit PH in First Half of this Year." *Xinhua*. Accessed September 1, 2017. http://news.xinhuanet.com/english/2017-08/19/c_136539108.htm.

"ZTE Controversy Timeline." *GMA*, September 18, 2007. Accessed April 6, 2011. http://www.gmanews.tv/story/61035/ZTE-controversy-timeline.

CHAPTER 6

Cambodia and the ASEAN Economic Community: Golden Opportunity for Ethnic Chinese in Cambodia

Touch Siphat

Introduction

The Cambodian government, as a member of the Association of Southeast Asian Nations (ASEAN) Economic Community (AEC), has committed to strengthen the economy by implementing certain changes and reforms. Those include adding trade regulations, complying with ASEAN's uniform codes for investment and tax, improving infrastructure and other facilities to attract more investment, and preparing businesses and laborers to become more competitive within the new environment by promoting national Small and Medium Enterprises (SME) for the ASEAN market. In addition to those changes, Cambodia is also seeking foreign investment and support on infrastructure and energy development from bilateral and multilateral partners.

T. Siphat (✉)
Cambodian Researcher for the Project of Chinese Capitalism in Southeast Asia coordinated by Chiang Mai University and funded by Thailand Research Fund, Phnom Penh, Cambodia

Y. Santasombat (ed.), *The Sociology of Chinese Capitalism in Southeast Asia*, https://doi.org/10.1007/978-981-13-0065-3_6

China is recognized by Cambodian leaders as 'the most trustworthy friend to Cambodia' and is a key and prominent supporter of development, investment, and trade. Those commitments will improve Cambodia's economy because the ethnic Chinese, who are a prominent influence in Cambodia, will grow by leveraging the ASEAN plus China incentives. This chapter reviews the framework designed by the Cambodian government for the AEC and how the ethnic Chinese in Cambodia prepare themselves to benefit from the AEC as they become key players. I discuss how Chinese capitalism is rooted and widely promoted among the overseas Chinese community and contend that this is behind the cultural, economic, and political rise of the Chinese on a global scale.

Cambodia's Economic Policy Response to the AEC

In response to the AEC framework, the Cambodian government has demonstrated strong commitment and has put effort into strengthening economic systems. Many high-level policy and strategy commitments demonstrate Cambodia's willingness and preparedness for the AEC. For example, one section of Rectangular Strategy-Phase III (2014–2018) of the Cambodian government titled "Deepening Cambodia's Integration into the Region and the World" states:

"The process of Cambodia's integration into regional and global communities will deepen especially through participation in the ASEAN Economic Community to be established in 2015, while making utmost efforts to effectively harness opportunities and the conductive environment stemming from regional integration to achieve maximum benefits for Cambodia, particularly through linking the Cambodian economy to regional production networks and global value chains."

The firm implementation of the Rectangular Strategy-Phase II (2008–2013) created a favorable environment and necessary conditions for Cambodia to move resolutely and confidently forward on a journey of reform and development, aimed at graduating from a low-income country to a lower-middle income status and further to become an upper-middle income country by 2030. The upper-middle income vision and the Rectangular Strategy-Phase III (2014–2018) have pointed to the structural transformation of the Cambodian economy in reaching the vision and considered the industrial sector as a key driver of its economic growth. To that end, the government prepared an Industrial Development Policy 2015–2025, approved by Council of Ministers at its plenary meeting on March 6, 2015. The policy is a guide for driving the development of the industrial sector in the country, which can contribute toward maintaining a sustainable and inclusive high economic growth. The industrial policy has been recognized as a New Economic Growth Strategy which stresses economic diversification, competitiveness strengthening, and productivity enhancement in line with the structural transformation of the domestic economy and the evolving global and regional economic architecture that has put focus on the utilization of national resources to its fullest potential.

The policy framework contains four strategic pillars. First, attracting foreign direct investment (FDI) and mobilizing domestic private investment for industrial development, export market development and expansion, and promotion of technology development and transfer. Second, developing and modernizing SMEs by way of expanding and strengthening the manufacturing base, modernizing and officially registering enterprises, promoting technology development and transfer, and strengthening industrial links between domestic and foreign enterprises specifically in the agro-industrial sector. Third, improving the legal environment to enhance competitiveness by way of improving the investment climate and promoting trade facilitation, providing market information, and reducing business transactional fees. Fourth, coordinating supporting policies such as human resource development, skills training and industrial relations improvement, implementation of land management, urbanization and land use plan in line with the Land Policy and the National Policy on Land Management together with infrastructure development, including transport/logistics system and digital connectivity, electricity, and clean water supply and other supporting public, social, and financial services.

Ethnic Chinese and Their Social and Economic Organization

The ethnic Chinese make up 1% of the total Cambodian population (National Institute of Statistics, Ministry of Planning 2008, 2014). Although many Chinese came to Cambodia between the seventeenth and early twentieth century and more recently in the 2000s, their presence in the country can be traced back to even before the Angkor Era (802–1431 AD). Currently, five different ethno-linguistic groups of ethnic Chinese reside in Cambodia (Edwards 2009). They are the Teochew (who are the majority), the Cantonese, the Hokkien, the Hakka, and the Hainanese. In Cambodia, the ethnic Chinese are referred to as "Chinese-the Cambodian", "Khmer-Chinese", "Raw Chinese (Original

Chinese)", "Chinese descendants" and/or "mixed Khmer-Chinese". They are generally well integrated with Khmers, many feel Khmer, speak the Khmer language, follow Khmer customs and many hold Cambodian citizenship. For example, they utilize Buddhist monks for their weddings and funeral ceremonies. However, ethnic Chinese groups have also kept strong links with their Chinese traditions. Some ethnic Chinese continue to use their dialect language, display ancestor culture in their houses, adorn spring festival couplets on their doors, and adhere to religious events according to the Chinese calendar. Many also practice Chinese culture in everyday life, they continue to use typical Chinese nomenclature: Ahear, Cher, Kou, Khim, Ning, Sau etcetera "Ahear (older brother)" or "Trea (uncle)", "Ache (older sister)" or "EE (aunt)", and eat Chinese food.

Ethnic Chinese social organizations have also played a key role in the maintenance of both Chinese culture and community and business networks in Cambodia. Established upon their arrival in the seventeenth century, those associations have survived all Cambodian political regimes, except for the 1970s and 1980s. Associations have also played a significant role in bridging business networks among ethnic Chinese businessmen/women in the Kingdom, as well as in ASEAN and the world. That is because those who set up and actively support associations are the wealthy business elite who are well connected with high-ranking government officers and other businessmen/women in the region. For example, the Lim Association is led by a business tycoon, Okhna Lim organized the 10th anniversary of the Lim Association of Cambodia and the 13th regional Lim Association Convention at the Diamond Island Convention Center, Phnom Penh in November 2010. The event was organized with Prime Minister Hun Sen's wife Bun Rany Hun Sen as an honored guest and 2200 distinguished guests of which there were approximately 850 delegates from 52 Lim member associations from 12 countries (Becker 2010). Similarly, the Huang Association of Cambodia with the Huang Association of the World gathered more than 1600 members from around the world at Diamond Island in Phnom Penh in 2012 (Becker 2012).

Within the association system, Chinese temples and schools have been established as centers for literature, tradition, customs, and history. Chinese education, media, and cultural practice are keys factors in keeping the ethnic Chinese united and strong in economics. Between 1901 and 1938 there were 95 Chinese schools established in Cambodia including two middle schools and 93 primary schools (Edwards 2009). The teachers were often recruited from China and brought new texts and ideas. In 1938, over 4000 students were enrolled at Chinese schools across the country (Edwards 2009). By 1938, the first Chinese newspaper 'Bo Yin Tai' (broadcaster) was opened, but collapsed in 1946. However, during that time, three other Chinese newspapers were in print including *Great China News*, *Chinese Commercial News*, and *China-Cambodia News*. Following Cambodia's independence in 1953, the number of Chinese schools notably increased around the country, and the Chinese press also expanded. By 1967, there were 170 Chinese schools and the number of Chinese students reached 25,665. In Phnom Penh alone, there were 27 Chinese schools with 11,350 Chinese students. In the 1960s, there were five Chinese newspapers in Cambodia (two were Teochew and three were Cantonese) including *Journal of Trade and Commerce*, *Mekong Daily*, *Khmer-Chinese Daily*, the express and afternoon news (Edwards 2009). All were uprooted in the 1970s and banned in the 1980s of Khmer Rouge and Vietnamese-based government. By the early 1990s, for reasons including the growing economic collaboration between China and Cambodia and the large investments being made by Chinese companies, the Khmer Chinese community was reopened and grew dramatically in the 2000s (Nyíri 2012).

Currently, there are five Chinese newspapers in Phnom Penh and Chinese-language schools have been mushrooming throughout Cambodia with Mandarin becoming the second most popular foreign language in the country after English. The huge growth in Chinese-language schools is due in large part to the Chinese government's support through donations to the Khmer-Chinese associations for Chinese native teachers, the production of textbooks (in Chinese) that incorporate Cambodian history and seminars for local Chinese teachers. Currently, there are reportedly 57 schools in Cambodia that teach the Chinese language, with a total of 40,000 students, many of whom are ethnic Chinese. One of these private schools, Daunhau, is allegedly the largest overseas Chinese schools in the world, with about 10,000 students (Nyíri 2012). That is probably because the Chinese language, particularly Mandarin, is an advantage in the job market. More and more Cambodian people are encouraging their children to study English and Chinese hoping it will help their children in finding a good job and starting a business.

"Chinese Capitalism" Rooted in the Cambodian Economic System

To make sense of ethnic Chinese business acumen and success in Southeast Asia, scholars have written extensively about a "Chinese way" of doing business and "Chinese capitalism". Redding (1990), for example, argued that Chinese businesses have their roots in a Confucian cultural tradition based on paternalism, personalism, and defensiveness, and that by means of family ties and guanxi networks—built on reciprocal social relationships and informal trust—Chinese entrepreneurs can expand their economic might and escape state disciplining. Characteristics such as personalism, informality, family business, patronage arrangements, and trust-based networking are features that may be rooted in Chinese cultural values but have evolved and adapted to the Southeast Asian context (Yeung 2004; Dahles 2010). In Cambodia, ethnic Chinese entrepreneurship is dually embedded in historically developed practices of Chinese business organization, on the one hand, and in the Cambodian socio-political and economic context, on the other. As such, the practices of ethnic Chinese business can only be understood as historically developing within the specific environment of Cambodia and are thus constantly in flux (Verver 2012).

The resilience and flexibility of ethnic Chinese people in various political regimes of Cambodia allowed them to dominate the country's economics. Thus, business activities have been recognized as a symbol of Chinese people or "Chineseness" in the country for many generations. 'Chinese Houses' [ផ្ទះចិន], 'Chinese Stores' [ហាងចិន], 'Chinese at Market' [ចិនផ្សារ], 'Borrow Chinese money' [ខ្ចីលុយចិន], 'Be careful of Chinese Save Your Head' [ប្រយ័ត្នចាញ់បោកចិនឬប្រយ័ត្នចិនកោ], for example, have been created by locals, particularly Khmer peasants who refer to Chinese people as sellers, business runners, or financers. Typically, Chinese migrants would start working as laborers for a family or doing business, and scrimp and save until they had enough to start their own cottage industry. From small beginnings—like making cakes or weaving fans and peddling them on foot—they would slowly build up enough to rent a market stall, then to open their own shop. In fact, many first-generation Chinese who were interviewed said they arrived in Cambodia with nothing. Kov, who sadly passed away in 2016, was 93 years old when interviewed and exemplifies that path. He escaped from Japanese troops and starvation in 1938. When he arrived in

Cambodia he started by living with and working for his uncle's family for about 6 months. He then traded agricultural products with the Khmer and Cham for a few years and married a Khmer-Chinese woman in 1947. Once he saved enough money, he bought a farm and grew cotton. The farm was a successful enterprise until the Khmer Rouge came into power in 1975. After the Khmer Rouge regime, his family opened a small grocery store in Speur Commune, Cham Kar Leur district, Kampong Cham province before finally retiring with his daughter's family.

Historically, thousands of Chinese migrated from southern parts of mainland China to Cambodia during what many call the "Dark Ages" in Cambodian history. From the fifteenth century, the cultural, political, and economic systems were weakened by powerful neighboring countries resulting in the "Dark Ages" of the seventeenth, eighteenth, and nineteenth centuries (Tully 2004). Most painful of all were the years between the 1780s and the coronation of Ang Duang in 1848, during which time the Khmer monarchy and national sovereignty almost vanished (Tully 2004). The Khmer were influenced by Theravada Buddhism. They relied on wet rice farming and natural resources and a sharing culture for living rather than making profit for a better life by looked-over commerce and manual labor. That was perhaps an opportunity for the new comers, the 'Chinese migrants' were able to develop their businesses and make a profit. As a result, Chinese-Cambodian have been able to control much of Cambodia's trade and commerce since then.

According to William E. Willmott (1967), Chinese people played a key role in Khmer economics. He stated that the Chinese, before the arrival of the French, were given the right to collect national revenue from farming activities, to monopolize businesses on gambling, drudge, alcohol, fishing, and logging. Under French administration, even though the Chinese communities were controlled, they could still work and run businesses. That included working as teachers, publishers, and owning hotels as well as others. The Chinese also had a great deal of autonomy-each Chinese dialect group had its own leader (chef de congregation), and those leaders were recognized by French authorities as having power over matters of immigration and emigration; movement between towns, schools, temples, and cultural societies; and actively engaged in commerce and trade. Ethnic Chinese elite unsurprisingly, therefore, dominated commerce in Cambodia from the time of independence in the early 1950s well into the era of the Khmer Republic in 1970.

Under the Khmer Rouge regime in the 1970s, most urban Chinese were perceived as capitalists, which resulted in upheaval. In the late 1970s the Chinese began trading activities months after liberation by traveling back and forth over the Cambodian–Thai border to buy foodstuffs, utensils, clothes, electronics, and bringing other consumer goods into the country (Chan 2005). By the early 1990s, under a commitment to transform the economic system from the planning stage to the market base, and a recognition of ethnic Chinese skills in doing business, the Chinese were encouraged to engage in the business sector. Mr. Chea Sim, the National Assembly Chairman at that time, told members of the preparatory committee of the new Chinese-the Cambodian umbrella organization-the Khmer-Chinese association that "most Khmers want to be government officials; they don't like business and are not good at it…You should unite and liaise with your relatives and friends overseas, attract foreign investment and become a bridge to developing the economy" (Nyíri 2012). That encouragement and opening for the ethnic Chinese was an opportunity for Chinese people to revitalize Chinese culture and economic practices which allowed them to become controllers of the current Cambodian economic system.

In the contemporary Cambodian context, Chinese-Cambodians have a considerable presence in the Cambodian economy and are estimated to own a vast share of it. Nearly all Chinese-Cambodians are involved in a business of one sort or another, ranging from small family-based shops to large companies. Their businesses always start off with small capital and are run by either the husband, wife, or father and son team or siblings-turned-partners or relatives working for relatives. Generally, many Chinese-Cambodian family businesses are still informal. They do not have clear plans, proper financial and account systems, and inherit their business from elders. An example of that is a Chinese mooncake bakery called LSH located in central Phnom Penh. The bakery owner's grandparents' family migrated from mainland China in the 1930s and opened a Chinese mooncake business. Their plan was to pass on the business to their first son. Business families often put a lot of effort into teaching their children how to be business people. They believe that in the Cambodian context, opening a business will earn them money and independence. Chinese families often give their children a store or a house and some financial capital as a marriage gift, which differs from rural Khmer families who often advise their children to study hard, and generally give their children a section of a rice field, or a pair of cattle and cows as gifts.

Chinese-Cambodian business capacity is reflected in the number of Chinese-Cambodian who are recipients of Oknhas. A list of Oknhas, recorded from 1994 to 2014, revealed there were about 704 Oknhas (business tycoons) in Cambodia and most of them were Chinese descendants and mixed Khmer-Chinese. Interestingly, all top ten predominant businessmen/women classified in the current Cambodian Chamber of Commerce (CCC), and who own a vast share of the nation's economy, are also descendants of Chinese migrants born in Cambodia (*Phnom Penh Post* 2011). Those Oknhas have close links to senior officials in various government institutions and are further bound together by marriages and business partnerships. They often support their family name association, dialect association, and actively share involvement in charitable activities such as the Cambodian Red Cross.

The AEC Integration and Opportunities for Chinese-Cambodians

This section discusses "local Chinese" and "international Chinese". Local Chinese are the ethnic Chinese of Cambodia who hold Cambodian citizenship. The international Chinese are ethnic Chinese from elsewhere in the world and the Chinese from mainland China heading to Cambodia for work and business. In terms of economics, the local Chinese have played a crucial role in the Cambodian economy and have acted as a bridge for the international Chinese to set up businesses in the country. Many shops, houses, and company buildings display Chinese altars and sign boards with Chinese characters. Most of those businesses are represented in Cambodian's 505,134 SMEs. The 2011 economic census of Cambodia does not reveal the identity of SME entrepreneurs, but from interviews and observation, most SME owners are ethnic Chinese or at least people who have Chinese ancestry.

The National Institute of Statistics (NIS) indicates that 72% of Cambodian enterprises have one to three employees and are family-run businesses (NIS 2008). In 2011, of 505,134 enterprises, only 3.5% were registered with the Ministry of Commerce. That means that most of the enterprises are run in a traditional way-relying on personal savings and informal sources for starting or expanding their businesses. The primary reason for SMEs to maintain their informal status is the perception that standard accounting practices are complicated and unnecessary.

Additionally, some SME prefer to keep informal financial records because it allows them to conceal their real profits and revenues from tax authorities.

To support the country's SME from AEC competition, the Cambodian government has established policies and strategies. Some key sectors that the government needs to reform and improve include trade facilitation; human capital; SME promotion framework and infrastructure development including transport/logistics system and digital connectivity; electricity and clean water supply; and attracting FDI and mobilizing domestic private investment for industrial development. Despite those incentives, it remains difficult for Cambodia to be independent of foreign aid. Cambodia seeks support in infrastructure development, energy, investment, and trading partners from bilateral and multilateral partners. China is one of Cambodia's key development players over the past decades (Vutha 2014).

Chinese-Cambodian Preparation for AEC Integration

Ethnic Chinese in Cambodia have been leaders in the nation's economics for many generations and are now keen to compete in the AEC market. In the private sector, which has been dominated by Chinese-Cambodians, there have been several associations formed to promote SME development, share information, and facilitate problem solving and include the Federation of Associations for Small and Medium Enterprises of Cambodia (FASMEC, established in 2010), the Cambodia Small and Medium Enterprises Association (established in 2006), the Phnom Penh Small and Medium Industry Association (established in 2004), CEO Master Club (business coaching, networking, and awarding platform in Cambodia established in 2004), and the Cambodian Women Entrepreneurs Association (established in 2011). Each of those associations has approximately 100 members and their goal is to have a role in providing information, training, and benefiting from international business societies connected to the members (Chan 2015).

FASMEC gathers various business associations and commercial enterprises throughout the country. It was organized by two businessmen (Oknha Te Taing Por and Oknha Hun lak) with support from the Ministry of Industry and Handicraft (MIH). Their members share the same vision and it is one of the most active SME associations. FASMEC commits to achieving the promotion of SMEs, acting as the main conduit for dialogue on SMEs issues with the government, seeks technical and financial support from the government and multilateral and bilateral aid agencies for SME improvement, providing relevant vocational training and capacity building for SMEs, partners with government institutions to improve productivity, standards, export procedures, assisting SMEs with business registering, licensing, and permits in the most efficient and cost effective ways (Chan 2015).

Cambodian businesses are joining forces to increase production and reduce the country's dependence on imports. The FASMEC, the MIH, and the CCC play a key role in encouraging SMEs to increase productivity. According to the federation, business in the country is booming with 530,000 enterprises across the country, and about 30,000 enterprises registered with the MIH. The president of the federation, Oknha Te, urged businesses to register by saying that "the government and the federation can provide support to businesses once they are registered" (Chan 2015). The federation is working actively to get Cambodian SMEs to register their businesses with the Ministry of Industry. In doing so, it is easier for the government, the federation, and other relevant organizations/partners to work together to set policies to assist them. Oknha Te stated, "Now they (SMEs) lack capital, so the federation has its microfinance institution (MFI) to support them financially…I will fly to China soon to promote local SMEs to Chinese counterparts, and will encourage them…to invest in Cambodia. The new government policies could make Cambodia more favorable to foreign (Chinese) investors. The government could encourage investment by waiving taxes on the import of raw materials for foreign investors operating here, as well as giving them three-year tax holidays." Oknha Te also mentioned that the federation could help address small businesses' lack of capital through its MFI, which had already loaned about US$2 million to its members and planned to inject about US$3 to US$5 million more in loans (Chan 2015).

Similarly, Nguon Meng Tech, Director General of the CCC told the *Khmer Times* that the CCC had invested in local SMEs, "Our role is to provide them with training and seminars, and to invite foreign investors to meet and discuss with local SMEs to find a way for collaboration in operating businesses in Cambodia." Mr. Tech said that "The big goal of CCC is to promote local and international investment. CCC tries to find the regional international investors to partner with local investment to boost the economic growth and to support to local SMEs."

From the local entrepreneurs' viewpoint, the regional integrated market of the AEC possibly provides some good opportunities; it could be a good prospect for local entrepreneurs to expand their businesses. Chy Sila, a General Director of CBM Corp and owner of Sabay Company, emphasized that he was happy to welcome the bigger single market, stating "My vision is to expand my businesses to the region as administration will be merged into one, it will be easy as I do not have to spend time understanding a lot of laws and regulations of different countries." Additionally, as it is a free flow of labor, he could outsource more qualified staff for his businesses. Keo Mom, Chief Executive director of Lyly Food Industry Co., Ltd., which is well known throughout Cambodia for producing snacks, said that she is ready for the AEC, and stated that "I am ready for 2015 because I have been preparing for the last few years. For my own company, I am preparing to defend against, as well as to compete with, other ASEAN member countries' products." Mom said that her company, which established in 2002 with US$100,000 in capital, now produces over 20 types of products and employs over 100 workers, an increase from the original three products and 25 workers.

The large enterprises, representing 1% of all enterprises in Cambodia, are particularly influential in the Cambodian import–export, banking, hotel, media, telecommunications, construction, and land concessions sectors (Ministry of Planning 2014). That trend emerged in the late 1980s and early 1990s. That group of entrepreneurs is well—connected with senior officials in various government institutions and is further bound by marriages and business partnerships. They developed their families into standard corporate businesses with a corporate business culture. That group is not only ready for regional and global competition, but they also play a key role in attracting foreign investors to invest in Cambodia. Those include investors such as the Royal Group Companies that is owned by the Sino-Khmer businessman, Oknha Kith Meng; the largest agro-industrial company in Cambodia owned by Sino-Khmer businessman, Oknha Mong Reththy; Attwood Import Export Co., Ltd., owned by Oknha Lim Chhiv Ho; Canadia bank and real estate developer, Overseas Cambodia Investment Corporation (OCIC), owned by Oknha Pung Kheav Se; as well as others.

The SMEs comprise approximately 2.2% of the total enterprises in Cambodia (Ministry of Planning 2014). They mostly emerged in the early 2000s and committed to transform their businesses from family businesses to businesses with a more standard corporate business culture by raising their quality and sustainability to benefit from the coming of ASEAN integration and globalization. That group generally has a business plan and strategies and looks for business partners and legal support from the government, financial capital from financial institutions, and registers their enterprises with the Ministry of Commerce. The group of medium entrepreneurs are busy preparing themselves for the AEC and are generally confident about market competition. However, some of them are still concerned about investment capital and capacity for regional competition. For example, the Lyly Food Industry Co., Ltd. owned by Keo Mom, is ready for the AEC. She is also as the vice president of PSMIA and the vice secretary-general of the Chamber of Professional and Micro Enterprises of Cambodia, and stated that most of the Cambodian SMEs, including hers, worry because they are family businesses and do not have enough financial capital to develop and buy modern materials.

Similarly, Ngov Heng Fish Sauce Factory, located in Kampot's Ta Ang Village and is owned by the Hainanese family, is well known throughout the country for producing fish, soy, and chili sauces and is one of the SMEs busy developing and enlarging its business for the AEC market. The owner of Ngov Heng Fish Sauce, said he has been making efforts to upgrade his products for almost ten years and his fish sauce will soon not only be well known in Cambodia, but also in the USA and throughout Southeast Asia. Ngov Heng Fish Sauce Factory began producing fish sauce in 1995, but at that time he could only produce about 1000 liters per month and only supplied it to Kampot province. He currently produces about 100,000 liters per month and ships to all provinces in Cambodia. For the AEC, he plans to buy a steaming machine to clean bottles and plans to build a new high-standard production chain that will cost about US$100,000. However, he said that as an entrepreneur, he will expand his products into the ASEAN market, but he is still concerned about his finances.

The micro enterprises make up about 97.7% of all enterprises in Cambodia. They are generally run by businessmen/women who are mainly retail sellers and shop keepers. They often convert their homes into streetside stores, sell goods in small market stalls, or are small handicraft family businesses. Those business practitioners generally began a business with very little money, were supported by their parents or relatives, operated as family businesses without proper governance, entrepreneurship, leadership, business plan, management operating systems, finance and accounting, and business skills, etc.

Many micro entrepreneurs recognize that ASEAN is made up of ten countries but do not know about the benefits of ASEAN. Many of them do not know what the AEC is. For example, the owner of the Mooncake Bakery said that the busiest time of year for her business is during the Chinese moon festival and during the New Year season. She does not want any more business because she is tired of managing the cake handicraft. She added that she will let her oldest son decide what to do with the business because he will be the one to continue with the business. Her son wants to expand the business, but he is not confident because he doesn't have much financial capital and the business has many local competitors. He said that "they already work very hard every day to produce the cakes for their existing customers, so it is very hard to expand because they do not have family members to help." That kind of micro entrepreneur has the will and characteristics to profit from the AEC but needs to be supported and provided with business skills and marketing training to succeed in the new environment.

China as Backbone for Cambodia with Eyes on ASEAN

China and Cambodia reached the Comprehensive Partnership for Cooperation agreement in April 2006 and achieved Comprehensive Strategic Partnership of Cooperation status in 2010, which marked a milestone of cooperation. Prime Minister Hun Sen described China as a "most trustworthy friend" for Cambodia. Under that relationship, China has become a major source of foreign assistance and investment, a top foreign investor, a major donor, and an increasingly important trading partner. In return for its financial support, China has exerted its influence on Cambodia by promoting its political, economic, and cultural interests. Politically, Cambodia strongly supports the "One-China Policy" and the "South China Sea Issues". Economically, besides benefits received from its loan provision, trading, and investments in Cambodia, China may see Cambodia as a bridge to more than 600 million people markets of ASEAN.

China has provided about US$3 billion in concessional loans and grants to Cambodia since 1992. Between 1994 and 2013, Chinese investment in Cambodia was about US$10 billion, focused mainly on agriculture, mining, infrastructure projects, hydro-power dams, and garment production. In addition to development aid, China has also provided a considerable amount of military assistance to the development of the Royal Cambodian Armed Forces (RCAF) (*Khmer Time* 2016). In recent years, China significantly increased military cooperation with the RCAF by providing loans and military equipment including trucks, helicopters, and aircraft, built military training and medical facilities, and donated uniforms to the RCAF (*Khmer Time* 2016).

Chinese development aid in infrastructure development has played a key role in Cambodia's national rehabilitation. With about ten long bridges and more than 2000 km of national road built by Chinese development aid, that infrastructure has significantly improved transportation and logistics for trading and business activities and for farmers' access to markets (*Khmer Time* 2016). In the state visit by President Xi Jinping on October 13–14, 2016, the two countries further tightened bilateral cooperation by presenting 31 agreements, including US$238 million in soft loans, US$89 million in debt forgiveness, and US$15 million in military aid related to various fields including the strengthening of international cooperation, economy and finance, taxation, law enforcement, industry and handicrafts, water resource management and irrigation, environment, and infrastructural construction (Sokheng and Willemyns 2016).

Mr. Sun Chanthol, the Minister of Public Works and Transport signed an agreement for three major construction projects with China that were expected to begin in 2017. The three new projects include the national highway projects from Phnom Penh to Sihanoukville, national road project No. 11 from Neak Loeung to Tnal Toteung, and a bridge construction project crossing the Mekong river, connecting Kroch Chmar to Steung Trang district. Deputy Prime Minister Sok An and Mr. Sun Yun, the chairman of Chinese state-run Yunnan Investment Holdings Ltd (YIHL), signed an agreement regarding construction of a new US$880 million airport about 50 km outside Siem Reap's provincial capital in Sonikum district. The project is a joint investment consortium formed by YIHL, the Yunnan Construction Investment Group, and the Yunnan Airport Group with an exclusive 55-year Build-Operate-Transfer (BOT). The construction will be located on 700 hectares of land provided by the government. The plan is to build a 4E class airport, with the possibility of expanding to 4F compliance, which means the airport could receive larger long-haul aircraft.

Investment in railway is also significant. The Cambodia Iron & Steel Mining Industry Group (CISMIG) and the China Railway Group Limited agreed to build a new railway line with 11 stations as well as an iron and steel factory in Preah Vihear province. The memorandum of understanding (MOU) between the groups is worth US$9.6 billion (May 2017). According to company statements, the railway will be 405 km long, from the mining area of Preah Vihear province through the southern provinces of Kampong Thom, Kampong Chnang, Kampong Speu and finally Koh Kong province. It will not connect to the existing lines of Toll Royal Railways. Zhang Chuan Li, Chairman of CISMIG told reporters at the signing ceremony that the US$9.6 billion will be used to build the new railway line, a new port, and a new bridge in Koh Kong. The planned iron and steel plant in Preah Vihear will cost US$1.6 billion. The company received 1300 km^2 of land concessions from the government and 10 km^2 would be needed for the factory in Preah Vihear (Kunmakara 2013). The factory, which will produce 1 million tons of steel and iron per year, will take two and a half years to construct. The raw material that is needed for construction will be taken from mines in Preah Vihear, Rattanakkiri, Kampong Thom, and Stung Treng provinces. Mr. Li explained that "with the factory we want to minimize the country's import of steel. We also plan to export to neighboring countries like Vietnam and Thailand." With this project information it is assumed that the project will connect to the massive gambling and tourist resort development project (Andreas and Touch 2016) which is under construction, covering on 45,000 hectares of coast area in Botum Sakor National Park, Koh Kong province with US$3.8 billion invested by the Chinese-owned firm, Tianjin Union Development Group for a sea port, airport, business complex, entertainment, casinos, etc.

Chinese-developed electric power attainments was considered a key factor in socio-economic development in Cambodia. Chinese companies had invested in seven hydroelectric power plants in Cambodia with a total cost of approximately US$2.4 billion, built under the concessional contracts of BOT (*Xinhua* June 02, 2017). Six of them were operational, producing a total of 928 megawatts, while the seventh one, Lower Sesan II hydropower plant with the capacity of 400 megawatts, was completed in September 2017. All hydropower plants in Cambodia are 100% Chinese investments, except for the US$781 million Lower Sesan II project that is a joint venture of Chinese, Cambodian, and Vietnamese companies. The Chinese firm holds 51%, the Cambodian firm (owned by Oknha Kit Meng, owner of the Royal Group and president of the CCC) controls 39%, and a Vietnamese company holds 10% (*Xinhua* November 10, 2016). Furthermore, Chinese firms have also constructed thousands of kilometers of electric power transmission lines. Another massive 700-megawatt coal-fired power plant that fuels the country's biggest industrial park in Preah Sihanouk province and feeds the national grid was set to be completed by the end of the year 2016. The plant, which was first approved in December 2010, is a development between the Cambodian People's Party Senator's Cambodia International Investment Development Group and the Chinese-based Erdos Hongjun Electric Power Co., with the US$383 million joint venture project operating under a 33-year build-own-operate scheme in Stung Hav district (Kotoski and Cheng 2016).

At the opening ceremony of the two-week fair of the Chinese-developed electric power achievements in Cambodia organized by the Electric Power Enterprise Association of the Chinese Chamber of Commerce in Cambodia in the complex of the Royal University of Phnom Penh in early 2017, Chinese Ambassador Xiong stated that "We are very happy to see Chinese enterprises actively engaged in the development of energy sector in Cambodia." He said, "We are confident that Chinese firms will invest more in the energy sector here." At the same time, the Cambodian Minister of Mines and Energy, Mr. Suy Sem stated that the "energy sector in Cambodia needs to base its destiny on Chinese investment, and if there is no Chinese investment, until now, we will not have electricity as we see today." The minister called on Chinese investors to help build more hydropower dams, coal-fired power plants, and power transmission lines in Cambodia by saying that the electricity demand goes up by about 20% every year. He highlighted that "Chinese investment in developing the sources of electrical energy is like the building of a new history for Cambodia." He claimed that the Sino-Cambodian cooperation in the energy sector is under the initiative backed by the Asian Infrastructure Investment Bank (AIIB) and the Silk Road Fund. The minister asserted that the Cambodian government has supported the initiative and that the country is also one of the AIIB's founding members and that "We will be able to borrow money from the bank for developing infrastructures, including infrastructure for the energy sector." He mentioned that the seven hydropower plants, power transmission lines, and sub-transmission lines in Cambodia were born from the One Belt One Road (OBOR) initiative (*Xinhua* 2016).

Lao Tip Seiha, under-secretary of state of the Ministry of Land Management, Urban Planning, and Construction announced recently that since the year 2000, foreign private investors from 18 countries have completed 287 real estate projects with a total estimated surface area of about 12 million m^2, resulting in an estimated capital investment of US$4.3 billion. When the figures were broken down, it was revealed that China is responsible for 110 projects out of the total 287 projects, bearing an investment capital of US$1.66 billion. That is followed by South Korea with 46 projects totaling an investment of US$1.59 billion, while Japan holds the third spot having overseen 34 projects valued at US$224 million (Meng 2016).

There are many skyscraper buildings under construction by Chinese companies in the city, such as the Sino Great wall. Another example is the construction on the island of Koh Pich-Diamond Island led by the OCIC-a local Chinese Oknha Se, run by the president of the Khmer-Chinese Association. The 2-km-long island, home to a golf driving range, the city's largest international exhibition center, a fire station, a new city hall, and a theatre, is unlikely to become the Chinatown that the Phnom Penh government has long hoped would attract more mainland tourists. Despite the Chinese capital flowing into the island's projects, Chinese tourists and residents are not a common sight in that part of the city. With street signs featuring the simplified Chinese characters used on China's mainland (elsewhere in Phnom Penh street signs are only in Khmer and English) and sales executives are fluent in Mandarin, Diamond Island seems ripe for Chinese investment (Horton 2014a).

Koh Pich is a 100-hectare, spit of land hugging downtown Phnom Penh's shoreline developed for more than 1000 condominiums, hundreds of villas, two international schools, and a replica of the Arc de Triomphe. "Mainland Chinese, especially Shanghainese, are very impressed," said Um Bun An, sales manager at Casa Meridian, a development that will feature two 33-story condominium towers. He pointed out that investors do not need loans but rather, they pay in cash. The island's largest project is the US$700 million Diamond Island Riviera, which is a joint venture between OCIC and the Chinese company Jixiang Investment. It will have three 33-story condominium towers supporting a 650-foot infinity-edge pool, a shopping mall, hospital, an international school, two pedestrian shopping streets, plus two additional 29-story condominium towers. In a nod to Chinese superstition, which considers the number four unlucky, the buildings will not have 4th, 14th, 24th, or 34th floors. Chinese buyers account for roughly half of the sales at Diamond Island Riviera, according to Brak Kim Seng, senior sales officer at the OCIC subsidiary Canadia Bank. "The majority of Chinese buyers are buying as an investment," Mr. Brak said in Mandarin,

"They'll hold on, and when prices rise, they'll sell off" (Horton 2014b). The Diamond One condominium project, a joint venture between the OCIC and Chinese developer Xin Tian Jian (Cambodia), is keeping to its planned schedule with its US$60 million investment. With 90% of its 372 units sold—70% to the Chinese and Taiwanese, 25% to locals, and 5% to Koreans and Japanese—the construction of Diamond One has been completed and awaits interior fittings, according to Yin Hai Ping, sales manager for the development (Halim and Harry 2016).

Chinese companies are also prominent in the Cambodian textile industry. They have enabled tens of thousands of Cambodians to work and make money, even though most of them are unskilled. China's investment in Cambodia has contributed to the garment and textile sector—with more than 3000 companies, which are the backbone of the Cambodian exports, accounting for 80% of all exports and employing about 500,000 workers (*Khmer Time* 2016).

Additionally, the Cambodia–China Business Forum is a new investment-promoting mechanism, officially opened by Prime Minister Hun Sen on December 1, 2016, it drew hundreds of Chinese investors to Phnom Penh to discuss opportunities to take a stake in Cambodia's developing economy. The forum reflected the continued growth of bilateral relations, which has seen significant Chinese investment in the major Cambodian economic and development projects. That high-profile investment conference, held under the tagline Cambodia: The Kingdom of Opportunity Along The One Belt, One Road was jointly organized by the Cambodian conglomerate LYP Group, owned by one of top ten Oknha; and by Cambodian People's Party Senator Ly Yong Phat, with China Minsheng Investment Group (CMIG), China's largest private investment group. There were representatives of more than 200 Chinese companies gathered at the hotel conference center, just a month after Chinese President Xi Jinping's visit (Ting and Sokhorng 2016).

The forum explored investment opportunities for Chinese companies in Cambodia, reviewed case studies of previous Chinese FDI, and ended with many investment deals signed. The biggest of those was a US$1.5 billion deal between the LYP Group and property developer SRE Group, a Hong Kong-listed subsidiary of CMIG, to develop the Cambodia–China Friendship City on 550 hectares of land in north of the capital. The development project will include an international five-star hotel, a television broadcasting studio, a sports stadium, an 18-hole golf course, and other entertainment facilities. Chen Yi Qin, Chief Operating

Officer of Zhejiang Provincial Energy Group participated in the forum, said that strong historic ties between China and Cambodia have given Chinese companies confidence in their investment in Cambodia. Moreover, Cambodia's rapid economic growth in recent years was creating fresh business opportunities for his company. "The energy industry in Cambodia has great potential for market growth in the near future," he said, "in every industry you need energy." Zhang Nan, Deputy General Manager of Sino-steel Corporation, a state-owned mining and metals trading firm, said the company was planning to expand its presence in the Kingdom. "We expect to sign an agreement next year for an industrial park," she said, "under our leadership as a central state-owned enterprise in China, there will be a lot of related enterprises and factories flocking over to Cambodia." Wrapping up the forum, the LYP Group signed an MOU with 14 Chinese banks to fund investments of the Cambodian industries and the OBOR project (Ting and Sokhorng 2016).

The agricultural sector will also see huge gains from Chinese investment. Cambodia signed an MOU for agricultural development with a Chinese company from East China's Shandong province in October 2016. The firm plans to invest at least US$2 billion in developing the country's first special economic zone (SEZ) geared entirely to agro-processing and storage, with sprawling zones factories and warehouses aimed at meeting the growing potential for Cambodia to export its agricultural products to buyers in Asia's biggest economy. "Since China's economy is growing, as well as its population, we are facing food shortage issues, while Cambodia could help provide the resources we need," Shen Chen, Chairman of Tian Rui, said following the signing of the deal (Sokhorng 2016b).

Tian Rui, a subsidiary of China's Qingdao Tian Rui Group, will develop a new SEZ in the Kong Pisey district of Kampong Speu province. According to Chen, the Council of Development for Cambodia approved a blueprint for the 100-hectare site in June, while the company has secured an adjacent 200 hectares for expansion. Tian Rui will construct an agricultural storage facility with a 30,000-ton capacity during the project's initial phase, while two 100,000-ton facilities will be added during subsequent stages. The master plan envisions 30–100 agro-industrial factories once the SEZ is fully operational in 5–10 years. "Ten Chinese companies have already registered to operate in the zone," Chen said. He explained that Tian Rui and other companies operating in the SEZ will source agricultural products from the surrounding countryside. "The company will work with farmers and buy their agricultural products," he said, adding that Tian Rui also has its own agricultural land for growing crops. Once fully operational, Chen expects the SEZ's tenants to export around 500,000 tons of agricultural products to China per year. Meanwhile, Mr. Veng explained that the cooperation between the ministry and the company will contribute to developing the Cambodian agriculture under the framework of the China-proposed Belt and Road Initiative. "The company will also help boost the exports of the Cambodian agricultural products to international markets, particularly to the Chinese market," he added (Sokhorng 2016b).

A giant sugar mill opened in Preah Vihear province in northern Cambodia in March 2016, which is another Chinese-owned agricultural company. With US$360 million in capital, Rui Feng (Cambodia) International Co., Ltd. is part of a closely linked group of Chinese firms with adjacent economic land concessions (ELCs) who built one of Asia's largest sugar processing facilities. They are now putting the finishing touches on its newly built sugar mill, which has a capacity of 20,000 tons per day. Kuy Yoeurn, an administrative assistant of the firm mentioned that the factory's single line was capable of processing about 20,000 tons of sugarcane daily to produce 2000 tons of refined sugar. A second production line will be added in the future. "The sugar mill is part of a US$1.5 billion project by the company and its four sister firms that include a power plant, fertilizer factory, and other infrastructures such as a hospital and school," said Um Sotha, spokesman for the MIH. "It is a huge project, and consists of much more than just a sugar mill," he said, "the factory that it is setting up here will produce large amount of sugar for the world market" (Sokhorng 2016a).

According to Poeng Trida, head of Preah Vihear's provincial agriculture department, Rui Feng has invested in constructing the sugar mill and refinery on 214 hectares, and expects to complete the remainder of the project within three years. The government granted Rui Feng an 8841-hectare ELC in 2011 for the cultivation of sugarcane, rubber, and acacia. The company has faced ongoing protests from villagers and indigenous hill tribes, who accuse them of land-grabbing. The adjacent ELCs are owned by Rui Feng's sister companies, Lan Feng, Heng You, Heng Rui, and Heng Nong. Collectively the Chinese-owned companies hold five separate ELC licenses covering a total of 40,000 hectares, effectively circumventing legislation that prohibits a single company from holding more than 10,000 hectares. The new mill and refinery will process sugarcane collected from the five ELCs, exporting raw and refined sugar to buyers in the European Union, China, and India. The waste generated by the factory will be processed into fertilizer or used for generating electricity (Sokhorng 2016a).

China is also an important trading partner for Cambodia. Trade between Cambodia and China has also dramatically increased, particularly after Cambodia became a full member of ASEAN in 1999. Bilateral trade between China and Cambodia will be worth more than US$5 billion by 2017, up from US$3.75 billion in 2014, according to estimates made public by the Ministry of Commerce. "According to Cambodia and China's cordial cooperation plan in the Cambodia-Chinese Economic Trade and Investment 5-year plan (2013–2017), Cambodia has estimated the bilateral trade volume to be worth US$4.21 billion for 2015, US$4.31 billion for 2016, and US$5.01 billion for 2017," Mr. Chhoun Dara, a secretary of state at the Ministry of Commerce said, according to a transcript of a speech he gave at the workshop on exporting products to China, held on June 22, 2015 (Ho and Sothear 2015).

All assistance and investment from China have boosted Cambodian economic growth over the past decades and have contributed greatly to Cambodia's integration into the AEC. The assistance China has provided in loans, grants, and investments in different sectors has created the connections between local and international Chinese and has strengthened the ethnic Chinese-Cambodian position in the economy. Furthermore, China can control Cambodia's economic and politic domains and benefit through loan interest, profits of investment, exportation of goods, and the creation of thousands of jobs for Chinese people. Notably, if traveling around some major cities, such as in the capital city of Phnom Penh, Preah Sihanouk Province and Seam Reap Province, new Chinese migrants doing business, like open restaurants, hotels, guest houses, condominiums, and entertainment clubs can be seen. According to Norn Thim, the Sales and Leasing Manager of Sihanoukville Property, the reasons for that dominance are that "currently, Chinese investors are dominating the real estate market in Sihanoukville with the goal of turning the province into a 'China Town' in the future," and further stating that Sihanoukville has previously been known as a hub for European investors—who accounted for 75% of the province's total investment. However, with the recent influx of Chinese investment, that is changing rapidly with the Chinese now holding 65% of the total. Casinos, condominiums, and hotel complexes are the major focus of Chinese investors (*Khmer Time* 2017). Consequently, China is benefitting by exercising its influence on Cambodia.

Conclusion

The ethnic Chinese have integrated into Khmer society, yet maintained aspects of their culture and traditions. They have developed a position within Cambodian sociopolitical circles and have been successful and prominent in Cambodia's commercial sector. The AEC will create further business opportunities for the Chinese-Cambodian as they become key players in the competitive regional market economy. Most of dominating business tycoons are Chinese descendants and have been well connected with powerful state groups controlling banking, micro financing, real estate marketing, export and import, transportation, media, telecommunications, construction, land concessions, largest agro-industrial special economic zones, and so on. Additionally, those powerful business tycoons are playing a very important role in connection with Chinese businessmen/women and investors for doing business in Cambodia. Most SMEs also belong to the ethnic Chinese. The Chinese-Cambodian have maintained the culture and business network through their social and business associations.

The Cambodian government's AEC commitments rely heavily on China's assistance under the Comprehensive Strategic Partnership of Cooperation. Such dependence will create golden opportunities for the Chinese-Cambodian capitalists to further promote their social, political, and economic influence. As "Cambodia's most trustworthy friend," China plays a key role in supporting the country's economic growth in the form of development aid, investment, and trade. The Chinese invested in the real estate sector, construction sector, agro-industrial sector, mining sector, electricity, garment sector, tourism sector, and most of physical infrastructures have been built with China's aid. However, China's agenda behind that assistance is to exert influence on Cambodia and to promote Chinese political, economic, and cultural interests. In effect, Cambodia continues to support the One-China Policy and has become a source of natural resources and raw materials for China. Cambodia is becoming an outsource of Cambodian products that are manufactured by the Chinese to reach the ASEAN market. Recently, many Overseas Chinese have been moving to Cambodia for work, business, and entertainment. That leads to a growth of Chinese cultural and traditional activities in Cambodia–reflecting China's rise in the region and the world at large.

Bibliography

AKP. 2012. "Press Conference a Launching of 'Khmer Economy' Magazine." akp.gov.kh. March 6, 2012. Accessed September 22, 2017.

ASEAN Secretariat. 2015. "A Blueprint for Growth ASEAN Economic Community 2015: Progress and Key Achievements," November 2015.

Becker, Alan Stuart. 2010. "Global Lims Descend on Cambodia." *Phnom Penh Post*, November 26, 2010. Accessed September 21, 2016.

Becker, Alan Stuart. 2012. "Local Chairman Welcomes Global Family." *Phnom Penh Post*, December 5, 2012. Accessed September 21, 2016.

Chan, Sambath. 2005. *The Chinese Minority in Cambodia: Identity Construction and Contestation*. Otawa: Library and Archives Canada.

Chan, Sok. 2015. "Local SMEs Keen to Replace Thai, Vietnamese Imports." *Khmer Time*, November 9, 2015. Accessed August 20, 2016.

"China's Influence in Cambodia." *Khmer Time*, June 29, 2016. Accessed August 20, 2016.

"Chinese Dominating Real Estate in Sihanoukville." *Khmer Time*, October 4, 2017. Accessed December 20, 2017.

Dahles, Heidi. 2010. "Ethnic Chinese Enterprises and the Embeddedness of Failure." *Journal of Enterprising Communities* 4, no. 2: 184–198.

Dahles, Heidi, and John Ter Horst. 2012. "Institutionalising Chineseness: Legacies of Chinese Commercial Hegemony in the Cambodian Silk Industry." *Journal of Contemporary Asia* 42, no 2: 210–229.

Edwards, Penny. 2009. "Ethnic Chinese in Cambodia." In *Ethnic Groups in Cambodia, Center for Advanced Studies*, 174–229. Phnom Penh, Cambodia: Center for Advanced Studies.

Halim, Hanamariya, and Catherine Harry. 2016. "Some Developments Yet to Reach Finishing Line." *Phnom Penh Post*, June 9. Accessed March 15, 2017.

Hamilton, Gary G. 2006. *Commerce and Capitalism in Chinese Societies*. London: Routledge.

Ho, Tsz-kwan, and Kang Sothear. 2015. "Cambodia-China Trade to Top $5 Billion by 2017." *Cambodiadaily*, June 23. Accessed March 25, 2017. https://www.cambodiadaily.com/business/cambodia-china-trade-to-top-5-billion-by-2017-86222/.

Horton, Chris. 2014a. "Koh Pich: Diamond in the Rough Slowly Comes Together." *Phnom Penh Post*, January 9. Accessed March 15, 2017. http://www.phnompenhpost.com/real-estate/koh-pich-diamond-rough-slowly-comes-together.

Horton, Chris. 2014b. "Giant Development in Cambodia Hinges on Chinese Buyers." www.nytimes.com, May 7. Accessed October 1, 2017. https://www.nytimes.com/2014/05/07/realestate/commercial/giant-development-in-cambodia-hinges-on-chinese-buyers.html.

Inserey, Khut. 2013. "Cambodia's Small Businesses Serve as Backbone of Sustainable Economy." *The Asia Foundation.*

Intor, Chav. 2012. "Map of the Cambodian Economic Development." *Khmer Economy Magazine*, March 1.

Kimsay, Hor. "Banker to Lead Khmer-Chinese Coterie," *Phnom Penh Post*, January 18, 2017. Accessed September 4, 2016. http://www.phnompenhpost.com/business/banker-lead-khmer-chinese-coterie.

Kotoski, Kali, and Cheng Sokhorng. 2016. "Giant Coal Plant Taking Shape in Sihanoukville." *Phnom Penh Post*, June 15, 2016. Accessed October 1, 2017. http://www.phnompenhpost.com/business/giant-coal-plant-taking-shape-sihanoukville.

Kunmakara, May. 2013. "China to Invest $9.6b in Cambodia." *Phnom Penh Post*, January 1, 2013. Accessed March 19, 2017.

Meng, Siv. 2016. "China Flexes Its Investment Muscles in the Cambodian Real Estate." *Phnom Penh Post*, October 20. Accessed March 17, 2016. http://www.phnompenhpost.com/post-property/china-flexes-its-investment-muscles-cambodian-real-estate.

National Bureau of Statistics of China. 2011. Statistical Communiqué of the People's Republic of China on the 2010, National Economic and Social Development, 2011.

National Institute of Statistics, Ministry of Planning, Cambodia. 2008. "General Population Census of Cambodia," August 2008.

National Institute of Statistics, Ministry of Planning, Cambodia. 2014. "Cambodia Socio-Economic Survey (2013)," July 2014.

Nay Pyi Taw. 2004. "ASEAN Community 2015: Integration for Whom?"

Neef, Andreas, and Siphat Touch. 2016. "Local Responses to Land Grabbing and Displacement in Rural Cambodia." In *Global Implications of Development, Disasters and Climate Change: Responses to Displacement from Asia Pacific*, edited by Susanna Price and Jane Singer, pp. 124–142. London and New York: Routledge.

Nyíri, Pál. 2012. "Investors, Managers, Brokers, and Culture Workers: How the 'New' Chinese Are Changing the Meaning of Chineseness in Cambodia." *Cross-Currents: East Asian History and Culture Review, E-Journal* no. 4: 94–118. http://cross-currents.berkeley.edu/e-journal/issue-4.

Phnom Penh Post. 2011. "Cambodia's-Top-Ten-Tycoons." Available at https://www.phnompenhpost.com/national/top-10-tycoons.

Redding, S. Gordon. 1990. *The Spirit of Chinese Capitalism.* New York: Walter de Gruyter.

Royal Government of Cambodia. 2005. Sub-committee on Small and Medium Enterprises SME Secretariat. *Small and Medium Enterprise Development Framework.*

Sokhorng, Cheng. 2016a. "Giant Sugar Mill Set to Open in Preah Vihear." *Phnom Penh Post*, February 4, 2016. Accessed March 19, 2017.

Sokhorng, Cheng. 2016b. "Agro SEZ to Grow China Exports." *Phnom Penh Post*, October 20, 2016. Accessed October 1, 2017.

Sokheng, Vong, and Alex Willemyns. 2016. "China's Xi Jinping Visits King, Hun Sen." *Phnom Penh Post*, October 14, 2016. Accessed October 17, 2016.

Ting, Joey Chua Xue, and Cheng Sokhorng. 2016. "Red Carpet for Chinese Investors." *Phnom Penh Post*, December 2, 2016. Accessed March 16, 2017. http://www.phnompenhpost.com/business/red-carpet-chinese-investors.

Tully, John. 2004. *A Short History of Cambodia: From Empire to Survival.* Crow's Nest, NSW: Allen & Unwin.

Verver, Michiel. 2012. "Templates of 'Chineseness' and Trajectories of the Cambodian Chinese Entrepreneurship in Phnom Penh." *Cross-Currents: East Asian History and Culture Review, E-Journal* no. 4: 23–50. http://cross-currents.berkeley.edu/e-journal/issue-4.

Vutha, Hing. 2014. Cambodia's Preparedness for ASEAN Economic Community 2015 and Beyond. *Development Research Forum Synthesis Report No.* 7, September.

Willmott, William E. 1967. *The Chinese in Cambodia.* Vancouver: University of British Columbia Press.

Xinhua. 2016. "Chinese Investment in Energy Creates New History for Cambodia: The Cambodian Minister." *China Daily Online*, October 11. Accessed March 19, 2017. http://europe.chinadaily.com.cn/business/2016-10/11/content_27023756.htm.

Xinhua. 2017. "Chinese-Developed Electric Power Achievements in Cambodia Displayed." *China Daily Online*, February 16. Accessed March 19, 2017.

Yeung, Henry Wai-chung. 2004. *Chinese Capitalism in a Global Era: Towards a Hybrid Capitalism.* London: Routledge.

CHAPTER 7

The Rise of China's Economy and Its Impact on the Ethnic Chinese Business Community: The Case of Cherry Automobile in Malaysia

Danny Wong Tze Ken and Miao Zhang

Introduction

The economic rise of China following market reforms has had huge ramifications for Chinese firms increasingly integrating into global markets. This chapter focuses on Malaysia as China's top trading partner in the Association of Southeast Asian Nations (ASEAN) between 2008 and 2014.

While China–Malaysia economic relations are continuing to strengthen at the macro-economic level, there has been little research on

Part of the findings in this chapter was published in *Journal of Contemporary Asia*, Volume 47, No. 5, 2017.

D. W. T. Ken (✉) · M. Zhang
Institute of China Studies, University of Malaya,
Kuala Lumpur, Malaysia

Y. Santasombat (ed.), *The Sociology of Chinese Capitalism in Southeast Asia*, https://doi.org/10.1007/978-981-13-0065-3_7

the impact of development at the microeconomic level. One major gap has been on the conduct of Chinese multinational corporations (MNCs) and their interactions with ethnic Chinese firms at host sites. Existing literature in this area has focused largely on outward investment and overseas mergers and/or acquisitions using macro-economic indicators (e.g. Athreye and Kapur 2009; Hymer 1975; Rasiah et al. 2010; Gu and Reed 2012). Those studies have offered little insight on how Chinese MNCs adapt their corporate strategies with the broader political economy environment at the host site, in specific sectors, to undertake their operations. Neither have they investigated the impact of the increasing flow of Chinese capitalism on small- and medium-sized enterprises in Southeast Asia. Therefore, there is a need to analyze the business practices of Chinese MNCs abroad to construct a reasonably consistent understanding of Chinese overseas investment. Such a study shall offer insights into Chinese investment into member states of ASEAN as well as markets in the rest of the world. A case study on Chinese automobile maker Chery in Malaysia provides insight for other Chinese MNCs abroad and how they interact with Malaysia national institutions and local suppliers.

By 2018, Malaysia had attracted US$15.9 billion of investment stock from China (China Global Investment Tracker 2014). Figure 7.1 provides sector distribution-based investment in Malaysia. Net foreign direct investment (FDI) inflows from China to Malaysia increased dramatically from 2005 to 2013, rising from US$56 million to US$616 million (China Global Investment Tracker 2014) and recording an average annual growth rate of 34% over the 7-year period. China invested in 17 manufacturing sectors by 2015 with capital stock amounting to RM1872 million (Malaysia Investment Development Authority 2015). Therefore, Malaysia provides a good sample for analysis given its relatively friendly environment for Chinese investment.

This chapter attempts to analyze the political economy factors that drew Chinese MNCs to Malaysia, and the interaction they have had with the local ethnic Chinese business society in the host site using a case study of Chinese automobile producer, Chery. We aim to provide an in-depth analysis of how Chinese MNCs responded to take advantage of the opportunities and challenges in Malaysia and investigate the interactions of Chinese MNCs with the local business society within Malaysia's ethno-political economy. The remainder of the chapter is

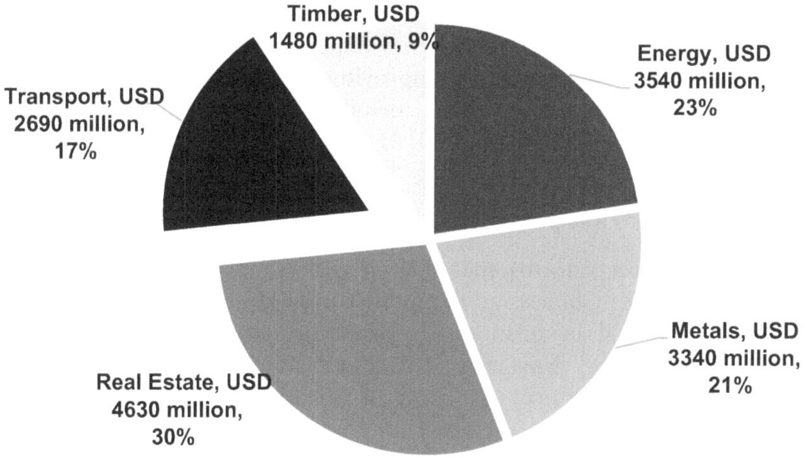

Fig. 7.1 China's outward investment stock in Malaysia by sector (2006–2014) (*Source* China Global Investment Tracker, (2014) online database: http://www.aei.org/china-global-investment-tracker/, accessed Dec 2016. *Note* mega project with investment over US$100 million and above)

organized as follows, the section after the introduction evaluates the institutional factors underlying Chinese investment in Malaysia; the next section analyzes Chery's experience in Malaysia and its impact on the ethnic Chinese business community; our findings are presented in the last section.

Push and Pull: Chery's Localization in Malaysia

As the motives pushing China's investment going abroad have developed from merely resource-seeking in the early days to asset- and market-seeking today, Chinese outward FDI in Southeast Asia has grown rapidly since 2000. An over-capacity in certain industries in China has driven Chinese firms to seek markets beyond its borders. Despite its large size, China's market for cars has become increasingly saturated, which has led to domestic firms taking advantage of the home government's Going-Out Policy to relocate production abroad (Statista.com 2016). China's economic reforms since 1978 have transformed the government's role from centrally controlled directives to one focusing on the management of regulatory functions (Zhang and Rasiah 2015). Since the reforms, the emphasis has shifted from central control to institutional change directed at improving coordination between government instruments and firms, including preferential policies and meso-organization (Rasiah et al. 2013).

Push Factors

Following market reforms that among others, attracted massive FDI from abroad, the Chinese government sought to balance inward FDI with outward FDI by encouraging domestic companies to think and invest globally. The firms with efforts to internationalize their businesses were predominantly state owned in the early days. Thus, as the majority owner, the state exercised its power to shape investment decisions to meet its political and economic interests rather than just targeting profit maximization (Kolstad and Wiig 2009). Outlined by former President Jiang Zemin at China's 16th National Party Congress in 2002, the Going-Out Policy was designed to 'encourage a number of strong Chinese firms with established brand names to become MNCs first' (Jiang 2002). In line with the propaganda pedaled by market economies, China assumed the slogan of 'market decides, government facilitates' to promote the internationalization of Chinese firms.

While strong political relations facilitated the expansion of Chinese MNCs across the globe, several major mergers and acquisitions were initially marred by massive inefficiencies and corruption. Hence, the Going-Out Policy was revamped to switch from reckless expansion abroad toward a focused approach built around exporting Chinese equipment and higher value goods and services, including high-speed railways and automobiles. While the reformers in the home government's administration have helped increase the efficiency of MNCs by emphasizing economic productivity, the Xi Administration began pursuing the political objective of westward expansion through the One Belt One Road (OBOR) Initiative (Wang 2016). In accordance with the strategy, MNC managers may have to juggle between striving for efficiency on one hand and the less profitable but strategically important contracts on the other (Cheong et al. 2014). In general, much of the Chinese outward FDI has gone to countries where a strong diplomatic relation exists with China. The localization of Chery in Malaysia can be viewed as a consequence of such policy initiatives.

Pull Factors

As with many countries trying to attract foreign investors to develop the economy, Malaysia has many incentive schemes in place. For example, income tax for technology transfer fees was exempted for foreign companies that transferred technology to Malaysian firms and individuals. Except for certain industries, the government allowed 100% foreign equity in the manufacturing sector thereby relaxing the need to allocate 30% equity to *Bumiputeras*[1] under the 1975 Industrial Coordination Act. The Malaysian government also offered special treatment to Chinese firms following the signing of the ASEAN–China Free Trade Agreement (ACFTA). For example, the Ministry of International Trade and Industry (MITI) organizes, at least twice a year, trade and investment promotion visits to China for investment. The Economic Corporation Working Group, comprised of high-ranking government officials, was formed to promote economic relations between the two countries. Additionally, measures have been taken to ensure smooth operation of Malaysia-China Qinzhou Industrial Park in Guangxi Province of China and China-Malaysia Kuantan Industrial Park in Pahang State of Malaysia. China and Malaysia have signed several mutually beneficial agreements to strengthen financial cooperation between the two countries. A classic example is the Bank of China (Malaysia) Berhad, which was authorized to conduct RMB clearing business in 2015 to facilitate cross-border RMB clearing transactions (Bank Negara Malaysia 2014).

The environment for the relocation of MNC subsidiaries from China to Malaysia improved tremendously following the signing of the Framework Agreement on Comprehensive Economic Cooperation between China and ASEAN (ACFTA) in 2002, which created the largest free trade area in terms of population with all members given favorable treatment related to trade and investment. Therefore, operation relocation in ASEAN has offered Chinese MNCs an opportunity to appropriate the favorable business conditions offered by the agreement. Furthermore, the goal of Chinese MNCs to upgrade their trade capacity and investment conditions through tentative ASEAN participation in the Regional Comprehensive Economic Partnership and the Trans-Pacific Partnership Agreement. See Fig. 7.2.

While the ACFTA agreement was instrumental in attracting Chinese FDI to ASEAN in general and Malaysia in particular, foreign automotive firms are subjected to heavy protectionist barriers erected by the

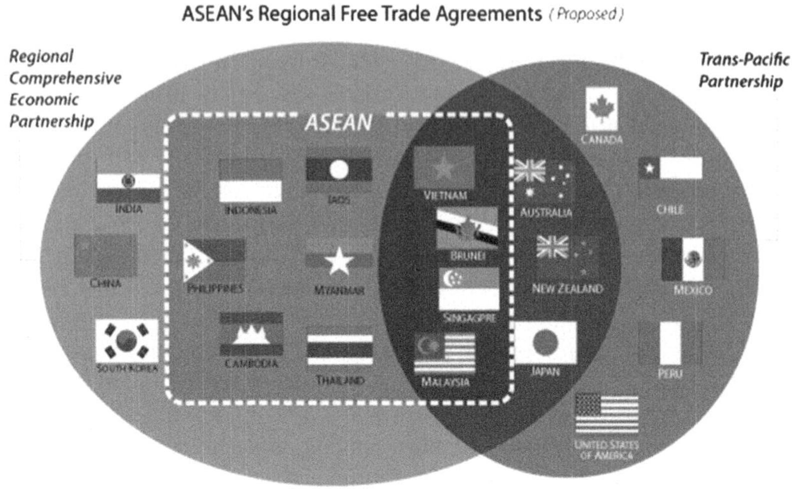

Fig. 7.2 ASEAN's FTA network (*Source* Compiled by the authors)

Malaysian government to protect national car makers and assemblers such as Proton, Perudua, and Naza Motors. Automotive products are listed as sensitive products, and therefore, have limited ACFTA capacity as a preferential trading arrangement to stimulate trade in the automotive industry. The tariff rates for completely built up (CBU) units imported and completely knocked down (CKD) units in 2010 were 28 and 15%, respectively (ACFTA 2010). Despite the heavy tariff on the finished unit, automotive parts and components are excluded from the sensitive product list. It offers an opportunity for foreign firms to start CKD assembly in Malaysia with imported parts and components. Therefore, the exports of automotive parts and accessories from China to Malaysia reached US$610 million in 2013, which accounted for 31% of the total trade in manufactured products between the two countries (Comtrade 2014). Furthermore, special-purpose vehicles have not been included in Malaysia's list of sensitive products, which allows Chinese firms a profitable access to the Malaysian market. Additionally, a tariff rate of 5% and less for intra-ASEAN exchange subject to the firms meeting the Rule of Origin[2] has also helped foreign firms in Malaysia obtain easy access to other ASEAN markets. Those fiscal instruments related to tariffs and trade have acted as a powerful pull factor to attract foreign operations.

In addition to formal policy arrangements, a common ethnic identity and cultural values have inspired the creation of business alliances between ethnic Chinese and MNCs from China, and thus resulted in an increasing investment from China to Malaysia. Although forging economic relations with Chinese firms is largely seen as economic rationalism, the business relations are further strengthened by tribalism and cultural identification which is deeply rooted in the value system of the ethnic Chinese. The presence of Chinese-Malaysian, who take up 23% of the total population in 2017, has in a way pulled Chinese MNCs to Malaysia. The traditional Chinese culture, and particularly the common language, have made Malaysia a relatively comfortable place for the inexperienced MNCs in the early days of China's open-up. For those reasons, Malaysia is more attractive for Chinese investors than the other countries that have a relatively small presence of ethnic Chinese in total population.

Case Study: Chery Automobile in Malaysia

The previous section presented socio-economic policies that encouraged the economic integration of Chinese MNCs into ASEAN in general and in Malaysia. China's Chery company is a beneficiary of those developments. However, any attempt to understand the conduct of Chery in Malaysia will require a profound in-depth assessment of its business strategy, its adaption to local policy, as well as its interactions with the Malaysian government and its local partner and suppliers. A blend of institutions shaped by political and cultural elements have influenced Chery's activities in Malaysia. Hence, this section attempts to elaborate why and how Chery established its business in Malaysia (including its coordination networks with its local partner and suppliers), how local socioeconomic conditions have shaped its business strategy in Malaysia, and the impact on the local ethnic Chinese business community.

Chery Automobile Co., Ltd. is a Chinese automobile manufacturing company headquartered in Wuhu, Anhui Province of China. It was founded by the Government of China in 1997 as a state-owned enterprise (SOE). Chery produced 590,000 passenger cars in 2012 and was ranked as the tenth-largest China-based automaker (Chery Official Website 2016). Since its founding, Chery has significantly upgraded its technological capabilities. In addition to owning its own production lines (e.g. plants for assembling cars, engines, and gearboxes), Chery had its own research and development facilities (e.g. Chery Automobile Engineering Research Institute and Automobile Planning and Design Institute). The firm employed 23,000 personnel and owned total assets of over RMB22 billion yuan in 2012 (Chery Official Website 2016).

Encouraged by China's Going Out Policy, Chery became China's first carmaker to export finished vehicles and components such as engines and chassis to foreign countries. While Syria became its first foreign export market in 2001, Chery also operates as the first foreign firm to produce cars in Iran in 2003. By 2005, Chery cars were imported by several countries including Russia, Egypt, Indonesia, and Malaysia.

It was Beijing's Going Out Policy that spurred state-owned Chery to relocate operations to Malaysia. Chery's top management officials who are appointed by the State-owned Assets Supervision and Administration Commission have strategized to achieve the political and economic objectives set by the government. While the home government's policy interests acted as the trigger, Chery chose Malaysia as a gateway to not only the ASEAN market, but also to a greater region by enjoying the preferential policies available to Malaysian due to its membership in various regional trade agreements. Therefore, Chery had earmarked Malaysia as its right-hand drive production hub. In addition to low tariffs on automotive parts and components, ASEAN Free Trade Area (AFTA) allows zero tariffs for Chery's CKD units to be exported to other ASEAN member states, providing Chery with a huge potential market (ACFTA 2010).

Following its initial investment of US$12 million (RM38.5 million), Chery-Alado planned to export locally manufactured cars to different markets in the ASEAN. Its CKD factory in Malaysia reflects Chery's global vision to tap other markets, such as Indonesia using Malaysia as an important production base. Chery's decision is based on two major factors. First, based on ASEAN Trade in Goods Agreement (ATIGA), Malaysia, as an ASEAN member state enjoys zero percent tariff when exporting locally assembled automobiles to other ASEAN countries. Second, Malaysia's relatively large domestic market with vehicle production is expected to reach 1.35 million units by 2020 (Automobile Industry Association of Malaysia 2014) and drove Chery to establish a regional base in Malaysia. Mr. Yin Tongyao, Chery's President and Secretary of the Party Committee expressed that,

> Malaysia is the largest passenger car market in ASEAN. It is also an important link for Chery to export cars to other ASEAN countries. (Ministry of Foreign Affairs 2008)

The regional executive chief officer, Mr. Paul Ng, recapped the company's strategy by noting that:

> Chery came to Malaysia in 2008 with a clear vision to establish our own factory to capture part of the ASEAN market. We have been waiting the policy on emission caps to be further relaxed. Chery intends to invest RM 300 million on a CKD factory with annual production capacity of 200,000 units in the coming 5 years. Actually, we had identified a location for the plant while awaiting government approval. To further open ASEAN market, we also aim to increase 40 to 50 authorized distributors in ASEAN, including Vietnam and Indonesia. (Ng 2012)

Merger with Local Partners

Chery's journey to ASEAN began in 2008 with a joint venture with Alado Corporation Sendirian Berhad, a private firm owned by prominent ethnic Malaysian-Chinese businessman, Tan Sri Cam Soh Thiam Hong. Cam Soh was born in Kuala Lumpur in 1962 and he is the third generation of his family in Malaysia. His grandfather came to Malaya from An Xi in Fujian Province, China when he was 16 years old. Originally, the Hokkien people[3] were the descendants of the earliest Chinese settlers largely originated from Fujian Province of China, who are arguably good at the import-export business. Soh's father is also unsurprisingly a businessman in trade. According to Soh, he made his first fortune from his mother to start a lorry business. Soh was like most boys and was interested in fancy cars, at age 20 he started his career by importing car accessories such as alloy wheels from foreign countries like Germany and Japan.

In 1996, after doing business in alloy wheel trading for over 14 years, and with his in-depth experience and knowledge of automotive products and business networks Soh decided to manufacture his own products. BSA International Berhad was then incorporated as a private limited company in 2000 and subsequently was converted to a public company in August 2000, which subsequently become listed on the Kuala Lumpur Stock Exchange on May 30, 2002. Heading the largest aluminum alloy wheel manufacturer and exporter in Malaysia, Soh was instrumental in spearheading the progress of the company and the development of its manufacturing capabilities, including establishing a manufacturing factory in China to cater to growing demands worldwide.

The establishment of CAM Automotive Manufacturing (Fushun) Co., Ltd in China in 2004 pushed Soh and Chery closer to bringing Chery's car to Malaysia. The company was set up by acquiring the manufacturing assets and inventories of Fushun Shunhua Aluminium in Fushun with an investment of US$22 million in 2004. Soh believed that with qualified engineers, lower labor cost, and reliable product, the company would prosper if it managed to install its own BSA alloy rims to at least 10% of newly registered cars in China. In fact, the annual alloy rim production at its new plant in Fushun was greatly enhanced from 720,000 pieces in 2004 to two million pieces by 2006.

Chery's success in producing and selling self-designed cars in China, in addition to its successful overseas experience in other countries such as Iran and Russia, inspired Soh to bring Chery to Southeast Asia. Soh was an ethnic Chinese himself and believed that overseas Chinese tend to favor and support endogenous car brands from China, due to which he saw a market potential in Malaysia. In 2005, when Soh started his efforts to persuade Chery to relocate to Malaysia, he found the domestic car market in China had become increasingly competitive and saturated, pushing him to start manufacturing Chery cars locally.

Soh's knowledge of automotive products and market coupled with good interpersonal skills enabled him to play a vital role in bringing Chinese car maker Chery to Malaysia in 2005. As an industrial veteran in the alloy wheel business for over three decades, Soh was adept at bringing his business knowhow to the automobile industry and business networks in both China and Malaysia. As a subsidiary of Chery Automobile Co., Ltd, Chery-Alado Malaysia (hereafter known as Chery-Alado) was officially established in May 2008 through an initial 50:50 partnership to export, assemble, and distribute CBU and CKD units. Taking advantage of Alado's sales network, Chery soon became the biggest Chinese car seller in Malaysia with more than 50 direct sales outlets and authorized dealers by 2009. Starting by importing fully assembled (CBU) Chery QQ cars, Chery-Alado extended the business further to assemble QQ cars and B14 minivans using Chery technology, parts, and components.

The joint venture between Chery and Alado resulted in Chery Automobile Co., Ltd. providing technological support and critical components, while Alado took charge of local distribution of the finished product. To undertake manufacturing and assembly, Chery-Alado Malaysia entered a business deal with Oriental Assemblers Sdn Bhd, a Malaysian vehicle manufacturer and assembler owned and managed by another ethnic Chinese family (Loh). Based in Johor Bahru, Oriental Assemblers (OA) was incorporated in 1967 as a subsidiary of Oriental

Holdings Bhd. With a great deal of experience in manufacturing and assembling of auto products (since 1967), OA was responsible for assembling two Chery car models, namely the Eastar MPV and the Tiggo SUV. Oriental Assembler sells auto parts and equipment such as engines and transmission parts for the local market with a workforce of over 200 employees in 2016. The firm has three major plants with each engaged in welding, painting, and assembly, respectively. To take advantage of ACFTA's low tariff on automotive parts and components, OA undertook locally assembling Chery cars by using imported parts and components. The firm's production of Chery vehicles increased from 716 units in 2008 to 2526 in 2009.

The decision to relocate to Malaysia as the entry point to the entire ASEAN market was heavily leveraged by Cam Soh's proactive role in forging the business alliance. The interpersonal relations as an informal institute is crucial in forging the nexus between key players and connecting ideas, strategies, and interests to form a business network of interdependent relations in the advancement of society development (North 1991). After several attempts by Alado to approach Chery before the deal was finally realized,[4] Chinese entrepreneurs' pragmatic approach and Soh's tacit knowledge (such as his networking with automotive dealers and the government) convinced Chery that a joint venture with Alado would be beneficial to their operations in ASEAN.

Chery made the decision to relocate to Malaysia and use it as a gateway to the whole of Southeast Asia despite its restrictive policies targeted at protecting the national automotive brands. Chery saw a local experienced partner in Alado that was strongly networked into the local cultural institutions, consumption behavior, and government policies that could be used productively to access Malaysia's domestic market and entire ASEAN region. Chery-Alado partnership suggests that Chinese MNCs tend to forge joint ventures with influential and well-connected local firms from host economies to connect appropriate local knowledge and networks of the domestic and regional marketplace (Lim 2015).

To solidify national support, Chery-Alado diversified its initial ownership structure by bringing a government-linked firm, Lembaga Tabung Angkatan Tentera (LTAT), as a passive investor. In 2009, Chery-Alado sold 20% of its shares to LTAT and offered it the task of distributing CBU units across the country. The participation of LTAT is an initiative to eventually meet the Industrial Coordination Act requirement of certain *Bumiputera* equity and gain further access to the domestic market. Malaysian Chinese businessmen were known to be good at establishing ties with the ruling party and forging alliances with *Bumiputera*-controlled government-linked companies (GLCs). That has been witnessed as early as 2005 when Soh, with Datuk Ayob Saad, helped Alado Bumi Automobile Sdn Bhd obtain 2496 Approved Permits to import foreign cars to Malaysia. Soh is among only a few non-*Bumiputera* businessman who successfully secured the Approved Permits. Although the Approved Permits scheme was introduced by the MITI in the 1970s as a method to help *Bumiputera* entrepreneurs in the automotive sector, ethnic Chinese Soh is among those who secured the most Approved Permits to import foreign cars.

Similarly, ethnic Chinese businessman Soh played a significant role in helping his business partners from China adapt their strategies to meet the political economy conditions prevailing in Malaysia. By so doing, Chery successfully forged an alliance between Chinese investors and the *Bumiputera*-owned GLC. The commercial ties established with government-linked and government-friendly organizations have offered Chery a solid footing in the Malaysian market. Although an inter-ethnic business collusion could be seen as rent-seeking, Soh's endeavor of forging ties with influential largely Malay-dominated GLCs helped Chery to deal with the government's policy restriction and protectionism over national car makers.

However, joining of LTAT, a government-backed GLC, has indicated that the business collusion with only Malaysian ethnic Chinese is not sufficient to overcome the policy restrictions. On the one hand, as the Malaysian government currently begins to realize the importance of Chinese investment, it is not impossible for the political elite to directly dialogue and engage with Chinese SOEs by bypassing the ethnic Chinese business community. In Chery's case, the ethnic Chinese businessman could not do not much but bring in a third party (a politically well-connected *Bumiputera* business entity in most cases) as an effort to assist the Chinese MNCs to overcome policy restrictions in the ethno-political context of Malaysia. On the other hand, Chinese multinationals also opt to collaborate with companies with a government background (such as GLC LTAT in this case) instead of firms privately owned by ethnic Chinese. Therefore, it is not surprising that Malaysian-Chinese businessmen act mostly as middlemen to forge business alliances between GLCs and Chinese investors.

Chery's experience in Malaysia reinforces Lim's finding (2015) that Chinese MNCs are at ease with the political economy of Malaysia by taking the government-linked LTAT and the ethnic Chinese businessman Soh as major shareholders in the joint venture (Michel and Beuret 2009; Lim 2015). Interestingly, interviews with officials of Chery show that Chery's experience in navigating a set of complex state-society relations in China enabled the firm to adapt quickly to Malaysia and established strong links with the host government. This finding supports Kolstad and Wiig's argument that the conduct of Chinese MNCs sometimes differs from MNCs from other countries, as the former are ready to relocate to developing countries where institutional settings are not necessarily established and well governed (Kolstad and Wiig 2009).

Interaction with Local Operations and Suppliers

One of the salient points we found from our interviews is that interactions with local suppliers tend to be very limited. It is reported that the parts and components of locally assembled cars are largely imported from China. Therefore, little production links have been established between Chery-Alado and its local suppliers in Malaysia. Minimal interaction with suppliers indicates that there is little knowledge flow from Chery-Alado to local firms which is in contrast to other international firms such as the Japanese automobile assemblers who have demonstrated significant localization of components and parts when establishing business in Southeast Asia in the 1980s. It means that Chery-Alado has largely remained a platform for the assembly of cars using imported components and parts. Nevertheless, because other foreign brands also demonstrated little links when they first relocated operations to the developing countries (Jenkins 1987), Chery may need a longer period to gradually see supplier networks fully established to support its operations in foreign locations.

For the same reasons, Chery's infancy in Malaysia may also explain why the firm has developed little engineering support to assist Malaysian manufacturers in the country. That experience is considerably different from the long-operating European and Japanese assemblers in Southeast Asia. Indeed, Chery did not have a large-scale assignment of technicians to train suppliers in meeting the demands of high-volume production and quality control procedures in Malaysia. In 2016, Chery reported that only three engineers had been assigned from the headquarters in Wuhu over the years to assist with assembly and quality control (Interview 2017). Furthermore, networking links between Chery and innovative companies and public research institutes such as research laboratories and universities are limited. Formal collaborative exchanges regarding technology and skills with Alado are drawn mainly from the headquarters through contracts. The limited two-way interactions between Chery and local suppliers and research and development organizations have resulted in limited collective leaning on the plants and suppliers in Malaysia.

Chery's strategy to partner with OA, a well-established auto producer in the local market, was to reduce the Malaysian operation's dependence on the headquarters for technological support. Given OA's familiarity with local conditions and experience in assembling vehicles, Chery opted to leave such production operations in the hands of its assembling partners. The firm reported that it opted to import rather than to manufacture parts and components because of the cheaper production costs in China.

Chery-Alado's experience in Malaysia suggests that Chinese car makers have not evolved enough to seek full integration into local production networks. It may be explained by Chery's SOE background which suggests that its internationalization and localization are more politically driven. Interviews suggest that Chery-Alado will gradually seek contracts with local firms to supply components and parts once long-term plans are laid out to produce passenger cars on a large scale.

Navigating a Highly Protected Market

While the ACFTA agreement has offered a broad platform to strengthen trade and FDI flows between China and Malaysia, restrictive policies to protect national assemblers have undermined Chery-Alado's plan to expand production in the country. To ensure the success of state-led import substitution industrialization in heavy industries such as automobile manufacturing, steel products, and cement, since 1981 when the Heavy Industries Corporation of Malaysia was launched, the Malaysian government has imposed import quotas and high excise and import duties to shield the domestic market from foreign competition (Chee 1985).

Because of the restrictions on cars that could be sold in Malaysia, Chery-Alado's sales in Malaysia have not been impressive compared with those in other countries. Chery-Alado only sold 3000 units in Malaysia in 2012, which rose from 2251 units in 2011 (Interview 2017). Cumulative sales over the period from 2008 to 2015 reached no more than 14,000 units, which is very low compared with its competitors in Malaysia, such as Toyota and Honda. Chery-Alado is now shifting away from assembling sedans[5] to avoid colliding with the host government's interests in protecting the national carmakers such as Proton and Perodua. Even with such a strategy, Chery-Alado is still disadvantaged because the host government has allowed it to sell only 40% of its production in the domestic market; the remaining 60% must be exported. According to Paul Ng, their Managing Director, although the current capacity for each model of 20,000 units annually could be reached, with only 4000 units that can be sold in Malaysia, the company must recalibrate its regional policy to comply with government regulations (Ng 2012). Because the sales networks in other ASEAN countries have yet to be fully developed, Chery-Alado has not taken advantage of the attractive regional tariff environment offered by AFTA to export to other ASEAN members.

Another barrier facing Chery-Alado is that the manufacturing license (ML) approved by the Malaysian government only allows the firm to assemble cars with an engine capacity of over 1800cc so as not to compete with the national assemblers. Although local automotive analysts foresee new incentives to attract FDI in developing energy-efficient vehicles, "only when the National Automotive Policy (NAP) becomes less restrictive can Chery-Alado give Malaysian consumers more choices. Right now, we can only offer them limited choices" (Interview 2017). With all those restrictions, Chery is now actively working to restrategize the company's policy by establishing a partnership with Proton, the national carmaker, to seek space for future development in ASEAN.

Substantial experience gained from managing complex business relations within a patron-client network in China and coordination with national partners such as Alado and LTAT have turned out to be insufficient to iron out Chery-Alado's dilemma in Malaysia. Nevertheless, initiatives to partner with Proton may be of help in removing the restrictions associated with sales quotas and ML. If that occurs, it will be an achievement for Chery-Alado in its efforts to comprehend and surmount the political economy conditions in Malaysia.

Conclusion

As the economies of Malaysia and China become increasingly integrated through trade and investment links, the leaders of Chinese MNC internationalization are dependent on interactions with the host government, local ethnic Chinese business partners, and suppliers in Malaysia. Through a push and pull factor analysis, we found that Chinese MNCs are highly motivated by China's national Going Out Policy (push factor) and the preferential trading arrangements such as ACFTA (pull factor) to relocate operations in Southeast Asia. Local ethnic Chinese businessmen, to some extent, have benefited from business engagement with China as their knowledge about China and the local market enable them to play an intermediary role in bringing Chinese investments into Malaysia, and subsequently forging collusion with influential Malay-dominated GLCs. Nevertheless, there is no evidence that the business environment facing ethnic Chinese business networks in Malaysia has significantly improved, particularly given the fact that collaboration between it and Chinese MNCs must eventually be consolidated with politically dominant ethnic groups to overcome certain policy restrictions. The impact of the increasing flow of Chinese capital does offer some benefit to local ethnic Chinese businesses, but has not fundamentally changed tense relations between them and the politically dominant ethnic groups in the host country.

Additionally, the case study indicates that local suppliers have hardly benefited from Chery's operations in Malaysia, as evidenced by the large imports of parts and components from China and the lack of supplier development strategies in Malaysia. With limited interactions between Chery and local suppliers and national research and development facilities, no large-scale collective leaning processes and production collaboration have emerged from the operations of Chery in Malaysia. Chery-Alado's current small production volume is largely a consequence of restrictive national policies to protect national assemblers and a lack of effort to expand sales outlets in other ASEAN countries. Therefore, Chery may need to embark on a more productive relationship with the national government by leveraging on a plan to expand sales in Malaysia and other ASEAN member countries. Its efforts to partner with the *Bumiputera* business entity may be a step in the right direction as it can then allow car sales in segments of 1800 cc and lower.

Chery's efforts to collaborate with not only ethnic Chinese partners but also the GLC body of LTAT, and the current negotiations to partner with Proton, another GLC company, show that the company's business strategy has developed to effectively navigate the political economy currents. While such a network was created to overcome hostile business and institutional constraints at the host site, China's MNCs, through the intermediation of ethnic Chinese business, have engaged in such patron-client relationships with indigenous state-supported capitalists to shield their interests (Gomez and Hsiao 2004).

Notes

1. Bumiputera in the context of Malaysia refers to Malays and other indigenous peoples in the country, which could be translated literally as "son of the land" or "son of the soil."
2. According to the Rule of Origin, a product with a minimum of 40% value added recorded cumulatively inside ASEAN can enjoy the preferential tariff of 5% or less in those ASEAN countries.
3. The Hokkien people are Han Chinese whose traditional ancestral homes are in South China and the people who speak Hokkien dialect in southern Fujian, Taiwan, and some Southeast Asian countries such as Malaysia and Singapore, and various locations across the world.
4. Interview conducted at Chery International headquarters in Kuala Lumpur, February 29, 2016.
5. One informant claimed that Chery had sold a few units of 11-seat vans as school buses in Sarawak in 2014.

Bibliography

ACFTA. 2010. "ASEAN-China Free Trade Agreement." *The ASEAN Secretariat*. Accessed June 2017. http://asean.org/?static_post=asean-china-free-trade-area-2.

Athreye, Suma, and Sandeep Kapur. 2009. "Introduction: The Internationalization of Chinese and Indian Firms Trends, Motivations and Strategy." *Industrial and Corporate Change* 18, no. 2: 209–221. https://ssrn.com/abstract=1372571 or http://dx.doi.org/dtp007.

Automobile Industry Association of Malaysia. 2014. "National Automotive Policy 2014." Accessed December 2015. http://www.maa.org.my/pdf/NAP_2014_policy.pdf.

Bank Negara Malaysia. 2014. "Bank Negara Malaysia and People's Bank of China Signs Memorandum of Understanding on Renminbi Clearing Arrangements in Malaysia." November 10. Accessed December 2017. http://www.bnm.gov.my/index.php?ch=en_press&pg=en_press&ac=1419&lang=en.

Chee, Peng Lim. 1985. "The Proton Saga-No Reverse Gear: The Economic Burden of Malaysia's Car Project." In *The Sun Also Sets: Lessons in Looking East*, edited by Kwame Jomo. Kuala Lumpur: Nadi Insan.

Cheong Cheok, Kee, Li Ran, Tan Chye Eu, Zhang Miao, et al. 2014. "China's State Enterprises, Economic Growth and Distribution: A Revisionist View." *China: An International Journal* 12, no. 1: 132–152.

Chery Official Website. 2016. "The Introduction of Chery Automotive Company Limited." Accessed December 2016. http://www.cheryinternational.com/corporate-overview.html.

China Global Investment Tracker. 2014. "Online Database." Accessed December 2016. http://www.aei.org/china-global-investment-tracker/.

Comtrade. 2014. "The United Nations Comtrade Database." Accessed January 2017. https://comtrade.un.org/.

Doner, R. Richard. 1991. *Driving a Bargain: Automobile Industrialization and Japanese Firms in Southeast Asia*. Berkeley: University of California Press.

Folker, Froebel, Juergen Heinrichs, and Otto Kreye. 1982. *The New International Division of Labor: Structural Unemployment in Industrialized Countries and Industrialization in Developing Countries.* Cambridge: Cambridge University Press.

Gomez, Terence, and Michael Hsin Huang Hsiao. 2004. *Chinese Enterprise, Transnationalism and Identity*. London: Routledge.

Gu, Lulu, and Robert W. Reed. 2012. "Chinese Overseas M&A Performance and the Go Global Policy." *Economics of Transition* 21, no. 1: 157–192.

Hymer, Stephen. 1975. "The Multinational Corporation and the Law of Uneven Development." In *International Firms and Modern Imperialism: Selected Readings*, edited by Hugo Radice. Harmondsworth: Penguin.

Jenkins, Rhys Owen. 1987. *Transnational Corporations and the Latin American Automobile Industry*. Bansingstoke: Macmillan.

Jiang, Zemin. 2002. "Jiang Zemin's Report at 16th Party Congress." Accessed July 2015. http://www.china.org.cn/english/features/49007.htm.

Kolstad, Ivar, and Arne Wiig. 2009. "What Determines Chinese Outward FDI?" *Journal of World Business* 47, no. 1: 26–34.

Lim, Guanie. 2015. "China's Investments in Malaysia: Choosing the 'Right' Partners." *International Journal of China Studies* 6, no. 1: 1–30.

Malaysia Investment Development Authority. 2015. "Malaysia Investment Performance Report: Driving Sustainable Growth." Accessed December 2017. http://www.mida.gov.my/home/administrator/system_files/modules/photo/uploads/20160301100315_MIPR2015-2.pdf.

Michel, Serge, and Michel Beuret. 2009. *China Safari: On the Trail of Beijing's Expansion in Africa*. New York: Nation Books.

Ministry of Foreign Affairs. 2008. "The Ambassador of China, P. R.C. in Malaysia Attended the Joint Venture Agreement Signing Ceremony Between Chery and Alado." Accessed December 2017. http://www.mfa.gov.cn/chn//pds/gjhdq/gjhdqzz/lhg_14/zwbd/t438341.htm.

Ng, Paul. 2012. "Chery to World: 'Here for the Long Term'." Interviewed by The Business Station, July 20. Accessed July 2016. http://www.bfm.my/chery-paul-ng.html.

North, Douglass C. 1991. "Institutions." *The Journal of Economic Perspectives* 5, no. 1 (Winter): 97–112.

Rasiah, Rajah, Peter Gammeltoft, and Yang Jiang. 2010. "Home Government Policies and Outward Foreign Direct Investment from Emerging Economies: Lessons from Asia." *International Journal of Emerging Markets* 5, no. 3: 333–357. https://doi.org/10.1108/17468801011058415.

Rasiah, Rajah, Zhang Miao, and Kong Xin Xin. 2013. "Can China's Miraculous Growth Continue?" *Journal of Contemporary Asia* 43, no. 2: 295–313.

Statista.com. 2016. "Car Sales in China (Passenger and Commercial) from 2008 to 2016." Accessed December 2016. https://www.statista.com/statistics/233743/vehicle-sales-in-china/.

Wad, Peter. 2009. "The Automobile Industry in Southeast Asia: Malaysia and Thailand." *Journal of the Asia Pacific Economy* 14, no. 2: 172–193.

Wang, Yong. 2016. "Offensive for Defensive: The Belt and Road Initiative and China's New Grand Strategy." *The Pacific Review* 29, no. 3: 455–463.

Zhang, Miao, and Rajah Rasiah. 2015. "Globalization, Industrialization and Labor Markets in China." *Journal of the Asia Pacific Economy* 20, no. 1: 14–41.

CHAPTER 8

Chinese Capital Going Global: Thai-Chinese Industrial Zone and Labor Conditions in Thailand

Romyen Kosaikanont

Introduction

One Belt One Road (OBOR) aims to link China, Asia, Africa and Europe like arteries and veins (Wang 2016). OBOR is a development strategy aiming to resolve the challenges facing the modern Chinese economy and to materialise China's peaceful rise. China hopes that OBOR will sustain its growth, restructure its economy, deepen the reform process, create a global business network, and expand its economic and political role on the global stage. This chapter provides two case studies to investigate how Chinese enterprises are using OBOR to their advantage and strengthen China's global position.

The first is a case study of the Thai-Chinese Rayong Industrial Zone. In 2006, the Thai-Chinese Rayong Industrial Zone was among the first batch of Chinese government-approved Overseas Economic and Cooperation Zone built in Thailand. In 2005, the joint venture was sealed in tandem with then Thai Prime Minister Thaksin Shinawatra's visit to China, which occurred when diplomatic ties between China and

R. Kosaikanont (✉)
School of Management, Mae Fah Luang University, Chiang Rai, Thailand

Y. Santasombat (ed.), *The Sociology of Chinese Capitalism in Southeast Asia*, https://doi.org/10.1007/978-981-13-0065-3_8

Thailand were regarded as optimal (Chinwanno 2009). The agreement came after a period of economic recovery following the 1997 Thailand financial crisis and the subsequent International Monetary Fund (IMF) economic measures (Kosaikanont 2003). This study discusses the establishment of the zone prior to the Thai government's announcement of the Eastern Economic Corridor in 2017 and China official announcement of the OBOR in 2013 and will be referred to as a zone.

The second case study is of Zhongce Rubber (Thailand) Co., Ltd., established in 2014. Zhongce is the largest rubber tire state-owned enterprise (SOE) from Hangzhou and was selected by the Chinese government to explore business opportunities abroad (*Thansettakij* 2016). The Zhongce case represents the SOE reform process that aims to expand OBOR and China's global market.

The chapter is organized into four sections. The first explains the history of the zone and the establishment of the Thai-Chinese Rayong Industrial Zone in 2006. It investigates the rationale behind Chinese enterprises opening an industrial zone in Thailand and supporting mechanisms. The second section looks at the Zhongce Rubber (Thailand) Co., Ltd. located in the Thai-Chinese Rayong Industrial Zone. The section investigates the motivations and strategies of the company and its utilization of services provided by the zone and Chinese government. The third section presents the impact of the Zhongce Rubber (Thailand) Co., Ltd. through an analysis and information gathered from the interviews of four employees and two suppliers. The fourth section is the conclusion.

The Thai-Chinese Rayong Industrial Zone

Situated 120 km southeast of Bangkok, the eastern seaboard and industrial zone was built in the 1980s during Prime Minister General Prem Tinsulanonda's administration. It was developed with Japanese financial support with the purpose of establishing a comprehensive network of infrastructure to augment industrial development of Thai products for global export (Unakul 2013). The then Secretary General of the National Economic and Social Development Board of Thailand, Sanoh Unakul, promoted the Eastern Seaboard Project with investments in infrastructure such as the Laemchabang Deep Seaport, upgraded roads and new highways, and an upgrade of the U-Tapao airport situated 40 km from the zone.

At present, the Eastern Seaboard has 23 industrial estates (IEAT 2017) which include estates such as Amata Industrial Estate, Hemaraj Eastern

Seaboard Industrial Estate, Maptaput, Asia Industrial Estate, RIL. Amata Group is the largest listed company on the Thailand stock market in the industrial estate sector. It was established in 1989 with a total land area of 3623 hectares. The Amata group industrial zone has fully equipped factories for rent, land for lease and sale, water treatment system, power plant, one-stop service information center, residential services and housing, recreational facilities, a hospital, and schools (Amata 2015) (Fig. 8.1).

Holley Group is a Chinese privately owned enterprise from Hangzhou, Zhejiang Province. Since 2000, the group invests in and operates an electrical parts production plant considered to be the first Chinese mainland enterprise in the Amata Industrial Zone. In 2005, the Holley Group signed a memorandum of understanding (MOU) with the Amata Group and established the Thai-Chinese Rayong Industrial Zone following a summit meeting in Beijing between Thai Prime Minister Thaksin Shinawatra and Chinese Prime Minister Wen Jiabao.

The Holley Group and the Amata Group were introduced by mediators trusted by both governments. Apipong Kunakornbodin, Senior Investment Promotion Officer and a former Director of the Board of Investment, Beijing Office, recalled that the Chinese government was first to express their interest to the Thai government and seek cooperation in the construction of the industrial zone in Thailand (Interview, January 15, 2017). Prime Minister Thaksin Shinawatra, when entering the office as Prime Minister in 2001, announced the foreign policy should engage more foreign investment in the region, particularly with China. The policy focused on development in the Mekong region and in the northern province and Chiang Rai as an industrial zone, not the eastern part of the country. To boost economic growth, China's investment in the industrial zone in the southeast seaboard was included. The construction of a new airport, Suvarnabhumi International Airport, was due to open in September 2006. The Holley group investment in Rayong was argued to boost economic activity showcasing the airport potential with endorsement from prominent figures in both Thailand and China at the MOU signing ceremony (Fig. 8.2).

After two decades of reform, China had attracted foreign direct investment (FDI) reaching 51 billion US dollars in 2003. At the time, controls were enforced limiting FDI to $US1.5 billion dollars in outgoing FDI to nurture domestic manufacturing and strengthen the domestic market. Controls included restriction of capital movement, fixed exchange rate, and dual pricing policies (Orlik 2011). With a low wage rate, the export

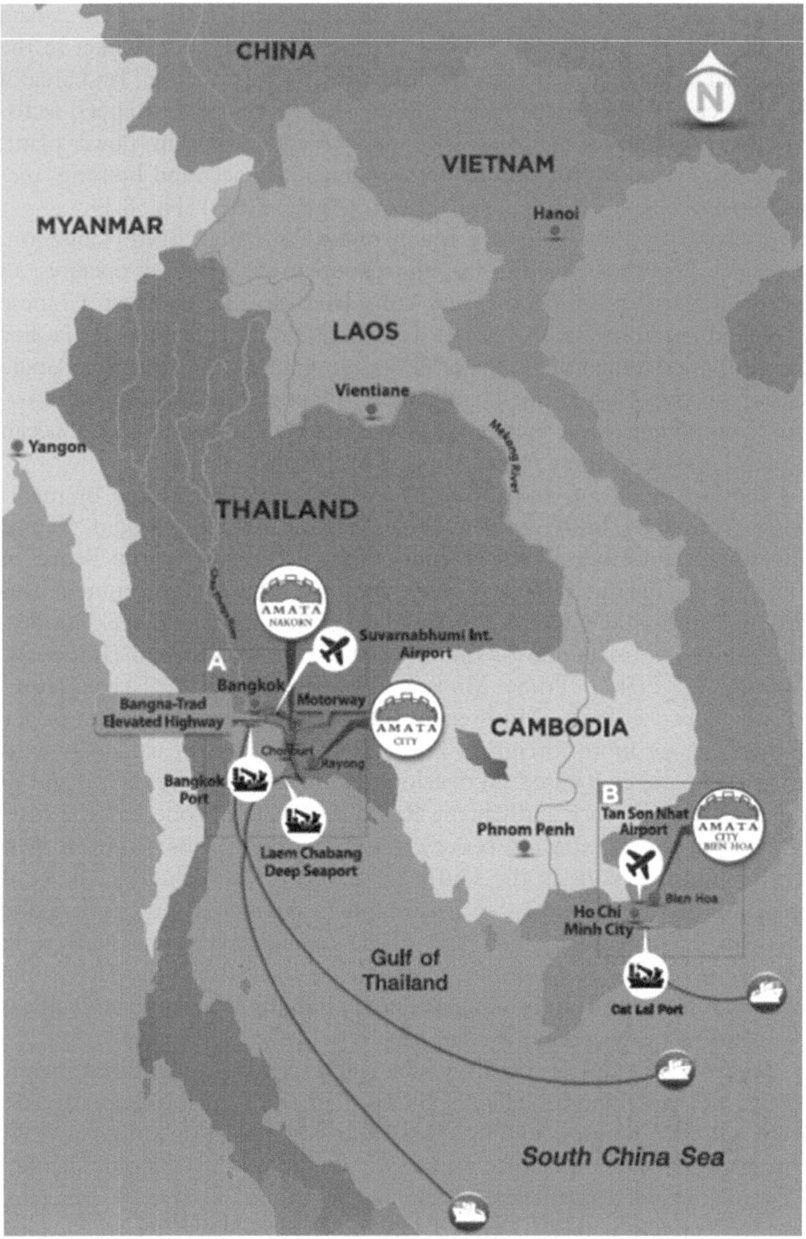

Fig. 8.1 Eastern seaboard of Thailand and Amata Group (*Source* Amata, undated http://amata.com/site/inside.php?m=locations&p=1)

Fig. 8.2 Signing Ceremony Agreement for an establishment of Thai-Chinese Rayong Industrial Zone (The occasion of the 30th anniversary of Thailand China diplomatic relation) (*Source* Amata 2015)

of Chinese-made products became highly competitive in the global market and became a major source of international reserves (Kosaikanont 2015). China committed to becoming a member of the World Trade Organization requiring liberalization of economic restrictions by 2001. Thus, their competitive advantage began to wane with overcapacity of manufacturing production, gradual rise in wage rates, and trade disputes and the early 2000s going out strategy and the 2010s OBOR were remedy to expand SOEs and investment overseas. Chinese enterprises were not experienced in running business in a liberalized global market posing new challenges. The Chinese government promoted joint ventures and investment in trade and cooperation zones to support new policies.

The Chair of the Greater Mekong Subregion Chamber of Commerce in Thailand, and member of the Advisory Committee of the National Think Tank on Thai-Chinese Strategy, explained that Chinese foreign investment risk is minimized by joint ventures with local companies to minimize the possible conflict with the local community especially over land access and acquire the best deals for arranging necessary infrastructure (Interview with Pattana Sittisombat, 2016). The Thai owner of Hi Tech Industrial Park explained that investing in the real estate and the industrial park in Thailand involved many risks and as a foreign investor, the risk was too great to overcome and that it is best if one can create a joint venture with key players in the industry (Interview with Tawit Techanawakul, 2017). The Thai government therefore endorsed and supported joint ventures such as the Holley Group.

Tawit Techanawakun is the owner of two industrial parks. During the interviews, he explained that the two main factors determining whether to invest in a particular zone or not are the privileges given by the government and the labor costs because those two factors have a direct impact on the cost of production. In the case of the Thai-China Rayong Industrial Zone, the application for the Board of Investment (BOI) of Thailand increased from the previous year of 12,306.5 million baht to 17,175.3 million baht in 2005 and 2006 respectively and received maximum tax and non-tax privileges from BOI because it was in the government-designated industrial estate. Those zones received corporate tax breaks for eight years, an additional 50% reduction in corporate income tax for five years, import duty reductions or exemptions on machinery and raw materials for up to five years, double deduction of public utility costs, and deductions for infrastructure and installation costs. Those tax privileges were bolstered with non-tax measures including land ownership rights, work permits, and visa fast track (BOI 2552).

According to Xu Genluo, the Executive Director of the Thai-Chinese Rayong Industrial Zone, the area has attracted approximately 80 Chinese enterprises with a total investment of US$2 billion. In 2016, the sale volume reached US$6.5 billion and generated more than 20,000 jobs for Thai workers and 2,000 Chinese workers (TAP 2017). The zone was built in three phases covering a total area of 12 km^2. Figures 8.3 and 8.4 show the first and second phase of the 1.5 and 2.5 km^2. The development has currently expanded into the third phase. The Zone will cover the general industrial area, bonded area, exhibition center, logistics base, and supporting commercial living facilities when construction is completed (Figs. 8.3 and 8.4).

According to the advertisement of the Zone by Holley Group, it is trying to attract Chinese enterprises that deal in auto parts, machinery, building materials, home appliances, and electronics sectors. According to the data published by the Thai-Chinese Rayong Industrial Zone office, there are currently 80 Chinese enterprises listed. Those enterprises are investing in photovoltaic, metal, heavy vehicles, electronics, chemical industry, food, and auto parts. Most of the enterprises are from Zhejiang, Shenzhen, Beijing, Heibei, and Shandong and they are both state-owned and privately owned enterprises. Currently, the largest SOE is Zhongce Rubber (Thailand) Co., Ltd. It is expected that in the third phase, the zone will be a base for 500 Chinese enterprises (sinothaizone.com).

The Thai-Chinese Rayong Industrial Zone and the extended phase of the Amata Industrial Estate are set up to attract Chinese investors and workers. Street signs, restaurants, residences, banks, and the name

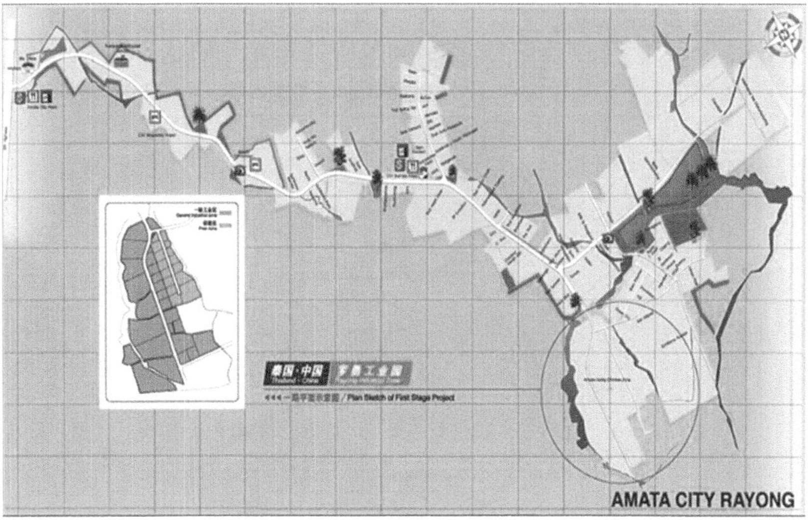

Fig. 8.3 Map of Amata City Rayong Industrial Estate and the Thai-Chinese Rayong Industrial Zone (*Source* www.sinothaizone.com)

of the companies are in Chinese, Thai and Chinese flags can be seen in front of each factory and most employees speak a Chinese language. Furthermore, facilities such as the Bank of China Limited Rayong branch and Chinese restaurants have been established to serve the needs of Chinese investors and workers alike.

The Thai-Chinese Rayong Industrial Zone received support from the Chinese government to demonstrate the benefits of OBOR, as well as facilitate and guarantee the success of Chinese enterprises going global. The government support included (1) advisory support and information for FDI and understanding host country-related policies and legal conditions, (2) operational services of namely company registration, fiscal and tax procedures, custom and human resources recruitment, and fringe benefits, (3) asset management, namely how to rent or buy property, construction, production, maintenance, medical matters, and living condition, (4) other support during emergencies, and (5) subsidies by state and local government for feasibility studies, site visits, negotiation with the host government, legal fees and insurance, as well as provision for a network of support services (COCZ 2017). The Chinese government, both at the state and local government level, has crafted means to financially

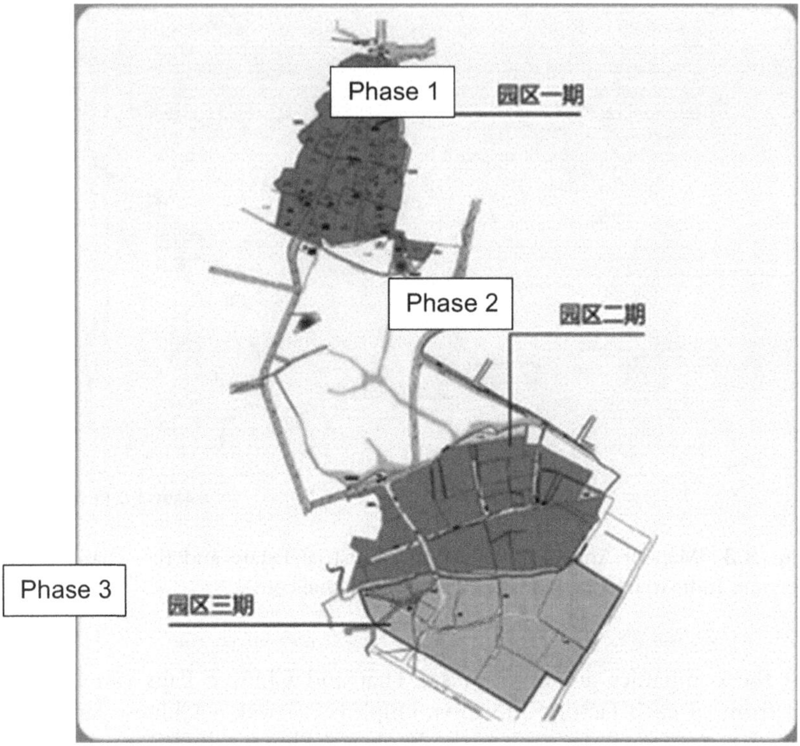

Fig. 8.4 Thai-Chinese Rayong Industrial Zone (*Source* www.sinothaizone.com)

support businesses in those joint ventures. The China Import and Export Bank and the China Development Bank provide localization of financial service, capital circulation channels, and an overseas investment fund. Apart from financial support, businesses participating in OBOR are insured for political unrest and natural disaster and are provided with information and research on the business environment of each country.

Brautigam et al. (2010) stated that in 2006 the Chinese government made the decision to establish up to 50 special economic cooperation zones in other countries as part of the Going Out Policy implementation. The Thai-Chinese Rayong Industrial Zone is one of the first of the eight Chinese enterprises to be approved by the Ministry of Commerce of China to establish a cooperation zone outside of China (see Fig. 8.5).

Country	Zone
1. Pakistan	Haier-Ruba Home Appliance Industrial Zone
2. Zambia	Chambishi Nonferrous Metal Mining Group Industrial Park
3. Thailand	Luoyong (Rayong) Industrial Zone
4. Cambodia	Taihu International Economic Cooperation Zone, Sihanouk Habour
5. Nigeria	Guangdong Ogun Economic and Trade Cooperation Zone
6. Mauritius	Tianli (now JinFei) Economic and Trade Cooperation Zone
7. Russian, Federation	St. Peterburg Baltic Economic and Trade Cooperation Zone
8. Russian Federation	Ussuriysk Economic and Trade Cooperation Zone

Fig. 8.5 China's official overseas economic and trade cooperation zones (*Source* Brautigam and Xiaoyang 2011)

In 2017, the Ministry of Commerce of the Department of Outward Investment and Economic Cooperation held a press conference and issued new data that revealed that 56 cooperation zones were set up worldwide-six more zones than the original target. Those cooperation zones were built voluntarily by the privately owned enterprises (POEs) or in some cases provincial authorities in support of the Going Out Policy and OBOR (MOFCOM 2017).

Among other reasons, Bongkot Anuroj, the Deputy Secretary General of the Board of Investment of Thailand and the former Investment Advisor to China explained that the specified clusters of Chinese enterprises are encouraged to go out because they have had trade friction or antidumping and countervailing duties imposed on them by various countries in recent years (Interview with Bongkot Anuroj, October 14, 2016).

Benjamin Zawacki (2017) claimed that for China, Thailand is viewed as the gateway to ASEAN. Hence, having the corporation zone in Thailand means that it can avoid the antidumping and countervailing duties and can use Thailand as a base to distribute products in ASEAN and the world.

The Thai-Chinese Rayong Industrial Zone is a government-approved cooperation zone outside of China. However, it is worth noting that the deal for the zone was closed in 2005, even before the Chinese government officially announced the economic and cooperation trade zone policy in 2006. The Holley Group explained that the zone was being used as a pilot for the Chinese government to experiment with the model of a POE joint venture in industrial zones with government support (Brautigam and Xiaoyang 2012).

In its economic development, the Chinese government often uses "crossing the river feeling the stone" or a gradual approach in implementation of new policy or strategy. The introduction of the approved support for the economic and trade cooperation zones of Chinese enterprises is no exception and the Thai-Chinese Rayong Industrial Zone is being used as a testing ground. The Chinese government set up an institutional infrastructure to facilitate the approval process and supporting measures for the cooperation zone through the Ministry of Commerce (MOFCOM). That may be an explanation of why there are more zones being built the world over because confidence and lessons were gained from operating industrial zone in various countries.

Now that the zones are somewhat successful in their operation in most countries, the process of granting approval is more institutionalized. The process for approving the overseas trade and cooperation zone begins with a MOFCOM announcement for an open call for proposals to any enterprises or province to make a bid (MOFCOM 2016). Selected bidders are called into submit full proposals and after the proposal screening, some are invited to present their proposals to a panel. The panel consists of independent outside experts comprising of officials from China's domestic industrial zones, university professors, and officials. The decision is made based on a feasibility study, documented evidence of support from the host government, the ability to finance the project, the ability to handle major construction, and engineering capacity. Once a project is selected, the implementation can begin immediately. Subsidies from the Chinese government are given to the enterprises if the construction has progressed at a satisfactory level. An inspection is typically carried out by senior officials of the Chinese government or by officials from local Chinese governments or municipalities. Additionally, the Department of Outward Investment and Economic Cooperation and MOFCOM are monitoring the overall picture of Chinese FDI and the progress of establishing the zone. The monitoring process is in place to measure progress and minimize any risk that might occur after the establishment or external factors.

The procedure to obtain subsidies includes completion of an application that needs to be evaluated by an official committee comprised of high-ranking officials from the Chinese government. In the case of the Thai-Chinese Rayong Industrial Zone, various high-ranking officials from China had paid a visit both to learn about the development of the zone and to evaluate its progress and some of those officials were State Councilor Wang Yong, who is also Chairman of Chinese People's Political Consultative Conference; Minister of Commerce Chen Deming; an official from the State-owned Assets Supervision and Administration Commission, as well as others. Both Wang Yong and Chen Deming are key and influential to the implementation of the OBOR, hence, having them visit the Zone meant that the zone was highly prioritized by the Chinese government.

The Chinese Embassy in Bangkok has been active in promoting the establishment of the Chamber of Commerce of Chinese Enterprises, Rayong branch. Ms. Zhang Peidong, the Counselor of the Chinese Embassy in Bangkok presided at the inaugural of the Chamber of Commerce Council and General Assembly meetings. During a meeting on June 9, 2017, she gave a speech that the Chamber of Commerce should be a platform for business information exchange including the latest development of the investment promotion policy of Thailand, as well as the national policy of China related to OBOR. She added that the Chamber of Commerce should also work closely to minimize business risks and that they should promote networking among Chinese enterprises through various types of activities. She continued by saying that having those three objectives in mind, the Chinese Embassy will ensure that the latest policies from the Chinese government are shared in a timely manner. The Embassy will also alert Chinese businesses of any political or economic risks. Ms. Zhang Peidong has continued to regularly visit the Zone, particularly during council meetings and for special occasions (Sinothaizone.com).

Xu Genluo played a significant role as the Executive Director of the Zone, known as the Honorable Life Time President of the Chamber of Commerce, Rayong Chapter. His 17 years of experience working with Thai counterparts, politicians, Thai officials, local communities, and businesses have made him an asset in building networks. Aksornsri Panichasarn, a renowned Thai economist and a Chinese economic observer believes that the Thai-Chinese Rayong Industrial Zone is a good example of state-supported Chinese FDIs. Chinese enterprises typically gain many supporters but the knowledge and networks within the host country are more important.

Wu Guangyun, Vice President of the Holley Group (Thailand), with reference to investment opportunities and the advantages of the Zone he stated that "there are many good reasons for Chinese companies to be situated here in comparison to other neighboring countries. These include (1) The size of Thai market is not only large but Thailand has capacity to distribute our goods to other ASEAN countries, (2) perfect infrastructural facilities namely highway and large seaports, (3) attractiveness of policy for FDI provided by government especially the exemption of personal income tax for eight years and tax holiday for machinery imports, (4) Thai people are kind and knowledgeable, (5) the political situation is gradually improving and stabilizing, and (6) the two countries have good relations" (Thaibiz.com).

In addition to attracting Chinese investors, the Thai perspective is that FDI is needed to finance the development and recovery of the Thai economy. In 2005, Thailand was experiencing its worst financial crisis that had begun in 1997. Following the refusal of the USA to bail out the country, Thailand was left with little choice but to seek assistance from the IMF which imposed harsh economic measures and 50 financial companies closed. The restructuring of the financial sector included high interest rates and credit restraints resulting in the country being left with limited resources to finance developments. The Thai government perceived China as not only an emerging market, but as a friend (Zawacki 2017) and Surakiart Sathirathai, the Minister of Foreign Affairs, stated that Thailand was pursuing proactive, economic diplomacy with "Asia for Asians" (MOFA 2006). Lada Phumas, the director of Division 4 of the Department of East Asia, Ministry of Foreign Affairs, in charge of China explained that good relations between Thailand and China during Shinawatra's administration prompted the offer from China to set up the financial architecture of the multilateral currency swap arrangement of the region to avoid dependency on IMF and the West and in May 2000 became known as the Chiang Mai Initiative (Phumas 2015).

Zawacki (2017) noted that the relationship between China and Thailand flourished during Thaksin Shinawatra's administration because of his personal satellite business deals with China, his profile as a Chinese descendant, and personal ties that he had established. McCargo and Pathamanand (2005) investigated Shinawatra and his business activities and pointed out that his telecommunication businesses profited from the policies that were implemented leading to concessions. Phongpaichit and Baker (2004) examined Shinawatra's power and profit and found his satellite business grew without limitations. Following many exchanged visits from top management, in 2004 the Chinese agreed to adjust their satellite's orbit to accommodate Shinawatra's family satellite, IPStar (Phongpaichit and Baker 2004).

Shinawatra's foreign policy of proactive, economic diplomacy that focused on Asians for Asia resulted in the creation of the Ayeyawady-Chao Phraya-Mekong Economic Cooperation Strategy with the goal of being a regional economic cooperation strategy under the Asia Cooperation Dialogue. Shinawatra offered Thailand as a bridge for China in ASEAN (Zawacki 2017).

The relationship of Thailand and China at the beginning of the twenty-first century is economic, political, and personal in nature. China's economic engagement in Thailand, particularly the establishment of the overseas trade and cooperation zone and subsequent investments of SOEs and POEs in the zone served as an economic path to recovery after the crisis. The Board of Investment of Thailand was assigned the task of promoting inbound foreign investors to Thailand. The Board of Investment and the China–Thailand Joint Committee on Trade, Investment and Economic Cooperation Meeting chaired by Deputy Prime Minister Somkid may have ignited the sealing of the Thai-Chinese Rayong Industrial Zone with staunch support by Prime Minister Thaksin Shinawatra.

After the coup d'état on September 19, 2006 and the displacement of Thaksin Shinawatra as a result, the relationship between China and Thailand has been less strong. As the West continues to put pressure on Thailand, China's position toward the coup d'état remains neutral. The government under General Surayud Chulanont continued to work with China although the political situation of Thailand has been rife with conflicts and division, but regardless, the Chinese government maintains and pursues their goal of OBOR.

In 2015, the Thai government, under the leadership of General Prayut Chan-ocha, announced a 20-year national vision and strategy under the premise of Stability, Prosperity, and Sustainability. The long-term vision and strategy was launched to address the problem of the middle-income trap. To escape that trap, the government restructured the economy through an innovation- and technology-driven economy and focused on infrastructure development for modern high technology and innovative production to promote regional and global connectivity.

To attract FDI, the BOI issued the Seven Year Investment Promotion Strategy (2015–2021) in January 2015, and subsequently, the new strategy for granting privileges to attract FDI was launched. Prior to 2015, the country had been divided into three investment zones for infrastructure and development according to their geographical locations. Each zone was provided with different tax and non-tax benefits to attract the appropriate investment and lessen the regional economic and development gaps. With the new strategy, the BOI would grant higher privileges to investors if the investment fit into one of the six following categories: (1) investment to enhance national competitiveness with research and development, innovation with inclusive growth; (2) activities that are environmentally friendly for sustainable growth; (3) investment that strengthens the country's value chains; (4) investment in borer provinces helping the local economy; (5) investment in the special economic zone or creating economic connectivity with ASEAN; and (6) Thai overseas investment (BOI 2015).

Although Amata City fell under zone 2 in the past, any investment in Amata City received maximum tax and non-tax privileges and the Amata City estate has two zones: the general industrial zone (GIZ) and the free zone (FZ).[1] The GIZ is for investors who are producing common manufacturing goods for the domestic market while the FX is more suitable for exporters. In the FZ, extra services, including 24-hour customs clearance and export friendly incentives are granted to investors. In addition to the benefits from GIZ, FZ, and BOI, foreign investors in Rayong and Thailand utilize the benefits from ASEAN and ASEAN Free Trade Agreement (AFTA) preferential tariffs according to the Rules of Origin. That is, if the products are sourced within ASEAN countries members and constitute at least 40%, the AFTA preferential tariffs can be applied.

In summary, the Thai-Chinese Rayong Industrial Zone was established as a Thai-Chinese joint venture with dedicated support from both governments. The investment was an experimental project for China, supporting the POEs to establish cooperation zones outside of China to seek a good model for institutional set up. Comprehensive support of the Chinese government in establishing the zone to facilitate other Chinese enterprises minimized the risk for Chinese FDI. Politically, the creation of those zones increased economic influence in production, networks of raw material, and cheaper inputs transformed into a new global production network directed by Chinese enterprises. It may be true that the zone generated new employment opportunities but the quality and the meaningful economic development must be assessed.

In the case of the Amata Group, the government recommended them because its business was fully equipped with the necessary services, had proximity to all infrastructure, access to all modes of transportation, and because it is listed in the stock market. Limited information of the personal relationship between Vikrom Kromdit, the owner of the Amata Group, and Prime Minister Thaksin Shinawatra and other ministers is limited. Vikrom Kromdit, like other businessmen from large corporations in Thailand seeking business partners, regularly joined the official trips to China (Interview with Peerapan Prempood, permanent secretary of the office of Prime Minister, 2017).

Case Study: Zhongce Rubber (Thailand) Co., Ltd.

After the MOU signing ceremony in 2005 between the Holley Group and the Amata Group in Beijing, the construction of the Thai-Chinese Rayong Industrial Zone began in 2006, with the zone starting to welcome POEs and SOEs from China in the late 2000s. Zhongce Rubber (Thailand) Co., Ltd. is the largest SOE and began construction in the zone in 2014. In China, Zhongce Rubber Co., Ltd., is recognized as the largest radial tires production enterprise in the People's Republic of China (PRC) and tenth largest in the world, according to their production volume. More than just a business run predominantly to make a profit, in its 60 years of existence Zhangce has become a source of employment and income for its Chinese workers (Sheng and Zhao 2013).

Zhongce Rubber (Thailand) Co., Ltd. was established in October 2014 with an investment of 26,400 million Baht, the largest Chinese SOE investments in Thailand. Zhongce Rubber (Thailand) Co., Ltd. is a joint venture partnering with Thai Hua Rubber with holdings of 85 and 15% shares, respectively. The primary business of Thai Hua Rubber is to produce latex, rubber sheets, and blocks (*Bangkok Post*, December 3, 2010). The plant occupies more than 49.92 hectares and was granted a BOI certificate in 2016. "Thailand is being chosen because of the strategic location and being a center of ASEAN region," according to Ms. Chen Hua who claimed that Thailand is a testing ground for the plant outside of China (Interview, October 13, 2016). In 2017, the Thai-China Rayong Industrial Zone produced a promotional video clip directed at Chinese investors coming to the zone. Ms. Chen Hua encouraged the Chinese investors to come and invest in the zone and to leave their footprint of the Chinese business brand on the OBOR.

During the interviews with Ms. Chen Hua, she made several claims that Zhongce Rubber had generated jobs for the local community and contributed to the Thai economy in terms of tax payments. However, the interview with Deputy Manager of Human Resources, a Thai middle-aged gentleman who has been working for Japanese companies since completing his formal education, said that the success of Zhongce Rubber stems from it being an SOE and having good connections with the Chinese government and influential people in the Thai government. Ms. Chen Hua elaborated that because the company is an SOE, it has received staunch support from the government. In Thailand, she has been assisted by Police General Chidchai Vanasatidya, the former deputy Prime Minister during Thaksin Shinawatra's administration, and currently serves as a consultant for the General Manager of Zhongce Rubber (Thailand) Co., Ltd.

Ms. Pancheewa Yoosabai, a Thai partner in a Thai-Chinese joint venture company and one of the trading partners and suppliers of Zhongce, elaborated that an SOE as large as Zhongce has its own bank to financially back its operation and that the company has access to information regarding the support for the Going Global companies provided by the Chinese government, which includes information on tax refunds, etc. SOEs have thus gained significant advantage in receiving support from the government in comparison with private enterprises.

Zhongce has always kept close contact with the Chinese Embassy in Bangkok and a picture of Ambassador H.E. Ning Fukui was hung on the wall in the executive dining room next to all the other pictures of senior high-ranking Chinese government officials. Zhongce Rubber (Thailand) Ltd. also remains connected with the Chinese Communist Party as well as the government. It can be argued that Zhongce is being used as a test for the SOE Going Global strategy in ASEAN and can be deduced from the numerous visits from high-ranking officials from the PRC (see Fig. 8.6).

Figures 8.6 and 8.7 show high-ranking officials and political leaders from China who came to support and show creditability and a close connection with the Chinese government and government support of SOEs Going Global in general. The Chinese Chamber of Commerce, Rayong Branch was established in 2015 within the Thai-Chinese Rayong Industrial Zone and Ms. Chen Hua became the president of the Chamber of Commerce in 2016. The Chamber of Commerce aims to be a platform for information and experience exchange, and a network

Fig. 8.6 Visit of Yu Zhengsheng to Zhongce Rubber (Thailand) Co., Ltd. (*Source* Picture was taken by Zhongce (Thailand) Co., Ltd., and presented at the job fair of Mae Fah Luang University, 2016)

platform for Chinese investors and a space for policy communication, particularly between the Chinese government via the Chinese Embassy in Bangkok.

Although Zhongce Rubber (Thailand) Co., Ltd. is an SOE and is supported by the Chinese government, other POEs within the zone also receive support from the state and local government in China to go global in clusters. Going global in cluster means that the whole supply chain of production can be exported and invested abroad while complimenting each other and minimizing the risks stemming from misunderstandings because of the business culture or language. Ultimately, the Chinese businesses abroad have more chance of success going out as a cluster. Focus is assigned to electronic parts, solar products, and rubber tires in Thailand; however, looking at it from the local economic perspective, having those clusters of the whole supply chain means that the local Thai businesses may not gain much from the establishment of new business (Interview with Pancheewa Yusabai, business owner of the Thai-Chinese Joint Venture of Kenner Knife Mould Manufacturing).

Fig. 8.7 Visit of Wang Yong to Zhongce Rubber (Thailand) Co., Ltd. (*Source* Picture was taken by Zhongce (Thailand) Co., Ltd., and presented at the job fair of Mae Fah Luang University, 2016)

The Impacts of Zhongce Rubber (Thailand) Co., Ltd. and the Local Community

According to the Department of Employment, Ministry of Labour, foreign companies can employ Thai and foreign employees with a ratio of 4:1. Statistics presented by Zhongce show that Zhongce employed 2,300 Thais and 527 Chinese, complying with the requirement of the Department of Employment. However, Thai employees are employed mostly in the production line or in junior management positions. As can be seen from the organizational structure (Fig. 8.8), there is only one management position in the office and one in the plant and both of those positions are filled by Chinese employees. The six-tier managerial positions (Chairman of the Board, General Manager, Vice General Managers), are also all filled by Chinese. The only exception is the position of General Manager Consultant and that position is occupied by the Thai Police General Chidchai Vannasadidya, the former Deputy Prime Minister during Prime Minister Thaksin Shinawatra's administration.

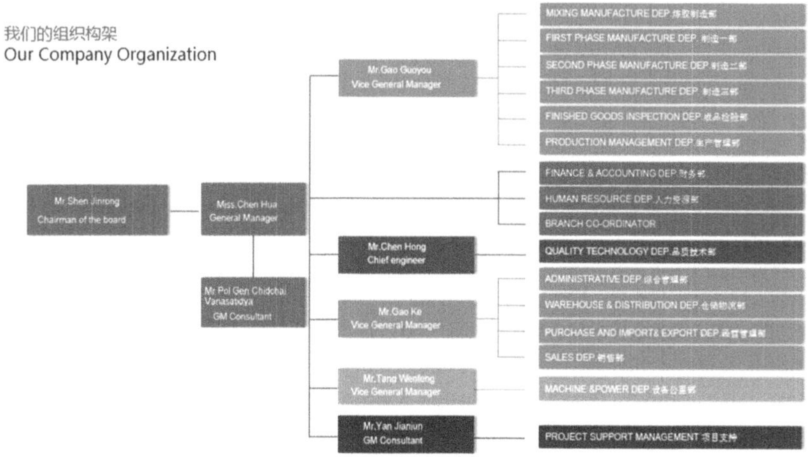

Fig. 8.8 Zhongce Rubber (Thailand) Co., Ltd. Organizational Structure (*Source* Zhongce Rubber (Thailand) Co., Ltd.)

Mr. Noppasorn Sukjun is the Assistant Manager of the Human Resources Department and currently holds the highest-ranking position in the company for a Thai employee. He explained in an interview that although he had held a senior position in a Japanese company prior to working at Zhongce, he understands that the working culture is different in the Chinese company and that it takes time and trust to be promoted. He believes that he must prove himself to the management of Zhongce. That differs from the Japanese companies where he was expected to be loyal and love the organization, to be disciplined, and to regularly report to his superior (Interview with Noppasorn Sukkun, October 13, 2016). Although there are no Thai nationals at the management level, he believes that the company will gradually let Thais take up higher positions once they have gained the trust of the Chinese management team. Ms. Chen Hua mentioned that she hopes that Mr. Noppasorn will one day take over for her (Interview with Chen Hua, October 13, 2016). It is important to stress, however, that absolute control of the firm will stay in the hands of the Chinese directive in Hangzhou. Hence, it is difficult to project whether delegating and appointing Thai employees to higher positions will occur in the not so distant future.

There are many translators working at the factory and the Chinese translators are placed on each production line which has created a division and eroded the trust of some Thai employees who believe they have been placed there to monitor their discussions, which reflects the level of trust between the Chinese companies and the Thai employees.

The Thai and Chinese employees can be grouped into two main departments, line production and office staff. However, in most cases, the Chinese hold higher positions than their Thai colleagues. Even when Thai and Chinese workers hold similar positions, the Chinese employees are not required to carry out certain less-valued and riskier tasks such as carrying heavy tires or operating heavy machinery (Interview with production line officers, August 12, 2017).

Thai line production operators' salaries increased from 9,000 baht to 9,300 baht a month in 2016. The salary of 9,300 baht a month complies with a newly issued minimum wage of 310 baht per day in Rayong province. The interviewees, Supan, Tak, and Karn were interviewed separately but all confirmed that it took the company a very long to make the wage adjustment and they were not paid for the missed wages from the previous months to reflect the increase since the announcement was made. The line production operators also receive a similar welfare package of rent, food, and transportation. Additionally, they can work overtime, with overtime pay being three times their basic standard wage per hour. However, in practice, the priority to carry out overtime work is given to the Chinese operators.

The differences in salary between Thai and Chinese employees and the perceived unfair treatment of Thai employees has caused a great deal of criticism and dissatisfaction. According to the female employees who had been interviewed, and who had all once worked for Japanese companies, they found that the Japanese companies provide their employees with clear career paths, they grade and test skills professionally, value education, and take those factors into consideration when negotiating salaries. However, none of that is in place at Zhongce (Interview, August 12, 2017). When the interviewees were asked whether they had ever tried to form a union, they claimed that when they had their job interviews with the company one of the first questions they were asked was if they had ever been part of a union. They were also told that those who protested had to leave the plant because starting a labor union was not allowed. For fear of losing their jobs, employees said they would prefer asking for equal and fair treatment quietly.

During the interviews with four employees, they often mentioned that the Chinese have their own style of working. When asked to elaborate, they explained that the Chinese working style focused less on people and quality and more on numbers, namely production targets. One interviewee, a 43-year-old single woman, compared Zhongce with her previous factory and pointed out that there is no training center. She claimed that without training center, one could not understand the entire process of production, how to be safe, how to produce good work, and how to understand quality control.

Two other interviewees, a 38-year-old woman and a 33-year-old woman, working on the production line shared similar opinions. They reiterated that the quality of work is not a priority for the firm. In the Japanese companies, the factory's policy, plan, work flow, as well as key performance indicators are clearly spelled out, communicated, and are accessible to all employees. Information and statistics of production and waste is systematically collected and continually analyzed to improve production and operation and to save costs. At Zhongce, the policy is never shared and the layout of the production floor is not well designed and organized. Safety is not a high priority and one woman talked about two cases where operators lost fingers and another where an operator got crushed by the forklift and broke an ankle, with Zhongce paying minimal compensation (Interview, August 12, 2017).

Based on those interviews, it can be perceived that Thai employees feel that the management style at Zhongce is not based on transparency. For example, in the previous year, many did not receive their annual salary raise and the management team never communicated why certain employees received raises and others did not. A bonus was supposed to be given at 1.5 months, but when the funds were finally deposited into employees' accounts, they found that it was not the correct amount. When the employees asked for an explanation, they were told that deductions were made for leave days. However, that information had not been communicated to the employees beforehand.

In a discussion about standards, one of the interviewees said that Zhongce would like to have an international certified standard to ease the pressure of exporting to international markets, especially to Europe and America. However, they are not willing to improve the layout of the plants and put in necessary measures to comply with industry standards. The company is happy instead to settle for average tires that meet the demand on time. The interviewees believe that type of thinking can be explained by the fact that Zhongce is a large SOE that has never had to comply with international standards or needed to be concerned with the efficiency of production.

The management of Zhongce also differentiates between Chinese and Thai employees in the way they organize space. Special zones are allocated for the senior management of the company, who are all Chinese, with even the dining room and rest areas being segregated. The interviewees found that the separation and unwillingness of the Chinese to learn the local culture or the Thai language shows their feeling of superiority.

Conclusion

The establishment of the Thai-Chinese Rayong Industrial Zone is a Chinese government experimental project created to support the POEs and SOEs in going global. Trade and cooperation zones such as those outside China require government approval and should be viewed in connection with the OBOR grand strategy and other policies, such as the internationalization of Yuan, Bilateral Swap Arrangement with the host country and the Confucius Institute and its offering of Chinese programs for the Chinese speaking workforce. The establishment of the zones not only brought down costs of production for China, but also eased trade tensions imposed by the external market and helped deepen multiple economic sector reform. The establishment of those zones by Chinese POEs, and subsequent investment of the SOEs in those zones, have transformed the global production network which is now dominated by China in terms of trade routes, flow of raw material, and finished products. Competition in global production and the market has become fiercer because the Chinese enterprises are supported financially through subsidies, connections with the host government, information, and facilities for Chinese investors.

From an economic rationale, both OBOR and the Thai-Chinese Rayong Industrial Zone can be viewed as a win-win situation for all involved parties. In effect, after the economic crisis in 1997, Thailand needed large investments to boost its economy. However, although the zone created job opportunities for the local community, working conditions and job satisfaction were lacking due to the Chinese enterprises' working and management culture.

Finally, China's large population and economic power means it faces very specific challenges. While OBOR may help China overcome her challenges, shared benefits with the host country and shared sustained and inclusive growth must be considered when such grand strategies and policies are implemented beyond its borders.

Note

1. Operating business in the Free Zone is considered operating outside of Thailand. Hence, all import duties are exempted if sourced from outside of Thailand. However, if the raw materials are sourced in Thailand, import duties are applied. Similarly, if the products are sold within Thailand, it will be considered as an export.

Bibliography

Aksornsri, Panitchasarn. 2011. *Settakij Chine Nai Mum Mong Nak Settasat Thai* [Chinese Economy from Thai Economist Perspective]. Bangkok: Openbooks (in Thai).

Amata. "Land Lease or Rent." 2015. Accessed June 15, 2016. http://amata.com/site/inside.php?m=locations&p=7&sub=29.

Angel, Curria. 2014. *Remarks of OECD Secretary-General Delivered at a Dinner with the Foreign Business Community*. Beijing: China Go Global.

Baker, C., and Pasuk Phongpaichit. 2014. *A History of Thailand*. Cambridge: Cambridge University Press.

BOI. 2015. Accessed January 12, 2018. www.boi.go.th.

Brautigam, Deborah, and Tang Xiaoyang. 2011. "China's Investment in Special Economic Zones in Africa: Overview and Initial Lessons." In *Special Economic Zones: Progress, Emerging Challenges and Future Directions*, edited by Thomas Forale and Golhan Akinci. Washington, D.C.: World Bank.

Brautigam, Deborah, and Tang Xiaoyang. 2012. "Economic Statecraft in China's New Overseas Special Economic Zones: Soft Power Business, or Resource Security?" *International Affairs*. 88: 4.

Brautigam, D., Thomas Farole, and Tang Xiaoyang. 2010. China's Investment in Africa Special Economic Zones: Prospects, Challenges, and Opportunities. *Economic Premise*, no. 5. Washington, D.C.: World Bank.

China Daily. "Zoning in on progress." 2014. Accessed June 25, 2016. http://epaper.chinadailyasia.com/asia-weekly/article-3520.html.

Chinwanno, C. 2009. "Rising China and Thailand's Policy of Strategic Engagement." In *The Rise of China: Responses from Southeast Asia and Japan*, edited by J. Tsunekawa. NIDS Joint Research Series, no. 4. Tokyo, Japan: The National Institute for Defense Studies.

Chinese Enterprises Enter "Go Global" Era 4.0. Accessed July 13, 2016. http://english.gov.cn/news/top_news/2016/04/11/content_281475325205328.htm.

COCZ. 2017. Accessed January 24, 2017. http://www.cocz.org/news/content-243504.aspx.

Convigton, and Burling LLP. 2014. *China Relaxes Approval Requirements for Outbound Investment*. Bejing: n.p.

Davies, K. 2013. "China Investment Policy: An Update." OECD Working Papers on International Investment, 2013/01, OECD Publishing.

EY. 2015. "Riding the Silk Road: China Sees Outbound Investment Boom: Outlook for China's Outward Foreign Direct Investment March 2015." Accessed June 22. http://www.ey.com/gl/en/services/specialty-services/china-overseas-investment-network/publication.

Garcia-Herrero, Alicia, Le Xia, and Carlos Casanov. 2015. "Chinese Outbound Foreign Direct Investment: How Much Goes Where after Round Tripping and Offshoring?" BBVA Research Working Paper 15/17, June.

Hall, Peter A., and David Soskic. 2003. *Varieties of Capitalism: The Institutional Foundations of Comparative Advantage*. Oxford: Oxford University Press.

Harvey, David. 2005. *A Brief History of Neoliberalism*. New York: Oxford University Press.

Huang, Yasheng. 2008. *Capitalism with Chinese Characteristics: Entrepreneurship and the State*. New York: Cambridge University Press.

IEAT. 2017. Accessed January 24, 2017. http://ieat.go.th/en.

Ieawsriwongs, Niddhi. 1984. *Pak Kai Lae Bai Rua: Ruam Kwam Rieng Wa Duay Wannakam La Prawatsat Ton Rattanakosin* [Collections of Literatures and the Early Rattanakosin]. Bangkok: n.p.

Irwin, Amos, and Kevin P. Gallgher. 2014. "Exporting National Champions: China's OFDI Finance in Comparative Perspective." GEGI Working Paper, June 2014.

ISS Contemporary Chinese Studies. 2014. *China's Outward Foreign Direct Investment Data*, edited by Tomoo Marukawa, Asei Ito, and Yongqi Zhang, n.p.

Kosaikanont, Romyen. 2003. The Impact of the Economic Crisis and Economic Structural Adjustment Programmes: Case Studies of the Urban and Peri-urban Communities in Northern Thailand. PhD dissertation, University of Bath.

Kosaikanont, Romyen. 2015. "The Internationalization of Renminbi: The Encroaching of the Variegated Dragon." In *Impact of China's Rise on the Mekong Region*, edited by Yos Santasombat, 227–256. New York: Palgrave Macmillan.

Lam, W. 2016. "Current and the Way Forward for Chinese Foreign Policy. Presented at Seminar on Challenges to the 'China Dream'." Organized by Institute of East Asian Studies, Thammasat University, August 8, 2016. Sukosol Hotel, Bangkok.

Laungaramsri, Pinkaew. 2012. "Frontier Capitalism and the Expansion of Rubber Plantations in Southern Laos." *Journal of Southeast Asian Studies* 23, no. 3, August: 463–477.

Li, Mengying, Athapol Ruangkanjanases, and Chenin Chen. 2014. "China's Foreign Direct Investment in Thailand—Current Status and Future Prospects." *International Journal of Trade, Economics and Finance* 5, no 4, August: 296–304.

Manarangsan, Sompop. 2009. "Thailand–China Cooperation in Trade, Investment and Official Development Assistance." Accessed June 24, 2016. http://www.ide.go.jp/English/Publish/Download/Brc/pdf/01_thailandandchina.pdf.

McCargo, D., and U. Pathamanand. 2005. *The Thaksinization of Thailand*. Copenhagen: Nordic Institute of Asian Studies.

MOFA. 2006. *Collected Speech of Minister of the Ministry of Foreign Affairs*. Bangkok: MOFA.

MOFCOM. 2016. "Official of the Department of Outward Investment and Economic Cooperation of the Ministry of Commerce Comments on China's Outward Investment and Economic Cooperation in 2015." Accessed May 5, 2017. http://english.mofcom.gov.cn/article/newsrelease/policyreleasing/201602/20160201251488.shtml.

MOFCOM. 2017. "China's Outward Investment and Cooperation in 2016." Accessed May 5, 2017. http://english.mofcom.gov.cn/article/newsrelease/policyreleasing/201701/20170102503092.shtml.

Nolan, Peter. 2012. *Is China Buying the World*. Cambridge: Polity Press.

Orlik, Thomas. 2011. *Understanding China's Economic Indicators: Translating the Data into Investment Opportunities*. Upper Saddle River, NJ: FT Press Science.

Phongpaichit, P., and C. Baker. 2004. *Thaksin: The Business of Politics in Thailand*. Chiang Mai: Silkworm Books.

Phumas, Lada. 2015. "Foreign Policy Directions of Thailand Towards PRC After 2015. Individual Study." Devawongse Varopakarn Institute of Foreign Affairs. Ministry of Foreign Affairs. Thailand.

Piketty, Thomas. 2014. *Capital in the Twenty-First Century*. Cambridge: Harvard University Press.

Santasombat, Yos. 2015. *Impact of China's Rise on the Mekong Region*. New York: Palgrave.

Sheng, Hong, and Nong Zhao. 2013. *China's State Owned Enterprises: Nature, Performance, and Reform*. Singapore: World Scientific Publishing Co. Ltd.

Sinothaizone. Accessed January 12, 2018. http://www.sinothaizone.com.

Siriphon, Aranya. 2010. *Poo Ka Jin Nai Chai Dan Lum Nam Khong* [Chinese Traders in Mekong Border]. Chiang Mai: TRF and Faculty of Social Sciences, Chiang Mai University.

Songprasert, Phuwadol. 2004. *Chine Pon Talay Samai Mai* [New Oversea Chinese]. Bangkok: Thaicoon Higher Press.

State Council. The People's Republic of China. 2016.

Suvakunta, Pittaya. 2010. "China's Go-Out Strategy: Chinese Foreign Direct Investment in Thailand." *Thailand Law Journal* 13, no. 1, Spring.

Thaibiz. Accessed January 12, 2018. http://www.thaibizchina.com/thaibizchina/th/.

Thammarat, Saroj. 2016. "Expansion of Chinese Capital and Its Impact on Thai Economy." IS Paper as Part of the EFAP Programme.

Thansettakij. 2016. "Thai-China Trade and Investment 2016: Perspective of Wu Zhui's." *Thansettakij* 35, December.

The Econmonist. Anonymous. 2013. "Let's Party Like It's 1793 Xi Jinping and the Chinese Dream and a Return to Greatness." *The Economist*, May 4. https://www.economist.com/news/leaders/21577070-vision-chinas-new-president-should-serve-his-people-not-nationalist-state-xi-jinping.

The Economist. 2004. "We Are the Champions: China's State Owned Enterprises Want to Make Their Mark on the World Stage." *The Economist*. Accessed May 16. http://www.economist.com/node/2495172.

Tiezzi, Shannon. 2015. "China Invests in the World." Accessed June 24, 2015. https://thediplomat.com/2015/06/china-invests-in-the-world/.

Unakul, Sanoh. 2013. *The Power of Technocrat*. Bangkok: Matichon Publishing.

Wang, Yiwei. 2016. *China Connects the World: What Behind the Belt and Road Initiative*. Shenzhen: China International Press.

Yeung, Henry Wai-chung. 2006. *Chinese Capitalism in a Global Era: Towards a Hybrid Capitalism*. Oxford: Routledge.

Zawacki, Benjamin. 2017. *Shifting Ground Between the US and a Rising China*. Chicago: Zed Books.

Interviews

*not a real name to protect the identity of the interviewee.

Apipong Kunakornbodin, Senior Investment Promotion Officer and a Former Director of the Board of Investment, Beijing Office, January 15, 2017.

Bongkot Anuroj, Executive Director, Investment Marketing Bureau, October 14, 2016.

Chen, CEO of Zhongce Rubber (Thailand) Ltd., October 13, 2016.

Dollaporn Atchaworakun, Director, Thailand Board of Investment (Beijing), January 31, 2017.

Karn*, Zhongce Rubber (Thailand) Co., Ltd., QC, August 12, 2017.

Noppasorn Sukkun, Deputy Manager of Human Resource of Zhongce Rubber (Thailand) Co., Ltd., October 13, 2016.

Nuntana Udomkij, Former Secretary to the Minister, Ministry of Commerce, August 21, 2017.

Pancheewa Yoosabai, A Business Joint Venture with Chinese Counterpart and Supplier to Zhongce Rubber (Thailand) Ltd., February 10, 2017 and August 20, 2017.

Pornprasit Denmolee, Former Executive Vice President of Haier (Thailand), October 12, 2016.

Supan*, Zhongce Rubber (Thailand) Co., Ltd., Staff Officer, August 10, 2017.

Tak*, Zhongce Rubber (Thailand) Co., Ltd., Operator, Production Line, August 12, 2017.

Tawit Techanawakul, Owner of Hi Tech Industrial Estate, Janurary 18, 2017.

Teerakul Niyom, Former Ambassador of Thailand to PRC, August 21, 2017.

CHAPTER 9

China's Economic Integration and New Chinese Immigrants in the Mekong Region

Chinh Van Nguyen

Introduction

The new migration from China to the Mekong region is examined in this chapter in the context of China's increasing economic-political influence in the region, and the special relations between the Mekong countries and China. The focus of the discussion is intended to capture the complexity of the new Chinese migration to the CLMV countries (Cambodia, Laos, Myanmar, and Vietnam) by looking at migration patterns, trends, and local policy response. This research was done to augment the understanding of previous research that Chinese migration is the consequence of domestic pressures that occur within Chinese society, such as high unemployment, rural-underemployment, and the rapid increase of what Rallu Jean Louis (2002) called a "floating population" and there is an increasing trend looking at the nexus between China's trade relations, foreign direct investments (FDI), and the new migration movement (Xerogiani 2006; Zhuang and Wangbo 2010; Chong 2013).

C. Van Nguyen (✉)
Vietnam National University, Hanoi, Vietnam

Y. Santasombat (ed.), *The Sociology of Chinese Capitalism in Southeast Asia*, https://doi.org/10.1007/978-981-13-0065-3_9

Chinese migration to the Mekong region has increased rapidly in recent years with the development of strong economic relationships. Early in the twenty-first century, Chinese companies invested billions of dollars in the Mekong countries focusing on infrastructure development, resource-exploitation, agricultural and cultural expansion, accompanied by establishment of Chinese educational institutions in the region. The economic reform of 1978 turned China from a poor, socialist and isolated nation into a workshop of the world, an accolade previously bestowed on Britain during the Industrial Revolution of the nineteenth century. The Going Out Policy launched by the Chinese Communist Party early in the twenty-first century saw the emergence of Red capitalists that began to invest abroad, with the goal of exploiting countries' natural resources and energy to feed the demands of China's domestic industries. FDI and economic cooperation between China and the Mekong region are the driving factors influencing the flow of migration to that area.

China's Economic Integration

For some time China had harbored a strong interest in forging close relations with the Mekong countries, but only in the last decade has its leadership been able to push forward a comprehensive cooperation and socio-economic influence in the region. China has promoted and increased its economic and political relations with the CLMV countries since the 1990s and has since then become their largest economic partner. A report published by China's National Development and Reform Commission on the 2008 Summit of the Greater Mekong Sub-region (GMS) stated that since the establishment of the China-Association of Southeast Asian Nations (ASEAN) Free Trade Area in 2010, bilateral trade between China and the GMS countries has gained a momentum of greater development, with a further improved trade structure and rapid increase in bilateral investment. That report further noted that bilateral trade and Chinese investments in the GMS countries had reached the highest levels recorded in 2010. In comparison with 2008, China's bilateral trade with Cambodia and Thailand increased by only 28%, while its trade with Vietnam, Myanmar, and Lao People's Democratic Republic (PDR) increased by 54, 68, and 150%, respectively (CNDRC 2011). China's main exports to the GMS countries were textiles, electromechanical products, hi-tech products, garments, steel, and agricultural products. Its main imports from those countries included raw materials such as natural rubber, garments, timber, coal, crude oil, agricultural products, and various minerals. Chinese companies also actively invested in the Mekong countries and its main industries are like the Mekong countries' industries that include textiles, light industry, machinery, electronics, building materials, and chemicals.

Bilateral China–GMS trade grew rapidly from early in the twenty-first century, with Thailand showing the largest increase in volume. In 1992, bilateral trade between Thailand and China was about US$13 billion and increased up to US$529 billion in 2010, and the growth rate made up 38.6% (Lu 2012). Several GMS countries have had a severe trade deficit with China, which is particularly acute in the case of Vietnam from 2001 forward where trade rose from US$188 million in 2001 to US$16.4 billion in 2012. Thailand is no exception and in 2010, Thailand had a trade deficit with China totaling US$13.45 billion (Chinh in Santasombat 2015). While China's share of each GMS country's trade is large, ranging from 10 to 25%, the share of GMS countries in China's foreign trade is approximately 1%.

The general trend in China–GMS trade relations is the growing dependence of the Mekong regional market on China. If the economic relations between the GMS countries and China were to decline, the effect on those countries would be far greater than the consequences suffered by China. In 2000, China officially became the FDI provider to the GMS countries which actively encouraged and supported investment activities overseas to utilize domestic and foreign resources and markets. By 2012, China had become the largest foreign investor in Myanmar, Laos, and Cambodia, and the fifth largest investor in Thailand. In the first 11 months of the 2012–2013 financial year, China was leading the FDI inflow in Laos with over US$1.33 billion worth of projects. By 2013, China had invested a total of US$14.1 billion across 52 projects in Myanmar, accounting for 41.7% of the newly liberalized country's cumulative FDI. That amount excludes investments from Hong Kong, where many subsidiaries of Chinese companies are registered. In 2008, Earth Rights International identified at least 69 Chinese multinational corporations involved in a total of 90 projects in Myanmar in hydropower, oil and natural gas, mining, jade, and other natural resources. In 2011, Chinese investments accounted for 60% of the total approved FDI for Cambodia. The size of the approved FDI from China continued to rise by 62% from 2012 to 2013, reaching US$427 million in 2013, compared with US$263 million in 2012.

China had become the largest investor in Cambodia in terms of cumulative FDI by 2013 which stood at US$9.6 billion in total from

1994 to 2013 (Xinhua 2014). Most large-scale investments are from the central Chinese enterprises targeting infrastructure, energy, and mining sectors, coupled with projects in the manufacturing and agricultural sectors. Along with outward FDI, China is also the largest source of loans and aid. Following the April 2013 visit to China of Cambodian Prime Minister Hun Sen, US$2 billion of loans and aid were received from China, followed by a further interest-free loan of US$33 million. Chinese companies are very active in tapping the hydropower market in Cambodia, which is expected to generate 77% of Cambodia's total electric-generating capacity by 2030 (IHLO 2014).

Chinese companies began expanding their investments in Thailand in the early 1990s. From 1995 to 2003, the Bank of Thailand registered an FDI inflow of US$114.9 million from China. As reported by the Thailand Board of Investment, 161 investment projects by Chinese companies were approved for the 1987–2005 period, with a total value of 31505.7 million baht, approximately US$900 million (Suvakunta 2007).

FDI from China is not as large in Vietnam as inflows from other international investors. During the period between 2002 and 2009, Chinese investments into Vietnam increased from US$2.5 billion to US$56.5 billion (Wenbin and Wilkes 2011). Most of those investments entailed funding for large-scale engineering, procurement, and construction (EPC) projects. EPC projects can also be perceived as special investments from China, which appear as a form of governmental support for its national investor and is the method preferred by Vietnamese investors since the Chinese government has created a special policy of preferential buyer's credit and concessional loans for EPC projects, which stipulates that the necessary equipment and technologies must be sourced from China. By the end of 2009, Chinese engineering companies were involved in projects worth US$15.42 billion, making Vietnam their largest EPC market in Southeast Asia (Le 2013).

Although Chinese investment activities in GMS countries are diverse, they tend to converge on three major sectors: (1) mining and resource extractions, (2) land concessions, and (3) infrastructure construction. Taking advantage of low infrastructure development in the Mekong region, Chinese companies were welcomed by local authorities. A typical example for that practice is the case of Lao PDR. When the decision was made for Laos to host the XXV Southeast Asian (SEA) Games in December 2009, the Lao government sought aid from the China Development Bank by applying for a loan to fund the necessary sporting facilities. The US$100 million loan was awarded on the condition that the Chinese company Suzhou Industrial Park Overseas Investment would be given a 50-year lease to develop 1640 hectares of central Vientiane and develop business centers, hotels, factories, and tourism facilities. That is perhaps the largest amount of aid linked to the Chinese government and may have led to the most well-known case of trade-offs that Laos has made in the name of development (Kenney-Lazar 2012). Consequently, it was agreed to bring 50,000 Chinese nationals into Lao PDR to populate the new satellite city. As part of the New City Development Project, the China Yunnan Construction Engineering Company Group Corporation imported thousands of Chinese workers to build the SEA Games stadium in Vientiane. The Lao government estimates that approximately 30,000 Chinese nationals already live in Laos, but most analysts believe the real figure to be perhaps ten times higher. Stores owned and operated by Chinese people have sprung up across northern Laos, while other Chinese have settled into remote villages as foremen and workers on commercial agriculture projects (Gunn and McCartan 2008).

The relationship with the Mekong region countries bordering China—Laos, Myanmar, and Vietnam—is strategic and important for China. China enjoys a long border with those countries and has easy access by road to natural resources. Chinese companies in the CLMV countries have gradually shifted their focus to the energy, resource extraction, infrastructure, and agriculture sectors in areas close to the border with China. Chinese financiers have moved into the region to take advantage of the favorable investment climate and the abundance of natural resources. Vietnam and Laos, and to a lesser extent Cambodia, are experiencing an unprecedented interest in their bauxite (aluminum ore) resources from China. The Lao mining industry (bauxite, copper, gold, lignite, tin, iron, zinc, gypsum) has been the main interest of Chinese investment over the last decade, responsible for more than 50% of Chinese FDI into the country. In 2008, there were 113 foreign companies operating in that sector, of which 33 were from China. Much of the demand is driven by China's need to feed its growing industry, and those Mekong countries are perfectly situated to bring the product to the market (Lazarus 2009).

Beginning in 2000, Chinese companies became particularly interested in land concession projects, many of which were granted to Chinese companies to increase agricultural and mining production. Concessions for 2–3 million hectares of land were granted (including domestic projects), representing up to 13% of the total land area of Lao PDR, in which the main investors were neighboring countries like China, Vietnam, and Thailand (GTZ 2009).

The economic relationship between Laos and China is expanding and currently, numerous provinces in the north of Laos function as economic zones for the southern Chinese province of Yunnan. Contract farming, especially for rubber plantations, forms a considerable part of the business ventures between the two countries. The massive expansion of rubber plantations by Chinese companies in north Laos stems from a mix of market demand and land constraints in China, as well as political incentives from both the Lao and Chinese governments (Haberecht 2009). Many new Chinese investors supplied Lao farmers with seeds and input for commercial production of sugarcane and rubber crops. As a result, competition for swidden (slash and burn) and fallow forests intensified, altering not only upland communities' customary relationships with the land and resources, but challenging the resource management framework established during the 1990s.

A comparable situation occurred in Cambodia. From 1995 to 2009, the Cambodian government granted 186,935 hectares of land to Chinese companies for 17 agricultural projects. The largest project seized an area of 10,000 hectares of land, taking 18% of a total 1,024,639 hectares of land granted to the economic organizations (Hem 2013). Capital flows from China into the Mekong region through bilateral trade, FDI, and EPC projects are facilitating the inflows of new waves of Chinese migrants into the Mekong region, and will be discussed in the next section.

New Chinese Migrants in the Mekong Region

Southeast Asia may be home to as many as 40 million people of Chinese descent, many of whose ancestors migrated to the area mostly from Guangdong and Fujian provinces (New World Encyclopedia 2003). The statistics vary according to the sources and definitions of Overseas Chinese. *The New World Encyclopedia*, for example, defines Overseas Chinese as people of Chinese birth or descent "who live outside the Greater China region, which includes territories administered by the rival governments of the People's Republic of China and the Republic of China" (New World Encyclopedia 2003). The same source estimates that the Overseas Chinese population is 7.1 million in Thailand,

1.3 million in Myanmar, 1.2 million in Vietnam, greater than 150,000 in Cambodia, and approximately 50,000 in Laos. The ethnic Chinese, therefore, make up more than 10% of Thailand's population, which World Bank figures put at 67.9 million for 2015 (World Bank 2016). For the CLMV countries, the ethnic Chinese make up 1–3% of the total population (SyCip 2001). Despite minority status, people of Chinese descent are known to play a dominant role in the economies of the region.

Recent waves of Chinese immigration into the Mekong region, particularly into Cambodia, Myanmar, and Thailand, play a vital role in China's economic engagement with the GMS. From the 1990s to the present, the Chinese community in Cambodia has grown to over 2 million, out of a total population of approximately 50 million. In Myanmar, 40% of the population in Mandalay province is identified as ethnic Chinese. The recent migrants to the region are thought to have close link with the Chinese mainland and its capital inflow. In *Migration and Trade*, Chinese researchers Zhuang and Wangbo (2010) from Xiamen University, claim that in the last 25 years the number of Chinese migrant arrivals in the Mekong region has reached 2.3–2.6 million, most of them labeled as "floating people".[1]

The Mekong region countries are historically the home of large ethnic Chinese communities, a possible factor behind the recent interest in the region by the new Chinese migrants. With the improved infrastructure connecting the Chinese economic centers in Yunnan, Guangxi, and Guangdong with the Mekong region, new Chinese migrants can reach those countries with fewer logistical challenges, particularly in an economic climate stimulated by increased commercial interaction between China and those neighboring countries. The following sections will explore the impact in each of the CLMV countries.

Cambodia

In Cambodia, people of Chinese descent are referred to as *Khmer kat Chen* or simply *Chen*. Under French colonial rule, the largest Chinese groups were from Hokkien and Canton, and Teochiu (also known as Chaozhou) had become the largest group by the middle of the twentieth century. Although the ethnic Chinese community in Cambodia experienced both abuse and assimilation, it displayed remarkable resilience in adapting to, responding to, and contesting the forces that tried to marginalize its members (Chan 2012).

Until 1970, the Overseas Chinese were the largest minority in Cambodia, numbering an estimated 425,000, a figure that by 1984 had dwindled to 61,000. Recently, the Chinese bilingual magazine *Khmer Economy Magazine* (2012) estimated that about one million ethnic Chinese may reside in Cambodia. A portion of those ethnic Chinese are descendants of settlers who migrated from southern China centuries ago, while others are arrivals from recent waves of migration.

Following the establishment of the State of Cambodia in 1989 as a transitional period until the restoration of the monarchy (1989–1993), Chinese education was restored in Cambodia, which was considered a step toward improved Sino-Cambodian ties. In December 1991, the Cambodian National Assembly accepted the reestablishment of the Khmer–Chinese Association in Cambodia—the first time that an Overseas Chinese Association had been officially recognized since 1973. That event was a turning point for the Khmer–Chinese of Cambodia, who can count on state legislation for their businesses and cultural activities, as well as education opportunities. Since then, the Overseas Chinese Association of Cambodia has grown rapidly. It currently has 22 branch offices in 24 provinces and approximately 140 offices at the district and commune levels (Siphat 2015). Those organizations are authorized to form their own associations and to build temples, schools, and cemeteries for the Chinese community. In 2000, Overseas Chinese in Cambodia set up *Chean Fra Media*, a Chinese newspaper headed by *Oknha* Duong Ch'hiv, Chairman of the Khmer Chinese Association. The newspaper's goal is to promote Chinese culture and education in Cambodia. In his position as a prominent figure in Cambodia, Ch'hiv collected funds from the Khmer–Chinese communities to build schools and to raise support for the poor and victims of natural disasters in Cambodia and China (Nyíri Pál 2013). The Chinese-language teachers were invited to teach Khmer–Chinese students at the schools run by the association. Chinese culture and education was also supported by the Phnom Penh branch of the Bank of China, through a special fund set up for that purpose to "not only contribute to developing the Cambodian economy but also [to] assist the country's education" (Van Chinh 2014a, b). That level of political support by the Cambodian government can help explain why Cambodia absorbed a high number of new Chinese migrants, which contributed to the revival of the local ethnic Chinese community.

New Chinese migration into Cambodia began around the 1990s, particularly after the Khmer–Chinese Association was set up. Although new

Chinese migrants into the country are diverse, they can be categorized into two major groups, namely, spontaneous migrants and organized migrants. Spontaneous migrants include petty traders, hawkers, traditional healers, farmers, marriage migrants, and small-scale business people who moved to the Kingdom in search of better opportunities. They traveled to Cambodia by independent means, running their own businesses and shouldering the risks and soon enough, Chinese cheap goods and technologies followed them. They set up businesses or obtained employment through networks with local Khmer–Chinese citizens or local Chinese associations. Those small-scale business people displayed a high degree of mobility, in that they would remain if their business prospered but did not hesitate to move out of Cambodia in search of better opportunities. Their movements involve frequent trips between Cambodia and their homeland of China.

The second group of organized migrants includes contracted workers, project managers, technicians, representative office staff, teachers, students, etc. Most of them work as salaried employees for Chinese companies with investment or contract projects in Cambodia. The National Bureau of Statistics of China reported that between 1995 and 2005, in the region of 43,070 Chinese technicians and laborers were brought to Cambodia for work (Zhuang and Wangbo 2010). They include two subgroups which include manual laborers recruited to work on the contracted projects or land concessions granted to Chinese companies; and professionals and people with higher education who work for Chinese investments, projects, representative offices, and Chinese schools.

By Cambodian law, new Chinese migrants who meet the necessary requirements can apply for Cambodian citizenship. Although no official statistics are available, during our fieldwork in many locations in Cambodia, we met dozens of recent migrants who had been granted Cambodian citizenship. Among the numerous Chinese employees who successfully applied for Cambodian citizenship, we were impressed by the circumstances surrounding Mr. Lam (personal names have been changed for anonymity), a 38-year-old man who had arrived in Cambodia from his native Kunming (Yunnan) in 2005 where he served as a soldier and upon his discharge from the army, decided to migrate to Cambodia. For the first two years after his arrival in the Kingdom, he worked in a garment factory but left in 2007 when a Chinese company in the Tong Min Group received a concession of 30,000 hectares of forestland for a 70-year lease. Mr. Lam applied for work and was recruited as an administrative manager for that large land concession based in Cambodia's Mondulkiri province. Mr. Lam enjoys a high salary and the relatively low living costs allow him to have savings. He visits his homeland once a year for 15 days. He married a Khmer woman who is also an employee of the Chinese company, and they have a child together. Mr. Lam believes that Cambodian citizenship will improve his personal status, enabling him to travel freely between China and Cambodia. In our interview, Mr. Lam stated that new Chinese migrants enjoy good relations in their host country and that is drawing many Chinese investors and workers into the Kingdom. In his opinion, although life and work in Cambodia are easy and less competitive than in China, to succeed in Cambodia a business person needs a powerful local backer, and must embrace certain unofficial local practices renowned for their ability to oil the wheels of business.

The greater the number of Chinese companies to be awarded projects by Cambodian investors, the greater the number of Chinese migrants likely to move into the country to find jobs as project managers, workers, and brokers for Chinese investors. With the increasing flow of Chinese capital under the umbrella of investment and aid, there is a high demand for materials and equipment for construction projects to be managed by Chinese companies, and consequently, large groups of Chinese workers and technicians are likely to follow that flow of capital into Cambodia. By way of example, in 2007, hydroelectric power accounted for less than 4% of Cambodia's 386 MW of energy-generating capacity, a level expected to rise to 77% by 2030 (US Energy Information Administration 2013). To date, much of Cambodia's hydroelectric power expansion has been financed by China. In December 2010, Sinohydro, a Chinese state-owned hydropower engineering and construction firm, completed the construction of the 184 MW Kamchay Dam project at a cost of US$280 million, with financing from the Export–Import Bank of China. Separately, at a cost of US$1 billion, China is sponsoring the construction of two mega-dams, Stung Tatay and Stung Russey, which upon completion will be among Cambodia's largest hydroelectric power projects (*The Jakarta Post* 2016). Cambodia plans to build ten dams between 2010 and 2019, adding 2045 MW of capacity with Chinese entities providing financing for six of those dams.

Because entry of new Chinese migrants into Cambodia is facilitated by Khmer–Chinese associations, the organization plays a prominent role in connecting new and old Chinese migrants on Cambodian soil. A society called *Oknha* was established by Khmer Chinese citizens, named after an honorific title bestowed by the Cambodian monarch to honor a chosen few. The title of *oknha* can be acquired by means of a donation of US$100,000 and a commitment to devolve funds toward the greater good. A recent estimate puts the number of *oknha* in Cambodia at just over 700, a significant increase from the 20 such titles recorded in 2004 (*The Cambodia Daily* 2014).

Lao PDR

The Chinese population in Laos has historically been smaller than the Chinese communities in other GMS countries. Although Laos shares a common border with China's Yunnan province, most of today's ethnic Chinese in Laos originate from other southern provinces of China, including Guangdong, Fujian, and Hainan, and settled in Laos around the second half of the nineteenth century. The Chinese accounted for 32,500 individuals in 1955, most of whom were Teochiu, followed by Hakka, Hainanese, and Cantonese groups. They owned approximately 50% (749 out of 1550) of the companies registered in Laos in 1959, however, their economic influence carried more weight as many were operating in Lao–Chinese joint ventures or under false Lao ownership (Halpern 1961). By the 1980s, the Chinese population in Laos had dropped to approximately 10,000, but is currently on the increase. The Overseas Community Affair Council, Republic of China (Taiwan) estimates there are 150,000 Chinese living in Laos. That estimate may include both older generations of ethnic Chinese, who settled in Laos in the middle of the nineteenth century, as well as new arrivals beginning in the 1990s. A recent study by Chiang and Cheng (2015) indicates that the number of long-term Chinese residents could reach 30,000 for the whole of Laos, of which up to 4000 are in Vientiane. The number of new Chinese arrivals has been estimated at between 200,000 and 300,000. In fact, it is difficult to obtain reliable data regarding the number of Chinese people in Laos because new arrivals are highly mobile, with large numbers returning to their native China after crossing into one of the northern Lao provinces for short periods of time. Lao administration systems at all levels are experiencing difficulties in obtaining official data and reports from local authorities.[2]

The revival of the Overseas Chinese community in Laos is believed to stem from the new wave of migrants arriving in the late 1990s on a scale that the country had never experienced before (Evans 2008). Most of those new Chinese migrants arrived and settled in the north of Laos and in the capital of Vientiane where many construction projects were granted to Chinese companies. An Asian Development Bank (ADB 2010) research project places the figure at 80,000 Chinese nationals working on Chinese-led projects. Available sources of information on specific locations indicate that the number of Chinese workers in northern Laos has increased dramatically. For example, in 2002, only 27 Chinese workers were recorded in the construction sector in Bokeo province but by 2007, the number officially registered by the provincial authorities was 1269 Chinese nationals (Tan 2011).

In many cases, Chinese migration to Laos is investment-linked, ranging from small shopkeepers' investments in their own stock, to Chinese multinational companies' investments in large-scale rubber plantations. From mining to rubber, transport, hydropower stations, and hospitality infrastructure such as hotels and casinos, China has currently invested heavily in several key economic sectors in Laos. This research indicates that at the smaller scale, Chinese investments in Laos, and their concomitant influx of laborers since the mid-2000s have also encouraged the arrival of spontaneous migrants who work as small traders, businesspeople, and farmers. They come in search of better prospects in a developing country. To better understand the situation of contemporary Chinese migration to Laos, we can analyze the facts of three projects: Golden Boten City, the construction of Route No. 3 on the North–South corridor, and the Hong Yue Market in Vientiane capital which is referred to as the "new Chinatown."

Golden Boten City is located on the border opposite the Chinese town of Mohan. Visitors to Boten may be forgiven for thinking that most of its inhabitants speak Mandarin Chinese as their native language. In 2002, the Golden Boten City "special zone" was built on a 1640-hectare free-trade zone, developed on a land concession project granted to a Chinese company, and leased for up to 90 years. The vision of the Chinese investors was of a border town suitable for conventions, entertainment, and sporting events, with business and transport centers that would become a trade hub in the region. The first project was a casino and hotel complex inaugurated in January 2007, which brought thousands of people from the People's Republic of China (PRC) into Boten every week. A few years later the Golden Boten City turned into an enclave of near lawlessness and was closed in 2010.[3] Another special economic zone appears to be replacing the Golden Boten City. Located in the Lao district of Tonpheung, Bokeo province, the Ton Pheung Special Economic Zone is built on an area of 867 hectares of land leased for a 50-year period (renewable lease) to the Chinese entity Myanmar Macao Lundun Co., which in 2009 employed over 1000 mostly Chinese workers (Tan 2011).

Route 3 is a 246-km road connecting Golden Boten City at the Lao PRC border with Houayxai on the bank of the Mekong in the province of Bokeo and opposite the Thai town of Chiang Khong. In December 2002, the ADB approved a US$30 million loan to the Lao government, for improvements to the road cutting through northwest Laos and feeding into an international North–South corridor linking Thailand and the PRC, with the Thai and Chinese governments co-financing the project to the amount of US$30 million each. The upgrading began in March 2008 and after two years of construction, the road linked two of the poorest provinces in north Laos (Luang Namtha and Bokeo) with the region's most dynamic economies, the southern region of China and Thailand. The completion of Route 3 has improved goods transportation and increased people's mobility. The number of people crossing in and out of the Lao PDR at Route 3 border points has increased significantly since the mid-2000s. Research by Lyttleton indicates that "at the PRC-Lao PDR border point of Boten, 13,433 people entered Laos in 1999 and 15,799 people entered in 2003. In 2006, however, 56,507 people (including 51,833 people from the PRC) crossed into Lao PDR at Boten. In addition, travelers and businesspeople from the PRC are increasingly traveling further into the Lao PDR on visas. In 2005, 9,851 people from the PRC entered Laos via Boten on passport visas (compared with 35,473 people on border passes). In 2006, this figure increased by 47%, with 14,449 people from the PRC using visas (compared with 37,244 people on border passes)" (Lyttleton 2009).

Hong Yue Market is another example of the pairing between Chinese money and manpower and the Lao government's open-door policy to foreign investments. The Hong Yue Market, formerly known locally as "Talat [market] Leng" and now the "New Chinatown," is located in the town center and was built by the Hong Yue Chinese state company on land leased for 25 years. The market contains 110 shop spaces and was inaugurated in 1996. Up to 1998, the Lao government invited Hong Yue to acquire more small entrepreneurs from the PRC and 97 small traders came and settled in Vientiane, taking over shop spaces previously left empty. Most of the traders and shopkeepers were from Hunan, while others were from Zhejiang and Jiangxi. Along with the Hong Yue market, the Chinese company Sanjiang opened the Sanjiang Market in 2008, a much larger shopping mall located on the road leading to the Vientiane airport. The new shopping mall was built at a cost of US$6 million. The new Chinatown has expanded the reach of the Vientiane capital further north, and the shopping mall has absorbed more Chinese migrants into the Lao capital.

The new Chinese migrants in Laos hail from different Chinese regions, not only from the southern provinces of Yunnan, Guangxi, and Guangdong, but also from Sichuan, Hunan, and Shejiang. The new Mekong economic corridor linking Kunming, the capital of Yunnan province, to Bangkok, via the completion of Route 3, has encouraged Chinese investors and businessmen to explore new and potential markets in Laos. Small traders also come to Laos along new paved feeder roads that reach previously inaccessible rural areas, to operate stalls in local markets, transporting their goods (easy-to-carry cheap consumer products) to places where they are likely to encounter less competition, particularly from other Chinese migrants. Chinese migrants have become important economic actors in those localities because they are often involved in various business activities and create jobs for local people. However, Chinese investments and their concomitant influx of laborers and traders are also causing some anxiety and resentment among Lao citizens, particularly in land concession areas where large stretches of land have been granted to Chinese companies, forcing local people to alter their livelihoods.

Myanmar

Myanmar has historically been an attractive destination for Chinese migrants. Migrants arrived throughout the era of British colonial rule, including nationals deserting China's political and economic upheavals during the twentieth century, such as the Sino-Japanese War and the long civil war. Most of the ethnic Chinese in Myanmar originate from Yunnan, Guangdong, and Fujian provinces. For the first half of the twentieth century, ethnic Chinese residing in Myanmar enjoyed peace and stability. The anti-Chinese riots of 1967 were followed by a campaign of assimilation under the "Burmese Way to Socialism," which forced

Overseas Chinese to integrate more deeply into mainstream Myanmar society. Estimates by Than and Khin Maung Kyi indicated that by 1983, Myanmar hosted about 234,000 people identifying themselves as Chinese (Than and Kyi 1997).

The new wave of Chinese migration to Myanmar began in the late 1980s, shortly after the military coup of September 1988, a date that can be regarded as a major factor in the emergence of a new wave of Chinese migrants as well as the acceleration of Myanmar–China ties. The cordial talks to establish Myanmar–China border trade on October 3, 1988, completed on December 1st of the same year, led to the open-border policy which facilitated cross-border business activities and the movement of people from both sides. The reopening of Chinese education, the approval of Chinese-language newspapers in Myanmar and, particularly, the re-establishment of the Chinese Chamber of Commerce that facilitated new business connections with Chinese investors across Southeast Asia, induced Chinese migrants, mostly from Yunnan, to pour into Myanmar in search of better prospects. According to Shannon and Farrelly (2014), the Chinese Embassy in Yangon estimated that by 2008, there were approximately 2.5 million Chinese living in Myanmar, most of whom had moved there in the late 1980s and early 1990s. The Chinese traders have played a prominent role in turning Myanmar into a new market, brimming with cheap consumer goods made in China, while Chinese entrepreneurs have become middlemen between local consumers and Chinese suppliers. Chinese traders and vendors, mainly from border areas, migrated into Myanmar and made their living by importing and selling cheap Chinese goods to local people. A trade route quickly emerged from southern Yunnan, through the border town of Muse, down to the Chinese hub of Lashio in northwestern Shan State, and then on to Mandalay, the bustling heart of Myanmar (Shannon and Farrelly 2014).

The close relationship between Myanmar and China has facilitated the expansion of economic relations, particularly bilateral trade through border towns in the two countries, and a massive inflow of Chinese investment which has brought Chinese migrants into Myanmar in its wake. On December 4, 1989, a Memorandum of Understanding (MOU) for economic and trade cooperation between the two countries was signed during the visit to Yunnan by the Myanmar Ministry of Trade delegation. Under that MOU, Yunnan province would open department stores in Mandalay and Lashio, branch company offices would be opened and Yunnan commodities would be sold in Myanmar, and tourism between

Yangon and Kunming would be encouraged. All those business activities, along with the government's economic liberalization, helped to stimulate Chinese migration into Myanmar (Tun 2015).

In contrast to the earlier movement of Chinese migrants to Myanmar, many of whom consisted of asylum seekers and citizens eager for resettlement, modern-day Chinese migrants are relatively affluent, with their sights firmly set on buying plots of land, establishing their own businesses, and engaging in investment projects and trading activities. Most of the gold and jewelry shops in central Mandalay are owned by Chinese or Myanmar–Chinese citizens. Large Chinese corporations and companies who have been awarded major development projects in Myanmar usually bring in their own employees from China, not just technicians but also unskilled laborers, the rationale being ease of communication.

Local people have expressed anxiety. In their view, Chinese investors have brought their wealth into Myanmar and then illegally invested in profitable sectors through Myanmar citizens descended from past generations of Chinese migrants. In some cases, new Chinese migrants married local women to gain access to local networks, and then registered their businesses in their Burmese wives' names. That may explain why modern-day Chinese migrants make Mandalay their primary destination, where they can take advantage of established social networks created by long-term Chinese residents. Some new migrants have sought to obtain Myanmar citizenship by various means, including approaching officials and authorities through unofficial channels. Some long-standing Myanmar–Chinese settlers are dissatisfied with the new wave of migrants, because, in their words, "We are quite different from them in cultural traditions. Previous settlers pay respect to the native citizens, and live modestly, not in a pompous lifestyle. In contrast, new settlers do not care about the native people. Even they look down on us" (Tun 2015).

Among the reasons for explaining how new Chinese migrants have been able to move to Myanmar in such large numbers since 1988, many locals believe that loose immigration rules and corrupt government officials are at the heart of the problem, with immigration officials in border towns known to issue Myanmar ID cards to Chinese migrants with relative ease. Some Chinese migrants pose as members of Myanmar ethnic minorities such as Shan, Shan-Chinese, Wa, or Kokang. The arrival of illegal Chinese migrants has been a cause for concern among members of the Myanmar Parliament. In 2013, a proposal was discussed to weed out fake new Chinese migrants by means of Burmese language tests.

Apart from a formal conversation and a new regulation for both Burmese and English to appear on advertising billboards instead of Chinese, no significant other steps have been taken.

In summary, since 1988 the movement of Chinese migration into Myanmar has been supported by connections with an open-door policy, in the absence of effective law enforcement, particularly in areas of cross-border migration between China and Myanmar. The economic liberalization, and particularly the facilitation for Chinese capital flow for trade, investment and aid, have provided opportunities for Chinese migrants to settle in Myanmar. As in other countries of the Mekong region, temporary Chinese migrants into Myanmar belong to different ethnic groups and places of origin, but the majority are Han Chinese from Yunnan, Guangxi, and Guangdong. They are investors, middlemen, project managers, small traders, and hawkers as well as free- and contracted-laborers working in the fishing, mining, and construction sectors or other heavy industry.

Vietnam

The population of ethnic Chinese in Vietnam prior to the 1979 China–Vietnam border war totaled 1.5 million, with 300,000 people located in the north of Vietnam (Tran 1994). During and after the 1979 war, approximately 300,000 people of Chinese descent left Vietnam for China or migrated to a third country. According to data published by Vietnam's General Statistical Office (GSO), the Vietnamese–Chinese population reached 862,071 in 1999. About 85% of ethnic Chinese live in the southern part of Vietnam. In Ho Chi Minh City alone, the Chinese population is believed to be approximately 500,000 (GSO 1999).

Historically, Vietnam was a traditional destination for Chinese migrants. The most prominent feature of Chinese communities in Vietnam is their preference for communal living in specific areas, thereby giving rise to their own communities and facilitating business dealings. Vietnamese historical sources, including family records, show that during the sixteenth to eighteenth centuries, many Minh Huong villages were established along the coastal southern reaches of Vietnam—evidence of Chinese migrants seeking to integrate by settling in new lands.[4] The *ChợLớn* (Chinatown market) is the most prosperous Chinese commercial center in the south, established in 1782 (Nguyen 2016).

The ethnic Chinese population played a significant role in southern Vietnam's economy until the post-1975 reforms. According to Tran

Khanh (1994), during French colonial times, Chinese ventures accounted for 21% of total foreign investments in the south, falling to 16% during the Vietnam–American war, but still the top foreign investor in both periods. Early in the 1970s, approximately half of the enterprises in the south were owned by ethnic Chinese who controlled most of the processing industries, including rice mills, as well as export and import companies (Nguyen 2016).

The new wave of Chinese migration to Vietnam began in the 1990s after the normalization of relations between the two countries, and can be broadly categorized into four types which are broad categories and are not always clearly defined. The first are contract laborers brought into Vietnam by Chinese contractors and enterprises. The second are professionals, business people, students at educational institutions, and staff at Chinese representative offices in Vietnam. The third are independent migrants who assume the risks of making their way to Vietnam to engage in small or medium trading, or engage in business in various sectors such as services, street vending, restaurants, and traditional herbal medicine. The fourth type is the daily cross-border circulation along the borderlands. While these four categories are helpful in identifying the specific groups of migrants, it is important to see them not as separate movements but as a larger and interrelated human flow from China to Southeast Asia (Nguyen 2016).

Aside from those who were previously recruited by Taiwanese companies, most Chinese workers have been brought in by Chinese contractors since the early 2000s. That form of labor migration is relatively new to Vietnam. The presence of Chinese migrant workers in the Mekong region reveals the growing economic integration between China and the region. An unpublished Ministry of Labour, Invalids, and Social Affairs report (2010) indicates that the number of Chinese workers in Vietnam increased from 21,217 in 2005 to 75,000 in 2010 (an increase of 3.5 times), although those figures are an estimate. Our investigation into nine actual work sites shows that only 21% of Chinese workers are legally registered with the local authorities. Those who are not registered are probably not included in reports (Van Chinh 2014a, b).

Chinese manual workers are mainly employed in major construction projects granted to Chinese companies. The Chinese contractors interviewed during our fieldwork reported that most of their workers were employed under short-term contracts of 3–12 months or longer, depending on the project. Many Chinese workers with whom we spoke had overstayed their permits by one year or more. Some workers at the Hai Phong

Thermo-Power Plant No. 1 had stayed in Vietnam more than five years, working at various projects across the country. Chinese employers usually move their workers from one worksite to another after three to six months to save on transaction costs. For instance, the Chalieco Company (Chinalco Corporation) was contracted to build an aluminum processing factory in Tan Rai Bauxite Mining of Lam Dong. The Chinese contractor brought in 700 workers when the project began in 2008. The number of workers was then doubled to 1400 in 2009 and decreased to 922 in late 2011. Most of the laborers working in Tan Rai were moved to Nhan Co aluminum factory in Dak Nong Province between 2011 and 2012, apparently working on similar tasks. Such shifting of workers ensures the availability of labor for Chinese contractors and saves the latter from reporting the presence of foreign workers to local authorities.

The wages and work conditions of Chinese workers in Vietnam vary depending on the type of job and employer. As discussed earlier, most of the EPC projects managed by Chinese contractors were awarded at the government-to-government level, with conditions tied to concessional loans. As a result, Vietnamese investors are not able to influence the Chinese workers' salaries.

Chinese petty traders and workers also cross the border into Vietnam for informal trade. During our fieldwork, we observed that 90% of the kiosks in Mong Cai Trade Center were rented to Chinese traders, most of whom cross over into Vietnam in the morning and return home to China in the afternoon. Interviews with people who live around the border gates reveal that cross-border human mobility benefited both Vietnam and China, particularly the residents on both sides of the border. Data provided by Mong Cai border gate administration indicate that the volume of Chinese migrants into Vietnam in the past ten years (1996–2006) increased by 33%, while the number of Vietnamese entering China rose by approximately 6%.

Cross-border farming is also popular among Chinese migrants in Vietnam. Chinese migrants lease land to plant cash crops and maintain aquaculture farms in Vietnam, with the produce shipped to China. It is difficult to obtain statistical data on seasonal migration from China to Vietnam, but my research indicates that mainstream media note that traditional, Chinese, small-scale cross-border cultivation can be found in many places in Vietnam. There are also aquaculture farms run by Chinese owners under the names of their Vietnamese wives or relatives along coastal Vietnam.

Chinese migrants offering traditional Chinese medicine and healing services are also very popular in Vietnam. Statistics provided by the Ministry of Health indicate that from 2005 to 2011, the government licensed a total of 168 Chinese clinics for operation in Vietnam. Chinese clinics are now present in 17 provinces and cities with most of them concentrated in Hanoi (52 clinics), Ho Chi Minh City (32 clinics), Can Tho (19 clinics), and Da Nang (13 clinics) (Van Chinh 2013). Among the 684 Chinese staff working at 168 Chinese clinics, we found 158 doctors who graduated from Guangxi Institute of Chinese Traditional Medicine and the College of Vietnam Traditional Medicine. Most Chinese healing practitioners have been working in Vietnam for several years but are still unable to speak Vietnamese and consequently must work through interpreters. Nevertheless, we did not meet professional interpreters in any medical clinic we visited and we more often found Chinese-language college students, or medical staff who could command some Chinese, acting as interpreters. The Chinese practitioners running clinics continually bring in their family members as health care assistants to write out prescriptions or work as bookkeepers.

Data from the Vietnam Chamber of Commerce and Industry show that in 2012 bilateral trade between Vietnam and China amounted to approximately US$30 billion, of which approximately one third (US$10 billion) was border trade. Chinese and Vietnamese petty traders operate through the three main border gates of Mong Cai, Tan Thanh, and Ha Khau, with Chinese merchants having the dominant role. Their presence is widely felt from small villages in the mountains to large cities in the plains (VECITA 2012).

In general, Chinese merchants tend to employ trade strategies for maximum benefit and minimize their tax liability by cooperating with local petty traders to run agencies to collect the goods at the site of manufacturing for further transport to the border gates; paying in advance via intermediary agencies or by investing directly in farming households to manufacture the goods they want to buy to keep the right to trade the products in which they have invested; and setting up agencies to collect products at commercial centers located at either border gates or borderlands and trade those products to China. Based on our observations in the field, by employing those practices, Chinese traders can buy almost all agricultural products available including fruit, coffee, rice, sweet potato, cassava, seafood, rubber, medicinal herbs, etc. They also collect small amounts of iron ore, coal, and various other minerals mined by family-run businesses or private groups, to be shipped to China for a high profit. At border markets, minerals are traded with the same ease that vegetables and other foodstuffs are bought and sold.

Unlike their ancestors, new Chinese migrants to Vietnam do not seem to seek long-term settlement or apply for citizenship. They will prolong their stay if conditions are favorable, but will leave for better possibilities in other places or return home to take advantage of new possibilities on the domestic market in China. As one Chinese petty merchant said to me in Mong Cai trade center during my interviews with him: "Anywhere we can make money so we stay for long. If not, we go home."

As discussed earlier, China is a major provider of concessional loans to Vietnam and has won major construction projects in the Vietnamese EPC sectors. By the end of 2009, Chinese companies were involved in development projects worth US$15.4 billion, making Vietnam their largest EPC market in Southeast Asia. The increase in the number and value of EPC contracts won by Chinese contractors is one of the most crucial factors driving the increasing flow of Chinese contract labor migration into Vietnam (Van Chinh 2014a, b).

Conclusion

How can we explain the new movement of Chinese migrants into the Mekong region and what could be the factors driving and influencing this movement? First, China's political relations with ASEAN in general, and the Mekong countries have improved. Since the 1978 economic reforms, the establishment of diplomatic relations with Thailand, normalization with Vietnam, and strategic partnerships formed with Cambodia, Laos, and Myanmar, China is no longer perceived as a communist threat but instead a friendly neighbor (although China's recent claims in the South China Sea have marred the relationship with Vietnam and with other ASEAN member states [*The Guardian* 2016]). China's economic aid and concessional loans provided to the region, as well as propaganda policies, also contribute to improving the image of China in the eyes of its neighbors.

Second, China's economic interactions with Mekong countries have expanded rapidly. Total bilateral trade increased by more than 20 times in just 20 years. The transportation infrastructure along the Mekong economic corridor between China and the Mekong region has been improved. Inexpensive Chinese-made goods, ranging from large machines to daily necessities, can be easily transported to Mekong countries and the Chinese traders supplying those goods appear to enjoy a degree of popularity among the local people. Small-scale Chinese vendors are spreading into many cities and towns in the CLMV countries.

Third, Chinese migration is closely related to Chinese investment and contract projects. Chinese enterprises prefer to bring technicians and administrative staff, as well as manual labor, from the floating population in the Chinese mainland. That policy helps China to solve the problem of domestic unemployment. Furthermore, construction projects in those countries, contracted by Chinese, depend on Chinese technicians along with skilled and unskilled workers from the Chinese mainland. Chinese migrants in CLMV countries play a prominent role in China's exports, foreign aid, and contract construction projects in the region.

Finally, those countries require coherent national immigration policies that take into consideration their social and economic development needs and interests. To better benefit from foreign workers in the region, and to avoid social problems, that national policy should address issues of the development of human resources, economic competitiveness, demographic transition, and industrial and social development. It is important to obtain accurate estimates of labor and vocational demand from different sectors. New Chinese migration into the Mekong region is linked with China's investments, trade, and economic aid. The migrants are not only motivated by employment and business opportunities but also spurred by, and facilitated by, Chinese government policies. There is currently no mechanism among CLMV countries and China to ensure the legal status and interests of migrant workers. Steps need to be taken to institute an MOU between each country and China on employment issues, and to establish a legal channel of recruitment for migrant workers.

Notes

1. "Floating population" or *liudong renkou* in Chinese, describes a group of people in a given population for a certain period of time and, for various reasons, are not generally considered part of the official census because they no longer reside in the countryside but are not yet city dwellers. See Francesco Sisci and Lu Xiang Sisci, 2003. "China's Achilles' Heel: The 'Floating Population'." *Asia Times*, May 17. http://www.atimes.com/atimes/China/EE17Ad01.html. Up to 2013, the number of floating people in China exceed 160 million. For more details see: Thomas D. Armstrong, 2013. "China's Floating Population." October 12. http://scrir.org/2013/10/chinas-floating-population/.

2. Regulations of the Lao PDR allow Chinese citizens to travel to the northern Lao provinces of Oudomxay, Luang Namtha, Bokeo, and Phongsaly for a period of ten days, extendable by a further ten days. On payment of a US$25 fee, Chinese visitors can extend their stay to a three-month business visa. Alternatively, they can pay a yearly fee of US$300 to obtain a 12-month resident's card for Laos. The cost of a tourist visa is US$20 for 30 days and can be collected on arrival at the international checkpoint of Boten, a Lao town bordering Mohan in China.
3. Reports claimed that casino concessionaires were locking up visitors unable to pay off gambling debts, forcing Chinese officials from Hubei Province to travel to Laos to negotiate the release of those captive nationals ("The Rise, Fall and Possible Renewal of a Town in Laos on China's Border," *The New York Times*, July 6, 2016. http://www.nytimes.com/2016/07/07/world/asia/china-laos-boten-gambling.html?_r=1).
4. The term "Minh Huong" (Ming loyalists) was used to refer to the refugees from the Ming Dynasty after the Qing takeover. Apart from the southern central coast, the Vietnamese Nguyen Dynasty also allowed them to settle in the Mekong Delta.

Bibliography

Armstrong, Thomas D. 2013. "China's Floating Population." *Southern California International Review*, October 12. http://scir.org/2013/10/chinas-floating-population/.

Asian Development Bank. 2010. *GMS Migration Policy Briefing. Extracts from an ABD Project entitled "Forecasting Migration Flows: The Relationships among Economic Development"*. Manila: Demographic Change and Migration in the Greater Mekong Subregion.

Cambodia Daily. 2014. *As Oknha Ranks Grow, Honorific Loses Meaning*. June 21, 2014. https://www.cambodiadaily.com/news/as-oknha-ranks-grow-honorific-losesmeaning-62057/.

Chan, Sambat. 2012. "The Chinese Minority in Cambodia Identity and Contestation." MA thesis, Concordia University.

Chiang, Bien, and Jean Chih-yin Cheng. 2015. "Changing Landscape and Changing Ethnoscape in Lao PDR: On PRC's Participation in the Greater Mekong Subregion." In *Impacts of China's Rise on the Mekong Region*, edited by Yos Santasombat. New York: Palgrave Macmillan.

China's National Development and Reform Commission. 2011. "Country Report on China's Participation in Greater Mekong Subregion Cooperation." *Xinhua*, December 17. http://www.china.org.cn/china/2011-12/17/content241806918.htm.

Chong, Terence. 2013. "Chinese Capital and Immigration into CLMV: Trend and Impact." *ISEAS Perspective*. no. 53.

Evans, G. 2008. "The Southward Drift of the Chinese." Paper presented at the 17th Biennial Conference of the Asian Studies Association of Australia, Melbourne, July 1–3, 2008.

Faming, Manynooch, and Vivien Wee, *New Chinese Immigrants in Laos*. Southeast Asian Research Center, City University of Hong Kong.

General Statistical Office (Tổng cục Thống kê Việt Nam). 1999. *Tổng điều tra dân số và nhà ở 1999* [General Investigation on Population and House (Census) 1999]. Hanoi: Thống kê.

GTZ (Deutsche Gesellschaftfür Technische Zusammenarbeit). 2009. *Foreign Direct Investment (FDI) in Land in the Lao PDR*. Germany: Federal Ministry for Economic Cooperation and Development.

Gunn, Geoffrey, and Brian McCartan. 2008. "Chinese Dams and the Great Mekong Floods of 2008." *Asia Times*, August 22, 2008. https://apjjf.org/-Geoffrey-Gunn/2865/article.html.

Haberecht, Svenja. 2009. "From Rice to Rubber: Development, Transformation, and Foreign Investment in Northern Laos—An Actor-Oriented Approach." Diploma thesis. University of Bielefeld.

Halpern, J. Martin. 1961. *The Role of the Chinese in Lao Society*. Santa Monica: The Rand Corporation.

Hem, Socheth. 2013. *Foreign Investment in Agriculture in Cambodia: A Survey of Recent Trends*. Canada: The International Institute for Sustainable Development.

IHLO (Hong Kong Liaison Office). 2014. *Briefer on Chinese Investments in Myanmar*. http://www.ihlo.org/CINTW/Burma.pdf.

Kenney-Lazar, M. 2012. *Land Concessions, Land Tenure, and Livelihood Change: Plantation Development in Attapeu Province, Southern Laos*. National University of Laos. http://rightslinklao.org/wp-content/uploads/downloads/2014/05/3-Land-Concessions-Land-Tenure-and-Livelihood-Change-Plantation-Development-in-Attapeu-Province-Southern-Laos.pdf.

Jakarta Post. 2016. *Why ASEAN Must Pay More Attention to the Mekong Delta*. Accessed June 10, 2016. http://www.thejakartapost.com/academia/2016/06/10/why-asean-must-pay-moreattention-to-the-mekong-delta.html.

Lazarus, Kate. 2009. *In Search of Aluminium: China's Role in the Mekong Region*. Geneva: Heinrich Bolle Stifling, WWF and International Institute for Sustainable Development.

Le, Hong Hiep. 2009. "The Dominance of Chinese Engineering Contractors in Vietnam." *ISEAS Perspective*, April. Accessed January 17, 2013. http://lehonghiep.net/2013/01/17/the-dominance-of-chinese-engineering-contractors-in-vietnam/.

Lu, Guangsheng. 2012. "Economic Relations between China and GMS Countries: Contents, Characteristics and Implications." The First Thai-Chinese Strategic Seminar. Bangkok.

Lyttleton, C. 2009. *Build It and They Will Come: Lessons from the Northern Economic Corridor for Mitigating HIV and Other Diseases.* Manila: Asian Development Bank.

McCartan, Brian. 2008. "New-Age Chinatown Has Laotians on Edge." *Asia Times,* July 26. http://www.atimes.com/atimes/Southeast_Asia/JG26Ae02.html.

MOLISA (Ministry of Labor, Invalid and Social Affairs) (Bộ Lao động). 2010. "Vấn đề lao động nước ngoài ở Việt Nam trong thời kì hội nhập quốc tế. Dự án Nghiên cứu." [The Question of Foreign Labor in Vietnam in the Period of International Integration: A Research Proposal]. Unpublished report. Hanoi.

New World Encyclopedia. 2003. *Overseas Chinese.* http://www.newworldencyclopedia.org/entry/Overseas_Chinese.

Nguyen, Van Huy. 2016. "Nguoi Hoa tai Viet Nam." *Nghien cuu Lich su,* October 14.

Nyíri Pál. 2013. "New Chinese Immigration and Capital in Cambodia." *ISEAS Perspective* 62: 25.

Rallu, Jean Louis. 2002. "International Migration in South-East Asia: The Role of China." Paper presented at the IUSP Conference on Southeast Asia Population in a Changing Asian Context held at Chulalongkorn University, Bangkok, Thailand, 10–13 June 2002.

Santasombat, Y. (ed.). 2015. *Impact of China's Rise on the Mekong Region.* New York: Palgrave Macmillan.

Shannon, Stephanie, and Nicholas Farrelly. 2014. "Ethnic Chinese in the Midst of Myanmar's Transition." *ISEAS Perspective* 9.

Siphat, Touch. 2015. "Patterns and Impacts of China Assistance." In *Impacts of China's Rise on the Mekong Region,* edited by Yos Santasombat, 195–226. New York: Palgrave Macmillan.

Sisci, Francesco, and Lu Xiang. 2003. "China's Achilles' Heel: The 'floating population'." *Asia Times,* 17 May. http://www.atimes.com/atimes/China/EE17Ad01.html.

Suvakunta, Pittaya. 2007 "China's Go-Out Strategy: Chinese Foreign Direct Investment in Thailand." *Thammasat Review* 12, no. 1, December: 116–145.

SyCip, W. 2001. "The Ethnic Chinese in Southeast Asia—The Past, Present and Future," September 17. http://www.wcec-secretariat.org/en/pdf/06/sycip_w_11.pdf.

Tan, Danielle. 2011. "Du communisme au néolibéralisme. Le rôle des réseaux chinois dans la transformation de l'État au Laos." (Volumes 1–2), Institut d'Études Politiques de Paris.

Tan, Danielle. 2012. "Small Is Beautiful. Lessons from Laos for the Study of Chinese Overseas." *Journal of Current Chinese Affair* 2: 61–94.

Than, M., and Khin Maung Kyi. 1997. "Ethnic Chinese in Myanmar and their Identity." In *Ethnic Chinese as Southeast Asians,* edited by Leo Suryadinata, 115–146. Singapore: Institute of Southeast Asian Studies.

Tran, Khanh. 1994. *The Ethnic Chinese and Economic Development in Vietnam*. Singapore: Institute of Southeast Asian Studies.

The Guardian. 2016. *South China Sea Dispute: What You Need to Know About The Hague Court Ruling*. Accessed September 15, 2016. https://www.theguardian.com/news/2016/jul/12/south-china-sea-dispute-what-you-need-to-know-about-the-hague-court-ruling.

Tun, Khine. 2015. "China-Myanmar: Toward a More Balance and Better Neighborhood." In *Impacts of China's Rise on the Mekong Region*, edited by Yos Santasombat, 167–194. New York: Palgrave Macmillan.

US Energy Information Administration (EIA). 2013. *Chinese Investments Play Large Role in Southeast Asia Hydroelectric Growth*. Accessed August 16, 2015. https://www.eia.gov/todayinenergy/detail.php?id=12571.

Van Chinh, Nguyen. 2013. "Recent Chinese Migration to Vietnam." *Asian and Pacific Migration Journal* 22, no. 1: 7–24.

Van Chinh, Nguyen. 2014a. "Chinese Labour Migration into Vietnam's Engineering, Procurement and Construction Sectors." *ISEAS Perspective* 46.

Van Chinh, Nguyen. 2014b. "Confucius Institutes in the Mekong Region: Soft Power or Soft Border?" *Issues and Studies* 50, no. 4: 85–117.

Van Chinh, Nguyen. 2015. "China's 'Comrade Money' and Its Social-Political Dimensions in Vietnam." In *Impacts of China's Rise on the Mekong Region*, edited by Yos Santasombat, 53–84. New York: Palgrave Macmillan.

VECITA (Vietnam E-commerce and Information Technology Agency). 2012. "Xuất nhập khẩu với Trung Quốc" (Import-Export with China). Accessed December 26, 2013. http://tttm.vecita.gov.vn/default.aspx?layout=body&do=detail&category_id=7&id=101.

Wenbin, Huang, and Andreas Wilkes. 2011. *Analysis of China's Overseas Investments Policies*. Bogo, Indonesia: Center for International Forestry Research (CIFOR), Working Paper 79/9.

World Bank. 2016. Thailand Overview. http://www.worldbank.org/en/country/thailand/overview.

Xerogiani, Theodora. 2006. "Migration Policy and Its Interactions with Aid, Trade and Foreign Direct Investment Policies." OECD Working Paper No. 249.

Xinhua Agency. 2014. "Chinese Investment in Cambodia Up in 2013." *Global Times*, 18 January. http://www.globaltimes.cn/content/838148.shtml#.UuHqNLQRXct.

Zhuang, Guotu, and Wang Wangbo. 2010. "Migration and Trade: The Role of Overseas Chinese in Economic Relations between China and Southeast Asia." *International Journal of China Studies* 1: 174–193.

CHAPTER 10

Floating in the Course of the ASEAN Economic Community and the Rise of China: The Case for Myanmar-Chinese Small and Medium Enterprises

Khine Tun

Introduction

In Myanmar, people of Chinese ancestry are widely believed to be superior to others at doing business. Myanmar citizens of Chinese ancestry (referred to in this chapter as Myanmar-Chinese) are descendants of an old wave of Chinese migrants who left China after the Myanmar colonialism. Additional massive migration occurred during the Sino-Japanese War and the Cultural Revolution in China. Despite arriving with few possessions, their savvy business acumen, similar religious beliefs, and intermarriages helped them integrate, set up businesses, and accumulate wealth. The businesses set up by the newly arrived migrants did not compete but complemented existing ones. Unlike many Myanmar businesses, these businesses were set up for long-term commercialization.

K. Tun (✉)
Asia Development Research Institute (ADRI), Yangon, Myanmar

Y. Santasombat (ed.), *The Sociology of Chinese Capitalism in Southeast Asia*, https://doi.org/10.1007/978-981-13-0065-3_10

The Enterprise Nationalization Law introduced by the military/socialist government in 1963 nationalized the Chinese migrant businesses, many of which had become well established and successful by that time. A brief period following nationalization, hundreds of thousands of Indians and Chinese migrants consequently left the country. The Chinese migrants who stayed were left poor but never gave up doing business. They recognized that it was impossible to have commercial possessions of wealth under a socialist regime. One coping strategy was to not grow small businesses (for example a grocery shop or micro-mart) but separate the businesses and create new venues under the name of other family members, which enabled household accumulation of wealth when the economy was somewhat opened in 1988. Although it was not a full-fledged market economy following the second military coup in 1988, the private sector could participate in a number of business activities and to expand without limitation. That enabled Myanmar-Chinese who had accumulated hidden wealth to combine and establish giant businesses with many different micro-mart branches merging and becoming supermarkets during that period.

Currently, various businesses owned by Myanmar-Chinese are actively competitive in the domestic market. Their influence can be found in all sectors, including construction, manufacturing, services, and trade. In this chapter, the impact and the changing relationships between Myanmar-Chinese businesses and the business networks with mainland China are analyzed within two specific events. The first is Myanmar joining the Association of Southeast Asian Nations (ASEAN) Economic Community (AEC) which brought with it the free flow of goods and services from other ASEAN countries and competition from the comparable exports from other ASEAN countries. Second is the rise of Chinese economic power brought about by the economic and political strategies, such as the New Silk Road and establishment of the Asian Infrastructure Investment Bank (AIIB). This chapter addresses the following research questions:

- How important is the AEC and China to Myanmar?
- How does the relationship with China affect the Myanmar-Chinese small- and medium-sized enterprises (SMEs)?
- What do the Myanmar-Chinese business owners think the possible impacts of the AEC and the rise of China will be on their businesses?
- How are SME owners preparing for those potential impacts?

To answer these questions, literature review, survey, interviews, and case studies are used to examine the impacts of the AEC and China's economic power on various businesses and their coping strategies. Significant limitations to note include the difficulty in selecting pure Myanmar-Chinese businesses for the questionnaire survey, and unwillingness to have their businesses referred to as the local Chinese owned.

Footprints of AEC and China's Economic Power in Myanmar

Myanmar joined ASEAN in July 1997. The idea for greater economic cooperation was initiated in 1992 with the agreement of six members. The idea was then deepened by the ASEAN Vision 2020 aiming at creating a stable, prosperous, and highly competitive market. Various steps were adopted in the Hanoi Plan of Action in 1998 with the purpose of achieving ASEAN Vision 2020 goals. The target date of 2015 for economic integration was brought forward by the 12th ASEAN Summit in 2007. The Summit specified the creation of the ASEAN Community based on three pillars of integration: ASEAN Political-Security Community, AEC, and ASEAN Socio-Cultural Community. The AEC was then officially launched on December 31, 2015.

ASEAN member states were responsible for accomplishing the AEC blueprint by the end of 2015 with full integration by 2018. While Myanmar, Lao People's Democratic Republic, and Cambodia were given three additional years of preparation to fully join the AEC, Myanmar still had to implement a number of reforms including liberalization and facilitation for trade, investment, and services in line with ASEAN standards. Economic integration is, at least theoretically, expected to increase economic welfare of member countries but the actual impacts of integration are more complicated.

Myanmar has not been able to achieve all the initiatives stipulated under AEC pillar one (i.e. free flow of goods, free flow of investment, and free flow of skilled labor). According to the ASEAN Trade in Goods Agreement, member countries must remove both tariff and non-tariff barriers within a designated timeline.

Immediate impacts of the AEC are expected from the free flow of goods, investment, and skilled-labor creating a single market and production base. Myanmar will not benefit from the free flow of goods and free flow of skilled labor because it is a net importer of merchandise trade with a shortage of qualified human resources. However, the country will benefit from a free flow of investments because Myanmar is viewed as the last resort for investment in the region (Khine 2008). See Fig. 10.1 for trade and investment flow over the past five years.

The authorities have conducted a series of public consultations on integration into the AEC. The private sector requested to put full integration on hold because of Myanmar's weak infrastructure, persistent corruption, and unskilled labor. Local industries were evaluated and were found to require additional time to effectively deal with challenges from the free flow of goods and skilled labor that will accompany integration.

As an extension of the AEC, the ASEAN–China Free Trade Area was agreed to on November 4, 2002 to establish a free trade area by 2010. Accordingly, both sides have dramatically reduced tariffs on imported goods, and the average tariff rate on imports from ASEAN to China decreased from 9.8 to 0.1%, while the average tariff rate on Chinese goods sold in ASEAN countries decreased from 12.8 to 0.6% starting on the first day of 2010.

Although there is an Agreement on Trade in Goods of the Framework Agreement on Comprehensive Economic Cooperation between China and ASEAN, China has a bilateral agreement of tariff reduction with individual ASEAN members. In the bilateral tariff reduction lists, Myanmar offers 16,757 items, while China offers 6654 items to reduce tariffs on imports. Because Myanmar is importing a wide range of Chinese products, Myanmar's tariff reduction covers many goods made in China. However, as Myanmar's export items to China are limited, China can avoid offering tariff reduction for major imports from

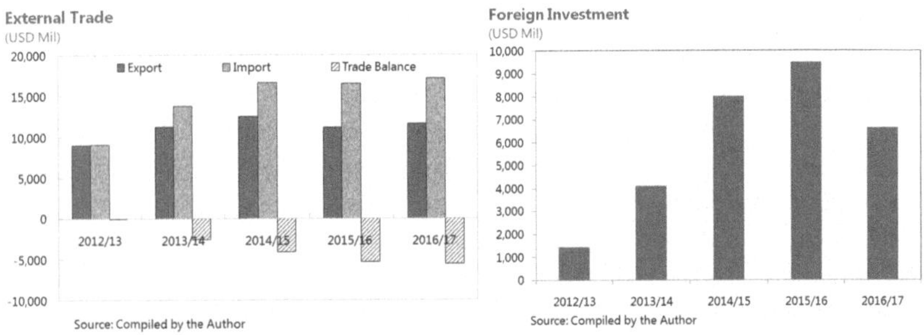

Fig. 10.1 International trade and foreign investment in Myanmar

Myanmar. For example, Myanmar's main export items to China such as jade, rice, and fishing products are not included in China's offered tariff reduction items, and are levied at 30, 10, and 20%, respectively. Therefore, the free trade agreement between ASEAN and China as an extension of the AEC is not beneficial to the SMEs that account for approximately 98% of business establishments in Myanmar.

China's Economic Power Expansion

China is the second largest economy in the world by gross domestic product, and according to International Monetary Fund data, has one of the highest global foreign exchange reserves. Along with rapid economic growth, China has also tried to export its investments to keep from economic overheating. Due to rising domestic labor costs, China's labor-intensive industries have been relocated to less developed countries. China has also become a creditor and source of official development assistance for developing economies in Asian and African regions. Furthermore, the creation of a new Silk Road, One Belt One Road (OBOR), and the establishment of the AIIB seem to be key strategies in China's power expansion in the region.

The original Silk Road is an extensive transcontinental inland network with several routes and contributed to China becoming a leader in trade with the Middle East, Asia, Europe, and Africa from 206 BC to 220 AD. With the advent of sea routes and maritime trade, the route became obsolete over time. The new Silk Road's purpose would go beyond just trade to include securing its trade routes from the threat of its rival, the USA, via allies including Japan and Korea. The inland route would not necessarily replace sea routes for China but would strengthen them and reduce China's dependency on maritime trade, particularly imports of energy products. The road would also reduce the numerous risks associated with sea trade, including piracy. Other purposes include:

(1) Facilitating access to neighboring countries with lower labor costs-many of which are easier to access via land route. Furthermore, China needs to seek new energy sources and raw material to sustain its domestic consumption and production requirements. Easy access to resource-rich neighboring countries will help fulfill China's thirst for energy and industrial raw materials.

(2) Focusing more on the emerging markets of the region. China's economy is currently in a decreasing trend and require readjustment. The cooling US economy and instability of European countries means China needs to start focusing more on emerging markets in the region. Asia and the Pacific is expected to be a leading economy in the future. ASEAN alone comprises 633 million people creating a huge market compared with Europe's population of 510 million.
(3) Balancing development in all regions and potentially reducing social tensions. Sea trade has increased inequality because it has mainly benefited coastal regions. Improved transportation networks could therefore aid in the development of a greater number of regions improving economic disparity.

Given the backdrop of China's power expansion, Myanmar will be an important part of the success of China's OBOR initiative. The link from Kunming, China to Kyaukphyu, Myanmar will minimize China's dependency on sea routes for energy imports for which about 70% pass through the Malacca Strait. Currently, crude oil from the Middle East and natural gas from Myanmar are beginning to be imported via the China–Myanmar oil and gas pipelines. The ongoing Dawei deep seaport and special economic zone projects will also support China's access to the Bay of Bengal via cross border road networks into Laos and Thailand. Additionally, the India–Myanmar–Thailand trilateral highway is a bonus for China's OBOR initiative which aims at connecting across Asia, Africa, and Europe. However, the question is to what extent Myanmar, and particularly SMEs, will be able to take advantage of the opportunities of OBOR.

Another Chinese project that will enhance China's power in the region is the AIIB, made known to Asian countries in October 2013. The memorandum of understanding was signed by 22 countries in October 2014 and agreed to locate the headquarters in Beijing. By the end of 2015 the number of prospected founding members increased to 57, and 13 more countries became members in 2017. The AIIB will therefore undoubtedly increase China's political and economic power in the region and beyond.

Myanmar joined the AIIB by signing the Article of Association on June 29, 2015 and ratified it two days later. Myanmar authorities are positive about the prospects of the AIIB and hope for rapid development of the country's poor infrastructure. The incoming loans from the AIIB and its associated infrastructure projects are expected to benefit Myanmar SMEs because improved infrastructure can support SMEs to form industrial clusters, to enhance capacity for subcontract from large firms, to establish corporate networks, and to introduce value chain to access international market.

However, the evidence currently shows that will not be the case. For example, Myanmar's first loan from AIIB of US$20 million for the country's energy project will be contracted out to the Singapore-based Sembcorp Industries. No local SME will therefore benefit from the AIIB loan.

China's Influence on the Myanmar Economy and General Impacts on SMEs

China's influence on the Myanmar economy stems back to the strong political ties of the two countries forged since Myanmar's 1988 military coup. Following the coup, many Western countries scaled back political relationships and imposed a series of economic sanctions. Myanmar's neighbors, India and Thailand, accepted the settlement of exiles and anti-government groups who had taken an active role during the 1988 uprising against the military. China became Myanmar's primary strategic partner. Chinese representatives were honored by military leaders who referred to them as "*Swe Myoe Pauk Phaw*" or "relative and sibling".

Trade between Myanmar and China was promoted by the People's Republic of China socialist government. In 1988, Myanmar initiated negotiations with Yunnan's authorities and in December signed the Agreement for Sale and Purchase of Goods between Myanmar Export Import Corporation and Yunnan Provincial Import Export Corporation. By opening border trade, the government began to liberalize the private sector to be able to engage in external trade previously monopolized by the state sector. China has since become Myanmar's largest trading partner with trade increasing to approximately 40% by 2015 (Fig. 10.2).

Myanmar is dependent on natural resource-based products for most of their exports. Imports are primarily substandard, single-use, and unsafe consumer goods. Trade with China is largely driven for the benefit of government foreign exchange with the export of natural resources under state-owned projects being replaced by consumer and household products. SMEs engage in direct border trade, sometimes undermining

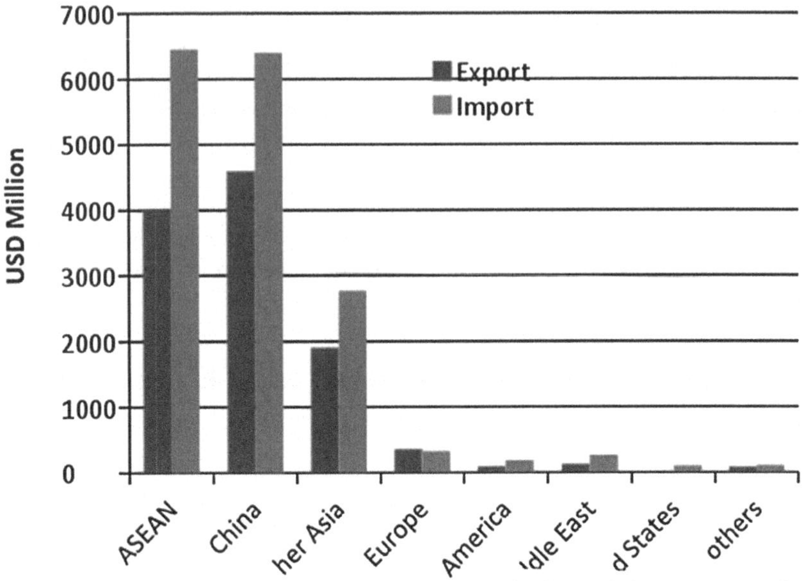

Source: compiled by the author based on trade data of the Ministry of Commerce

Fig. 10.2 Myanmar's external trade with respective trading partners in the fiscal year 2015–2016

small manufacturers who cannot compete with the price of imported goods from China (Tatlow 1999).

One of the first moves by the military government was the enactment of the Foreign Investment Law in December 1988. However, there were only a limited number of investors who responded to the government's invitation, most of which came from Asia and a few from Europe. China's investment was negligible until 2007 with a share of about 5% of total investment being approved. China's foreign direct investment (FDI) doubled to 10% with the state-owned enterprise (SOE) joint venture to build the Shweli Hydropower project on the border with Yunnan. In 2012, the approval of the construction of Myitsone hydropower dam project in the Kyaukphyu deep seaport included the development of an oil and gas dual pipeline and the transfer of the Letpadaung copper mine project from the Canadian mining company Ivanhoe to the Chinese company Wanbao. That investment increased the FDI share

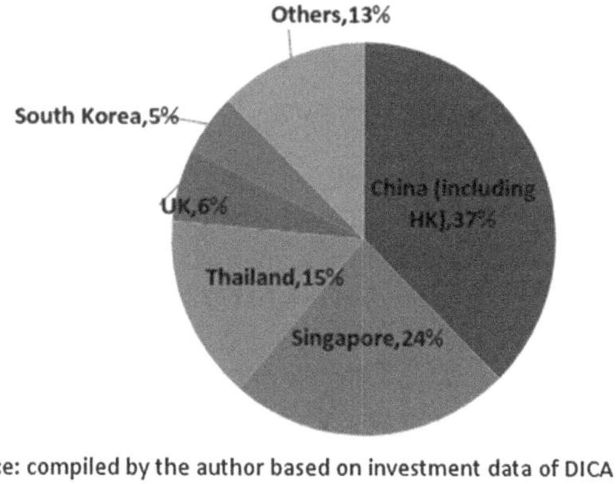

Fig. 10.3 Foreign direct investment in Myanmar as of March 2017 (*Source* Myanmar's Directorate of Investment and Company Administration (DICA))

of Chinese investment to almost 50% of total foreign investment in Myanmar, according to data released by the Directorate of Investment and Company Administration (DICA). In subsequent years, Myanmar's transition to civilian government administration led to an easing of economic sanctions by many Western countries. While that led to more FDI in Myanmar, China remains the largest trade partner maintaining a 40% share of FDI (DICA). See Fig. 10.3.

Foreign investments can be beneficial to recipient countries in terms of growth, productivity, job creation, and technology transfer, provided the investments flow into the proper sectors. Local SMEs can benefit through domestic infrastructure and trade. Unfortunately, the benefit to local SMEs and the public is rare because Chinese investments are concentrated in SOE resource extraction or resource-based production. For example, the Shweli Hydropower project is a joint venture with the Myanmar Electric Power Enterprise and the Letpadaung Copper Mine project with the Union of Myanmar Economic Holding. Subcontracts or any outsourcing to Myanmar SMEs were not observed. The only private sector involvement in those hydropower projects is the Asia World Group, one of the largest conglomerates in Myanmar, founded by an ethnic Kokang Chinese businessman.

Another important economic affiliation with China has been through foreign loans. Termination or postponement of loans by both bilateral sources and multilateral institutions during the time of the military government made China the major source of loans for Myanmar. By 2005, China had provided Myanmar with over US$400 million in aid and US$1 billion in loans through the Exim Bank of China (Reeves 2016). China continued to provide loans to the civilian government even following the transition from the military administration. China's Exim Bank offered a US$600 million loan at 4.5% interest in 2013, and another US$3 billion loan to construct a highway connecting Kyaukphyu (where China–Myanmar oil and gas pipeline starts) with Ruili of Yunnan Province. Another US$600 million in loans for the Yunnan–Kyaukphyu highway was not approved. By December 2015, total loans owed to China reached US$4.3 billion, equivalent to 47% of Myanmar's total external debt. Because the private sector has been restricted access to foreign loans until 2013, almost all loans received were to the government sector. See Fig. 10.4.

Most loans were obtained to finance infrastructure projects implemented by either government enterprises or large-scale private companies like Asia World Group. Some loans were for financing establishments or expansion of SOEs and associated with the purchase of Chinese machines or products. Occasionally, SMEs do benefit from those loans. For example, Exim Bank's loan to the (former) Ministry of Cooperatives benefited local farmers and SMEs and members of cooperative societies including farmers.

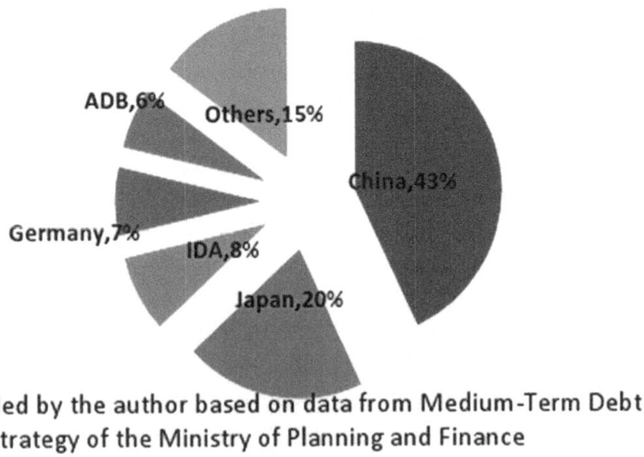

Fig. 10.4 Foreign loans to Myanmar as of November 2016

Chinese influence on the Myanmar economy in the form of trade, investment, and financing has been significant and its impact on the country's SMEs has varied. Trade agreements and FDI have contributed to trading businesses but have been harmful to small manufacturing businesses. Investments from China have not benefited the various types of SMEs because Chinese investment is mainly focused on resource extraction and not on the production process of raw resources. Financing through loans and aid has also not had significant effect on SMEs because only minor portions of those loans have been allocated to a select few, namely members of cooperatives.

Business Channels Between Mainland Chinese and Myanmar-Chinese

The transactions between mainland Chinese businesses and Myanmar-Chinese SMEs are difficult to track. Whereas FDI and large business transactions are more transparent and tracked by government agencies, there is little data available about the transactions between small business and SMEs. The private sector, such as SMEs in the Myanmar economy, have unrecorded or underrecorded numbers so that the extent of their business activities, trade, and investments are not known. To shed some light on the nature and extent of those transactions, key informant interviews in Yangon and Mandalay provide qualitative data about the micro-level relationship with China.

Many of the Myanmar-Chinese in Yangon are descendants of Cantonese and Hokkien migrants from Guangdong and Fujian province. There have been many clan associations and respective temples established to serve the social and cultural needs of families. Temple committees organize traditional events such as Lunar New Year, Hungry Ghost Festival, Birthday of Guan Yin, etc. Some temples provide training courses for younger generations on Chinese language and culture including lion dancing and dragon dancing. The temples in Yangon are financially supported by donations from members and businesses of their respective clans. Some associations and temples have accumulated relatively substantial amounts of funds but those funds are kept in banks as savings. Associations and temples in Yangon generally avoid getting involved in business or commercial activities.

A member of the trusteeship of the Leong Sun Tong Society clarified that the society was originally founded and established in Yangon prior to the year 1875 by the early Chinese settlers of the *Khoo* and *Chan* clans who came to Myanmar from the four villages of Chanya, Hawwa, Napoonkhen, and Sinwa of Fujian province. Although the names of *Chan* and *Khoo* are different, they are from the same ancestry. The trust was founded for religious and charitable purposes, including encouraging educational studies by paying school fees, scholarships, and prizes, starting educational institutions, and donations or financial aid for funeral expenses, poor widows, and aged and poor members.

However, interviews with business owners and temple trustees indicate that those businesses in Yangon do not seem to have many commercial ties with China. However, in-kind support, such as consignment deals and credit sales are done on consignment. Informal wholesale dealers of Chinese products, including fashion clothing, a variety of bags, fancy goods, and sportwear—that did not pass import quality control—are sold in Myanmar at discounted prices. Those rejected products are then traded to neighboring countries.

The situation is different in the northern town of Mandalay. Most of the Myanmar-Chinese originate from Yunnan province with a few from Fujian and Kokang. With diverse clan associations, the Myanmar Mandalay Chinese Yunnan Association is the most dominant in Mandalay City. There are a number of small temples throughout the city but they are very small compared with the Yunnanese Buddhist Temple established by the Association. Myanmar-Chinese in Mandalay are more active than those in Yangon. They organize regular events, meetings, and gatherings in their respective temples. Clan associations in Mandalay are reported to play a significant role in business among local businesses as well as with trade in China.

Associations are used to create funds by businessmen. The temple association acts as a guarantee for loans disbursed to members to start or expand their small businesses. Those loans are offered at a higher interest rate than in China. The bank interest rate in China averages 5% whereas in Myanmar it is 13%, but those informal association loans can be as high as 36% interest.

There are a few notable cases where some Chinese associations are acting as financial intermediaries between exporters from Mandalay and importers from Yunnan province. Goods that are not allowed for trade in the formal market, such as rice, are traded cross-border. Bank transfers cannot be used therefore agents travel across the border to conduct financial transactions. The associations sometimes accommodate those transactions. An example of that is wax import. Myanmar imports wax from China as the raw materials for candle production. Wax exporters from China provide credit to Myanmar-Chinese wax importers at the amount guaranteed by the designated association. The Myanmar-Chinese importers must settle their credit either with the association or Chinese exporters.

In conclusion, the interviews revealed that the business channels between China and Myanmar-Chinese in Yangon are different than those in Mandalay and is a result of several various factors including proximity to the border, origins of migration, timing of migration, intention of temple trusteeship, and interconnection of each clan. Some similarities did emerge between the two societies. For example, in both cases temples and clan associations are important and respectable for each society but they play varying roles. It can be concluded that the associations in Mandalay are used for business, trade, and finance more than they are in Yangon.

Impacts of AEC and China's Rise on Myanmar-Chinese SMEs

The AEC was to be fully implemented by the end of 2015. However, the countries grouped as CLMV (Cambodia, Laos, Myanmar, and Vietnam) were given an extension for full implementation until 2018. It is therefore too early to assess the impact of the AEC in Myanmar. Whereas the rise of China in the form of formal and informal trade, investment, and development assistance can be evaluated, it is too soon to make an accurate assessment regarding the impact of the recent centralization of China, the development of the new Silk Road initiative, and the establishment of the AIIB.

Surveys provide some indication of perspectives and expectations from SME owner predictions for Myanmar joining the AEC, the AIIB, and China's OBOR. Surveys were conducted in Yangon and Mandalay but barriers limited the number of respondents. Limitations included resistance of firms to participate, identifying Myanmar-Chinese businesses, and reluctance to respond to questions. A total of 31 firms (17 from Yangon and 14 from Mandalay) responded to the survey. About 50% (14 out of 31 firms) were Myanmar-Chinese SMEs. The surveys did not ask for identifiers, and sampling was based on the type of business and location.

According to the 1990 Industry Law, a firm is a small enterprise if it employs 10–50 employees, while it is a medium enterprise if it employees 51–100 employees, and it is a large enterprise if it employs more than 100 employees. Included in the survey are two manufacturing firms with over 100 (but less than 300) employees. Out of 31 respondents, ten firms were in the production industry, seven in the service industry, and 14 in the trading sector including retail sales. More firms from manufacturing and trading sectors were selected because the service sector is impacted less by the AEC and China's rise.

Apart from one of the service firms, all other firms said they knew about the AEC and that Myanmar is to allow free flow of goods and services. The owner of the service firm that responded "No" said he had seen the word AEC in newspapers and journals but he did not try to fully understand what the AEC meant for his business. Although a high percentage of respondents (96.8%) answered "Yes", some firm owners, especially from Mandalay, needed hints to jog their memory on the subject. Various government departments have been educating people about the AEC through state-run newspapers and ministerial websites, but most of respondents said they learned about the AEC mostly from private-owned journals, private sector seminars, and Facebook. Out of 31 respondents, one manufacturing firm (candle production), five service firms (two air-con services, two mobile phone services, and one auto workshop), and three trading businesses (rice exporter, jiggery trading, and cloth shop) replied that they did not recognize any impact of the AEC on their business. However, another two rice exporters said that they anticipate impact of the AEC.

Most of the respondents have an optimistic perception about the AEC affecting the acquiring of raw materials (55% of respondents), operating business (50%), marketing their products (50%), financing for their business (77%), and importing (59%). Only 36% of firms think that increased competition from neighboring countries will have a negative impact. Most respondents perceive no impact in acquiring technology (82%), acquiring technicians (55%), acquiring general labor (73%), and exporting (59%).

Many of the businesses that are engaged in export, import, or local markets responded that they must rely on the import of finished goods, raw materials, or equipment. For example, if exporting rice then they import fumigation pills, moisture equipment, and color-sorting machines. Those businesses welcome the AEC which will provide easier access to raw materials and equipment as well as finance. On the other hand, other industries such as slipper manufacturing, are concerned about the impact on access to raw materials (rubber) if the AEC opens rubber exports leading to scarcity in the domestic market. Table 10.1 shows the average scores of the respondents.

While most firms (55%) have a positive view of acquiring raw materials after the AEC, many of them are getting ready to seek new more

Table 10.1 Respondent scores on perception of the Association of Southeast Asian Nations Economic Community impact to business

	Lowest	*Low*	*Medium*	*High*	*Highest*	*Total scores*
1. Find new raw material suppliers	1	2	3	4	5	81
2. Study the requirement of new markets	1	2	3	4	5	20
3. Study the probability to move business base	1	2	3	4	5	64
4. Improve the logistics system	1	2	3	4	5	18
5. Improve competitiveness in new markets	1	2	3	4	5	33
6. Study the new business competitors	1	2	3	4	5	48
7. Improve the manufacturing processes	1	2	3	4	5	22
8. Increase business strength and reduce weaknesses	1	2	3	4	5	33
9. Improve customers' loyalty	1	2	3	4	5	37
10. Generate skilled workers' loyalty	1	2	3	4	5	97
11. Create partnership with other countries	1	2	3	4	5	13
12. Increase salary and wages to protect worker move out	1	2	3	4	5	99
13. Improve workers' skills	1	2	3	4	5	66
14. Develop an operating system	1	2	3	4	5	77

If you answered "Yes" to question 7, in what areas have you seen the biggest effect? (you can tick more than one)

a. Migration by Chinese people [28/31]
b. Investments by Chinese people [24/31]
c. Investments by the Chinese government [20/31]
c. Financing by Chinese people [2/31]
d. Financing by the Chinese government [2/31]
d. Imports from China [31/31]
e. Exports to China [31/31]
f. Other(s) please specify [1/31]

affordable suppliers. On the other hand, a high total score indicates readiness to generate laborers loyalty, many firms plan to increase salary and wage. At the same time, improving workers' skills is also a factor of consideration of the firms to be able to employ skilled labor in response to anticipated competition resulting from AEC.

Awareness and Preparation Over the Rise of China

Those interviewed consider China's influence on the market as much more severe than the impact of AEC. All 31 survey respondents admitted that they recognize the influence of China on the economy while only 50% (16:15) said that China directly effects their business. While they are being informed about the AEC mostly by state-run media, the influence of China, Chinese people, Chinese investment, and Made-in-China products is covered by private media and social networks. Almost all have had to engage with China or Chinese products in one way or another (Table 10.2).

Most respondents believe that a positive impact brought about by China's rise will be on acquiring raw materials (75%), followed by operating business (60%), exporting (69%), and importing (63%). For example, the improvement of China's oil refinery industry could produce petroleum wax which is an essential raw material for Myanmar's candle production firms. Similarly, China's trade liberalization contributes to the ease of export and import activities with China. On the other hand, negative impacts were believed to be rising competition (78%) and difficulty finding

Table 10.2 Perception of China's impact on business

	Positive (%)	*Negative (%)*	*Neither (%)*	*Total (%)*
a. Acquiring raw materials (such as wax for candle production)	75	25	0	100
b. Operating business	60	40	0	100
c. Marketing your products	30	30	40	100
d. Financing for your business	0	0	100	100
e. Competition	22	78	0	100
f. Acquiring technology	0	0	100	100
g. Acquiring technicians	16	0	84	100
h. Acquiring general labor	10	80	10	100
i. Exporting	69	31	0	100
j. Importing	63	37	0	100

labor (80%). All participants stated that there is no effect on financing to their business and acquiring technology from the rise of China.

All firms are aware of China's influence on exports and imports, while 90% of firms and 77% firms recognize Chinese migration and investments. Although the Chinese government has made large-scale project investments in Myanmar, about 65% of respondents recognized that Chinese were involved in the state-owned investments. Regarding financing from China, only 6% could identify the source of people and government. An area of influence, other than those in the survey, was cited as human trafficking, especially of the practice of seeking brides or forced marriages. Brokers persuaded Myanmar women to find jobs with good income in China but then sold them to Chinese men who wanted brides.

Respondents were asked to state their level of preparedness for the rise of China. SMEs felt most prepared to improve customer loyalty and generating skilled labor. They do not feel prepared to build partnerships (Table 10.3).

Table 10.3 Preparedness for the rise of China

	Lowest	*Low*	*Medium*	*High*	*Highest*	*Total scores*
1. Find new raw material suppliers	1	2	3	4	5	67
2. Study the requirement of new markets	1	2	3	4	5	51
3. Study the probability of moving the business base	1	2	3	4	5	50
4. Improve the logistics system	1	2	3	4	5	61
5. Improve competitiveness in new markets	1	2	3	4	5	67
6. Study new business competitors	1	2	3	4	5	62
7. Improve the manufacturing processes	1	2	3	4	5	52
8. Increase business strength and reduce weaknesses	1	2	3	4	5	63
9. Improve customers' loyalty	1	2	3	4	5	74
10. Generate skilled workers' loyalty	1	2	3	4	5	72
11. Create partnerships with other countries	1	2	3	4	5	45
12. Increase salary and wages to protect worker move out	1	2	3	4	5	57
13. Improve workers' skills	1	2	3	4	5	52
14. Develop an operating system	1	2	3	4	5	48

In conclusion, the survey indicates that SME business owners perceive both positive and negative impacts with implementation of AEC and the rise of China. Most of the respondents have a positive perception and many anticipate easier access to acquiring materials, financing, operations, and trade. The negative perception is related to competition and acquiring domestic labor.

The next section presents two case studies to demonstrate the impacts of AEC and China. The first case study is of an export business while the second is active in the domestic market.

Case Study 1: Export-Oriented Myanmar-Chinese SME

The first case study is about a medium-sized garment factory located in Yangon that employs about 300 employees. The owner is a fifth-generation migrant Chinese. His parents own a traditional weaving business in a small town located in upper Myanmar. After his graduation in 1994, his parents wanted him to move to Japan or to America where their relatives live and work. Per his parents' wish he attended an English four-skill teaching course where he met a senior graduate working in a Korean garment factory. He worked as a part-time auditor at the Korean garment factory to learn and study the business. Realizing that was a profitable business for earning foreign currency, he decided not to go abroad but instead opened a garment factory in Myanmar.

With financial support from his parents, in 1996 he rented an empty warehouse building in a government compound in Yangon. That was an optimum time to start a garment company in Myanmar because garment factories in middle-income countries such as Malaysia were scaling down their businesses because of the rising cost of labor, and second-hand sewing machines were imported into Myanmar and available to buy on credit. One of his friends helped him acquire garment technicians to start operations. It was a booming period for the Myanmar garment industry from 1996 to 2000, and he enjoyed high rates of return which allowed him to establish a larger-sized business on his own land in an industrial zone.

The business was going well until the US economic sanction of 2003. The sanctions froze all financial transactions with Myanmar and blocked import of all products made in Myanmar. Accordingly, international buyers of Myanmar garments massively reduced their orders. To keep the business going and get around the sanctions, he changed the country of origin on the garments labels. He did not have any direct contact with Chinese buyers from China, however, another large garment factory that arranged order processing was owned by a Myanmar-Chinese and believed to be backed by Chinese investment. Even though that large garment factory owner was also Myanmar-Chinese, it did not favor his business relationship with them. He had to attach the Made in China labels on items but on container boxes the garments were described as Made in Myanmar. As transaction costs increased, order prices and his income dropped, by as much as about half from the time of the garment booming period. He tried to obtain direct buyers from China and Japan but it was very costly so he had to continue to rely on Chinese-backed companies as intermediaries.

The business environment improved after the transition from military rule to civil government in 2011. The US and the European Union (EU) countries began to relax their sanctions and showed eagerness to open trade and investment channels with Myanmar. The business owner in the case study was especially optimistic about the EU's promise to restore the Generalized System of Preferences status for Myanmar imports, which favors imported products by lowering tariffs. In practice, however, business did not become that much easier. Development partners, investors, donors, and tourists pushed up general prices and living costs, including the price of land and labor which also made the investment environment more competitive. Foreign investors opened new garment factories—or expanded existing ones-partnering with local businesses which put competitive pressure on available labor.

In response to the new labor market, the business owner brought in employees from rural areas and provided in-house training. Training can add up to six months with costs in addition to monthly wages. Maintaining staff is a challenge because the larger garment factories recruit employees after they are trained, offering higher wages and better facilities. Laborers often prefer the larger factories, even if the wages are the same.

Although the business owner in this case study has not felt direct impact from AEC, he has heard that it will result in increased competition due to the free flow of goods. He stated that, "so far, I have felt no significant impact from the AEC on my business but have felt the compound effects of globalization, Myanmar's openness to FDI, and the interest of international investors. It is now difficult to hire skilled people at a low cost and this is the result of the compound effect, but not only of the AEC" (Interview, 2017). When discussing the impact of China in Myanmar, he reflects that:

> There are both positive and negative impacts of Chinese investments in the garment sector on my business. As they have direct contact with overseas buyers, smaller garment factories like mine can enjoy spillover of garment orders. Another advantage of Chinese garment orders is that they do not care much about quality control while Japanese garment orders are very sensitive about the quality of both process and output. The negative impact is labor recruitment and sustainability has become more challenging because Chinese garment factories usually take trained workers from me.

He recognized that there are rumors of increased competition because of Chinese products in local markets and illegal migration, but did not feel the impact directly on his business. He was not aware of the OBOR or AIIB. However, he had heard that Chinese garment factories in Myanmar are operating with loans from Chinese banks with lower interest rates and better terms. He observed that, "We have to rely on local bank loans which charge high interest rates and short loan terms. If we could get a loan from AIIB, it would be great for us."

In an interview with a different SME garment factory owner in Yangon, the greatest perceived impact of the AEC and China will be on the labor market. Although industries will be affected differently, those that are export-oriented seem less vulnerable to the change. One example is a small cutting, making, and packaging export firm that will not compete with imported products but is concerned that with the opening of new factories, labor will be in high demand without enough supply and it will be harder to retain current employees. He sees that the AEC will open ASEAN countries for Myanmar exports, possibly becoming a main destination for the garment industry.

Case Study 2: Domestic-Oriented Myanmar-Chinese SME

This case study is of a sweater-knitting manufacturer, established more than 35 years ago. It is one of over 50 knitting firms in a hill town called Pyin Oo Lwin located on the China–Myanmar highway trade route and about 42 miles from Mandalay City. The owner of the firm, a Myanmar-Chinese, is originally from Lasho Township who moved to Pyin Oo Lwin to establish this family business. Initially it was a retail clothing shop selling various types of ready-made dresses. As Pyin Oo Lwin is located in the mountain range and the weather is cold, warm clothing like winter coats were in high demand.

The family decided to start a knitting business to produce wool sweaters. They hired ten knitters, including family members. From 1990 to 2010 it was a golden age for wool sweaters from Maymyo (now Pyin Oo Lwin). The company grew to 30 non-family member employees. They introduced rabbit fur in addition to wool, both of which were bought from a wholesaler in Yangon. During that time the business changed production from hand-made to machine-based production, increasing production to up to ten pieces a day (versus 10–20 days to hand make one sweater). The company had to hire a technician and machinist to supervise the process and fix machines. With the introduction of computerized machines, designs are changed quickly to respond to trends, however, those machines are expensive and require back-up generators.

In 2010, the industry was impacted with a rapid inflow of Chinese-made sweaters entering the Myanmar market. Less expensive, modern-design sweaters took over the market, causing local production to decrease significantly. Currently, an estimated 70% of the domestic market for sweaters is supplied by China. Myanmar producers rely on imported raw materials—yarn from China and rabbit fur from Thailand—driving up the price. Regardless, some customers still prefer the locally made sweaters saying that they are better quality. It is currently difficult to find employees who will create hand-made sweaters.

The interviewee said that she is concerned that locally produced sweaters will be losing the entire market within 5–10 years if local entrepreneurs are unable to meet customers' preferences or compete with the price of Chinese goods. She has diversified her business to now include a travel agency responding to the new popularity of Pyin Oo Lwin as a destination for Chinese tourists crossing at the nearby land border points.

These two case studies represent different experiences with the rise of China and anticipated introduction of AEC. Export businesses are less impacted but are concerned about the labor supply. Domestic market businesses are threatened by the increased market share taken by less expensive products imported from China.

Conclusion

Myanmar's economic relationship with ASEAN countries is based on multilateral trade agreements and integration, whereas the relationship with China is driven by preferential trade, institutional finance, and regional expansion policies including the OBOR and establishment of the AIIB. Both will have a significant impact on Myanmar's economy.

China remains Myanmar's largest trading partner. The impact—both positive and negative—on SMEs is variable due to exclusion from China's trade agreements and finance opportunities. On the other hand, the AEC can impact SMEs by opening export markets for Myanmar-made goods and increasing business opportunities, albeit there is an impact on labor supply because of increased competition for small manufacturing businesses. China is the largest source of FDI in Myanmar and China investment is directed to large-scale state-owned projects effectively excluding SMEs from investment opportunities other than a few loan opportunities through SME cooperatives.

Direct financial support to Chinese-Myanmar businesses differs between Yangon and the northern town of Mandalay. Temple associations play an integral role in the cultural and educational societies of both cities, but they also play an informal financing role in Mandalay. The associations thereby have more influence and prominence in Mandalay, when compared with Yangon.

A perception survey and interviews of business owners in the two cities provides some insight into the perceived impacts of the AEC and rise of China. SMEs have varying responses based somewhat on the industry they are in. Those in manufacturing for export are less impacted than those in the domestic market seeing competition from Chinese imports. Those reliant on import of raw materials see benefit from AEC to improve access, operations, quality, and financing for goods manufactured in Myanmar. Whereas with the allowance of businesses and investments from China and ASEAN, there is pressure on the labor market with the demand exceeding the supply of skilled workers. The SMEs interviewed provided some coping strategies that include identifying new suppliers, increasing labor payments to retain skilled laborers, developing modern operating systems, and building customer loyalty.

The two case studies presented provide insight into coping mechanisms among SME owners in response to both AEC and the rise of China because both have experienced an impact on labor and supply because of competition from larger factories and imported goods. One business diversified to respond to a growing tourism market.

In conclusion, the AEC and the rise of China both have an impact on SMEs in Myanmar. Theoretically, that economic integration should benefit all participating countries. In practice, however, Myanmar is challenged with integration that will benefit all people, including those in small businesses who are affected by increased competition and have limited access to capital investments and technology.

Bibliography

ASEAN Secretariat. 2008. *ASEAN Economic Community Blueprint*. Indonesia: ASEAN Secretariat.

Central Statistical Organization. 2012. *Statistical Yearbook 2010*. Nay Pyi Taw: Ministry of National Planning and Economic Development.

Central Statistical Organization. 2016. *Statistical Yearbook 2015*. Nay Pyi Taw: Ministry of Planning and Finance.

Central Statistical Organization. 2017. *Statistical Yearbook 2016*. Nay Pyi Taw: Ministry of Planning and Finance.

Economic Research Institute for ASEAN and East Asia. 2012. *Mid-Term Review of the Implementation of AEC Blue Print*. Jakarta: ERIA.

Ei Moet Moet Khaing. 2016. "Firms in Mandalay Industrial Zone Begin to Fall." *Modern News Journal* 11, no. 50, December: 11 (in Myanmar Language).

Government of Myanmar. 2015. *The Small and Medium Enterprises Development Law*, April 9, 2015.

Htwe, Khin Maung, Win Win Maw, and Myat Sandy. 2017. "Interview with Chinese Ambassador to Myanmar." *Myanma Alinn*, February 5, 2017. Yangon, Myanmar, 21–22 (in Myanmar Language).

Ito, Takatoshi. 2015. "The Future of the Asian Infrastructure Investment Bank: Concerns for Transparency and Governance." Occasional Paper Series No. 75, Center on Japanese Economy and Business. Columbia: Columbia University Press.

Khine, Thandar. 2008. "Foreign Direct Investment Relation between Myanmar and ASEAN." IDE Discussion Paper No. 149.

Myanmar News Agency. 2016. "Myanmar Will Cooperate with ASEAN Members and China to Accelerate Cooperation in Multi Sectors." *Myanma Alinn*, September 12, 2016. Yangon, Myanmar (in Myanmar Language).

Myanmar Marketing Research and Development (MMRD). 2015. "Mandalay Investment Opportunity Survey Report." Unpublished. *Study Planned by MIC and JICA and Prepared by MMRD*, Yangon.

Myoe, Maung Aung. 2007. "Sino-Myanmar Economic Relation Since 1988." Asia Research Institute Working Paper, no. 86.

Oh, Su-Ann, and Philip Andrews-Speed. 2015. *Trends in Southeast Asia: Chinese Investment and Myanmar's Shifting Political Landscape*. Singapore: ISEAS Publishing.

Page, Christ, and Pwint Thet Wah. 2015. *Survey of Trade-Related Private Sector in Myanmar*. Mandaluyong City: Asian Development Bank.

Reeves, Jeffrey. 2016. *Chinese Foreign Relation with Weak Peripheral States: Asymmetrical economic power and security*. New York: Routledge.

Su, Chuanzhi. 2016. "Myingyan 225 MW Combined Cycle Gas Turbine (CCGT) Power Plant Project, Myanmar." Unpublished. *Project Summary*, Asian Infrastructure Investment Bank.

Tatlow, Dermot. 1999. "China's Shadow." *Asiaweek*. Accessed October 8, 2015. http://edition.cnn.com/ASIANOW/asiaweek/99/0528/nat4.html.

Wheeler, Andre. 2016. "The New China Silk Road: Changing the Face of Oil & Gas in Southeast Asia." *CROSSROADS*, no. 8, Information Matrix Co., Ltd., Yangon, Myanmar.

CHAPTER 11

Chinese Migrant Traders in Pakse, Champasak Province, Laos: Trajectories and Business Future

Wasana La-orngplew

Introduction

The Greater Mekong Subregion (GMS) is mentioned in China's "Vision and Actions on Jointly Building Silk Road Economic Belt and twenty-first Century Maritime Silk Road" as one of the targeted regions that will be connected to China through China's Yunnan Province. The region is "a pivot of China's opening up to South and Southeast Asia" (NDRC 2015). China has already enhanced the connectivity between Yunnan Province and the GMS through various infrastructure development projects. The Kunming–Bangkok Express highway and the improvement of the upstream channels of the Mekong River are some of the largest projects. China provided US$30 million to Laos for construction of an 85 km highway which is currently part of the North-South Economic Corridor in Laos. That fund accounted for one third of the project's total cost. In 2004, China provided a concessional loan of US$200

W. La-orngplew (✉)
College of Interdisciplinary Studies, Thammasat University
(Lampang Campus), Lampang, Thailand

Y. Santasombat (ed.), *The Sociology of Chinese Capitalism in Southeast Asia*, https://doi.org/10.1007/978-981-13-0065-3_11

million to Cambodia for the construction of two bridges and two highways. Four years later, it provided more than US$200 million for two additional highways (Zhu 2009). Recently, China provided 50% of the funds needed for construction of the Houayxay-Chiang Khong Bridge (Lin and Grundy-Warr 2012).

China has become a major economic partner of GMS countries and is currently the largest source of foreign direct investment in Laos, from 1989 to 2015 valued at approximately US$5.49 million (Ministry of Planning and Investment 2016). In 2014, China became Myanmar's largest trading partner and Vietnam's second largest trading partner (China Britain Business Council 2015) even though the One Belt and One Road (OBOR) Initiative had not yet come into full effect in the region, China's influence is obvious. Leaders of GMS countries generally welcome the OBOR Initiative even though it is still unclear how it will impact the region. A Vice President of the Laos–China Cooperation Committee recently stated that:

> Laos always supports China's development policy, especially the Belt and Road Initiative...There is a saying in Chinese that 'If you want to get rich, build a road first,' but for Laos, it would be 'If you want to get rich, build railway first.' Therefore, Laos will actively support the Belt and Road Initiative. (Sindavong 2017)

Lao leaders expect OBOR to turn its land-locked country into a land-linked country. In December 2015, a groundbreaking ceremony was held in Vientiane as a formal start to construction of the Laos–China Railway, a Chinese-backed project linking the Laos–China border to Vientiane.

Over the past decade, China's influence in Laos has significantly increased. One of the most visible signs of Chinese influence in Laos is the presence of Chinese migrants and Chinese wholesale and retail shops, which can be found throughout the country. The arrival of Chinese migrant traders and cheap Chinese products are a cause for concern for the future of local businesses. There is a worry that the local businesses may be taken over by the new Chinese migrants (Ku 2016). This chapter seeks to respond to that concern. It traces trajectories of new migrants' petty trade in southern Laos and examines the extent to which local businesses have been affected by the arrival of new migrants. The chapter also brings attention to the migrants' business future in Laos. The author interviews Chinese migrant traders in one of the Laos economic centers,

Pakse, Champasak Province. The chapter begins with an overview of Chinese petty traders and their businesses in Pakse and then moves on to examine the nature of business operations found among Chinese migrant traders, their relations with the locals, and their business future.

Chinese Traders in Pakse

The exact number of new Chinese migrants in Laos is somewhat vague. It was estimated that from the late 1980s to 2006, there were approximately 100,000 new Chinese migrants residing in Laos (Zhuang and Wang 2010). The Chinese embassy data indicate that there were 30,000 migrants officially living in Laos but their exact number could be ten times higher (The Nation 2007). The GMS Migration Policy Briefing records indicate that by 2008, around 80,000 Chinese were working on Chinese-led projects (ADB 2010 cited in Tan 2012: 67). A new Chinese migrant who runs a hotel in Oudomxai Province, northern Laos estimated that there would be more 20,000 Chinese migrants arriving Laos to work for the Laos-China railway project (Perlez and Feng 2013). The pioneer group of Chinese migrants came to Laos in the mid-1990s as contracted workers and technicians working for road construction and industrial development projects with cooperation between the Chinese and Lao governments. Many had stayed and set up businesses in Laos. They were later joined by new migrant traders coming from mainly Hunan, Yunnan, Sichuan, and Zhejiang (Tan 2012). The flow of Chinese migrant traders to Laos is closely related to China's "Going Out" policy, which encourages Chinese enterprises to seek investment abroad and regional integration. China and Laos are closely connected through the "Going Out" policy and the Greater Mekong Subregion Cooperation. Chinese foreign aid, investment, and migrants in Laos have significantly increased after the turn of the century (Tan 2014).

It is difficult to estimate the exact number of new Chinese migrants in Pakse, the capital city of Champasak Province of southern Laos. Leaders of the Pakse Chinese Association[1] estimated that there were approximately 3,000 new migrants residing in Pakse and the surrounding areas in 2015. The new migrants generally arrived in Pakse after 2000. A Hunan woman, who runs a Hunan restaurant and works for the Hunan Chamber of Commerce, stated that there were roughly 800 new Chinese people registered with the Chamber in 2014 (Interview,

CL, May 25, 2015) and that registered number is far below the actual number of new Chinese migrants. It appears that only business owners have registered with the Chamber and many Chinese migrants who work as shop assistants, or migrants who visit their friends and relatives, are absent from the Chamber's record. An owner of a hardware store mentioned that he has not informed the Chamber about his fellow villager who is assisting him in running his shop. That is because the assistant is only staying temporarily with him: "He comes to explore his chances. He won't be with me for a long period of time. He will soon move to another place or set up his own business somewhere" (Interview, MB, April 27, 2015). Some shop owners have registered themselves with the Chamber although they have some non-registered migrants, either family members or friends, staying with them (Interview, EF, October 2, 2015; Interview, VM, April 5, 2016).

The area with the most noticeable Chinese migrant community in Pakse is the Dao-Heuang market and surrounding area (see Fig. 11.1). The market was established in 1995 by the Dao-Heuang Group, one of the largest and most progressive business groups in Laos, led by Leuang

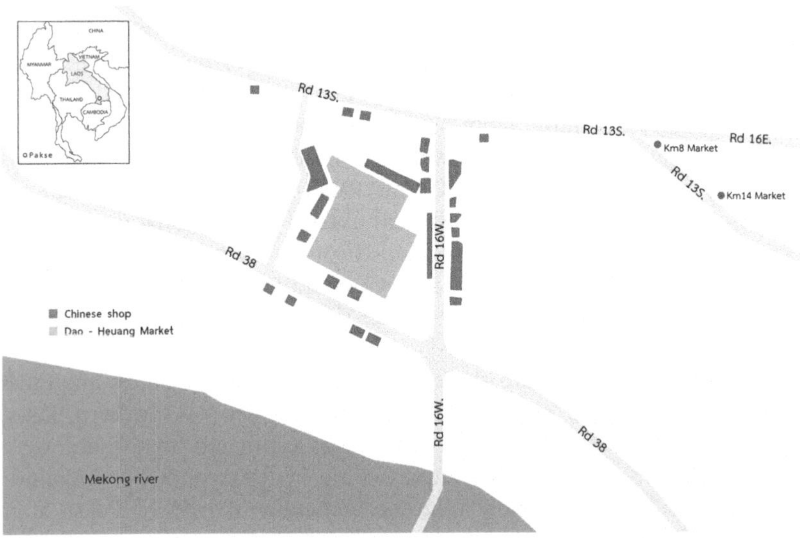

Fig. 11.1 Dao-Heuang market and Chinese shops (2016) (*Source* Author's fieldwork)

Litdang, a well-known Vietnamese-Lao businesswoman. The market is located next to the intersection of Road No. 38 and Road No. 16W. Road No. 13 is the most important highway in Laos and begins at the Laos–China border in Boten, Luang Namtha Province and connects the main cities in Laos from the north, central, and southern regions to the Lao-Cambodian border, and is also within walking distance of the Dao-Heuang market. The market is about 2 km from the city center where the old Chinese market, Pakse's economic center before the 1975 revolution, is located. That 35,000 m^2 market has stalls that sell both food and non-food items. The Dao-Heuang market has become the new commercial center of Pakse.

Trading in the Dao-Heuang market is mainly in the hands of local Laos, Overseas Chinese, and Vietnamese Laos. However, the presence of new Chinese merchants is clearly visible in the market (see Fig. 11.1). The crowded Road No. 16W is lined with Chinese shops. Some of the Chinese shops are located at the back of the market but they remain easily accessible through the market's back entrance. There are remarkable numbers of Chinese petty traders who are mobile. Those mobile merchants usually load commodities onto trucks and drive to several rural villages. Some take their goods to local market fairs.

It is common that while Chinese migrants have Pakse as their current business base, they all have close relatives, friends, or co-villagers running businesses elsewhere, either in Laos, China, or other countries. A Chinese man from Hunan Province who runs a hardware store in Pakse mentioned his brothers and sisters operate hardware shops in Vientiane, Savannakhet, Bokeo, Luangprabang, and Muang Khong, another district of Champasak Province (Interview, HM, July 19, 2015). Another Hunan lady who runs a shop selling televisions and stereo equipment noted that her parents and sister are all doing business in Laos. Her sister runs a mobile phone shop in Vientiane while her parents have a shop selling hardware products and agricultural tools in the KM8 market. Her parents-in-law also have a shop in Muang Ta Oy, a rural district of Salavan Province, which is about 190 km from Pakse. Her husband's uncle has a hardware store in Vientiane and he also has some relatives running a shop in Stung Treng, Cambodia (Interview, DF, April 3, 2016). Through those networks, Chinese migrants get updated on business opportunities in other places.

The main commodities that are sold in Chinese shops are street products. Nearly 100% of the goods are imported from China and only a few shops have products made in Laos, Thailand, or Vietnam. The Dao-Heuang Group's record reveals that the main commodities sold in Chinese shops are clothes (19 shops), bags (16 shops), and hardware products (ten shops). Other goods the Chinese traders sell include motorbikes, home appliances, mobile phones, cosmetics, car and motorbike parts and accessories, and sports equipment (Dao-Heuang Group no date). The Group's records indicate that clothes and bags are the main products sold by new Chinese migrants. The author's survey, however, found only a few clothing and bag shops. The clearly visible commodities are hardware products, agricultural tools, home appliances, and motorbike parts and accessories. Owners of Chinese shops explained that some of them have changed commodity types without informing the Dao-Heuang Group. Of the 26 Chinese businesses surveyed, it was found that there were seven hardware shops, five motorbike parts and accessories shops, four home appliances stores, and three agricultural equipment shops. The remaining businesses are a mobile phone shop, a motorbike shop, a hotel and restaurant, and a consumer products and groceries shop. Each shop sells a wide variety of commodities. One shop, for example, offers hardware products, shoes, agricultural tools, clothes, and home appliances.

It is recorded that the Overseas Chinese who migrated to Southeast Asia before the 1990s had their roots in coastal provinces, particularly Guangdong, Fujian, and Zhejiang (Zhuang and Wang 2010; Wong 2013). However, only a few Chinese migrant traders in Pakse came from those areas. Interviewing 26 Chinese shop owners in the Dao-Heuang market and its adjacent areas, the author found only two traders who had come from Zhejiang Province and only one Chinese indicating Guangdong Province as his origin. There was also only one shop run by a Chinese from Yunnan Province, while the other 22 shops were owned by Hunan migrants. Chinese migrants also confirmed that most of the Chinese shops in the area belong to Hunan. That observation is consistent with previous records on Chinese petty traders in other parts of Laos. Aranya Siriphon's (2012) work recorded that many new Chinese traders in a Chinese market in Bokeo Province, northern Laos, also indicated Hunan as their hometown. Bien Chiang and Jean Chih-yin Cheng (2015) noted that the biggest group of Chinese migrant merchants running businesses in Laos came from Hunan Province, with more than 10,000 Hunan running businesses in the Laos capital of Vientiane. Hunan merchants dominate the wholesale and retail businesses in Laos associated with Hunan's industry sector and Hunan Provincial government's policy. Following China's "Go-West" strategy, Hunan has become one of the leading places for hardware and mechanical and electrical products. Engaging with China's "Going Out" policy, the Hunan Provincial government has encouraged and provided financial support to Hunan enterprises to access overseas markets. Commodities available in Chinese shops in Pakse are mainly from Hunan Province. The presence of Hunan migrant traders in Pakse, as well as in other areas of Laos, is related to the success of the pioneer migrants who initially set up a Chinese shop in northern Laos and many convinced their relatives and friends to join them in Laos. Some have extended their business networks to other parts of Laos; they set up a new shop and sent their family members to look after the shop. The pioneers' stories of success attract other Chinese to find business opportunities in Laos.

Many migrants arrived in Laos when they were quite young. Fifteen of the 26 interviewees indicated that they first came to Laos at the age of 25 years or younger, while only six traders arrived at age 35 years or older. The youngest arrived at the age of 14 years, while the oldest was 52 years old. Most of the migrants arrived in Laos after 2000, with the peak period of migration from 2000 to 2005 with 11 out of the 26 traders arriving in Laos during that period, and only seven migrants arrived in Laos after 2010. However, many new migrants did not head directly to Pakse, most of them attempted to make their fortune in other parts of Laos before relocating. There were only five shop owners who had come directly to Pakse; only seven Chinese migrants settled in Pakse between 2000 and 2005; and 12 migrants arrived in Pakse after 2010.

Trajectories of Chinese Traders in Pakse

The trajectories of Chinese petty traders who operate shops in Pakse can be classified into three different categories. The first and most common category is the establishment of business through interpersonal connections with pioneers. The second category involves new migrants who are employed as wage laborers in Chinese shops to accumulate capital for future business investment. The third and least common category is that of the migrants who travel to and explore the potential for business investment in Laos.

Interpersonal networks play a significant role for new Chinese migrants to explore and start businesses in Laos. Most of the shop owners indicated that they came to Laos because some of their family members, relatives, or friends from the same villages or towns had arrived previously. Those origin-based networks are a crucial source of business information for new migrants. Business information and tips that the pioneers provide for the new migrants depend on how close they are. In general, newcomers learn the business environment, potential business locations, commodity types, commodity sources, and business networks in Laos from the pioneers. In addition to providing business information for new migrants, interpersonal networks shape the ways Chinese petty trade is established.

That pattern is common among Chinese migrants. Many traders mentioned that they first came to assist their family or relatives who had previously established a shop in Laos. At the family's shop, they learned business skills and the business environment in Laos. They also saved cash and explored the possibility of setting up their own business in the future. A Hunan male aged 29 years stated that he had spent 8 years in Vientiane helping his brother run a motorbike spare parts and accessories shop. He opened his own shop in Vientiane in 2011 selling the same types of products as his brother. The shop was set up with the support of his brother, who negotiated with wholesalers on his behalf. His first shop in Vientiane did not go well due to the number of competitors there, and he then relocated to Pakse in 2012 (Interview, JM, October 3, 2015). A 36-year-old lady from Zhejiang Province referred to the business of her sister, who has run a textile store in Vientiane for more than 10 years. Prior to coming to live in Laos, she visited her sister's shop on several occasions and stayed a few months each trip. She came to Vientiane again in 2011, staying one year while assisting her sister in the shop. She opened her own shop in Pakse in 2012, selling clothes and Lao sarongs made in a garment factory in China (Interview, GF, October 4, 2015).

Some successful Chinese traders also expanded their business from one place to another. Those traders tend to send some of their relatives, those who had previously assisted them in one locale, to look after a newly established shop. AM, a 27-year-old man from Guangdong Province, explained that he came to Laos when he was only 17 years old and worked in his uncle's curtain shop in Vientiane. Because his uncle's business has grown in size, more young nieces and nephews have come to work in the shop. AM's uncle always encourages all of his nieces and nephews to have their own business. Seeing a business opportunity in Pakse in 2008, his uncle set up a mobile phone shop for him. The uncle also set up a hardware store in Vientiane for AM's cousin, who previously assisted in the curtain store (Interview, April 25, 2015). Establishment of a business relies heavily on family ties, which provide start-up capital and various elements of support for migrants who arrive later.

Village-based networks played a crucial role in the recent expansion of Chinese petty trade in Laos. A considerable number of Chinese shop owners indicated that they first came to Laos through networks of friends and co-villagers. IM, a 53-year-old man from rural Hunan, is one such example. He is one of only a few Chinese who headed directly to Pakse after leaving home from China. He had a garment shop in Hunan's rural village, but business was not good. He was convinced by his co-villager, who had opened a stereo and home appliance store in Pakse, to seek his fortune there. He traveled to Pakse and stayed with a friend for almost a month. Apart from doing some work in his friend's shop, he also explored the potential of Pakse for his own business. On other trips, he visited his village friends and relatives who had shops in Sawannakhet and Khammouan, exploring business possibilities in those towns. He finally decided to go to Pakse with his 30-year-old daughter, leaving his wife to look after his clothing shop in Hunan. He used the family's savings and borrowed some money from two relatives to set up a shop in Pakse. He initially wanted to open a clothing shop, as he had established networks with the wholesalers. However, there were already many clothing shops in Pakse and that business was unlikely to be successful. His village friend again suggested that he sell stereos and televisions. His friend introduced him to stereo wholesalers and negotiated with some wholesalers for lower prices for the products (Interview, April 4, 2016).

That pattern of migration is still prevalent among new Chinese migrants. About 50% of shop owners indicated that they have friends visiting them. The newcomers generally stay with the pioneers and help them with some of the tasks in the shop. The pioneers provide not only accommodation for their newly arriving friends, but also business information and advice. Shop owners commonly do not pay new Chinese migrants for the assistance they provide in their shops, and the new Chinese migrants do not expect to get paid. A Hunan man, an owner of a hardware store, who has one visitor staying with him, noted that, "It's kind of mutual help between a shop owner and newcomers. It's not really a matter of money. We help each other. We are friends" (Interview, PM, April 4, 2016).

There are some new migrants who want to have their own business in Laos but have capital constraints and thus need to first seek work in

Laos. New Chinese migrants often work as low-skilled shop assistants, and those poor migrants generally find jobs in Chinese shops through their networks of relatives or village-based friends. They mainly get jobs through referrals from pioneers or by word of mouth and the new migrants generally get hired in Chinese shops owned by relatives or co-villagers. The migrants stay with their employers and have long working hours. One migrant, who had worked in a Chinese shop in Vientiane for 5 years, remembered that she received very low pay and had to work from 5 AM to 8 PM (Interview, PF, April 4, 2016). New migrants gather business information and, in some cases, establish business networks while they are working as shop assistants. Some migrants later set up their own businesses, using savings and business networks and information they acquired while they were at the shop. A 26-year-old Hunan woman noted that her parents, who were poor farmers from rural Hunan, had worked in a few Chinese shops in Vientiane for 14 years before opening their first business in Ta Oy district of Salavan Province. Her parents decided to open a shop in a faraway rural area, about 190 km from Pakse, because establishment costs in Ta Oy were far lower than in urban areas. Having more savings from the business (selling customer goods and hardware products) in the peripheral area, her parents moved to Pakse in 2009 (Interview, DF, April 3, 2016).

There are only a few Chinese traders who indicated that they did not know anyone when they first came to Laos. Those Chinese migrants arrived in Laos as tourists and stayed at Chinese-run guesthouses. They gathered business information through the Chinese they met, usually at guesthouses and restaurants, which became information centers for Chinese migrants. Few Chinese visitors stayed for extended periods of time at each place. Their length of stay was generally shorter than those shop assistants mentioned earlier. Some stayed for only a week or two before visiting a new place. Many of them traveled back and forth between China and various places in Laos, making several trips before opening their shops. One Hunan man, an owner of a small hardware store, mentioned that he had visited and explored business possibilities in Oudomxai, Vientiane, Savannakhet, and Khammouan before deciding to set up a shop in Pakse (Interview, MN, October 5, 2015). Many Chinese bring goods with them while they are traveling. One shop owner noted that he brought mobile phones from China with him and sold them to Chinese shops located outside the city. That invisible trade allowed him to earn some money to pay for exploring business opportunities in Laos

(Interview, DM, October 3, 2015). Another Hunan shop owner said that she brought clothes with her and she sold them at the morning or evening markets in the towns she was exploring (Interview, JF, April 3, 2015).

Nature of Chinese Business Operations

Two common strategies that Chinese migrants use for running a business are using interpersonal networks and using (often exploiting) family labor.

Interpersonal ties, based on family and place of origin, are vital not only for establishing businesses but also for keeping businesses running smoothly. Through networks of relatives and co-villagers, new migrants can gain access to suppliers or factories in China. Having strong connections with the pioneers, new petty traders are likely to be able to negotiate for lower prices on goods. By contrast, new traders without connections may struggle to find cheap commodities. Many cannot access wholesale suppliers in China and they must purchase goods at higher prices from other Chinese traders. Some migrant merchants mentioned that at the initial stage of business, they had to visit wholesale markets or factory outlets in Changsha, Hunan Province to purchase goods themselves. They also attempted to establish relationships with Chinese suppliers at that stage as well. Later, purchases could be made in two ways. First, orders can be placed through networks of family or friends in China. Typically, merchants in Laos send details of products they want to their relatives or friends through chat programs. Their friends or relatives then manage to get the goods for them. Second, they visit suppliers in China and finds goods themselves. An owner of a motorbike spare parts store stated that he travels back to China for that purpose two to three times each year; each trip takes about 10–15 days (Interview, NM, April 5, 2016). When the order is made, they normally are required to pay no less than 50% of the cost. The remaining cost is expected to be paid when the goods arrive. Few migrants indicate that they are offered credit from their suppliers in China. Some goods are delivered from China via road directly to Laos, while other commodities are shipped to Bangkok first, then later delivered via road to Laos. It is expected that delivery costs will decrease when the Laos–China railway begins operation.

Networks linked through webs of family and place of origin are also important for new traders to get to know their potential Chinese customers.

One Hunan who opened his home appliances store in 2014 indicated that his main customers are Hunan traders from other small towns. His shop has become popular in a very brief period because he has extended business networks and stated that, "most of my customers are Hunan traders in other towns. They come to my shop because other Hunan gave them a referral to my shop. No need to pay for advertisement. It's just word of mouth. I am just being honest and trustworthy. When they are impressed, they recommend me to their friends and relatives. Some of my customers come very far. Some come from Salavan or Attapeu" (Interview, IM, April 4, 2016).

One condition behind the persistence of Chinese petty business is a credit relationship between traders and their customers. Selling on credit to other Chinese traders is prevalent. Almost 100% of migrant traders indicated that they sell on credit to their Chinese customers who have shops in other districts or in rural villages. There is only one trader selling on credit to local Laos. The migrants admitted that they do not want to sell on credit but that they must. Three conditions that determine the duration and amount of credit Chinese traders give to their customers are (1) the relationship between the two parties, (2) the migrants' capital, and (3) the migrants' perception of the customers' solvency. One trader stated that he sells on credit to about 14–15 customers. The maximum credit each customer receives varies, ranging between 2000 and 10,000 RMB (approximately US$300 and US$1500), with a duration of two to six months (Interview, IM, April 4, 2016). Another trader sells on credit to only a few friends and relatives, fewer than ten customers total. The maximum amount of credit for each customer is no more than 2000 RMB (US$300) (Interview, JF, April 3, 2015). It should be noted that while Chinese traders tend to sell on credit to their friends and relatives, it cannot be interpreted that co-villagers, friends, and relatives receive credit from sellers automatically. Many Chinese merchants insisted that trading on the credit system is based on trust built between themselves and their customers, "I won't sell on credit to anyone just because he is my relative or he originally came from the same village. Selling on credit is applied only to a person I can really trust. Of course, it takes time to learn who I can trust" (Interview, JF, April 3, 2015). However, some traders admitted that they feel uncomfortable denying credit to certain customers who are their relatives or friends. "It's easy not to give credit to non-relatives, but for close friends or close relatives, it's difficult. They expect credit from us, but we cannot offer it. I am sometimes happy to sell to unfamiliar customers more than relatives. It's easy to say no" (Interview, CF, October 3, 2015).

Credit relationships are important for the existence and survival of poorer Chinese traders who usually have a shop, or only a stall, in peripheral areas. That group of traders is generally limited in capital, thus accessing credit from Chinese wholesalers permits them to have more goods to show in their shops and to increase their chances of earning profits. When they have accumulated a certain amount of capital, they tend to move to a commercial center, hoping they can earn more profit. Another group of migrants benefiting from access to credit are mobile traders. Like Chinese traders in rural villages, mobile traders have limited capital and cannot set up shops in a city center. Those poor migrants generally purchase goods from Chinese shops and take those goods around to many rural villages and rural markets. An owner of a motorbike spare parts shop, who was a mobile trader previously, noted that he had credit relationships with a few wholesale traders. Some allowed him to pay only one third of the cost up front, while others required 50%. He also remembered that the cost of goods he bought on credit was higher than normal. However, limited capital did not allow him to have many options (Interview, KM, October 3, 2015).

It is clear that the operation of Chinese petty business relies heavily on the utilization of family members for labor, especially during the pioneering days of the business. The business is usually established by one or only a few Chinese, in most cases male. If a business goes well or more labor is required, more family members join them. Many traders indicated that there were only family members helping them run a shop at the initial stage of the business. The families were dealing with suppliers and customers, managing shop accounts, seeking newer or cheaper goods, checking stock, keeping the shop tidy and clean, stocking shelves, and more. Another advantage of having family members as co-workers is the element of trust in allowing that person to take care of the business when the settlers are away on business trips, meaning that shop operation is not interrupted by the absence of the owner. One Hunan noted that he travels back and forth between Laos and China 3–4 times a year. He can make several trips because his daughter oversees the family's stereos and home appliances store. That trader also has a clothing shop in Hunan Province, which his wife operates. Having no worries about the shop, he can travel to China to meet wholesalers and seek newer or cheaper products (Interview, IM, April 4, 2016).

When the business grows and families cannot provide a sufficient labor supply to the shop, non-family labor is recruited. Some shops employ local Laos to help in their shops. The Chinese traders, however, prefer to hire

Chinese laborers instead of Lao workers. There is a common perception among Chinese petty traders that Lao workers are lazy and feeble. One migrant trader expressed his impression that Lao workers "are extremely lazy. They just sit and look around. They do not tolerate hard work. Many were with us only a few days and left. They said the work is too hard. They are not patient. It is very difficult to find any good Lao worker" (Interview, FM, October 3, 2015). Chinese labor is mainly recruited through networks of village-based friends and relatives. They are assigned to take care of various types of unskilled duties that were previously handled by the owners and their families. The shop setters and families focus mainly on dealing with accounting, suppliers, or wholesale customers. However, the owners continue to keep an eye on their employees at all times.

Chinese migrant traders appreciate the habit of hard work by their co-villagers or relatives. As mentioned earlier, poor newcomers consider getting hired in the pioneers' shops as a significant route to building up savings, gathering business information, and eventually opening their own business in the future. The two groups of migrants are generally connected through their family or village-based networks. There is some tension between the shop owners and new migrants. Some Chinese laborers feel that they are exploited by shop owners. One Hunan, who arrived in Pakse at the age of 22 years in early 2015, noted that he was recommended to work in a hardware shop owned by his brother's friend. He did not get paid for the first month of his work and was required to work from early morning until late at night, seven days a week. The young Hunan did not want to continue working with his current employer but because he was connected with the shop owner through his brother's ties, he could not leave the shop immediately as he wished. "He is my brother's friend. He recruited me because of my brother's recommendation. I have to work with him for a while, to keep my brother's face" (Interview, April 6, 2016). Although interpersonal networks are important for labor management, there is also a downside to them.

Chinese Migrant Traders and the Locals

Prior to the arrival of Chinese petty traders and Chinese commodities, the commodities offered in Laos were mostly imported from Thailand and, less often, Vietnam. There is widespread perception among the Lao population that Thai products are the best quality, but that the prices are also high. Many poor Laos are unable to afford Thai goods. In contrast,

Chinese commodities are much cheaper than Thai products and the Lao people always comment on the inferior quality of the Chinese products. However, Chinese goods are popular among the Lao population because their affordable prices. It is said that Chinese products are in every single house in Laos. Houses belonging to local traders who consider Chinese migrant traders as their competitors are without exception.

Increasing numbers of Chinese petty traders are cause for alarm for local merchants. Some local traders who sell goods imported from Thailand have described that local traders have not yet been fully displaced by Chinese merchants. However, they have started to worry about the future of local business. One Lao lady who runs a consumer store expressed her concern: "We have already lost some customers to Chinese shops, largely the poor. Prices of Thai goods are too high for the poor. When the Chinese come, they provide a cheaper choice for poor Laos. Many customers have moved from my store to Chinese shops" (Interview, JK, March 7, 2015). Another Lao, who is running a shop selling motorbike spare parts and accessories imported from Thailand, shared a similar story. He mentioned that his business was doing well in the past, as the motorbike market was dominated by Thai motorbikes. Currently, Chinese motorbikes are found all over Laos and have gradually superseded Thai motorbikes. That situation occurs due to the price difference between Chinese and Thai motorbikes. In general, a Chinese motorbike costs only about one third of the price of a motorbike imported from Thailand (Interview, SY, October 6, 2015). A Chinese migrant trader who runs a motorbike shop noted that while both Thai and Chinese motorbikes are offered in her shop, Chinese motorbikes are far more popular than Thai motorbikes. She usually sells about 80–90 Chinese motorbikes each month, but no more than 20 Thai motorbikes or even less than ten in some months (Interview, EF, October 2, 2015). Some local traders, both Laos and Overseas Chinese, are worried that they might be displaced from the market because they cannot afford high rents like the Chinese migrants can. To survive, some local traders have Chinese goods placed in their shops alongside Thai and Vietnamese goods. It is likely that in the future, Chinese goods will be prevalently offered not only in Chinese shops, but also in shops owned by locals.

The Overseas Chinese in Pakse have different perspectives on the rise of Chinese influence in Laos. The Laotian Chinese who run small businesses, such as grocery shops, agricultural tools shops, motorbike repair shops, and clothing shops express their worries about their business future after the arrival of Chinese petty traders. With limited capital and business networks, those Overseas Chinese may not be able to handle the arrival of Chinese migrant traders. The situation of the Overseas Chinese who have a large amount of capital or have strong business networks is different. Some of them have begun to establish business connections with Chinese from mainland China, mainly through the links of a dialect or hometown-based Chinese association. Some Laotian Chinese import products from China. Some have sent their children to a school or a university in China; they expect that their children will obtain not only an education but also business networks with the Chinese. One Overseas Chinese, who owns a hotel, a building materials store, and a motorbike spare parts shop, mentioned that he has two children studying in China. The main reason for sending his children to China instead of a western country is to gain business networks in China.

> Education in a western country might be better than in China. My children might have a chance to develop English language skills. But China has a massive population and large domestic market. It has more business opportunities. I thought going to China might be the best choice. I persuaded my children to go to China. I told them that they could learn the Chinese language which would be an important business language in the future. They could make friends with their Chinese classmates. These would be crucial for business dealing or investing in China in the future. (Interview, GM, April 26, 2016)

While some Overseas Chinese attempt to establish links with people in mainland China, they generally have no willingness to establish relations with Chinese petty traders. The Overseas Chinese, whose ancestors migrated from China (mainly Guangdong Province) in the early twentieth century, differentiate themselves from new migrants. One of the committees of the Overseas Chinese Association in Pakse pointed out that:

> They came from China like our ancestors but we are not the same. They speak Chinese but have different accents, which are not easy to understand. We have settled here considering Laos as home. But new migrant traders have not settled yet. They see China as their home, not Laos. They are not members of our [Overseas Chinese] association. They do not join any activities with us. There is nothing we do together. (Interview, ZY, March 21, 2015)

Another Overseas Chinese also commented on the ways that new migrants operate a business:

> Their goods are cheaper than ours, but they sell very poor-quality goods. Look at the mobile phones they sell. How long can you use it? New Chinese just come to make money from selling crappy products. They keep moving from one place to another all the time. What else can you do if there is a problem with your phone? You go back to the shop and find that they have already left. What can you do? They do not care much about customers here. They just come to make money. But we are here. We have houses and families here. We cannot run away from home. We cannot do business like that. We have to operate our business with honesty and integrity. (Interview, GS, March 21, 2015)

New migrant traders themselves do not express their willingness to engage with Lao society. While Laos is seen to be the place they can seek their fortune, it is an unpleasant place to live. Some common complaints they have include, “the market is dirty,” “the school quality is low,” “hospital services are poor,” and “people are poor and lazy.” Thus, they send their kids back to school in China. When they have health concerns, they seek Chinese doctors in another town or even return to China. Nearly 100% of the interviewees insisted that they would stay in Laos only on a temporary basis. Some migrants’ length of temporary stay is almost 20 years; however, they still have strong intentions to go back to their homes in China in the future. Unlike Overseas Chinese who enjoy their Lao citizenship, new migrants prefer to hold a People’s Republic of China passport.

The situation of Chinese migrant traders in Pakse is thus like what Danielle Tan noted, that integration of new Chinese migrants to Lao society is limited (Tan 2015). New migrants have very limited contact with local communities. Only a few of them have established contacts with local Laos or Overseas Chinese. They tend to stick together. When the shop closes in the evening, they spend their free time with their neighbors, who are often their relatives or co-villagers. Playing Chinese Mahjong together in front of a shop is a familiar sight. Some watch Chinese television shows. Many contact their families in China, mainly via the internet and chat programs.

It should be noted that levels of interaction between Chinese migrants and local communities are related to migrants’ investment level. Bien Chiang and Jean Chih-yin Cheng noted that for migrant petty traders who run a small shop, their business relies mostly on assistance of the relatives, friends, or co-villagers who came earlier (Chiang and Cheng 2015). Assistance of Overseas Chinese may be unnecessary for their business operations, however, for Chinese migrants who seek to invest in large-scale enterprises such as setting up large-scale plantations or mining, they need to obtain concessions from the government. Thus, assistance of the locals is indispensable. Without assistance of Overseas Chinese, new Chinese migrants can hardly establish personal connections with Laos' political elite and government officials (ibid., 2015). One Chinese migrant noted that he could obtain rock mining concession from the government through the assistance of an Overseas Chinese who has good connections with high-ranking officials in Champasak (Interview, AM, April 25, 2015). Another migrant, who is a mobile phone distributor in Champasak Province, also mentioned an Overseas Chinese in Vientiane who had assisted him in negotiating with the company (Interview, XM, April 6, 2016). However, even this group of migrant merchants have limited cultural integration into Lao society.

Uncertain Future of Chinese Migrant Traders

There is increasing competition among Chinese petty businesses as more new traders arrive in the already crowded Chinese shops. Many migrant traders indicated that they were hesitant to invite new migrants to join them in Pakse because, "the business here is not as good as it was. Many have already lost their money. I do not want to upset them. I do not want them to lose money" (Interview, KF, April 3, 2016). Another shop owner gave a straightforward view: "There are already too many traders here. Nobody wants more competitors. We are already struggling to earn money" (Interview, YF, April 6, 2016). Although current Chinese traders see that the future railway linking Kunming and Laos will minimize transportation costs of their goods, they are concerned that the train will bring more migrants, thus more competitors, to Laos. Their business is likely to be tougher in the future.

Even though the train has not yet arrived in Laos, many migrant traders, particularly those who run wholesale shops, have already experienced stiff competition from other Chinese shops. One area of concern is caused by a credit system. The credit relationship is embedded in Chinese business practices and shop owners are expected to offer credit to their customers. The migrant traders do not want to sell on credit and try to avoid that relationship with customers. However, running a business in a highly competitive environment, they must involve themselves in the system to maintain their customers. Selling on credit becomes a serious problem for traders with limited capital because those traders cannot offer long-term credit or substantial amounts of credit in the same way that big shops can. Most of the wholesale traders have experienced losing money from selling on credit, even when they carefully consider the customer's background.

Petty traders have a mixed image of Laos. The country is viewed as an attractive destination to seek business success. Of course, many new migrants have become successful traders and have expanded their businesses. However other migrants have suffered losses. Over the past few years, some Chinese shops have been closed or sold to new migrants. More than ten shop owners have returned to China, or moved to another location on Laos, having had little to no success. Some traders have complained about the Lao government's attempts to control Chinese businesses: "We are required to pay lots of fees. We are not so sure how long we can run a shop" (Interview, KM, October 3, 2015). Regulations and enforcement regarding the business operations of foreign migrants somehow overlap. Legally, migrant traders are required to register with the Lao government. Although most of the migrant traders have registered with the Hunan Chamber of Commerce, only some have registered with the government. The government has achieved limited potential to enforce the regulations which leaves room for negotiation between migrants and local officials. Migrant traders were informed in 2013 that the Lao government would actively enforce the rules. Local officials visited Chinese shops and checked their business licenses and visas. The owners could, however, negotiate with officials to stay and operate their businesses in Laos on the condition that they register and pay a fee to the government. That solution adds cost and puts more pressure on their businesses. Some Chinese migrants are under the impression that the Lao government will impose the regulations on them more strictly than on Vietnamese migrants. Surprisingly, many migrants do not feel that the Chinese government has provided support for their businesses. Many heard about the financial support that the Chinese government provides for Chinese overseas investments, however, none of them could access that support. Migrant petty traders have the impression that large-scale investors can better access financial support from the Chinese government than small-scale merchants.

Conclusion

This chapter explored the background of the current Chinese migrant traders in Pakse, southern Laos. A considerable number of migrants first came to Laos between 2000 and 2005, after the implementation of China's "Going Out" strategy which has led to an increase in China's aid and investment in Laos. However, it was only after 2010 that Pakse became a new and popular destination for Chinese migrant traders where they could set up Chinese shops in Pakse's commercial center and the surrounding areas.

Those new Chinese migrants have different backgrounds from the Overseas Chinese who migrated to Southeast Asia in the early twentieth century. The previous wave of migrants mainly came from the coastal areas, mostly Guangdong Province. New Chinese migrants in Pakse mostly arrived from Hunan, an inland province. The educational background of the migrant entrepreneurs is also different from the Overseas Chinese who migrated to Southeast Asia during the colonial period. Unlike the old wave, many of the new migrants have a university degree and some have a high school diploma.

Having Pakse as a current business base, migrant traders have family members, friends, or co-villagers running businesses in other parts of Laos. Those interpersonal networks are important for business establishment and operations. Many migrant traders set up their businesses through networks of pioneer migrants who provide various forms of support, such as business information, business networks, and financial support. Being a laborer in a Chinese shop when they first come to Laos is another means Chinese migrants use to earn savings, gather business information, and establish business networks before establishing their own businesses. Some traders, who do not have links with the pioneers, explore their business opportunity in Laos through Chinese migrants they meet at Chinese guesthouses and restaurants-unofficial Chinese business centers. Those migrants generally travel with small-item goods to many places before deciding on their business location.

Interpersonal networks are crucial for Chinese migrants' business operations. Migrant traders can access business information, networks, and particularly business credit through their interpersonal networks, mainly based on family, friends, or a common village or township. Another common characteristic found among the migrant traders is that they heavily rely on family labor. When their businesses expand and more labor is needed, they try to recruit another member of the family to join them rather than employing locals. However, while interpersonal networks play a significant role in migrants' business operations, they can create more tension. For example, financial problems emerged under the credit relationship among migrant traders.

New migrants have had limited success engaging both local Laos and Overseas Chinese. Their cheap commodities are welcomed in Pakse but the migrants themselves are not. Although some oversea Chinese attempt to reestablish the links with mainland China for their business opportunities, they express no willingness to get involved with the Chinese petty traders. The migrant traders have not shown themselves willing to integrate into Lao society or the Overseas Chinese community. Migrant traders, especially those who run small shops, rely more on migrants' networks than Overseas Chinese's assistance.

Migrants who arrived with substantial amounts of capital to invest in Laos, however, attempt to establish business relationships with Overseas Chinese or local Laos. Through connections with the locals, they can gain access to government officials and political leaders, and in such a way, obtaining official permission or concession from the government is possible. Even though the locals are of assistance to the operation of their business, their cultural engagement with the local communities remains limited. Migrant traders typically consider Laos a place of temporary residence and express their intentions to return home to China.

The presence of Chinese migrants and cheap Chinese products has led to concern over the future of local businesses. Some local merchants have lost customers to Chinese shops. Some are attempting to make their business survive by ordering Chinese goods for their shops, and other local traders are concerned that they will be replaced by Chinese traders in the future. Evidence from Pakse suggests that Chinese business is not always bright. It is true that some migrants become successful and can expand their businesses. New migrants, especially those who came late or have limited capital and networks, are facing business difficulties or suffering losses, mainly caused by a highly competitive business environment. Additionally, many petty traders are concerned that when Laos and China become more connected through the Laos-China railway, there will be more new migrants arriving in Laos and their business is likely to suffer. According to the migrant traders, China's policy and development projects seem to provide benefits for large-scale business enterprises rather than their small businesses.

Note

1. This is an association of the Overseas Chinese ancestors who migrated to Laos in the twentieth century and have become Lao citizens.

Bibliography

Chiang, Bien, and Jean Chih-yin Cheng. 2015. "Changing Landscape and Changing Ethnoscape in Lao PDR: On PRC's Participation in the Greater Mekong Subregion Development Project." In *Impact of China's Rise on the Mekong Region*, edited by Yos Santasombat, 85–115. New York: Palgrave Macmillan.

China Britain Business Council. 2015. *One Belt One Road: A Role for UK Companies in Developing China's New Initiative Opportunities in China and Beyond*. n.p. China Britain Business Council. Accessed June 15, 2015. http://www.cbbc.org/cbbc/media/cbbc_media/One-Belt-One-Road-main-body.pdf.

Dao-Heuang Group. no date. *Statistic on Chinese Shops in Dao-Huang Market in 2015.* Unpublished Document.

Gray, Dennis D. 2008. "Laos Fear China's Footprint." *AP*, April 6, 2008. Accessed December 5, 2010. http://www.freerepublic.com/focus/f-news/1997633/posts.

Ku, Samuel. 2016. "China's Rising Influence in Laos." *The Diplomat*, March 3, 2016. Accessed September 3, 2016. http://thediplomat.com/2016/03/chinas-rising-influence-in-laos/.

Lin, Shuan, and Carl Grundy-Warr. 2012. "One Bridge, Two Towns and Three Countries: Anticipatory Geopolitics in the Greater Mekong Subregion." *Geopolitics* 17, no. 4: 952–979. http://dx.doi.org/10.1080/14650045.2012.662556.

Ministry of Planning and Investment, the Government of Laos. 2016. *All Approved Investment Project by Country*. Online: Ministry of Planning and Investment. Accessed March 5, 2016. http://www.investlaos.gov.la/images/Statistics/rpt_Invest_Summary_Country1A1989-2015.pdf.

National Development and Reform Commision (NDRC), People's Republic of China. 2015. *Vision and Actions on Jointly Building Silk Road Economic Belt and 21st-Century Maritime Silk Road*. Online: National Development and Reform Commission, Ministry of Foreign Affairs, and Ministry of Commerce of the People's Republic of China. Accessed March 2, 2016. http://en.ndrc.gov.cn/newsrelease/201503/t20150330_669367.html.

Perlez, Jane, and Jane Feng. 2013. "Laos Could Bear of China Railroad." *The New York Times*, January 1, 2013. Accessed March 12, 2018. https://www.nytimes.com/2013/01/02/world/asia/china-builds-a-railroad-and-laos-bears-the-cost.html.

Shanghai Institutes for International Studies. 2016. *Assessment and Prospect of China-Laos Development Cooperation*. Shanghai: Shanghai Institutes for International Studies.

Sindavong, Vichit. 2017. "Laos Actively Supports China-Proposed Belt and Road Initiative." Interview by Jianhua Zhang. *Xinhua*, April 22, 2017. Accessed June 2, 2017. http://news.xinhuanet.com/english/2017-04/22/c_136228120.htm.

Siriphon, Aranya อรัญญา ศิริผล. 2012. "Phu kha chin kap itthiphon chin nai chai daen lum nam Khong" ผู้ค้าจีนกับอิทธิพลจีนในชายแดนลุ่มน้ำโขง [Chinese Merchants and Chinese Influence in the Mekong Borderlands]. In *Chon chai daen kap kan kao kham phrom daen* ชนชายแดนกับการก้าวข้ามพรมแดน [Borderlanders and Cross-Border Practices], edited by Yos Santasombat ยศ สันตสมบัติ, 149–183. Chiang Mai: Biodiversity and Indigenous Knowledge Studies, Center for Research and Sustainable Development, Faculty of Social Sciences, Chiang Mai University.

Tan, Danielle. 2012. "Small Is Beautiful: Lessons from Laos for the Study of Chinese Overseas." *Journal of Current Chinese Affairs* 41, no. 2: 61–94.

Tan, Danielle. 2014. "China in Laos: Is There Cause for Worry?" *ISEAS Perspective* 31: 1–16.

Tan, Danielle. 2015. *Chinese Engagement in Laos: Past, Present, and Uncertain Future*. Singapore: Institute of Southeast Asian Studies.

The Nation. 2007. "Chinese Investors Invade Laos." October 8, 2007. Accessed April 2, 2013. http://www.nationmultimedia.com/home/2007/10/8/region/-Chinese-investors-invade-Laos-30051701.html.

Wong, Diana. 2013. "Introduction: The New Chinese Migration to Southeast Asia." *Asian and Pacific Migration Journal* 22, no. 1: 1–6.

Zhu, Zhenming. 2009. "China's Economic Aid to CLMV and Its Economic Cooperation with Them." In *A China-Japan Comaprison of Economic Relationships with the Mekong River Basin Countries, BRC Research Report No.1*, edited by Kagami Mitsuhiro, 69–106. Bangkok: Bangkok Research Center, IDE-JETRO.

Zhuang, Guotu, and Wangbo Wang. 2010. "Migration and Trade: The Role of Overseas Chinese in Economic Relations between China and Southeast Asia." *International Journal of China Studies* 1, no. 1: 174–193.

Lists of Interviewees

New Chinese Migrants

AM (an owner of a mobile phone shop, a Chinese restaurant, and a stone mining company). Interview by author. Pakse Laos, April 25, 2015.

CF (an owner of an agricultural equipment shop). Interview by author. Pakse Laos, October 3, 2015.

CL (an owner of a Chinese restaurant and a volunteer at the Hunan Chamber of Commerce). Interview by author. Pakse Laos, May 25, 2015.
DF (an owner of home and electrical appliances store). Interview by author. Pakse Laos, April 3, 2016.
DM (an owner of a toy and mobile phone shop). Interview by author. Pakse Laos, October 3, 2015.
EF (an owner of motorbike shops). Interview by author. Pakse Laos, October 2, 2015.
FM (an owner of a motorbike spare parts shop). Interview by author. Pakse Laos, October 3, 2015.
GF (an owner of a clothes and blanket shop). Interview by author. Pakse Laos, October 4, 2015.
HM (an owner of a hardware and agricultural tools shop). Interview by author. Pakse Laos, July 19, 2015.
IM (an owner of a home appliances and audio equipment store). Interview by author. Pakse Laos, April 4, 2016.
JF (an owner of a clothes and mobile phone shop). Interview by author. Pakse Laos, April 3, 2015.
JM (an owner of a motorbike spare parts store). Interview by author. Pakse Laos, October 3, 2015.
KF (an owner of a Chinese grocery shop). Interview by author. Pakse Laos, April 3, 2016.
KM (an owner of a motorbike spare parts shop). Interview by author. Pakse Laos, October 3, 2015.
MB (an owner of a hardware shop). Interview by author. Pakse Laos, April 27, 2015.
MN (an owner of a hardware shop). Interview by author. Pakse Laos, April 5, 2016.
NM (an owner of a motorbike spare parts shop). Interview by author. Pakse Laos, April 5, 2016.
PF (an owner of a hardware shop). Interview by author. Pakse Laos, April 4, 2016.
PM (an owner of a hardware shop). Interview by author. Pakse Laos, April 4, 2016.
PS (a hardware shop's employee). Interview by author. Pakse Laos, April 6, 2016.
VM (an owner of a motorbike spare parts shop). Interview by author. Pakse Laos, April 5, 2016.
XM (a mobile phone distributor). Interview by author. Pakse Laos, April 6, 2016.
YF (an owner of a hardware shop). Interview by author. Pakse Laos, April 6, 2016.

Oversea Chinese

GM (an owner of a hotel, a motorbike spare parts store, and a construction material store). Interview by author. Pakse Laos, April 26, 2015.

GS (an owner of gold stores and the Pakse Chinese Association's committee). Interview by author. Pakse Laos, March 21, 2015.

KS (an owner of gold shops). Interview by author. Pakse Laos, March 8, 2015.

ZY (an owner of a construction company and the Pakse Chinese Association's committee). Interview by author, March 21, 2015.

Local Lao

JK (a Lao businesswoman who runs a grocery shop). Interview by author. Pakse Laos, March 7, 2015.

SY (a Lao businessman who owns a motorbike shop). Interview by author. Pakse Laos, October 6, 2015.

CHAPTER 12

Developing Entrepreneurship Under the Rise of China: Chinese Migrant Entrepreneurs in Tourism-Related Businesses in Chiang Mai

Aranya Siriphon

Introduction

This chapter identifies entrepreneurial strategies developed by Chinese businesses engaged in the tourism sector and located in Chiang Mai, Thailand. The research presents case studies of small- and medium-sized enterprises (SMEs) with transnational business practices. Chinese entrepreneurs in the region utilize new strategies that are common among multinational enterprises in Southeast Asia. This generation of migrants benefit from political, economic, and social networks with direct and indirect support from the Chinese government.

Distinctive to the northern Thai province, Chinese migrants often come from a middle-class background utilizing modern approaches similar to entrepreneurs from a higher socio-economic class with established large-scale businesses (Chen et al. 2006). They represent a new

A. Siriphon (✉)
Faculty of Social Sciences, Chiang Mai University,
Chiang Mai, Thailand

Y. Santasombat (ed.), *The Sociology of Chinese Capitalism in Southeast Asia*, https://doi.org/10.1007/978-981-13-0065-3_12

generation with an average age of 25–40 years and are the descendants of government officials working in state-owned enterprises (SOEs) who now operate domestic and international businesses. A comparative analysis of Chinese SMEs provides insight into similarities with Chinese owned multi-national private enterprises in Taiwan and Vietnam (Chen et al. 2008) and Hong Kong (Wong 2008). Both demonstrate a combination of risk taking and utilization of technology to advance and manage their business (Milton-Smith 1999; Foo and Foo 2000; Liu 2012). They also use modern western management practices and organizational structures (Wong 2008; Chen et al. 2008; Yarzebinski 1992). One difference is that SMEs in Chiang Mai tend to value small business without the ambition for growth and expansion that are driving multi-national firms based in Hong Kong and Taiwan. Chiang Mai entrepreneurs tend to diversify their investment in several types of businesses and are redefining the nature of traditional *guanxi*. Furthermore, the research considers those transnational entrepreneurs in the context of contemporary Thai state policies and the concept of dual embeddedness (Ren and Liu 2015).

The emergence of new modes of entrepreneurship is demonstrative of China's growing influence in Southeast Asia. Chinese entrepreneurship and transnational business networks in modern Asia are complex and not always transparent (i.e. intra-ethnic competition or the dark side of *guanxi*) (Chan and Ng 2001; Chan 2000; Gomez and Hsiao 2001; Menkhoff and Gerke 2002). Chinese capitalism can be viewed as hybrid capitalism which is open and fluid in nature instead of the ethnic and cultural commonalities or cooperation defined as ethnic Chinese (Yeung 2004). Hong Liu (2012) proposed deeper elaboration on the roles of the state, society, and capital in Chinese business. He argued that transnational Chinese networks and state interaction has been significantly shaped by the dynamic rise of China and the rapid economic regionalization of the Asia Pacific region. That reinforces transnational embedded networks and facilitates the emergence of transnational Chinese entrepreneurship among a new generation (Liu 2012; Ren and Liu 2015).

Transnational Entrepreneurs in Chiang Mai

The number of Chinese entrepreneurs establishing businesses in Thailand has risen rapidly since 2012. The Thai Department of Business Development reports a total of 8905 Chinese companies registered

(2016–2017) under the Foreign Business Act B.E. 2542 (A.D. 1999). Bangkok is the most popular province for Chinese business with 4690 companies (75%) registered. The northern province has 570 companies registered with 381 concentrated in the provincial capital of Chiang Mai. Eighty-three of those companies are in the tourism-related sector with a total investment of US$86 million in the past year (Table 12.1).

Fieldwork conducted from November 2015 to July 2016 includes in-depth and key informant interviews, participant observation at a new Chinese Association established by the *Qiaoban* Center of Beijing, and extensive literature review. Ten key informants represent newly settled Chinese migrant entrepreneurs in Chiang Mai and are typical of middle-class Chinese coming from professional or government jobs (Hays 2015). They invest outside of China with high ambitions for success based on innovative entrepreneurial risk (Zhou 2010; Graceffo 2016), are both male and female, and most have college degrees.

The emerging class of Chinese entrepreneurs in Chiang Mai come from all regions of China such as Guangxi, Kunming, Shanghai, Shenzhen, Fujian, Henan, Qinghai, and Beijing. That distinguishes them from migrants who settle along the Thai border arriving overland

Table 12.1 Chinese companies operating in various tourism-related businesses in Chiang Mai during 2016–2017

Business type	*Total numbers of companies*	*Investment values (THB million/USD)*
1. Real estate business	40	2742/79,000,000
2. Accommodations and food services business	33	198/6,000,000
3. Shipping, transportation, and logistics companies	9	27/772,000
4. Arts, entertainment, and recreation business	1	1/28,571
Total	**83**	**2968/85,800,571**

Source Data from the Department of Business Development, Ministry of Commerce 2017, http://www.dbd.go.th/main.php?filename=index (Retrieved March 30, 2017) These numbers do not include individual/private Chinese entrepreneurs or main street entrepreneurs (Doody et al. 2016: 858–876) who run various types of tourism-related businesses in Chiang Mai such as hotels, resort guesthouses, lodges, restaurants, spa and massage shops, travel agencies, souvenir shops, and even those who are freelancing as tour guides or running online market businesses that send Thai products to China and beyond.

from the southern regions of China, primarily Yunnan (Siriphon 2015, 2016). The Chiang Mai entrepreneurs take advantage of modern technology and transportation, making them mobile and flexible, with many traveling throughout Southeast Asia and back to China. Six out of ten respondents have a similar level of professional experience. At least six have run similar businesses in China or elsewhere. Table 12.2 depicts the diversity of experience and backgrounds ranging from Shanghai to Canada. Some entrepreneurs are new to business, coming from public service, teaching, or journalism in China and moving to Chiang Mai to start a new life.

Related to the content of Tables 12.2 and 12.3 demonstrates the commonalities and differences in applying entrepreneurial strategies. All ten respondents have utilized various strategies commonly seen in contemporary multinational firms. Wong (2008) and Chen et al. (2008) identified that the commonality in Asian multinational firms is rationality and efficiency in corporate governance structures to protect shareholders, employees, customers, and other stakeholders. That approach is utilized by many of the key informants who were interviewed. They recruit professionals and local experts and put them in management positions. For example, Interviewee 2 hired an English-speaking Thai employee to manage her antique shop and deal with the export of Thai products and English-speaking customers. Interviewee 3 hired a Chinese chef as a senior cook to serve Chinese fusion cuisine and a Thai general manager. Interviewee 7 hired a Muslim-Chinese chef from Xingjing to serve specialized noodles to her customers. Many of those entrepreneurs collaborate with Thai investors for joint SMEs and hire communications and marketing professionals to service customers in many languages.

Digital technology is used by all the respondents to both manage their business from a distance and open markets to new customers. Online management tools allow for business owners to oversee accounting, payroll, bookings, and other administrative tasks virtually from anywhere in the world. For example, Interviewees 2, 3, 6, and 7 all use online platforms such as WeChat pay and Alipay to manage their accounts as they travel between China and Thailand.

Online booking systems are used for hotels as well as electronic bill paying systems. Some business owners install closed circuit television surveillance to remotely monitor employee performance. The internet,

Table 12.2 Interview profile of ten case studies, recent Chinese entrepreneurs in the tourism-related business in Chiang Mai

KI	*Age/general background in China*	*Professional background*	*Business in Thailand*
1.	• Female, 28 years old, single, north China, B.A. graduated from Beijing, came alone to Thailand	• One year Chinese language teacher in Bangkok, enjoys traveling	• Export Thai products (cosmetics, souvenirs) in Nimmanhaemin area.
2.	• Female, 29 years old, single, Shanghai, B.A. in Journalism, came alone to Thailand	• Former journalist, volunteer in disaster in Guangdong, India, Nepal • Loves traveling worldwide	• Antique shop at Ban Tawai area, touristic place of Chiang Mai
3.	• Female, 30 years old, married, Guangxi, M.A. in Economics, came with husband at first	• 6 years foreign affairs staff of Qiaoban in Quangxi and in Chiang Rai, Thailand • Travel to Laos, Myanmar for tourism and business	• Chinese restaurant in city
4.	• Female, 40 years old, married, Kunming, high school, with family (family go back and forth)	• Shipping, logistics company in Kunming	• Shipping, logistics business
5.	• Male, 38 years old, married, Shenzhen, B.A., came with his wife	• Logistics and hotel business background in Shenzhen • Enjoys traveling as a tourist and businessmen in Southeast Asia	• Owner, small-scale hotel
6.	• Male, 32 years old, single, Fujian, B.A. in Business Management, Canada, worked in Shanghai (overseas Chinese from Canada)	• Hotel business background in Shanghai (home in Canada), overseas Chinese • Enjoys traveling worldwide	• Manager, shareholder of a hotel resort

(continued)

Table 12.2 (continued)

KI	*Age/general background in China*	*Professional background*	*Business in Thailand*
7.	• Male, 42 years old, married, Qinghai, B.A. in Physics	• Former teacher in Beijing, gold and mineral surveyor in Laos and Indonesia, restaurant owner, real estate investment background in Beijing • Enjoys traveling in Southeast Asia and Chiang Mai	• Resort hotel, noodle restaurant (Halal food)
8.	• Male, 30 years old, Henan, single, B.A. in Management	• Staff member of Chinese real estate company working in China for 6 years, and later the same position working in Chiang Mai branch for 2 years • Enjoys traveling, sharing experience (in China, Southeast Asia)	• Real estate company (sells condominiums, houses) and offers a consulting service in buying land, doing business in Thailand
9.	• Male, 40 years old, married, south China, B.A. in China, came with family	• Opened tour agency for Chinese tourists	• Export Thai products (rubber pillows, dried fruits, cosmetics)
10.	• Male, 30 years old, single, south China, B.A. in Thai University, Lampang, and graduated with M.A. from Thai University	• Former Chinese language teacher in Lampang	• Logistics company, shipping Thai products (fruits, rubber, pillows, cosmetics, etc.)

particularly social media, is used for marketing to promote their services and products. Young Chinese entrepreneurs in Thailand use technology to gain a competitive advantage. They use online communication via various platforms (such as chat rooms) as well as digital payment or electronic money transfers with online transaction processing. All ten respondents have taken advantage of advanced internet marketing tools and technologies to target wider markets, and have been able to do so on a small budget.

The difference between the SMEs based in Chiang Mai and Asian multinational business strategies is their investment diversification strategies. Diversification usually involves long-term returns while minimizing risk. Chinese entrepreneurs based in Chiang Mai treat diversification as a backup plan for unexpected situations to balance the risk of running a small business. Some young Chinese entrepreneurs diversify their business by adopting several modern techniques and management strategies. Others choose to diversify by expanding to other related products, research their potential, and make an entry into the new market. They also diversify their investments across different geographies. All ten cases have diversified their businesses and investments both in China and abroad. Most have investments in the Chinese stock market and domestic businesses. They all responded that those investments are crucial to provide passive income and reduce the risk of bankruptcy. They prefer investing in stock markets over savings accounts in banks as the Chinese stock market is known to be dominated by retailers and entrepreneurs seeking long-term gain to balance high-risk short-term investment.[1]

Aiming to diversify their investment, all respondents operate their primary business investment in Thailand or in China and are also shareholders in other businesses. For example, Interviewee 6 is a manager and owner of a hotel branch in Chiang Mai, but he is also a shareholder of a hotel corporation based in Shanghai where he used to work. Interviewee 4 owns shares in a logistics company in Kunming, while also setting up her own logistics company in Chiang Mai. Interviewees 1, 2, and 3 all maintain shares in previously owned businesses and guesthouses based at tourist destinations in China, such as Dali, Lijiang. Investment in the tourism sector in Thailand is another strategy. For example, Interviewee 8 runs a real estate company selling condominiums and houses in Chiang Mai for Chinese customers and rents a building for a small-scale hip-style hotel. He has a dream to meet foreigners and share travel experiences. Interviewee 10 has his own logistics company and an import-export venture to trade in Thai products. Table 12.3 represents the diversification and entrepreneurship strategies used by the key-informants.

The Chiang Mai entrepreneurs gradually expand their businesses throughout northern Thailand by renting land. However, that can pose vulnerabilities and risks because there are restrictions to foreign property ownership in Thailand. Sometimes nominee shareholders are used to create joint ventures for the sole purpose of owning property, which is illegal and authorities have recently cracked down on the practice. Thai property owners have limitations regarding leasing to non-citizens but business people have found a way around that through investment in Thai-owned businesses to obtain long-term leases or property. Most Chinese entrepreneurs are forced to rent space for their business. According to Private Property Law and Civil and Commercial Law of Thailand, the Thai owners have the right to decide the fee and rental period of the lease. Normally contracts are 1–2 years with annual renewal options. Should they want a 3-year contract, the tenants need to register with the Provincial Land Office.

Another difference in managerial styles between SMEs and large firms is the use of *guanxi*. *Guanxi* is considered the spirit of Chinese entrepreneurship and is regarded as an essential element of Chinese culture and social structure deeply rooted within Confucianism and the values of kinship, family, trust, loyalty, reciprocity, and harmony (Weidenbaum 1996; Redding 1995; Fei 1992). Some scholars contend that *guanxi* has emerged from within a set of social institutions like other socialist economies marked by scarce resources and elite control. Other management scholars see *guanxi* as human capital that helps gain competitive business advantages (Tsang 1998; Yeung and Tung 1996) and improves economic efficiency (Nee 1992). Scholars have demonstrated the way in which *guanxi* has developed as a cultural aspect of Chinese entrepreneurs in facilitating their business within unpredictable economic and political constrain (Whitley 1992; Hefner 1998; Weller 1998). Others (Yang 1994; Kipnis 1997) have proposed a more multidimensional analysis of *guanxi*, noting that the principle of trust (central to *guanxi* practices) can operate in several ways in transnational networks, including beyond ethno-national lines.

In modern business practice *guanxi* strategies are used to a lesser degree because formal transnational trade using modern technology, along with more relaxed regulations for foreign investment, create new pathways for entrepreneurs. Although *guanxi* is currently less

Table 12.3 Ten case studies of Chinese migrant entrepreneurs and their business strategies in various tourism-related business sectors in Chiang Mai city

KI	*Business and investment diversification*		*Entrepreneurship*	
	Primary business	*Extra business*	*Business operation*	*Technology support and design*
1.	E-commerce exporting Thai products (cosmetics, souvenirs, clothes)	Shareholder in a guesthouse business in Dali, China	• Rents two small rooms for product stocking and display space • Modern business, target online shopping market, Chinese customers and worldwide	• e-commerce online shopping markets • Using WeChat and various online platforms, selecting luxurious items for different online shopping customers
2.	Antique shop at Ban Tawai	Shareholder in a guesthouse/bed and breakfast business in Lijiang, China	• Rents a large warehouse space • Mix traditional + modern (on-site shopping + online commerce) • Company registration under Thai Law	• Hire a foreign manager, modern administration/decoration • Online market (website, email contact, and ordering) • Closed circuit television surveillance for security, distance management
3.	Chinese restaurant in city	Ph.D. study, investing in stocks market, shareholder in guesthouse in China	• Renting a 2-floor building in Tapae rd. for Chinese restaurant • Mix traditional business + modern management	• Hire Thai professionals, employees for routine, specific work (accounting—use *gimu*, WeChat and other digital payment providers) • Closed circuit television surveillance for being a distance owner, taking care of the shop
4.	Shipping, logistics company	Exporting Thai products by order Shareholder in logistics company	• Rents a large space in the *Ban Tawai* area • Company registration under Thai Law	• Closed circuit television surveillance for security, global positioning systems for logistics examination • Strategically logistic routes (R3A, different ports and roads due to border flexible regulation

(continued)

Table 12.3 (continued)

KI	*Business and investment diversification*		*Entrepreneurship*	
	Primary business	*Extra business*	*Business operation*	*Technology support and design*
5.	Owner, small-scale hotel	Shareholder in logistics company in Kunming	• Rents a 3-floor building for 8-room hotel from Thai business owner	• Mobile manager and owner • Modern management, hiring Thai professionals, employees for routine specific task • Online booking, digital payment
6.	Manager, shareholder of resort hotel	Shareholder in 5-star hotel in Shanghai	• Rents land, old resort from Thai owner • Manager and shareholder • Company registration under Thai Law • Using Thai-Chinese friend network for company registration	• Modern management setting as a company (human resources, accounting, sales marketing) • Hiring Thai professionals, employees for routine specific tasks, online-booking, walk-in customers, digital payment, old-styled personality + knowledge (trust, good relation, diligent, learning knowledge acquirement)
7.	Resort hotel, noodle restaurant (Halal food)	Shareholder in real estate investment and restaurant in northern China	• Rents land, old resort from Thai business owner for 9 years • Company registration under Thai Law • Using Thai-Chinese friend network for company registration	Online-booking, walk-in customers, digital payment and cash Modern management, hiring Thai professionals, employees for specific tasks (Thai manager and staff who speak Chinese/English, cook from Qinghai, Thai waitress)
8.	Real estate company (sells condominiums, houses) Consulting service in buying land, business in Thailand	Education service, stock market, guesthouse owner	• Company registration under Thai Law • Using Thai friend network (who have been working together) for company registration	• Modern management, hiring Thai professionals, employees for specific tasks (human resources, sales marketing in 3 different languages), Thai shareholder works for land arrangement, Chinese and Lee work on Chinese market arrangement, Aware of Thai legality, trust

(continued)

Table 12.3 (continued)

KI	*Business and investment diversification*		*Entrepreneurship*	
	Primary business	*Extra business*	*Business operation*	*Technology support and design*
9.	E-commerce, export Thai products (rubber, pillows, dried fruits, cosmetics)	Tour agency, direct sale, shareholder with Thai-Chinese friend for cosmetics import-export business	• Rents a 2-floor home office for family house and office to stock product and display space, Modern business, go for online shopping market, Chinese customers and worldwide	• E-commerce based online shopping markets • Using WeChat and various based on quality/class items online platforms for different online shopping customers • Change Thai products for exporting in 2–3 years
10.	Logistics company, shipping Thai products (fruits, rubber, pillows, cosmetics, etc.)	Tour guide Shareholder in tour company	• Company registration under Thai Law	• Closed circuit television surveillance for security, global position system for logistics examination, online order, telephone • Different shipping routes depend on Thai products

important, it may still be used in some cases. *Guanxi* networks, such as Thai-Chinese citizens known for many years or their Chinese partners who came to Thailand over years past, assist entrepreneurs with information and communication. Interviewee 6, for example, rented land and took over an old resort from a previous Thai owner who he heard about through a close Chinese friend. The friend knew the Thai owner through a Thai-Chinese national network. That type of *guanxi* network does not represent the dark side of *guanxi*, rather it is used as a type of shortcut to save time and costs to facilitate business development. It is worth noting that this kind of *guanxi* network is not necessarily used in all cases because entrepreneurs have access to people and opportunities via their formal trade channels and the internet. For example, entrepreneurs can find information about places for rent through online advertisements written in Chinese posted on online platforms.

However, some informants have uniquely redefined *guanxi* on a philosophical level rather than on a strategic one. For example, Interviewee 6 defines *guanxi* as the ability to gain trust from customers by providing good services which guarantees that customers come back to his business. He insists that young Chinese entrepreneurs should be diligent, peaceful, and professional and always gain new knowledge to advance. *Guanxi*, in that sense means cultivating both a good personality for self-improvement and growth (Fei 1992) and evokes the principle of trust (Yang 1994).

The Role of Government

Both the Chinese and Thai governments play a significant role in the success or failure of the transnational Chinese entrepreneurs' business ventures. Barabantseva (2011) argued that the Chinese Communist Party (CCP) has a desire to build a strong state and a prosperous society to overcome the legacies of imperialism and invasion and the dilemma of modernization. Those have been the underlying themes of state-led nationalism in China. One mechanism that the CCP uses with inbound and outbound Chinese subjects of mainland China is deterritorialized nationalism (Duara 1997, 2005). China has initiated transnational cultural politics by which it trans-nationalizes the Chinese identity among the diaspora and instills a sense of Chinese nationalism in the Overseas Chinese community (Nyiri 2001; Callahan 2006; Barabantseva 2011). On the one hand, deterritorialized nationalism helps to strategically refine the Chinese nation-state establishing codes of communication with both the state and societal forces transnationally. On the other hand, along with the "Going-Out" policy, the reemergence of Overseas Chinese nationalism employed by the Chinese state can increase the number and facilitate *xin yimin* (new migrants) (Zhuang 2007; Nyiri and Saveliev 2002; Nyiri 2007; Liu 2005; Callahan 2008; Siriphon 2015). For the increasing flow of Chinese migrant entrepreneurs into the Mekong region, the People's Republic of China not only effectively influences local and national economies of the host countries, but actively asserts its symbolic and ideological presence in the region. Thus China can expand its presence in the region through Chinese migrant entrepreneurs.

The increasing Chinese entrepreneur capitalism in China and beyond was stimulated after the 1990s by the Chinese state and the market-oriented reforms initiated by Chinese leader Deng Xiaoping (Smart and Smart 2005). The growing Chinese entrepreneur capitalism in China emerged partly from the economic reform policy regarding business loss of SOEs in China which were replaced by small and medium non-SOEs. Meanwhile, after 2000, SMEs were supported by promoting technological innovation policies and development, granting financial support for SME development by tax incentives, and improving the financing environment for SMEs (Chen 2006; Liu 2008). Since then, urban collective enterprises, town and village enterprises (TVE), and the private and self-employment sector have been growing and flourishing throughout China. The TVE is recognized as the main driving economic mechanism of China's economic development. After 2010, the China-ASEAN Free Trade Area, along with the Chinese government's announcement of the Going-Out strategy, encouraged domestic enterprises including SMEs to invest overseas. The policy has been a success in promoting China's local SMEs participating in foreign management and competition in various forms. China's Ministry of Commerce reported that at the beginning of SME promotional policies in 2003, there were more than 20,000 enterprises that participated in foreign investment, 70% of those were SMEs. Foreign direct investment (FDI) policies for SMEs have become the major part of transnational management of China's enterprises, whose failure or success is determined by the accomplishment of One Belt One Road (OBOR) (Wang 2014).

Chinese migrant entrepreneurs in Thailand are part of the Chinese government OBOR that encourages domestic entrepreneurs, including

SMEs, to invest overseas. The Chinese state is explicitly proactive in helping create transnational entrepreneurship and a business-friendly environment through effective relevant policies and strategies operating in and outside China and advancing technological telecommunication to indirectly support and facilitate transnational Chinese business.

The Thai government plays a less active role in regulating transnational Chinese entrepreneurship in Thailand and that less active role has had a negative effect on Thai groups of small- and medium-sized tourism-related businesses. A notable example is how the Thai government has failed to do anything about the gaps in Thai law relating to ownership. The Thai government said that it would obstruct business environment in Thailand. The private property law, Civil and Commercial Law of Thailand, and the Foreign Business Act of 1999, have resulted in using nominee shareholders to create illegal joint ventures for the sole purpose of owning property in Thailand. At the end of 2016, the Thai government took steps to stop illegal business practices. The Ministry of Commerce, Department of Tourism, Department of Business Development, and Department of Special Investigation of Royal Thai Police, collaboratively began monitoring businesses that they suspected were operating illegally. Recently, the Thai government reported that the monitoring would continue and extend to 17 provinces from ten provinces.

The Thai government has focused on launching economic policies and strategies to assist big firms and larger scale business and investment. For example, to attract FDI, the Board of Investment of Thailand (BOI) created several promotion measurements, including tax incentives focusing exclusively on foreign firms' large-scale investments, and exemptions of corporate income tax for the first 8 years of investment in Thailand. The BOI also offered a 50% corporate income tax reduction for up to 5 years and includes an exemption for foreign investment companies to have 100% shared ownership when the investment is for export. In the event of investment in the industrial sector establishing a headquarters or international branch in Thailand, it is permitted to own 100% of the land and bring skilled workers and experts to work in promoted activities (BOI 2017).

China is actively creating incentive policies to support the economic growth in and outside China for both small- and large-scale investments. The Thai government, on the other hand, focuses only on economic policies and strategies to assist larger-scale businesses and investment. Those policies do not provide sufficient room for Thai entrepreneurs in small- and medium-scale businesses to compete. The results have proved that Thai laws are often one step behind in preventing aggressive strategic policy to stimulate growth of other countries whose nationals are attempting to penetrate the Thai market.

Chinese entrepreneurs provide a new competitiveness for Thai business, which is especially so in the handicraft manufacturing, hotel, logistics, and shipping industries formerly run by Thai business owners in Hang Dong and San Kam Paeng districts attracting tourists to Chiang Mai. During this research, at least five Thai SMEs closed their businesses or sold them to Chinese entrepreneurs (Interview, November 2015). Other Thai businessmen rented or leased their businesses, while still others sought emerging markets by building new networks, however, that requires investment and can be constrained by new Thai regulations.

Conclusion

There are two significant findings to better understand Chinese diaspora and transnationalism in Thailand. The first is a new type of recent Chinese entrepreneurs from middle-class backgrounds who run small transnational businesses. The second is the role of the Chinese and Thai policies. While the Chinese state has played a proactive role in advancing policies and strategies to encourage Chinese emigration and investment, the role of the Thai state has been less active in promoting Thai entrepreneurs, and especially in handling transnational Chinese entrepreneurs' business in Thailand. Thai policy has been slower and narrower than Chinese policy in creating incentives that can support business development and growth equitably. The Thai government, with its less proactive approach and narrow-minded policies, causes insecurity in the Thai economy. With the intense competitive atmosphere driven by the growing transnational Chinese entrepreneurs in Thailand, that can potentially harm Thai entrepreneurs of small- and medium-sized tourism-related businesses to the point where they can hardly share any part of the market.

Note

1. According to Reuters, about 85% of the Chinese stock markets in Hong Kong, Shenzhen, and Shanghai are traded by Chinese individual retail investors rather than institutional investors. It is everyday Chinese citizens that dominate the market which is unlike many of the world's stock markets. See more details at http://www.reuters.com/article/us-china-stocks-idUSKCN0PI04Q20150708 (accessed on February 12, 2017).

Bibliography

Barabantseva, Elena. 2011. *Overseas Chinese, Ethnic Minorities, and Nationalism: De-centering China*. New York: Routledge.

BOI (Thailand Board of Investment). 2017. "A Guide to the Board of Investment 2017." Accessed December 24, 2017. http://www.boi.go.th/index.php?page=guides.

Callahan, William A. 2006. "History, Identity, and Security: Producing and Consuming Nationalism in China." *Critical Asian Studies* 38, no. 2: 179–208.

Callahan, William A. 2008. "Chinese Visions of World Order: Post-hegemonic or a New Hegemony?" *International Studies Review* 10, no. 4: 749–761.

Chan, K. Bun, ed. 2000. *Chinese Business Networks: State, Economy and Culture*. Singapore: Prentice Hall.

Chan, K. Bun, and B.K. Ng. 2001. "Singapore." In *Chinese Business in Southeast Asia: Contesting Cultural Explanations, Researching Entrepreneurship*, edited by Terence E. Gomez and Hsin-Huang Michael Hsiao, 38–61. London: Routledge.

Chen, Dung-Sheng, Sue-Ching Jou, and Hsin-Huang Michael Hsiao. 2008. "Transforming Guanxi Networks: Taiwanese Enterprises' Production Networks in Thailand and Vietnam." In *Chinese Entrepreneurship in a Global Era*, edited by Raymond Sin-Kwok Wong, 149–165. London: Routledge.

Chen, Guangjin, Jun Li, and Harry Matlay. 2006. "Who Are the Chinese Private Entrepreneurs?" *Journal of Small Business and Enterprise Development* 13, no. 2: 148–160.

Chen, Jia. 2006. "Development of Chinese Small and Medium-Sized Enterprises." *Journal of Small Business and Enterprise Development* 13, no. 2: 140–147.

Doody, Sean, Victor T. Chen, and Jesse Goldstein. 2016. "Varieties of Entrepreneurial Capitalism: The Culture of Entrepreneurship and Structural Inequalities of Work and Business Creation." *Sociology Compass* 10, no. 10: 858–876.

Duara, Prasenjit. 1997. "Nationalists among Transnationals: Overseas Chinese and the Idea of China, 1900–1911." In *Ungrounded Empires: The Cultural Politics of Modern Chinese Transnationalism*, edited by Aiwha Ong and Donald Nonini. New York: Routledge.

Duara, Prasenjit. 2005. "The Legacy of Empire and Nations in East Asia." In *China Inside Out: Contemporary Chinese Nationalism and Transnationalism*, edited by Pal Nyiri and Joana Breindenbach, 35–54. Budapest: Central European University Press.

Fei, Xiaotong. 1992. *From the Soil: The Foundation of Chinese Society*. Translated by Gary G. Hamilton and Wang Zheng. Berkeley: University of California Press.

Foo, Check-teck, and Check-tong Foo. 2000. "Socialization of Technopreneurism towards Symbiosis in Corporate Innovation and Technology Strategy." *Technovation* 20: 551–562.

Gomez, Edmund T., and Michael Hsiao, eds. 2001. *Chinese Business in South-East Asia: Contesting Cultural Explanations, Researching Entrepreneurship*. Surrey: Curzon Press.

Graceffo, Antonio. 2016. "A Look at China's Middle Class." PhD diss., Shanghai University of Sport, China PRC.

Hays, Jeffrey. 2015. "Facts and Details Middle Class in China". Accessed March 2017. http://factsanddetails.com/china/cat11/sub70/item156.html.

Hefner, W. Robert. 1998. "Introduction: Society and Modernity in the New Asian Capitalism." In *Market Cultures: Society and Morality in the New Asian Capitalisms*, edited by Robert W. Hefner, 1–38. Oxford: Westview Press.

Kipnis, Andrew. 1997. *Producing Guanxi: Sentiment, Self and Subculture in a North China Village*. Durham, NC: Duke University Press.

Liu, Hong. 2005. "New Migrants and the Revival of Overseas Chinese Nationalism." *Journal of Contemporary China* 14, no. 43: 291–316.

Liu, Hong. 2008. "Immigrant Transnational Entrepreneurship and Linkages with the State/Network: Sino-Singaporean Experience in a Comparative Perspective." In *Chinese Entrepreneurship in a Global Era*, edited by Raymond Sin-Kwok Wong, 118–148. London: Routledge.

Liu, Hong. 2012. "Beyond a Revisionist Turn: Networks, State and the Changing Dynamics of Diasporic Chinese Entrepreneurship." *China: An International Journal* 10, no. 3: 20–41.

Liu, Xiangfeng. 2016. "SME Development in China: A Policy Perspective on SME Industrial Clustering." In *SME in Asia and Globalization*, edited by H. Lim, 37–68. ERIA Research Project Report 2007. Accessed September 10, 2016. http://www.eria.org/SME%20Development%20in%20China_A%20Policy%20Perspective%20on%20SME%20Industrial%20Clustering.pdf.

Menkhoff, Thomas, and Solvay Gerke, eds. 2002. *Chinese Entrepreneurship and Asian Business Networks*. London: Routledge Curzon.

Milton-Smith, John. 1999. *The Making of Technopreneur*. Singapore: ITE Alumni Association.

Nee, Victor. 1992. "Organizational Dynamics of Market Transition: Hybrid Forms, Property Rights, and Mixed Economy in China." *Administrative Science Quarterly* 37: 1–27.

Nyiri, Pal. 2001. "Expatriating Is Patriotic? The Discourse on 'New Migrants' in the People's Republic of China and Identity Construction among Recent Migrants from the PRC." *Journal of Ethnic and Migration Studies* 27, no. 4: 635–653.

Nyiri, Pal. 2007. *Chinese in Russia and Eastern Europe: A Middleman Minority in a Transnational Era*. Abingdon, Oxon: Routledge.

Nyiri, Pal, and Igor R. Saveliev, eds. 2002. *Globalizing Chinese Migration: Trends in Europe and Asia*. Burlington, VT: Ashgate.

Ong, Aiwha. 2005. "Anthropological Concepts for the Study of Nationalism." In *China Inside Out*, edited by Pal Nyiri and Joana Breidenbach, 1–34. Budapest: Central European Press.

Redding, Gordon S. 1995. *The Spirit of Chinese Capitalism*. Berlin: De Gruyter.

Ren, Na, and Hong Liu. 2015. "Traversing between Transnationalism and Integration: Dual Embeddedness of New Chinese Immigrant Entrepreneurs in Singapore." *Asian and Pacific Migration Journal* 24, no 3: 298–326.

Santasombat, Yos. 2015. "Introduction." In *Impact of China's Rise on the Mekong Region*, edited by Yos Santasombat, 1–22. New York: Palgrave Macmillan.

Siriphon, Aranya. 2015. "'Xinyimin', New Chinese Migrants and the Influence of the People's Republic of China (PRC) and Taiwan on the Northern Thai Border." In *Impact of China's Rise on the Mekong Region*, edited by Yos Santasombat, 147–166. New York: Palgrave Macmillan.

Siriphon, Aranya. 2016. "Border Guanxi: *Xinyimin* and Transborder Trade in Northern Thailand." In *Chinese Encounters in Southeast Asia: How People, Money, and Ideas from China Are Changing a Region*, edited by Pal Nyiri and Danielle Tan, 59–79. Settle: University of Washington Press.

Smart, Alan, and Josephine Smart, eds. 2005. *Petty Capitalists and Globalization: Flexibility, Entrepreneurship, and Economic Development*. Albany, NY: State University of New York Press.

Tsang, Eric W.K. 1998. "Can Guanxi be a Source of Sustained Competitive Advantage for Doing Business in China?" *Academy of Management Executive* 12, no. 2: 64–73.

Wang, Qianfeng. 2014. "Analysis on the Policies of FDI from SMEs about Chinese Out-Going Strategy." *International Journal of Business Administration* 5, no. 6: 61–64.

Weidenbaum, Murray. 1996. "The Chinese Family Business Enterprise." *California Management Review* 38, no. 4: 141–156.

Weller, R.P. 1998. "Divided Market Cultures in China: Gender, Enterprise, and Religion." In *Market Cultures: Society and Morality in the New Asian Capitalisms*, edited by Robert W. Hefner, 78–103. Oxford: Westview Press.

Whitley, Richard. 1992. *Business System in East Asia*. London: Sage.

Wong, Raymond Sin-Kwok. 2008. "Introduction: A New Breed of Chinese Entrepreneurs? Critical Reflections." In *Chinese Entrepreneurship in a Global Era*, edited by Raymond Sin-Kwok Wong, 3–26. London: Routledge.

Yang, Mayfair. 1994. *Gifts, Favors, and Banquets: The Art of Social Relationships in China*. Ithaca, NY: Cornell University Press.

Yarzebinski, J. 1992. "Understanding and Encouraging the Entrepreneur." *Economic Development Review* 10, no. 1: 32–35.

Yeung, Henry Wai-chung. 2004. *Chinese Capitalism in a Global Era: Towards Hybrid Capitalism*. London: Routledge.
Yeung, Irene Y.M., and Rosalie L. Tung. 1996. "Achieving Business Success in Confucian Societies: The Importance of Guanxi (Connections)." *Organizational Dynamics* 25, no. 2 Autumn: 54–65.
Zhou, Xiaohong. 2010. "Who Are China's Middle Class?" Retrieved March 2, 2017. http://www.china.org.cn/china/2010-01/23/content_19293900.htm.
Zhou, Xiaohong. 2017. "Who Are China's Middle Class?" 2010. Accessed March 2, 2017. http://www.china.org.cn/china/2010-01/23/content_19293900.html.
Zhuang, Guotu. 2000. "Policies of the Chinese Government toward Overseas Chinese Since 1978." China Area Studies Series, no. 10. Tokyo: Ministry of Education, Science, Sports and Culture, Scientific Research in Priority Areas 113, Structural Changes in Contemporary China.
Zhuang, Guotu. 2007. "China's Policies towards Overseas Chinese." In *The Encyclopedia of the Overseas Chinese*, edited by L. Pan, 2nd edition. Singapore: Didier Millet.

CHAPTER 13

Negotiating the Rise and Vice of People's Republic of China Transnational Entrepreneurs: Multiple Strategies by Thai-Yunnanese Small and Medium Enterprises in Chiang Mai

Kian Cheng Lee

Introduction

This chapter posits that Thai-Yunnanese entrepreneurs from small and medium enterprises (SMEs) utilize multiple strategies to mitigate the challenges and seize opportunities posed by People's Republic of China (PRC) transnational entrepreneurs in Chiang Mai, Thailand. The author has chosen to explore the versatile and diverse strategies adopted by Thai-Yunnanese SME entrepreneurs against the backdrop of the recent rise of PRC transnational entrepreneurs. Chiang Mai was chosen as a site due to its prominence and cultural significance in northern Thailand. The city has industries, including agriculture, tourism, food

K. C. Lee (✉)
School of International Affairs, Faculty of Political Science and Public Administration, Chiang Mai University, Chiang Mai, Thailand

Y. Santasombat (ed.), *The Sociology of Chinese Capitalism in Southeast Asia*, https://doi.org/10.1007/978-981-13-0065-3_13

and beverages, and household products. These industries are business interests for many PRC transnational entrepreneurs.

Association of Southeast Asian Nations (ASEAN)–Sino policies have sought to facilitate ethnic Overseas Chinese business in Chiang Mai as a bridge between Thailand and China. On the surface there seems to be a growing, vibrant, and promising relationship between ethnic Overseas Chinese entrepreneurs and PRC private companies promoting a flow of investments. However, the win-win situation painted by the Overseas Chinese Multinational Corporations (MNCs) has inadvertently concealed the devastating impact of expanding PRC transnational business on the local Thai socio-economic and environmental landscape. Hence, the primary research objective of this chapter lies in the elucidation of the strategic interactions by the Thai-Yunnanese SME entrepreneurs against the masking effect generated with the rise of the PRC and the implementation of the ASEAN Economic Community (AEC). The guiding research questions are: Will China's economic growth advance or jeopardize a favorable environment of ethnic Chinese business networks in Southeast Asia? In what ways do the PRC Chinese transnational entrepreneurs enhance or encroach socio-economic, cultural, and environmental spheres in Chiang Mai province of northern Thailand? How do Thai-Yunnanese SME entrepreneurs perceive and utilize AEC?

Historical Context and Changing Sino-Thai Politico-Economic Relations

The first Chinese economic activities in Thailand were reported during the Sukhothai era (1238–1419) (Wu and Wu 1980). Between the years 1405 and 1433, China sent vast fleets, under the command of Admiral Zheng He, to Southeast Asia with the purpose of exacting tribute for the Ming Dynasty (Levathes 1994). By the end of the nineteenth century, Chinese involvement gradually extended from manufacturing and commercial sectors to agriculture and mining, which eventually expanded into the entire economy (Wu and Wu 1980). However, with the 1939 proclamation of Ratha Niyom ("a patriotic movement"), measures were designed to restrict Chinese activities (Wu and Wu 1980). In chronological order, those measures are as follows: (1) the 1951 restriction on remittances to PRC; (2) the 1956 requirement of firms to employ Thais for at least 50% of the positions; (3) the 1972 control of alien populations; and (4) the 1974 implementation of Thai nationals to hold 51% of the stock in joint ventures with alien-owned firms (Wu and Wu 1980). Surprisingly, it was the Cambodian Conflict (1978–1991) that forged close ties between Thailand and the PRC throughout the 1980s (Chinvanno 2015). In the 1990s, security-focused relations were broadened and deepened as trade, which culminated with the signing of Joint Declaration on the Cooperation Program of the twenty first century in 1999 (Freedman 2014).

During the past decades, the Chinese diaspora in Southeast Asia has significantly grown. Approximately 40 million ethnic Chinese residing outside of Mainland China, Hong Kong, Macau, and Taiwan in 2003 had reached over 60 million by 2014 (Dalpino and Steinberg 2003; Liu and Dongen 2016). It is worth noting that Thailand has the largest Overseas Chinese population in any Southeast Asian country (Jacques 2009). Recent migrants differ from their predecessors in terms of maintaining extensive networks as well as cultural and political attachments to the PRC (Santasombat 2015). They identify themselves as Zhongguo Ren or Chinese nationals/citizens and are supported by regional economic policies and regional cooperation (Siriphon 2015). Siriphon (2015) highlighted three factors related to economic and political conditions that explained that migration to Thailand: (1) the opening of the PRC to the world through Chinese economic reform in the 1980s; (2) the regionalization of the Greater Mekong Subregion, which has connected the PRC to mainland Southeast Asia since the early 1990s; and (3) Chinese soft power as part of the PRC government's foreign policy for countries in Southeast Asia. In recent years, Thailand has engendered a sense of confidence and affection for the PRC, garnered through the PRC support of Thailand's security and economy during times of crisis. For instance, Thailand asked China to purchase surplus agricultural products such as rice, rubber, and fruit, and encourage tourists to the Thai market which may lead to Thailand's unrealistic expectation, verging on dependency, with the PRC (Chinvanno 2015). Thailand's policymakers must be aware of the socio-economic and political realities on the ground and develop policies accordingly.

In recent years, the PRC has emerged as the second largest economy in the world and foreign direct investment (Tong 2014). Unlike past warlike ascending great powers, the PRC has a strategy that depends on an international environment of peace to achieve the main goal of economic development (The State Council Information Office 2005). The tone of the PRC's global intentions seems to have strengthened under the leadership of President Xi Jinping (Chinvanno 2015). On November 29, 2012, President Xi announced the "Chinese Dream" and a future where the PRC will "forge ahead like a gigantic ship breaking through strong winds and heavy waves" (Xi 2014). China has since touted itself as a new model of development and political discourse in an unprecedented wave of change with win-win interests for all mankind (Zhang 2012). On April 22, 2016, President Xi received a new title as commander-in-chief of China's new joint battle command center which could be a move to consolidate his power over the military (Ramzy 2016). According to state media, he stressed that battle command capacities should be measured by "the standards of being able to fight and win wars" (Ramzy 2016). Those collectively raised the possibility of China as a "potential hegemon in the region" (Chinvanno 2015). How will this "potential hegemon" impact Southeast Asian countries?

Many scholars in Southeast Asian Chinese studies view the rise of the PRC from a favorable perspective. Qiu (2000) argued that the rise of China and the economic development in Asia-Pacific will provide Chinese with favorable circumstances. According to Viraphol (2006) and Astarita's (2008) review of Wong (2006), the PRC's economic rise will prove "to be not only a new engine for development in the Asian region, but also a catalyst for integrating the Southeast Asian economies" (Viraphol 2006). Unwittingly, the PRC's economic development has been perceived as vital for the mobilization of global resources of capital, market, know-how, and talent by overseas Chinese entrepreneurs (Astarita 2008; Viraphol 2006). However, Santasombat (2015) cited some scholars and activists who have criticized PRC strategies to secure a steady supply of energy and raw materials through the expansion into new markets, creation of economic partnerships, and forging political alliances with individual countries. Other scholars have lamented the struggle for soft power in Asia, especially from the PRC, arguing that such struggle might aggravate rather than ameliorate tensions in the region (Hall and Smith 2013). This chapter seeks to unravel the contesting perspectives within the dialectic presence of opportunities and threats.

Appadurai (2000) articulated the idea of deterritorialization whereby money managers seek the best markets for their investments, independent of national boundaries. Citing the example of the impact of rich Arabs in Bombay, Appadurai (2000) described the substantial alteration of the local price of mangoes and the profile of hotels, restaurants, and other services. Similarly, yet distinctively, there are some PRC transnational entrepreneurs in Chiang Mai who are deterritorializing natural and economic resources.

The following section provides interviews with Chiang Mai-based business owners and academics to reveal contrasting views of the impact of PRC involvement in the agriculture market. According to some interviewees, the predatory business practices of the PRC transnational entrepreneurs are primarily in the agriculture industry. One example is the monopolization of agriculture trading centers and orchard acquisitions and a restrictive customs department. However, some respondents disputed those arguments as over-exaggerated and proposed positive alternatives to embrace the rise of the PRC. That imbroglio of opposing perspectives reveals the complexity of embedded motivations and provides the space for diverse strategic responses.

Interview with a Director at a Research Institute of Chiang Mai University

The respondent elaborated on deterritorialization as practiced by some Chinese transnational entrepreneurs. During Thailand's agricultural harvest, fruit growers conduct their business on a free carrier basis and deliver their freight to a trading center where fresh fruits are purchased by traders. Some transnational entrepreneurs set up trading centers through transnational marriages with local Thai workers. Those Thai local wives are instrumental in insulating them from legal and financial woes when their companies, which are registered under their Thai wives' names, face bankruptcy. Having established their first trading centers, the PRC transnational entrepreneurs acquire other Thai-owned trading centers. If the Thai owners refuse to sell, they wage a price war by paying more money to the Thai fruit growers. As a result, their "join or die" strategy forces Thai owners to concede. Through such aggressive tactics, some PRC transnational entrepreneurs have already taken over a sizeable part of the longan trade in Chiang Mai, which is considered one of the best in the world.

For the past few years, adverse weather conditions and other factors combined with an ailing economy have led Thai growers to resort to leasing out their orchards to transnational entrepreneurs from the PRC. To accelerate growth for harvest, the entrepreneurs sometimes inject chemicals into the soil. While that generates a bountiful harvest for the first few years, the destructive method expels nutrition from the plants and renders the soil useless after a few years. Additionally, they often use pesticides that leave substantial residue on the crops and contaminate the rivers and canals which cause health issues.

The director explained that the restrictive PRC Customs Department is discriminatory toward Thai traders and exporters. There are five big Chinese shipping companies at the checkpoints, known as the "five tigers," who are designated to assist foreign fruit exporters to clear food customs. However, if one chooses not to pay them nor engage their services, they create problems including unreasonable rejection or delays due to an extended administrative process, such as getting approval documents from Beijing. In contrast, the PRC transnational entrepreneurs easily clear customs and import Thai fruits into the PRC. One example of overcoming that hurdle is a cooperative of Thai exporters of dried longan who took a bank loan of about 20 million baht (US$600,000) and set up a company, Longan Thai-China Amata Co. Ltd, in China. However, that company was recently ordered to shut down by the Chinese provincial government after less than two years of operation.

Interview with a Thai-Yunnanese Director of an Import–Export Company

As a Thai-Yunnanese entrepreneur, the respondent is the founder and director of an import–export company. He shared candidly about the competition saying, "Just last year, I lost about 60 million Thai baht due to competition with PRC Chinese who had booked entire orchards. But we need to fight this battle. It goes like this. Having seen the lucrative opportunity, these PRC Chinese came with massive force. They didn't just buy but they rented parcels of land…for 3 or 5 years. Just recently, there was a Shanghainese who rented over 3000 rai which is equivalent to 4.8 million square meters for over 3 or 5 years…I have about more than 30 PRC transnational entrepreneurs, who used to be my clients, have come over to rent orchards directly dealing with Longans, Mangoes, Durians and Mangosteen…Thus, those who rented orchards have already gained superior advantage and raised capital. This is because everybody is competing to purchase fruits as fruits harvested in Thailand are of excellent quality. So as an exporter, I need to purchase fruits as well. Hence, with the increased selling price, I suffered" (Interview, June 7, 2016).

He further explained the ecological impact of those agricultural practices, as well as the restrictive and prejudicial treatment by the customs department: "Another thing is that when the Chinese came over to rent the land, they would use pesticides to accelerate the growth of the plants…For instance, while the limit might be set at 0.5 kg, they could liberally increase till 2 kg. Consequently, the soil is destroyed. So 3 years later, the trees no longer become fruitful because for over 3 years, they'd been forcing the plants to bloom daily. Hence, in my opinion, down the road, this would greatly impact Thai agricultural industry…When I was importing fruits into Guangzhou China, the PRC customs complained that the residual sulfur dioxide component on my Longans is too high. Someone has lodged a complaint there. There are some people who specialized in finding faults. The irony behind this is that the goods imported by the PRC transnational entrepreneurs into China had far more sulfur dioxide content but were granted approval successfully by the PRC customs! Consequently, one of my subsidiary companies was banned for a year while another was banned for about 8 months. They actually didn't stipulate timeframe of banning. So you need to write letters of appeal to Beijing and await their clearance" (Interview, June 7, 2016).

Interview with a Vice Dean at Chiang Mai University

Another perspective of PRC transnational entrepreneurialism is provided by a Vice Dean at Chiang Mai University. Having previously done research in the agriculture-related field, the professor provided an alternative perspective to the behaviors of the entrepreneurs. He explained that there are many instances of overexaggeration and prejudice. For instance, with regard to the utilization of pesticides and chemicals to accelerate growth, he argued that some of those practices have also been carried out by Thai locals. He shared how Thais should not merely engage the rise of transnational entrepreneurship by traditional methods or rely on governmental support. On the contrary, Thais should be innovative in e-commerce to better engage with the emerging transnational market. In the digital age, it is crucial to understand and catch up with the transforming landscape in agriculture business.

AEC and Production Fetishism

The AEC has its implementation challenges. When first introduced, there was little awareness and understanding in the private sector (Das 2012a). Existing domestic political forces hinder the implementation of the AEC at the national level with different business practices, non-tariff barriers, policy and protections, sub-regional agreements, external free trade agreements, and dispute settlement and institutions (Severino and Menon 2013). Nipon Poapongsakorn (2012) highlighted that Thailand ranked above average in the implementation of AEC in measures of a single market and production base, economic competitiveness, economic development, and integration into the global economy. In the analysis of Thailand's challenges in pursuing liberalization commitments under the AEC blueprint, Nipon Poapongsakorn (2012) argued that weak government and conflicts of interest in government agencies are the most crucial factors affecting the liberalization of the services sector. Appadurai argued that production and consumer fetishism are today's contemporary adaptations of Marx's commodity fetishism. He defined production fetishism as "an illusion created by contemporary transnational production loci, which masks trans-local capital, transnational earning-flows, global management, and often faraway workers" (Appadurai 2000). Production fetishism can produce an "imagined region" through the production of socio-economic and political imagination, constituted by so-called regional interests. In other words, although the implementation of AEC measures seems to serve as regional economic integration to improving lives, strengthening leaders' legitimacy and sending positive signals to the international business community, it has masked the struggles and maneuvers of Thai-Yunnanese entrepreneurs (Severino and Menon 2013).

Another view is that of Das who stated that "so far the top-down approach to establishing a single market and productive base has been carried out. But realizing an AEC also requires a bottom-up style that involves the interests, requirements, opinions, and actions of the business sector, considering the market forces in operation (Das 2012b)." This section examines local Thai-Yunnanese SME entrepreneurs' multiplicity of strategies, with and without the AEC implementations, used to mitigate the challenges and opportunities brought about by the PRC transnational entrepreneurs in Chiang Mai.

Versatility of Thai-Yunnanese Entrepreneurs in Chiang Mai Province

Thai-Yunnanese SME entrepreneurs demonstrate great versatility in PRC entrepreneurs' adaption. Thai-Yunnanese transnational entrepreneurs in Chiang Mai simultaneously possess multiple sets of identities in what Eidheim (1971) labeled dichotomization and complementarization (Lee 2015). Those entrepreneurs have simultaneously distinguished themselves as Thai, Thai-Chinese, and Thai-Yunnanese, while constructing commonalities with PRC Chinese transnationally and Yunnanese trans-locally (Lee 2015). Those forms of identifications are politico-economically situated in capital accumulation and transformation against the backdrop of historical marginality. Succinctly, they have actively employed economic cultures of guanxi in capital interaction to shed their past social stigma and gain class mobility through symbolic power (Lee 2015). Finally, from a linguistic perspective, Thai-Yunnanese have an advantage over other Thai-Chinese because many of them can speak Mandarin.

This research takes on an actor-oriented qualitative approach through in-depth interviews with several respondents. Four individuals were selected for the case studies because of their prominent social standing, different industrial affiliations, as well as their distinct modes of interactions with the PRC transnational entrepreneurs.

Resistance Strategy: Case Study of a Thai-Yunnanese Entrepreneur

This is a study of a Thai-Yunnanese transnational entrepreneur who became the founder and director of a company at the age of 36 years. The company exports fresh fruits, such as longan, mangosteen, durian, lychees, and tamarins, as well as dried longan to Indonesia, China, and Taiwan.

The interviewee has not seen any substantial benefits brought about by the AEC. Some less significant benefits of the AEC observed include an opportunity to accumulate cultural capital and improved access to resources, such as regional labor. He shared: "I would like to talk about cultural exchange. This is something which I felt that is not too bad in the AEC. I am referring to knowing more languages. I felt it is good that through the AEC there is a greater exchange of languages and thinking perspectives from different countries. Without the AEC, countries like Laos and Myanmar were considered as closed-up countries. With the AEC, they have to open up their doors" (Interview, June 7, 2016).

In other words, the AEC provided a stimulating platform in which the respondent could acquire new languages and perspectives. At the same time, the AEC could also assist him in his business expansion. With the opening of certain countries, he found that it was now easier to access resources, he could employ regional workers. "With AEC opening up, Myanmar workers now have passports to travel. All they need is to get their passport stamped in order to cross over here. And they can come here to work for me. Besides, there are also workers from Cambodia and Laos as well" (Interview, June 7, 2016). Hence, he has employed up to several hundred regional workers during certain peak seasons for about three months for different fruit harvests. In so doing, he has a more flexible and relatively cost-effective workforce.

This particular respondent utilizes institutional and interpersonal networking to resist the predatory business practices of PRC transnational entrepreneurs. For instance, he commented that he has joined Thailand Fruit Export Trade Association (泰国水果出口商协会), which is organized mainly by Thai-Chinese export companies. The association discussed and reported the orchard issue mentioned above to the Thai government officials. With regard to that incident of the PRC Customs Department banning a total of 34 Thai export companies, the association also discussed that in their biannual meeting and reported to the Thailand Agriculture Department. As a result, the authorities sent delegates to pay the PRC Customs Department a visit, which proved to be effective as the ban was subsequently lifted (Interview, June 7, 2016). He explained that although it was simply a routine visit, the PRC Customs Department seemed to "have gotten the message." In that manner, the local institutional networking as an association has further been elevated into a viable form of politico-economic force at the bilateral institutional networking level. In response, the respondent actively adopts an interpersonal networking strategy in his metaphorical battle. According to him, there is a team of people who actively assist him in sourcing orchards. Although they are not directly employed by him, they share a strong relationship with him. He explains: "I have known them for more than 20 years. Hence, this is my competitive advantage. The PRC Chinese do not have such deep relationships and feelings with them. Human beings ultimately need to have relationships and feelings. This can only be achieved over an extended period. For instance, if they have difficulties in the family or when they are facing times of poverty, I would help them. Therefore, this is the key difference between money and relationships forged over the years" (Interview, June 7, 2016).

While the PRC transnational entrepreneurs have deterritorialized Thai fruit orchards through their shifting "hit and run" tactics, the respondent has utilized local knowledge to overcome the challenges. With regard to that, he shared: "There are both strengths and weaknesses in this. The disadvantage in this method is that in theory, it might seem easy but it would be difficult to handle in actual operations. So, in my speculation, the PRC transnational entrepreneurs would have a "headache" this coming year. Why? First, there might be drought in Thailand due to a lack of rain. Just like the saying goes, "man proposes, God disposes" (谋事在人,成事在天), I am sure they would definitely suffer losses this year...And also, when they rent the fruit orchards, they will need reliable workers to tend them. So, they will ultimately need to depend on the heavens (老天) if they want to reap a good harvest...All we need to do is to cherish our strengths. We know the geography of our country, Thailand. We know where the places in Thailand are that can produce fruit crops; in terms of speed efficiency and in terms of good quality. We are the local people and definitely this gives us our superiority and our competitive advantage over them. Such local knowledge requires substantial time to be cultivated. We have grown up here so we are more familiar with the geography of Thailand...Yes, we are always a step faster than them. For instance, when the PRC entrepreneurs come over, they need to look for local people to bring them around. Thus, they would be in a precarious situation for these local people might not be genuinely working for their interest" (Interview, June 7, 2016).

Apart from diverse local knowledge, he broadened his business networks to other countries and places to mitigate the challenges brought about by the PRC transnational entrepreneurs. For instance, he exports lychees to Indonesia and he actively seeks new places to export his durians. Although there are those who have stopped taking supplies from him, he still maintains a sizeable pool of customers in China. He stated: "Not everyone comes over to Thailand. Perhaps, only 1 or 2 from each city come over" (Interview, June 7, 2016). In a non-linear diversification approach, he actively seeks to ensure that his PRC customer base expands while networking to other localities.

Collaboration Strategy: Case Study of a First-Generation Thai-Yunnanese

The second case is a first-generation Thai-Yunnanese who successfully switched from the jade business to the food and beverage industry about a decade ago. He has started Curry Pot Restaurant, Hoja Restaurant, and Vanilla Café at Kad Suan Kaew Shopping Centre in the city of Chiang Mai.

As a businessman, he has sought to abide strictly to Thai laws while seeking to collaborate with the PRC transnational entrepreneurs. In fact, Thai laws serve as a protection for successful partnerships. In an interview (June 19, 2016) he referred to PRC transnational entrepreneurs as doing "many messy stuff following the old communist ways." By that he refers to those who started their Chinese restaurants without following the legal means. He explained: "If they really want to go into the catering business (餐饮业), they will need Thai locals to invest with them. If they don't, they will find anyone to be pseudo partners who, in actual practice, do not invest. In such cases, the immigration officers might inspect and ask to see their Thai counterparts. And if they cannot get them, they are seen to have committed offences" (Interview, June 19, 2016).

During the interview he cited a case of a PRC transnational entrepreneur who chose not to collaborate with a reliable Thai national and failed in complying to corporate laws. With a retiree visa, this budding PRC Chinese eagerly employed a Thai legal advisor to help him set up a company for his restaurant. Conveniently, the Thai advisor roped in some unknown Thai nationals to be his nominal pseudo-partners without any financial investments. Without checking legal issues carefully, he immediately rented and renovated a place to set up "麻辣宝宝," a Chinese restaurant catering to PRC Chinese tourists. Having started this business in less than a month, the Immigration Office conducted a routine inspection on the restaurant and he was slapped with a heavy fine for three charges: (1) Working with a retirement visa but without a proper working permit; (2) Does not even know the name and location of Thai partner; and (3) Transferring Myanmar workers from another company without proper transfer documents. As a result, the owner was forced to close the restaurant.

While the AEC does not seem to have any effect on him, he recognized the importance of opening and utilizing the Thai legal framework to his advantage. With the rise of China, there will inevitably be many transnational entrepreneurs who might move to Chiang Mai. However, instead of seeing it as a competition, he viewed it as an opportunity for collaboration: "To me, Thailand is a lawful place. We are Thai nationals and so it is more convenient for us to start companies here. However, when transnational entrepreneurs come over here to start companies, they need Thai citizens to collaborate with them-with a Thai-PRC ratio of 51:49. It is only when the Thais have started the company, that they can then invest in it. After this has been done, they can bring the documents to the Thailand Embassy in China (for instance, Kunming, Yunnan). It is only after they have processed visa issues there that they can come back here to conduct their business. If he wants to be a chef, then he needs to come here with a chef identity. If the person did not come with the correct visa, then they might be caught by immigration officers who check on them. So, in other words, if he comes with a tourist visa and does business, it is illegal. Thus, he can apply for the appropriate visa only when the company has been established. In this way, their entrance into Chiang Mai is beneficial to the Thai economy and won't have any bad effects" (Interview, June 19, 2016).

The respondent capitalized on his Thai citizenship to gain the upper hand. He relied on the stringent Thai policy on business collaboration with foreigners. Apart from his Thai nationality, he utilized his local knowledge of Thai legal matters to ensure a smooth business setup. He shared that: "It is a lawful business partnership unlike those fake ones where one party is not around. This is because we have a mutual contractual agreement. We look for a Thai lawyer who specializes in business setups at the provincial government level. For purely Thai business, one would go to Chiang Mai City Governmental Office but for those whose partnership involves foreigners, then they would have to apply at the Chiang Mai Provincial Office. So with regards to my partnership with the Chinese, we had to proceed to the provincial office. However, for my existing personal Thai company, I did it at the city office. So, for those who don't know about the intricate details, they simply look for any lawyers and consequently, they will lose money" (Interview, June 19, 2016).

This model of collaboration works particularly well in that case because of his vast knowledge of the intricate details related to legal matters in setting up a company. As a veteran experienced in running his own businesses, he is not easily fooled nor taken advantage of. Being the major shareholder, he was very confident of the collaboration strategy, which is beneficial to the Thai economy.

To achieve a successful business partnership, building trust is a crucial component. That applies mutually to both partners. When he was asked to share the process in which the collaboration was forged, he stated: “In the past, I never had any experience in doing business with them. It is only in recent times that they came over. To begin with, my son runs a car rental company for foreigners like the westerners and the Chinese. As a family, we also recommend houses for them to rent during their stay here. In most cases, these Chinese have to sign a contract to stay for a year with a monthly rate of 20,000 Thai Baht and the middleman extract a commission of a month’s rental rate. As for us, we are the middleman. Yet, we don’t do this intentionally as a money-making business. Let me explain. In the case of my collaboration, it actually started off with a woman who is my eldest daughter’s friend. She brought her child here to study. She is a proper woman so we helped her find a place to stay. It is a relatively cheap place and she is very happy. We also did not get any commission from her. In so doing, she has also found us to be very honest and law-abiding. Hence, even if the authorities inspect us, they have nothing to fear because we run proper business, unlike those who don’t have legal means. My daughter opened a tourist agency. This woman helps bring Chinese tourists and also sometimes she wants to get some dried longans. She also asked my daughter to help. She has been here for a couple of years. She actually knows my daughter through another mutual friend. Her husband also came. He had previously bought the latex pillows here to sell them in China. After knowing us, he also felt that he should do restaurant business” (Interview, June 19, 2016).

In this account, the respondent demonstrated his active engagement in networking and building trust through the business connections of his son and daughter. In so doing, he has involved his trusted loved ones as an additional precautionary measure to help him ascertain the credibility of his potential partners. On the other hand, through providing free services such as recommendation of places for accommodation, he has secured the woman’s trust which subsequently led to her husband becoming a business partner.

There are also advantages to having cultural and culinary knowledge. Being in the fluid landscape of the catering business for more than a decade, he has largely captured the taste buds of the locals, as well as Chinese tourists. As such, he can capitalize on this local knowledge: “In terms of food taste, we are asking to learn how to prepare the taste that is suitable for Chinese tourists and we would also research Thai flavor.

Our restaurant intends to cater to both Thai and Chinese taste buds" (Interview, June 19, 2016). Their restaurant is in a prominent district in Chiang Mai city attracting tourists and locals.

Mutual Exploitation: Case Study of a Tour Company

The interviewee in the third case runs a newly-opened tour company. She takes an approach the author calls "mutual exploitation". That is an approach where both parties benefit from each other while remaining autonomous. With regard to the AEC, the respondent candidly shared that it did not have any direct impact on her business. She felt that perhaps the timing was not ripe for her to reap any benefits. She attributed it to the unstable political situation in Thailand and pessimistically stated that it might take a while for her business to experience the AEC's positive outcomes.

Her diverse networking can be seen in the way she founded her company. From a networking perspective, her three business partners have wide and diverse connections: (1) A Thai citizen whose Thai husband works in Dubai; (2) A Thai citizen who works in Taiwan and often travels between both places; and (3) A Thai citizen who works as a tour guide. Those networks have provided a healthy stream of tourists from those places. She adopts both affective and instrumental networking approaches in various forms to secure business connections for her tourism business. First, she is sincere when assisting new PRC migrants. In one instance, she helped a Chinese woman, who was a mother accompanying her daughter to study (陪读妈妈) in Chiang Mai, Thailand. She gave her practical help with housing, transportation, schooling, and other parenting matters, and soon their friendship became a trusted and instrumental business relationship. They started discussing bringing Chinese tourists into Chiang Mai for mutual benefits. With that arrangement, she draws profit from a regular stream of customers while her friend earns a commission through the price difference between the price charged by the tour agency and the marked-up fees collected from tourists. That "mutual exploitation" strategy provides profit for both parties while offering freedom and flexibility to each without any long-term legal entanglements.

To enrich the "mutual exploitation" strategy, the respondent employs a niche marketing approach to tourism. She expands her conventional tour packages and caters to nontraditional but creative niche versions to meet emerging needs. For instance, she develops an education tour package known as "charity education" (爱心教育). In that model, she targets children who have "lacked culture and ethical values due to their communist upbringing environment" (Interview, July 2, 2016). In the same vein, her agency organizes rural and countryside tours for the children to view nature and do simple horticulture art for donating to the charity. Beyond education tourism, she has also explored new concepts such as health and retirement tours to attract the older group.

Romanticization Strategy: Case Study of a Mobile Café

The last case is of a business owner of a mobile café, as well as a self-employed transnational multilevel marketer with Addwell Beauty (Thailand) Company Ltd (Interview, March 1, 2016). In contrast to the previous cases, her example demonstrates drawing of optimal gratification from the inherent advantages of the AEC and the rise of China, termed as the "romanticization strategy." The respondent is full of praise for the AEC. She believes that the AEC has ushered Chinese capitalism and tourism into the region and has brought prosperity to the entire economic landscape. From a transnational business perspective, the AEC has opened regional markets where she can sell herbal sanitary pads and other skin beauty products to other countries such as Myanmar, Cambodia, and Laos. She believes that in the broader context, through the AEC, ASEAN countries could help one another more with their respective unique strengths.

Aside from the economic benefits, she thinks that the AEC has "forced us to develop ourselves" (Interview, March 1, 2016). With a more open regional ecosystem, there is greater interaction where one must adaptively learn without remaining complacent in insularity. She explains, "Look at the PRC. They are very industrious because they would not have food to eat if they were lazy. But the Thais can wake up as late as they want" (Interview, March 1, 2016). She started reading up on ASEAN and other regional countries to learn about their different values and strengths. She has also started picking up the English and Chinese languages. While embracing the positive impact of open regionalization, she thinks that the AEC has served as an impetus for her to appreciate and capitalize on Thai cultural strengths. For instance, she is aware that many Laotians are big fans of Thai celebrities and Thai pop culture in the same way as many Thais are obsessed with Korean pop culture. She believes that Thai people need to preserve their "Thainess" and typical characteristics such as gentleness and their warm hospitality. Additionally, she also believes that Thai people need to be proud and safeguard their cultural heritage of handicrafts, which cannot be duplicated elsewhere.

She works to establish networks with PRC Chinese. She genuinely looks out for them when they are setting up businesses in Chiang Mai and she takes the initiative to caution and guide them. She shared: "Whenever a Chinese business seems to flourish, some of the neighboring Thai rivals will not be happy. They will report to the immigration department, which will send officials to interrogate and thus interrupt the business. In a certain case, the Thai competitors spread rumors and ganged up on the Chinese. Consequently, many Chinese have bad experiences even though they have legitimate companies. Hence, I often advise them to make sure that they employ reliable and capable Thai nationals" (Interview, March 1, 2016).

In that way, she gradually secured many lasting and trustworthy networks through providing practical tips for business survival to the Chinese. Moreover, she strengthened networks by providing Chinese with her time and care. In one particular instance, she volunteered herself as an educator and babysitter to the Chinese. She shared: "Once, I saw a child of a Chinese woman misbehaving quite badly in public. The mother was quite distraught and helpless. I felt that I could help her. I then offered to spend at least an hour of personal time with the child over a period of time. I taught the child good values and helped him to be gentle and polite instead of being aggressive and ill-behaved" (Interview, March 1, 2016).

This example illustrates the kind of care she provides the Chinese, and has helped to build her network effectively with the newcomers. Finally, she is protective over the foreigners. She often thinks that any negative encounters experienced by foreigners will reduce economic opportunities for Thailand. Hence, she hopes that Thai laws will be evaluated and tightened to protect foreigners from unfair treatment.

Because of her optimism, she adopts several innovative and diverse perspectives to capitalize on the growing transnational PRC market in Chiang Mai. For instance, she is taking a course that will enable her to acquire an official license to be a tour guide. She can then tap into the opportunities brought about by the phenomenal growth of tourists in Chiang Mai. In the same train of thought, she is preparing to set up homestay services for Chinese travelers, which will provide a safe and authentic immersive experience for them. She intends to extend her sales of herbal sanitary pads and skin beauty products into the Chinese markets through subsidiary PRC marketers.

Conclusion

The case studies in this chapter are not meant to be exhaustive and the strategies are not static and rigid. They are but a sampling of the multiplicity of responses adopted by Thai-Yunnanese entrepreneurs in Chiang Mai to mitigate the rise and business practices of Chinese transnational entrepreneurs in Chiang Mai. The table in Fig. 13.1 summarizes the various strategies against the social topographies (Urry 2000) of region, network, and fluids in capital accumulation.

The multiplicity of strategies shown in this research has aptly demonstrated the flexibility involved in mitigating the challenges and seizing opportunities posed by the Chinese transnational entrepreneurs in Chiang Mai. There is a need to reevaluate the underlying assumptions in the existing policies and perspectives. One respondent commented:

	Resistance	**Collaboration**	**Mutual Exploitation**	**Romanticization**
Region (AEC)	*Cultural exchange and capitalizing regional resources through the AEC*	*Utilizing Thai legal framework to gain superior ground in collaboration*	*No immediate benefits from the AEC*	*Rich opportunities in economic benefits and self-development through the AEC*
Network (Inter-connectedness)	*Mitigating through institutional and interpersonal networking tactics*	*Networking through family model in multiple services*	*Variegated forms of networking for business connections*	*Genuine, intricate and protective care in networking*
Fluids (Non-linear movements)	*Local knowledge and diversification in mitigating uncertain factors*	*Local and translocal dimensions in food and geographical knowledge*	*Niche tourism as alternative measures*	*Innovative and diverse avenues to capitalize on growing transnational PRC market*

Fig. 13.1 Summary of strategies and capital accumulation in social topographies as compiled by the author

"Indeed, AEC has an impact on my export trading business. For instance, under the AEC implementation, there is zero tariff (零关税). With such an implementation, there will naturally be a reduction of revenue for the government bodies that will affect the officials operating on the ground. This inevitably poses many barriers. With lesser income, customs officers would either accuse you for not meeting certain standards, or that your pesticide content has exceeded the limit, or that the insects found in your goods have been excessive. These would not have happened in the past. Back then, you would have easy access within these ten countries because the customs officers would be happy to serve you since they received adequate revenue due to the imposed tariffs. However, their income has been reduced since the tariffs have been removed under AEC implementation. Hence, without such revenue, they begin to find fault with you either hoping to get some money from you privately or simply venting their frustrations on you" (Interview, June 7, 2016).

The respondent feels that although the AEC has facilitated the opening of the region, it is pertinent to consider the impact on the ground. As far as business operations are concerned, the ASEAN countries should still retain their tariff collection which will sustain the revenue for the customs officers, who will ensure that operations run smoothly. Hence, there is a need to critically evaluate whether the existing policies are facilitating or obstructing SMEs. There are other existing stereotypes with regard to the transnational entrepreneurs that need critical evaluation. On one hand, they are viewed as wealthy saviors to the ailing Thai economy developing a false crippling sense of overdependence. For example, one respondent stated:

"Currently, Thailand's economy is very bad. However, at the marketplace (Talat Mongmai), there are many Thai locals selling vegetables and fruits. With the arrival of Chinese, these Thai sellers are very happy. On the contrary, if the Chinese fail to come, businesses would truly be hard…if there are no Chinese, then they would surely perish" (Interview, June 19, 2016).

On the other hand, there are those who labeled the Chinese as predators who should be avoided at all cost. There is a need to strike a balance and seek to evaluate the underlying assumptions to find the appropriate strategy in meeting the challenges and capitalizing on the opportunities.

Most of the respondents appreciate the AEC from a cultural exchange perspective. They view AEC as an opportunity for them to learn new languages, cultures, and other perspectives from other countries. While this is significantly true, it is equally important to identify, cherish, and strengthen local strengths. In this research, the respondents' unique local geographical and cultural knowledge and networks provide them with a competitive edge. Hence, it is crucial to return to local roots and further add value to them.

Interestingly, one respondent talked about a national industry heritage that the Thai government needs to pay attention to. He shared that: "For the food and beverage industry to prosper, I believe that the farmers need to have their earnings and do well economically. For instance, in Thailand, bananas are on the decline. Consequently, the economy becomes bad. Also, when it comes to staple food like rice, farmers also do not earn much. Hence, the only way now is to help the rice farmers to have income. Traditionally, Thailand relies on agriculture such as rice, rubber, grains etc., thus if they prosper then they will generate economic growth. So, the Thai government needs to think of ways to help them, especially in terms of export. If there are more orders from foreign countries, it would be better…Thus, Thai government needs to help them. And they would be able to lead the growth engine for the country. However, if they don't, then it will affect everyone else. So, the AEC must try to help. The earnings of the farmers are very crucial" (Interview, June 19, 2016).

The respondent could see not only the interconnectedness between industries but saw agriculture as a core strength of the nation. In other words, in a fast globalizing world with competing and distracting agendas, there is a need to stay sound in assessing one's core strengths while learning new things from other countries. Another respondent reflected: "I think the world is smaller now than before. I think we have to think international. If the Chinese people were to come, then we should have some laws to manage them. While we do not want to obstruct them from entering Thailand, we should control the amount of profits, which they would like to transfer out of the country. This is crucial because we want to retain their investments. We should implement some measures that will reasonably cap the remittance amount gained from their profits to their families in China. This is what is happening in China. If you are doing business or selling your products in China, then you could not simply bring your profit out. If you have made 1 million yuan, then you would have to buy something from China. This was the case with Walmart. In the case of Walmart, they earned a lot from Chinese people in China but they could not bring their money back to USA. They had to import Chinese goods back so as to sell the Chinese products in USA! Chinese laws are very smart. Hence, in the similar fashion, we have to create a law to control and stop the flow of cash out of Thailand" (Interview, June 21, 2016).

The above comments best sum up the critical approach that is needed in crafting and implementing policies. Instead of blanket policies in a "one size fits all" approach, there is a need for policymakers to prepare smart options to a certain degree of sophistication. This chapter has tried to demonstrate the multiplicity of negotiation strategies utilized by the Thai-Yunnanese SME entrepreneurs in response to the transnational entrepreneurs from the PRC.

Bibliography

Anderson, Benedict. 1983. *Imagined Communities: Reflections on the Origin and Spread of Nationalism*. London: Verso.

Appadurai, Arjun. 2000. "Disjuncture and Difference in the Global Cultural Economy." In *Readings in Contemporary Political Sociology*, edited by Kate Nash, 100–114. Oxford: Blackwell.

Astarita, Claudia. 2008. "Leo Suryadinata, ed. Southeast Asia's Chinese Businesses in an Era of Globalization: Coping with the Rise of China. Singapore: Institute of Southeast Asian Studies, 2006, 374." *China Perspectives* 2008/1: 117–118.

Castells, Manuel. 1996. *The Rise of the Network Society*. Cambridge, MA and Oxford, UK: Blackwell.

Chinvanno, Anuson. 2015. "'Rise of China': A Perceptual Challenge for Thailand." *Rangsit Journal of Social Sciences and Humanities* 2, no. 2: 13–18.

Dalpino, Catharin, and David Steinberg. 2003. "Southeast Asia Looks North." In *Georgetown Southeast Asia Survey, 2002–03*, edited by Catharin Dalpino and David Steinberg. Washington, DC: Georgetown University.

Das, Sanchita Basu. 2012a. "Introduction: State of Readiness of ASEAN Economies and Businesses." In *Achieving ASEAN Economic Community 2015: Challenges for Member Countries & Businesses*, edited by Sanchita Basu Das, 1–9. Singapore: ISEAS Publishing.

Das, Sanchita Basu. 2012b. "Conclusion and Recommendations for an Effective AEC." In *Achieving ASEAN Economic Community 2015: Challenges for Member Countries & Businesses*, edited by Sanchita Basu Das, 327–332. Singapore: ISEAS Publishing.

Eidheim, Harald. 1971. *Aspects of Lappish Minority Situation*. Oslo: Universitetsforlaget.

Eriksen, Thomas Hylland. 2010. *Small Places, Large Issues: An Introduction to Social and Cultural Anthropology (Third Edition)*. New York: Palgrave Macmillan.

Freedman, Amy L. 2014. "Malaysia, Thailand, and the ASEAN Middle Power Way." In *Middle Power and the Rise of China*, edited by Bruce Gilley and Andrew O' Neil, 104–125. Washington, DC: Georgetown University Press.

Hall, Ian, and Frank Smith. 2013. "The Struggle for Soft Power in Asia: Public Diplomacy of Regional Competition." *Asia Security* 9, no. 1: 1–18.

Hannigan, John. 2002. "Culture, Globalization, and Social Cohesion: Toward a Deterritorialized, Global Fluids Model." *Canadian Journal of Communication* 27: 277–287.

Jacques, Martin. 2009. *When China Rules the World: The End of the Western World and the Birth of a New Global Order*. New York: The Penguin Press.

Lee, Kian Cheng. 2015. *Rethinking Chinese Capitalism: Economic Cultures, Guanxi and Identities of Thai Yunnanese Transnational Entrepreneurs in Chiang Mai City*. PhD diss., Faculty of Social Science, Chiang Mai University.

Levathes, Louise. 1994. *When China Ruled the Seas: The Treasure Fleet of the Dragon Throne 1405–1433*. New York: Simon & Schuster.

Liu, Hong, and Els van Dongen. 2016. "China's Diaspora Policies as a New Mode of Transnational Governance." *Journal of Contemporary China* 25, no. 102: 805–821.

Poapongsakorn, Nipon. 2012. "Achieving the AEC 2015: Challenges for Thailand." In *The ASEAN Economic Community: A Work in Progress*, edited by Sanchita Basu Das, Jayant Menon, Rodolfo Severino, and Omkar Lal Shrestha, 138–160. Singapore: ISEAS Publishing.

Qiu, Liben. 2000. "The Chinese Networks in Southeast Asia: Past, Present and Future." In *Chinese Business Networks: State, Economy and Culture*, edited by Chan Kwok Bun, 193–206. Singapore: Prentice Hall, Pearson Education Asia Pte Ltd.

Ramzy, Austin. 2016. "China's President, Xi Jinping, Gains a New Title: Commander in Chief." *The New York Times*, April 21, 2016. https://www.nytimes.com/2016/04/22/world/asia/china-xi-jinping-military-commander.html.

Santasombat, Yos. 2015. "Introduction." In *Impact of China's Rise on the Mekong Region*, edited by Yos Santasombat, 1–24. New York: Palgrave Macmillan.

Severino, Rudolf C., and Jayant Menon. 2013. "Overview." In *The ASEAN Economic Community: A Work in Progress*, edited by Sanchita Basu Das, Jayant Menon, Rodolfo Severino, and Omkar Lal Shrestha, 1–30. Singapore: ISEAS Publishing.

Siriphon, Aranya. 2015. "*Xinyinmin*, New Chinese Migrants, and the Influence of the PRC and Taiwan on the Northern Thai Border." In *Impact of China's Rise on the Mekong Region*, edited by Yos Santasombat, 147–166. New York: Palgrave Macmillan.

Sung, Hsing-Chou. 2015. "China's "Comrade Money" and Its Social-Political Dimensions in Vietnam." In *Impact of China's Rise on the Mekong Region*, edited by Yos Santasombat, 23–54. New York: Palgrave Macmillan.

Tan, Chin Tiong. 2013. "Foreword." In *The ASEAN Economic Community: A Work in Progress*, edited by Sanchita Basu Das, Jayant Menon, Rodolfo Severino, and Omkar Lal Shrestha, vii–viii. Singapore: ISEAS Publishing.

The State Council Information Office. 2005. "China's Peaceful Development Road." *People's Daily Online*, December 22, 2005. http://en.people.cn/200512/22/eng20051222_230059.html.

Tong, Chee Kiong. 2014. "Rethinking Chinese Business." In *Chinese Business: Rethinking Guanxi and Trust in Chinese Business Networks*, edited by Tong Chee Kiong, 1–20. Singapore: Springer.

Urry, John. 2000. "Mobile Sociology." *British Journal of Sociology* 51, no. 1: 185–203.

Viraphol, Sarasin. 2006. "The Emergence of China's Economic Power and Its Implication for Chinese Businesses in Southeast Asia." In *Southeast Asia's Chinese Businesses in an Era of Globalization: Coping with the Rise of China*, edited by Leo Suryadinata, 38–48. Singapore: Institute of Southeast Asian Studies.

Wong, John. 2006. "China's Economic Rise and Its Implications for Southeast Asia: The Big Picture." In *Southeast Asia's Chinese Businesses in an Era of Globalization: Coping with the Rise of China*, edited by Leo Suryadinata, 13–37. Singapore: Institute of Southeast Asian Studies.

Wu, Yuan-li, and Chun-hsi Wu. 1980. *Economic Development in Southeast Asia: The Chinese Dimension*. Stanford: Hoover Institution Press.

Xi, Jinping. 2014. "Achieving Rejuvenation is the Dream of the Chinese People." *The Governance of China*, 37–39. Beijing: Foreign Languages Press.

Zhang, Weiwei. 2012. *The China Wave: Rise of a Civilizational State*. Hackensack, NJ: World Century Publishing Corporation.

CHAPTER 14

Chinese Capital and Chinese Cultural Capital: A Case Study of Singkawang, West Kalimantan, Indonesia

Bien Chiang and Jean Chih-yin Cheng

Introduction

This chapter addresses how the Sino-Indonesian community contributes to economic and business development in the city of Singkawang, West Kalimantan, Indonesia. Based on ethnographic case studies, the authors illustrate how "Chineseness" work as both a liability and an asset to business operations. Sino-Indonesian entrepreneurs convert accumulated cultural capital into fiscal capital, and vice versa, to ensure business success. The Sino-Indonesian community has accomplished economic and political status after surviving decades of government persecution, social expulsion, and the coming of a new wave of Chinese diaspora. The chapter argues that cultural capital is a significant asset to the Sino-Indonesian business community in Singkawang and is behind their current economic success.

B. Chiang (✉)
Institute of Ethnology, Academia Sinica, Taipei, Taiwan

J. C. Cheng
National Tsinghua University, Hsinchu, Taiwan

Y. Santasombat (ed.), *The Sociology of Chinese Capitalism in Southeast Asia*, https://doi.org/10.1007/978-981-13-0065-3_14

In the discussions of Chinese socio-economic history, four major issues stand out:

(1) China had well established autochthonous monetary, market and production systems before the coming of Western capitalism in the eighteenth century. Then the Chinese economic and political superiority had been severely eclipsed by the Western capitalism. Why there was autochthonous capitalism development in China?
(2) The inter-relation between European colonization of Southeast Asia and Oversea Chinese economic achievements in this area.
(3) The cultural factors (whether or not the neo-Confucian values) that are supposed to be behind the rise of "Four Little Dragons" in the second half of the twentieth century.
(4) The role of Oversea Chinese business communities in the liberalization of domestic economics and the global economic expansion of the People's Republic of China: whether or not it is justifiable to view the Oversea Chinese businesses as PRC's economic "Fifth Column" in their respective hosting countries.

David Faure (2006) argued that the economic prosperity of China in the sixteenth and seventeenth centuries was in part attributable to kinship and acquaintance networks in absence of institutional instruments needed for the development of capitalism. He argued that it took the entire twentieth century for China to establish the legal and institutional apparatus needed to create an environment where capitalism could flourish. In previous centuries, China had developed a rather mature monetary system with a somewhat influential mercantile social class, however, it had not nurtured the idea of capital that could assume a status independent from the person or social grouping who generated or owned it. It was not possible for corporations to be established purely on the pooling of capital without the social or legal institutions dedicated to regulating the flow of capital. Therefore, monetary capital was never fully distinguished from social capital or networks. Faure argued that there were always certain social prerequisites of capital in a traditional Chinese economy. An example is socially based capital pooling, the seeking of external patronage, and the expenditure of capital in socially obligated or culturally sanctioned manners. That may explain the economic success of the Overseas Chinese in Southeast Asia. Their economic success is driven by social networking, familial solidarity, political patronage, business disposition, and a culture of frugality. Indeed, most Chinese immigrants to

Southeast Asia in the nineteenth and early twentieth centuries did not possess much capital to invest and their economic security was a factor of cultural capital[1] rather than financial or "Chinese capitalism".

Another important point of view regarding the economic prominence of Southeast Asian Chinese is that western capitalism in Southeast Asia provided Chinese immigrants with opportunities to develop business interests beyond the constraints of cultural morals. Overseas Chinese were attracted to the region during the colonial period when they could capitalize on that system. Dutch historian Leonard Blussé (1991) argued that the expansion of western powers in the region paved the way for the expansion of Chinese trade. European colonialism became an enabling factor for capitalism to flourish in the region. When Chinese migrated to Southeast Asia they found a niche and thrived by adapting their business practices to capitalist norms in host countries. In this new-found niche in western-colonial capitalism, however, some traditional Chinese cultural norms remain powerful. The accumulation of material wealth was often burdened with social (or familial) responsibilities and overshadowed by moral skepticism. Pure material wealth and capital accumulation seldom represented moral value and was not invested with social agency found in other capitalist systems. Material wealth and capital was used to facilitate alliance, consolidate group loyalties, and affect decisions of political authority. Money was an asset to the economically powerful yet it was still morally bounded by social agencies.

For centuries, Chinese people had been familiar with the principle of exchange and the usage of currency in daily life. Even traditional Chinese religious rituals were often centered on negotiating, pledging, receiving and rewarding between the mortals and the immortals, mediated by objects in either material or monetary forms. Calculation and profit making were central to the grass-root common-sense knowledge that a large part of Chinese population grew up with. However, the moral value of material wealth had always been problematic. This is evident not only in the elitist Confucian teaching but also in the common codes of conduct of the populace. For example, in one of the Chinese temples in Pontianak, we found a rather common decorative bamboo scroll, the kind of scroll you will likely find in many shops and offices in Chinese societies. On the upper half of the scroll, there is a portrait of "the three legendary sworn brothers", Liu, Guan and Chang, which symbolizes the virtue of "*yi*" (義), meaning "commitment and trustworthiness toward friends" (see Fig. 14.1). The lower half of the scroll is printed with "Valuable Advices for Merchants". A very common set f grass-root knowledge or code of conduct for business peoples. The "Advices" were believed to be composed by the legendary entrepreneur Tao Zhu (536~448 B.C.) (Plate I and II). In addition to teaching "good business senses", it also includes the following advices:

- Be able to know about people, tell good from bad, book will be balanced;
- Be able to receive people properly, treat people with courtesy and civility, social connection will grow;
- Be able to deliberate; accumulate wealth the right ways and enlighten those who are ignorant (so they can follow your ways);
- Don't be coarse and raucous; befriend with the vulgars and you will lose good companions;
- Don't be harshly argumentative; treating people with a turbulent heart and disasters will be unavoidable.

In their analysis of neoliberalism of the late twentieth and the early twenty-first centuries, Comaroff and Comaroff (1999, 2001) propose to label the phenomenon "millennial capitalism" and focus on one of its prominent features: "occult economy". They defined occult economy as "the deployment,

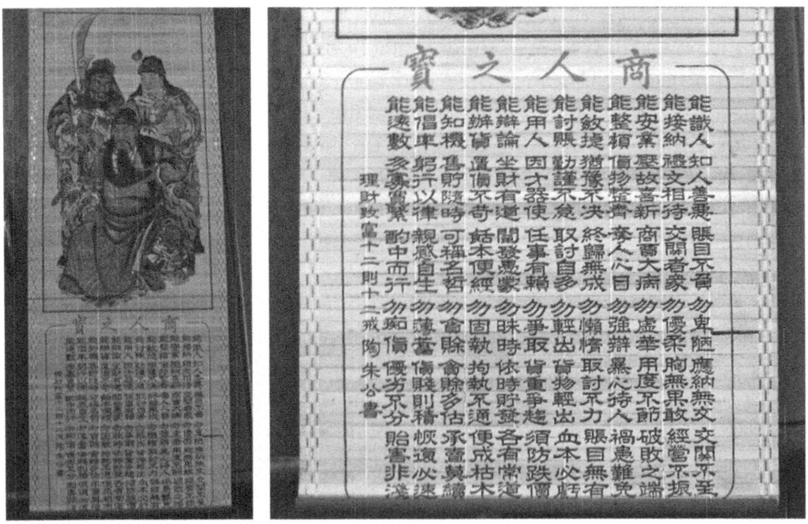

Fig. 14.1 Scroll found in one of Pontianak's Chinese Temples. Plate I: Bamboo scroll with *yi* icons and "Valuable Advices for Merchants"; Plate II: Contents of "Valuable Advices for Merchants"

real or imagined, of magical means for material ends" (Comaroff and Comaroff 1999: 279) and relate that to the social insecurity and mystification of capitalism in a neoliberal world. While a significant aspect of occult economy is the commodification of cultural things (rituals, heritages, and social memories), a recognized feature of neoliberalism following the invasion of market idioms and market principles into other domains, such as kinship, politics, and religion (Comaroff and Comaroff 2000; Coronil 2000; Lima et al. 2000), the Comaroffs proposed the concept of occult economy mainly to highlight the "darker" side of neoliberalism as reflecting the experience of the underprivileged population about government corruption, economic scams, precarious market, and widening of the income gap, and resorting to occult means as a form of resistance (Ortner 2011; Taussig 1980).

The ethnographic case study presented in this chapter provide examples of occult economy, but they also propose an expansion of the application of the concept. The most prominent revival of traditional festival-cum-tourist attraction in Singkawang in recent years is the festival of *Chap-Go-Meh*, celebrated on the fifteenth day of the first month of the Chinese lunar calendar. The festival features processions of hundreds of spiritual mediums down the streets to rid the city of evil elements. The thriving economic strength of Singkawang's Sino-Indonesian community[2] is behind this ever-enlarging celebration.

The Sino-Indonesians of Singakawang are considered economically prosperous when compared with other ethnic groups in the community. Their success is despite decades of political persecution. The Sino-Indonesian of Singkawang, not unlike those in other parts of Indonesia, have a history of being politically marginalized and insecure, who began to thrive at the turn of the twenty-first century relying on their familiarity with monetary and market economy, along with their cultural and fiscal capital to take advantage of emerging markets in an era of Chinese capitalism. Based on the concepts of cultural capital, commodification of culture things and occult economy, we now turn to the current economic practices of the Sino-Indonesian community of Singkawang.

Singkawang: A History of Persecution and Prosperity

The coastal city of Singkawang has a population of 192,844 (according to the 2014 census) with 42% Sino-Indonesian, 28% ethnic Malay, and 7% Dayak (indigenous tribes), the remaining 24% are ethnic Javanese, Bataks, Madurese, and Ambonese. The city is known as "the city of thousand (Chinese) temples" in part due to the majority Sino-Indonesian population. Because of its remote location from Jakarta and a more relaxed manner of the local authority in the enforcement of central government policies, the temples have survived the rather oppressive Suharto era and have flourished under President Wahid's 2001 decree which allowed the public display of Chinese characters, customs, and rituals.

Singkawang was one of the main points of entry for immigrants from China to work the gold mines of northwestern Kalimantan during the eighteenth century. In the nineteenth century, the port served to import Chinese goods and export gold. The Chinese community in Singkawang experienced some of the worst atrocities in modern Indonesian history. During World War II, the Japanese authorities carried out large-scale arrests and executions of prominent community leaders of all ethnic groups in West Kalimantan in 1943 and 1944. It is estimated that over 20,000 people were killed in the so-called "Pontianak Incident" or "Mandor Affair" (Hui 2011). The massacre left a long-lasting psychological scar on all the residents of the northwestern part of West Kalimantan and a monument was built in the 1970s to commemorate the incident. After Indonesia achieved independence, Sukarno issued a Presidential Regulation in 1959 banning all foreign nationalities from operating retail businesses in the rural areas which resulted in the relocation of tens of thousands of Chinese from the West Kalimantan interior to the coastal cities. After Suharto assumed the presidency, ethnic Chinese were targeted again because of their presumed connection to the communists.

A series of arrests and expulsions of Chinese took place in West Kalimantan as part of the nationwide communist purge. The expulsions were often carried out by the Dayak after being instigated by government or military agents. "Estimates of refugees range from 50,000 to 117,000, while the number of those killed range from a few hundred to about 2,000–3,000" (Hui 2011: 131). A large number of ethnic Chinese fled to the coastal cities of West Kalimantan and the influx of refugees made it difficult to find jobs or make a living in those places. After some years, many of those refugees, and particularly their children, chose to move to places like Jakarta or West Java to find a better future. In the early 2000s, many of the refugees, or secondary migrants, from West Kalimantan achieved financial security for themselves and their families in Jakarta. They established the *Yayasan Bumi Khatulistiwa*

(Equator Foundation) to assist the development of their hometowns in West Kalimantan and around Singkawang. That foundation represents the secondary diasporic Singkawang Sino-Indonesians whose interest focuses on the development of cultural and education affairs. Currently, many of the committee members of the foundation are renowned entrepreneurs in both Jakarta and Singkawang and are particularly active in promoting the cultural and social connections between Jakarta and Singkawang. Although the official mission of the Equator Foundation is to promote education by providing scholarships for students to continue their secondary and higher education, it is instrumental in the successful staging of *Chap Go Meh* celebration. Because it serves as a platform to connect successful entrepreneurs from Singkawang and now living all over the places. When there is a financial need, the organizing committee of *Chap Go Meh* would first turn to the Equator Foundation in order to reach potential benefactors. This has become a pattern in recent years.

Neoliberalism in West Kalimantan: Culture as a Commodity and as Capital

West Kalimantan is not considered an economically advanced province of Indonesia. According to Indonesia Investment Coordinating Board, in 2014, West Java received the largest amount of foreign direct investment (FDI) (US$6561.9 million) while Gorontalo of northern Sulawesi received the smallest (US$4.1 million). West Kalimantan received US$966.1 million, ranking the tenth among the total of 34 provinces. Available information of FDI from the People's Republic of China indicate that those investments are almost exclusively in natural resources extraction: rubber, palm oil, and bauxite. As a tourist destination of Indonesia, Kalimantan is popular for river boating and jungle trekking, while West Kalimantan is usually not highlighted. In this context, the people of Singkawang aim to put their city on the tourist map as a destination "to experience Chinese cultural heritage" in Indonesia. Following we will discuss two cases of commodification and capitalization of Chinese cultural heritage. The first one is the Chinese festival, *Chap Goh Meh*, which is an iconic event the city of Singkawang has to offer to the international tourist market. The second one is a privately owned and operated theme park, the Poteng Water Theme Park, which utilizes the notion of *Feng-shui* (geomancy) and artificial landscaping to offer local residents a destination for weekend outing and bridal photo taking.

Chap Go Meh Festival in Singkawang

According to the traditional Chinese lunar calendar, the fifteenth day of the first lunar month marks the end of the New Year celebration. Lanterns are the theme of this holiday ranging from handcrafted lantern-making and contests, exhibitions, and processions, to a lantern riddle contest. Lanterns symbolize light and the force capable of driving away evil elements in the community. The festival is therefore an occasion of ritual cleansing.

In addition to the reputation of being "the city of thousand temples", Singkawang is also known for the considerable number of spiritual mediums practicing in and around the city (Hui 2011; Chai 2017). Ever since the lifting of the ban on public display of Chinese cultural heritage, the routine practice of spiritual mediums in healing, fortune telling, and session of trance (being possessed by guardian deities) entered a period of revival. The celebration of *Chap Goh Meh* in Singkawang is known for featuring the procession of numerous spiritual mediums from their respective household shrines, neighborhood temples, and regional temples to pay respect to the Central Pak Kung Temple in downtown Singkawang. While all the spiritual mediums are in trance, indicating the embodiment of their respective guardian deities, each medium (along with his/her entourage) performs a ritual cleansing, whereby collectively cleansing the city of any evil elements. The spiritual mediums wear colorful, almost theatrical-like, costumes to represent the deities that they impersonate and, while possessed, perform assorted marvels to demonstrate their spiritual power. Because of those extravagant ritual performances, *Chap Goh Meh* in Singkawang has gradually earned fame among cultural tourism destinations of Southeast Asia.

In 2009, the Indonesian government started listing *Chap Goh Meh* as an item on the national tourism agenda (Chai 2017) and subsidized the celebration with government funds.[3] Since then, two events have been added to the festival: a lantern and floats procession on the evening of the thirteenth day and a gathering of hundreds of spiritual mediums in front of the Mayor's office to launch an all-out parade down the main streets on the fifteenth day. In addition to those officially endorsed and financed events, the more authentic rituals of spiritual mediums paying respect to Central Pak Kung (as well as some of the more prestigious temples that have relationship with the mediums) is scheduled for the fourteenth day. Household and neighborhood shrines performing neighborhood cleansing and blessing to individual clients lasts for a week.

Hui (2011) called the spiritual mediums parade of *Chap Goh Meh* a performance of multiculturalism. Chai (2017) documented in detail the life stories of some prominent spiritual mediums in Singkawang. Both researchers are impressed by the presence of Dayak mediums in what is largely categorized as Sino-Indonesian religious life. The presence of Dayak spiritual mediums is, however, not limited to the festival; they are also part of people's daily lives, performing regular services befitted to their role in both traditional and contemporary settings. A common interpretation of the "syncretic" phenomenon resorts to the commonality between the traditional religions of the Dayak and the Chinese, because both retain strong animistic features in their cosmologies and ritual practices, plus a long tradition of *Datuk Kong* (Deity of Locality, an indigenous deity in Southeast Asian context) worship in Chinese temples in Malaysia and Indonesia. However, another noteworthy fact, as commonly known by the local residents, is that the costume worn by a medium represents the character of his/her guardian deity or the deity that possesses the medium during that particular session. The ethnic background or ethnic identity of the medium, on the other hand, is not really crucial in the determination of the appearance or the origin of the deities that he/she works with. In other words, there are mediums that are categorically Sino-Indonesian in terms of ethnicity but occasionally or frequently possessed by Dayak deities and therefore dress in Dayak costume in these sessions. Conversely, there are ethnic Dayak mediums that regularly work with deities of Chinese origin and dress accordingly in Chinese costume.

In terms of organization, each year behind the *Chap Go Meh* celebration there is an *ad hoc* committee of three invited by the mayor or volunteered by community leaders and then mandated by the mayor. With the mandate from the mayor, the committee recruits and organizes a work team as well as invites other socially and financially resourceful community leaders to join the committee. The funds for each year's celebration come partially from the city government and partially from private donation. Having resourceful and respectable persons on the committee becomes a crucial factor for the success of that year's celebration. For the year 2017, the total budget for the festival was said to be around 4.7 billion IDR or US$350,000. According to some sources, the government has furnished between one to two billion IDR this year, and the balance is made up of private donations, including lesser amounts from local businesses and bigger sums from prominent enterprises that are either based in Singkawang or in other parts of Indonesia or Asia but who have a Singkawang background.

In 2017, over 500 spiritual mediums, with entourages consisting of ten to 20 people each, signed up for the official parade, which had about 200 more units from the year prior but less than the year 2009, which is said to have had around 800 units. The 2016 committee was thought to be corrupt and was boycotted by some of the local religious groups. This year, each spiritual medium unit is awarded 1.5 million IDR for their attendance-a sum that many complain is hardly enough to cover the expenses. "But this is not entirely for the money, right? It is our heritage!" said a number of participants. While the figure of government funding, number of spiritual mediums taking part in the parade, and the amount of donations from the private sector can vary from year to year, one thing remains constant: the main corpus of funding for the festival comes from the business owners of the Sino-Indonesian community especially those sizable enterprises of former Singkawang residents who now operate elsewhere. Many of those business owners are members of the Equator Foundation.

One of such benefactors is Mr. Pui Sudarto, President Director of the PT. Pulauintan Bajaperkasa Construction Company, which is based in West Jakarta and is one of the major construction companies in Indonesia. The Company joined with PT Bauing Construction Group Indonesia (a joint venture between Bauing Construction Group, Shenzhen China, and Sioeng's Group Inc, Indonesia) to build an army hospital, the cornerstone laying ceremony of which in 2015 was attended by Indonesian President Joko Widodo. The group is also the construction company of the major industrial park invested by Chinese company, the Indonesia China Integrated Industrial Zone, in West Java. On February 11, 2017, the Pulauintan Company hosted a grand opening for the 117 rooms of the Hotel Swiss Belinn, Singkawang (the first international chained-brand in Singkawang), which is attached to the Grand Mall (the first modern shopping mall in Singkawang) that had opened two years before, also built by the Pulauintan. The grand opening is scheduled to coincide with the main parade of *Chap Goh Meh*. The hotel will accommodate at least 26 foreign diplomats and dignitaries who are Mr. Pui's personal guests for the festival. Mr. Pui started this gesture of hospitality a few years ago as chairman of the *Chap Goh Meh* committee.

Although Singkawang has a majority Sino-Indonesian population and the area is generally spared from recent anti-Chinese strife in Indonesia, interethnic tensions, mainly between the Muslim and the non-Muslim groups, are never deep beneath the surface. Not only does the city's landmark dragon statue become the focus of protests and become the victim of vandalism, the size of the *Chap Goh Meh* celebration fluctuates according to the general political atmosphere or the precarious situation of the local election. Although recognized by the central government as one of Indonesia's public holidays, and promoted by the local government as one of the city's major tourist attractions, that does not guarantee the celebration is without interference, at least in the minds of many Sino-Indonesians. One strategy is to recognize the celebration as multicultural and widely known internationally to safeguard its continuation. Although Mr. Pui does not publicly claim that that is his intention, the hospitality he extends to foreign diplomats and dignitaries is in line with that strategy. It helps to consolidate the legitimacy of the festival as an annual official event of the city.

According to Mr. Lim, a mid-size import-export business owner in Singkawang, and a member of the Equator Foundation, most of the funds for *Chap Go Meh* come from individual donations including from local enterprises, businesses, and temples. The fundraising capacity differs from year to year, depending on the social standing and connection of committee members. The fluctuations in the amount of funds raised in recent years also depend very much on the general economic situation of the nation, and there is also a political factor to be considered. Says Mr. Lim:

> This year is the election year. Usually the national government does not want to see too much excitement among the local communities during the election year. So they (the government) want us to size-down the celebration this year. But we resist the demand on the base that the *Chap Go Meh* has become the representative festival of Sino-Indonesian nationwide and the most important tourist attraction of the city. Tourists from Hong Kong, Singapore, Malaysia and even China and Taiwan are all coming and expecting to see a grand celebration! How can we size it down?
>
> Beside, with the effort of Mr. Pui, who has invited all these foreign dignitaries to *Chap Go Meh* in recent years, now the whole world is watching the *Chap Go Meh* of Singkawang!

In 2017, among the much advertised tourist attractions, there is a 178 meters long dragon in the parade; it is said to be the longest ever. According to Mr. Lim, each year one organization would step forward to sponsor the main dragon for the procession. The dragon sponsor would finance its making and recruit people for its playing. This year the dragon is sponsored by Santo Yosep School alumnus society. Listed on the *Chap Go Meh* celebration brochure is the "burning of dragon" ritual in front of a Chinese temple on the outskirts of the city on the sixteenth day. In the afternoon of February 11th of 2017, watched by a huge crowd-amid beating of gongs and drums-the dragon is set ablaze and consumed by fire in a matter of minutes. It has become a custom that the dragon should be made anew each year by different sponsor. According to Mr. Lim, one year the senior craftsman who made the dragon passed away. Fearing that no qualified craftsman would be able to continue the making of new dragons, the organizers of that year decided to keep the dragon for future use. The following year witnessed at least a dozen fires in the city and many houses were destroyed. People sought divination and learned that the dragon was mad because it was prevented from returning to heaven. They hurriedly burnt the dragon and ended the chain of misfortune.

Chap Go Meh is therefore still a ritual loaded with magical potency, regardless of its appropriation in recent years by civil, economic, and ethnic-political motivations. The recent development of the *Go Meh* celebration in Singkawang is both a combination of civil and corporal agencies commodifying culture for economic gains in a neoliberal world, and a boom of occult economy among a still somewhat marginalized and insecure ethnic group in Indonesia, the Sino-Indonesian.

Poteng Water Theme Park

Another much publicized tourist project in Singkawang is the Poteng Water Theme Park. The park is located 7 km southeast of the city center of Singkawang. Originally called "Swallow Garden" because of the bird's nest houses surrounding the park, it is now also popularly known as "Pajintan Love Park" because of the park's landscape partially targeting the growing market of bridal photos. The 90,000 m^2 park features a swimming pool, a splashing pool, a set of water slides coming out of a big dragon mouth, some rafting channels, a hotel, and a café.

The Park's most amazing landscaping feature, however, centers on the integration of the surrounding mountains with manmade landscape. The main visitor center building faces a lake at the center of the park; and from the waterfront balconies of the building, visitors can have a panoramic view of Mt. Poteng. In *Feng-shui* terms, mountain ridges are commonly interpreted as lying dragon or dragon ridge. The auspiciousness or un-auspiciousness of a site is, to a large extend, decided by its relationship with the "dragon" in its vicinity. While standing on the balcony of the main visitor center building, appreciating the tranquil scenery of the nearby water and the distant mountains, one would be struck by the sight that at one end of this lying "mountain dragon" stands a man-made dragonhead that is over 20 meters high, bright red and constructed with rebar and cement. Although the mountain dragon is at a distance and the dragonhead is in the Park, about 200 meters from the viewing spot, perspective of the viewers connects the mountain dragon with the colorful man-made dragonhead. A set of 70-meter-long water slides extend out of the mouth of the dragonhead. That is a uniquely envisioned and executed appropriation of *Feng-shui*. Combining two auspicious elements, dragon and water (both symbolizing prosperity), the park provides a surrounding that is filled with heavenly bliss for wedding couples to take photographs and share the auspiciousness. According to the owner of the park, the *Feng-shui* of the site was investigated and interpreted by a consultant from Taiwan.

The visionary-cum-owner of the Park, Mr. Chen Chao-sheng, is a native Sino-Indonesian of Singkawang who left West Kalimantan in the 1970s. He established his business in Jakarta as an authorized dealer of China-made computer-controlled embroidery machines. He still considers Singkawang his hometown as both of his parents were buried here. The Poteng Water Theme Park is his pet project for a semi-retired life. Originally the project had three shareholders, both of who were Chen's good friends. After a while the other two lost interest in the project and withdrew their investment. It opened on December 25, 2016 but is still under construction. The project has cost him 50 billion IDR. Mr. Chen is rather happy with its current business which usually breaks even and sometimes makes a small profit. Mr. Chen likes to entertain guests, as well as staying in the Park by himself for a night every now and then, to enjoy the exquisite *Feng-shui*.

The lakes that constitute the main attractions of the Park are pit lakes from the gold-mining era. Surrounding the park's premises stand six bird's nest houses (see Fig. 14.2). They were once also Mr. Chen's projects, but was not profitable. Therefore, the scene at the park is a representation of the various phases of the economic history of the Sino-Indonesian community in the area. The gold mining of the eighteenth and nineteenth centuries, continuing with culturally invested enterprises such as bird's nest farming of the late twentieth century (Chiang and Cheng 2017) and then moving into tourist industry of the twenty-first century.

There are two tasks in *Feng-shui* profession: (1) the interpretation of landscape according to a set of systematic knowledge, and (2) the evaluation of a particular site in the landscape according to a scale of

Fig. 14.2 View from the balcony of the main building, Poteng Water Park, Singkawang (*Source* Author's picture)

auspiciousness to decide whether or not this site would bring good fortune to the appropriator. *Feng-shui* knowledge has been available to be hired in Chinese society for a long time. A good *Feng-shui* site, either for grave or for house, can fetch a much better price in real estate market. *Feng-shui* is not only a commodity of the traditional time but also a commodity with ever-increasing demand in the occult economy of a neo-liberal Chinese market. Being able to discover and to appropriate a good *Feng-shui* site is a sign of a person's possession of abundant cultural capital. Now in addition to the appropriation of good *Feng-shui* for the benefit of himself and his family in an occult way, Mr. Chen invests real fiscal capital into *Feng-shui* and turns the place into a money-making project. The market that Mr. Chen has in mind mainly consists of the domestic and international Ethnic Chinese customers who can appreciate the *Feng-shui* that is encode in the scenery. However, from our observation in the park and interviewing Mr. Chen, currently it seems that he would also need the patronage of local non-Chinese customers to balance the book.

Conclusion

Both the *Chap Goh Meh* festival and the Poteng Water Theme Park represent cases of commodification of culture. The Sino-Indonesian community, and to some extent the Dayak community, upholds the celebration as a symbol of ethnic identity in a precarious socio-political context. When we shared findings and understandings with Dayak friends in Pontianak about the relationship between culture and the economy, the occult appearance in many of the economic activities, and the status of Sino-Indonesian community in Singkawang, one Dayak friend sighed and commented: "All peoples have their cultural heritage, and all peoples have their cultural interpretations of the environment. But only the Chinese people can turn these things into tourist attractions in such a big scale."

Chinese business practices are invested with cultural values and social responsibilities. The persecution and marginalization that the Sino-Indonesians of Singkawang experience have become: (1) the historical causes of resorting to occult activities, (2) a reason for secondary diaspora and fortune seeking in other place, both inside Indonesia and abroad, and (3) the foundation for demonstrating hometown loyalty through investing in the improvement of Singkawang's economy and education. The cases demonstrate that Sino-Indonesians from Singkawang link their identity to the area, and those with financial means use that to reinforce Chinese identity as a kind of cultural capital. These two cases demonstrate that occult economy is not limited to underprivileged people but that financially affluent people also resort to occult activities, both as a psychological protection and a cultural fulfillment. Occult activities can be transformed into occult economies that serve not only internal customers as clients but also external customers as tourists. These cases also demonstrate the tendency for commodification of cultural heritage in a neo-liberal environment.

Notes

1. Bourdieu (1977, 1984, 1986) proposed the concept of cultural capital in his analysis of social mobility. Cultural capital consists of speech, dress, lifestyle, knowledge, and taste (mostly through family background and up-bringing). Cultural capital is used to enhance one's chance of social mobility. The concept is also useful in the discussion of cultural factors behind business success (Purwanto 2016).
2. Dr. Hui Yew-foong (personal correspondence) points out that the Sino-Indonesians of Singakawang should be divided into three classes: the very rich, the petite bourgeoisie, and the majority poor, and that each class would have distinct roles and different shares in the economic gains brought about by the celebration. The point is well taken but a full investigation of the internal differentiation would need to wait for further research.
3. Officials of Singkawang municipal government and the Sino-Indonesian are both organizers of the celebration and they both emphasize that the government fund is spent exclusively on the "civil celebration" parts of the festival, for example the lantern procession, procession of spiritual mediums in front of the Mayor's office, advertisement and public relations operations, etc., and never on the religious rituals.

Bibliography

Blussé, Leonard. 1991. "In Praise of Commodities: An Essay on the Cross-cultural Trade in Edible Bird's Nests." In *Emporia, Commodities and Entrepreneurs in Asian Maritime Trade c. 1400–1750*, edited by Roderich Ptak and Dietmar Rothermund. Stuttgart: Franz Steiner Verlag.

Bourdieu, Pierre. 1977. *Outline of a Theory of Practice*. Cambridge: Cambridge University Press.

Bourdieu, Pierre. 1984. *Distinction: A Social Critique of the Judgement of Taste*. London: Routledge.

Bourdieu, Pierre. 1986. "The Forms of Capital." In *Handbook of Theory and Research for the Sociology of Education*, edited by John Richardson. Westport, CT: Greenwood.

Chai, Elena. 2017. *Of Temple and Tatung Tradition in Singkawang*. Kota Samarahan: UNIMAS Publisher.

Chiang, Bien, and Jean Chih-yin Cheng. 2017. "Ethnic Chinese Enterprises in Indonesia: A Case Study of West Kalimantan." In *Chinese Capitalism in Southeast Asia: Cultures and Practices*, edited by Yos Santasombat. Palgrave Macmillan.

Comaroff, Jean, and John Comaroff. 1999. "Occult Economies and the Violence of Abstraction: Notes from the South African Postcolony." *American Ethnologist* 26, no. 2: 279–303.

Comaroff, Jean, and John Comaroff. 2000. "Millennial Capitalism: First Thoughts on a Second Coming." *Public Culture* 12, no. 2: 291–343.

Comaroff, Jean, and John Comaroff. eds. 2001. *Millennial Capitalism and the Culture of Neoliberalism*. Durham: Duke University Press.

Coronil, Fernando. 2000. "Towards a Critique of Globalcentrism: Speculations on Capitalism's Nature." *Public Culture* 12, no. 2: 351–74.

Faur, David. 2006. *China and Capitalism: A History of Business Enterprise in Modern China*. Hong Kong: Hong Kong University Press.

Hui, Yew-foong. 2011. *Strangers at Home: History and Subjectivity among the Chinese Communities of West Kalimantan, Indonesia*. Boston and Leiden: Brill.

Lima, Luiz Paulo, Scott Bradwell, and Seamus Walsh. 2000. "Millennial Coal Face." *Public Culture* 12, no. 2 (Spring): 453–55.

Ortner, Sherry B. 2011. "On Neoliberalism." *Anthropology of this Century*, Issue 1. http://aotcpress.com/articles/neoliberalism/.

Purwanto, Antonius. 2016. "Cultural Capital and Business Success among Entrepreneurs." *Ventura* 19, no 2: 227–36.

Taussig, Michael. 1980. *The Devil and Commodity Fetishism in South America*. Chapel Hill: The University of North Carolina Press.

Index

Y. Santasombat (ed.), *The Sociology of Chinese Capitalism in Southeast Asia*, https://doi.org/10.1007/978-981-13-0065-3

X

Y

The manufacturer's authorised representative in the EU is Springer Nature Customer Service Centre GmbH, Europaplatz 3, 69115 Heidelberg, Germany. If you have any concerns regarding our products, please contact ProductSafety@springernature.com

Printed and bound by CPI Group (UK) Ltd, Croydon, CR0 4YY
25/09/2026
02222902-0011